Industrial clusters and innovation systems in Africa

UNU-MERIT is the United Nations University Maastricht Economic and social Research and training centre on Innovation and Technology. It integrates the former UNU Institute for New Technologies (UNU INTECH) and the Maastricht Economic Research Institute on Innovation and Technology (MERIT). UNU-MERIT provides insights into the social, political and economic contexts within which innovation and technological change is created, adapted, selected, diffused and improved upon. The Institute's research and training programmes address a broad range of relevant policy questions dealing with the national and international governance of innovation, intellectual property protection and knowledge creation and diffusion. UNU-MERIT is located at and works in close collaboration with Maastricht University in the Netherlands.

Website: http://www.merit.unu.edu

**UNITED NATIONS
UNIVERSITY**

UNU-MERIT

Industrial clusters and innovation systems in Africa: Institutions, markets and policy

Edited by Banji Oyelaran-Oyeyinka and
Dorothy McCormick

**United Nations
University Press**

TOKYO · NEW YORK · PARIS

The views expressed in this publication are those of the authors and do not necessarily reflect the views of United Nations University.

United Nations University Press
United Nations University, 53-70, Jingumae 5-chome,
Shibuya-ku, Tokyo 150-8925, Japan
Tel: +81-3-3499-2811   Fax: +81-3-3406-7345
E-mail: sales@hq.unu.edu   general enquiries: press@hq.unu.edu
http://www.unu.edu

United Nations University Office at the United Nations, New York
2 United Nations Plaza, Room DC2-2062, New York, NY 10017, USA
Tel: +1-212-963-6387   Fax: +1-212-371-9454
E-mail: unuona@ony.unu.edu

United Nations University Press is the publishing division of United Nations University.

Cover design by Leslie Fitch

Printed in Hong Kong

ISBN 978-92-808-1137-7

Library of Congress Cataloging-in-Publication Data

Industrial clusters and innovation systems in Africa : institutions, markets, and
policy / edited by Banji Oyelaran-Oyeyinka and Dorothy McCormick.
    p.   cm.
Papers from an author's workshop funded by UNU-INTECH (now
UNU-MERIT) and held in Maastricht, the Netherlands at the end of July 2004.
Includes index.
ISBN 978-9280811377 (pbk.)
    1. Industrial clusters—Africa—Congresses. 2. Technological innovation—
Economic aspects—Africa—Congresses. 3. Industrial location—Africa—
Congresses. 4. Regional planning.—Africa—Congresses. 5. Africa—Economic
policy—21st century—Congresses. I. Oyelaran-Oyeyinka, Oyebanji.
II. McCormick, Dorothy, 1941–
HC800.Z9D55   2007
338.8′7—dc22   2007007189

Contents

Figures

Tables

Contributors

Catherine Nyaki Adeya, formerly a research fellow at UNU-INTECH, is now an independent consultant based in Nairobi, Kenya.

Justin Barnes is the managing director of Benchmarking and Manufacturing Analysts, a benchmarking and cluster facilitation company, and an associate of the School of Economics, University of Cape Town.

Samah El-Shahat is an independent consultant based in London.

Rose Kiggundu works on innovation systems and development. She is based at the International Livestock Research Institute, Ethiopia. Her research interests include livestock and financial innovations for development.

Mary Njeri Kinyanjui is a senior research fellow at the Institute for Development Studies, University of Nairobi, Kenya. She is an economic geographer with a focus on industrial development, MSMEs and gender.

Kaushalesh Lal is a researcher at UNU-MERIT. His research interests include the adoption of information and communication technologies and their consequences in different institutional environments.

Jochen Lorentzen is the chief research specialist at the Human Sciences Research Council in Cape Town.

Dorothy McCormick is an associate research professor at the Institute for Development Studies, University of Nairobi, Kenya, where she has worked since 1988. She currently serves as the Institute's director. She was educated at Trinity College, the University of Pennsylvania and the Johns Hopkins University School of Advanced International Studies. She has a long history of research and teaching in the area of industrialization and enterprise development in Africa. Her work has dealt with institutions and enterprise development, enterprise clusters, value chains and, most recently, the impact of the rise of China and India on African enterprises and workers.

Winnie V. Mitullah is an associate research professor at the Institute for Development Studies, University of Nairobi, Kenya. She is a political scientist with research and teaching interests in local livelihoods, local government and urban development.

Mike Morris is a professor in the School of Economics, University of Cape Town, and the School of Development Studies, University of KwaZulu-Natal, South Africa.

Flora Mndeme Musonda is a research fellow at the Economic and Social Research Foundation, Dar es Salaam, Tanzania.

Lynn K. Mytelka is a professorial fellow at UNU-MERIT and former director of UNU-INTECH. She is also a distinguished research professor at Carleton University in Ottawa, Canada.

Banji Oyelaran-Oyeyinka is a senior researcher and professor at United Nations University (UNU-MERIT). He received his postgraduate education at the University of Toronto, Canada, and the Science Policy Research Unit, University of Sussex, UK. His research interests include small and medium enterprise and industrial clusters and systems of innovation and development. His most recent books are *Learning to Compete in African Industry* (Aldershot, UK: Ashgate, 2006) and *SMEs and New Technologies* (Houndmills, UK: Palgrave, 2006).

Glen Robbins is a researcher at the School of Development Studies, University of KwaZulu-Natal, in Durban, South Africa. He works on urban economic development.

Preface

The idea for this book came out of discussions between Banji Oyelaran-Oyeyinka, Dorothy McCormick and Lynn Mytelka during the Regional Conference on Innovation Systems and Innovative Clusters in Africa held at Bagamoyo, Tanzania, in February 2004. The three were resource persons at the conference, which was organized to generate greater awareness of the role of clusters and innovation-systems concepts in Africa. It was a follow-up to the September 2003 Competitiveness Institute Conference on Innovative Clusters in Gothenburg, Sweden, where the need for more in-depth deliberation on the role of innovative clusters in Africa was recognized. Both conferences were supported by SIDA/SAREC and were part of an on-going collaboration between three engineering faculties, namely the University of Dar es Salaam in Tanzania, Makerere University in Uganda and Eduardo Mondlane University in Mozambique. At the end of the Tanzanian conference, we recognized the need for deeper analytical studies of the subjects and UNU-INTECH (now UNU-MERIT) subsequently funded an authors' workshop that brought the contributors to this volume together in Maastricht, the Netherlands at the end of July 2004.

Acknowledgements

This book owes its existence to the willingness of the various actors to make a contribution. We therefore express our appreciation to all our colleagues who not only agreed to write, but endured the usual pains of peer review. We also wish to thank UNU-MERIT (formerly UNU-INTECH, under which the project started) for supporting the authors' workshop with financial and logistic resources. Our sincere appreciation to Eveline in de Braek, who did a superb job as always in coordinating the authors' workshop, following through various revisions and formatting the manuscript. We are also grateful to two anonymous reviewers for very valuable suggestions that improved the manuscript significantly.

Finally, the usual caveat: The editors take responsibility for all shortcomings.

1

Introduction: Clusters and innovation systems in Africa

Dorothy McCormick and Banji Oyelaran-Oyeyinka

Every locality has incidents of its own that affect in various ways the methods of arrangement of every class of business that is carried on in it: and even in the same place and the same trade no two persons pursuing the same ends will adopt exactly the same routes. The tendency to variation is a chief cause of progress; and the abler are the undertakers in any trade the greater will this tendency be.[1]

Regional agglomerations of industrial activity have long been recognized as potential sources of innovation as well as of general economic growth. At the turn of the twentieth century, proximity was absolutely necessary for rapid communication and cooperation among firms. Thus it is not surprising that Marshall (1890, 1919) took great pains to explain the localization of particular industries and the benefits of industrial districts. Revolutions in transport and communication may seem to have reduced the need for firms to operate near one another, yet scholars continue to argue "locality matters" (Schmitz, 2004).

Locality matters to industrial development in several different ways. Some observers have focused on the regional context in which industry operates, emphasizing the importance of local governance and in particular meso-level policy (Messner, 2004; Scott, 2002; Scott and Storper, 2003; Storper, 1995). The rich literature on industrial clusters, more about which will be said in chapter 2, highlights the availability of external economies and opportunities for joint action arising from proximity (Beccatini, 1990; Pyke and Sengenberger, 1992; Schmitz, 1995, 2004; World Development, 1999). Porter's (1990, 1998) slightly different use of the

Industrial clusters and innovation systems in Africa: Institutions, markets and policy, Oyelaran-Oyeyinka and McCormick (eds), United Nations University Press, 2007, ISBN 978-92-808-1137-7

term "cluster" underscores the importance of local synergy and rivalry as sources of industrial development. Attempts to examine the difference between developed and developing country clusters are yet another way of looking at the importance of locality. Schmitz and Nadvi (1999) pointed out that the former are frequently global leaders that play a decisive role in innovation and product design; furthermore, they are standards makers, whereas firms in developing country clusters are standards takers and tend to work to specifications set elsewhere. While this dichotomy surely oversimplifies a wide range of cluster capabilities in both developed and developing countries, it serves to highlight the very important issues of industry leadership, product and process quality and linkages between global standards and local realities. Nevertheless, locality does also seem to matter for innovation. Studies of innovation systems also point to the impact of local institutions in shaping patterns of innovation and technical change (Edquist, 1997; Lundvall, 1992; Smale and Ruttan, 1997; and Mytelka in this volume).

Locality can be understood to mean anything from the whole of the developed or developing world to a very small local neighbourhood. We choose in this volume to focus on industrial clusters. These vary in size, but are most often sub-national in extent.

The notion of clusters fits into the innovation systems framework given its systemic, networking features as well as reliance on institutions as sources of dynamism. However, clusters are not necessarily innovation systems (Mytelka and Oyelaran-Oyeyinka, 2000; and Mytelka in this volume) and transforming clusters into innovation systems requires sustained policy support. The process of policy learning is itself heuristic, while strengthening local actors takes time and requires explicit investment in learning. An important lesson for developing countries is the fact that traditional sectors in advanced industrial countries have made the transition from low technology sectors into successful innovative clusters.

Despite the usefulness of the cluster approach, however, it has, like all abstractions from reality, its fundamental weaknesses. One such weakness is the assumption of homogenized relationships between the different-sized firms in the cluster. In other words, the cluster theory assumes that all firms are equal in the status and power they wield in the cluster. This underplays the inevitable confrontation, friction or domination by powerful actors of other firms. This assumption builds into the framework a naive hypothesis on the reality of collective learning that takes as given that all actors in the cluster benefit from interactions. This presupposes that actors will be unified in interest and behaviour, putting the collective above the individual. It is for this reason that "joint action" is unintentionally selective, because, evidently, its applicability to cluster actors will be differentiated and uneven (Kennedy, 1999). The case study of Domiatt furniture in this book shows that there are differentiated relationships between firms and this is reflected in confrontations over power, knowledge and income. The types of links between actors in the cluster are a reflection of their differences in power relations. More importantly, not all interactions, even in cooperative relationships or in the creation of new knowledge, are beneficial to all actors. The case study shows that where there is a negative asymmetric power relationship, interaction could lead to deskilling where dominant actors force an unprofitable learning trajectory.

The second theoretical approach in this book, the systems of innovation framework, has received widespread attention in the last two decades (Freeman, 1987; Lundvall, 1992; Nelson, 1987). A national system of innovation is the "elements and relationships which interact in the production, diffusion, and the use of new, and economically useful, knowledge ... and are either located within or rooted inside the borders of a nation state" (Lundvall, 1992: 12).

A system of innovation framework is essentially undergirded by the theory of institutions and this book appropriately places a strong premium on institutions and institutional change. In studies of technological change, institutions may be conceptualized narrowly or broadly,[2] but in both cases they take on a wide range of functions. These include managing uncertainty, providing information, managing conflicts and promoting trust among groups (Edquist, 1997; North, 1989).[3] Institutions in these areas are necessary for innovation for two reasons. First, the innovation process is characterized by considerable uncertainty. For example, institutions provide stability by regulating the actions of individuals and enforcing contractual obligations. Second, the creation, validation and distribution of learning and knowledge, which are prerequisites of economic change, are mediated by institutions. These institutions operate in such areas as research and development (R&D), finance and investment, intellectual property rights, patent laws and so on.

As with clusters, innovation systems have spatial and geographic dimension. An innovation system could be national, regional, local or sectoral. In other words, the persistent and uneven distribution of the capabilities of firms to innovate could be identified across sectors, countries and regions. This skewed effect of innovation performance is a function of specific national or sectoral factors and as such the competitive advantage of sectors and nations depends greatly on how advanced the system of innovation (SI) is and how well it has generated coherence and interactions. From the above, this approach places emphasis on knowledge flows, interactive learning and the role of institutions.

To sum up, an industrial cluster is a dense sectoral and geographical concentration of enterprises comprising manufacturers, suppliers, users

Box 1.1 Definitions and stylized facts on clusters and innovation systems

- An innovation system is defined as the network of institutions in the public and private sectors whose activities and interactions "initiate, import, modify and diffuse new technologies" (Freeman, 1987);
- A cluster is defined as a sectoral and geographical concentration of enterprises (Schmitz, 1995);
- A cluster is characterized as a geographically and sectorally bounded entity akin to a (local) innovation system but differing in that the latter emphasizes the networking of individuals, firms and organizations whose interaction fosters the innovative performance of firms. The roles of individual firms (intra-firm capability) and organizations therefore matter, in contrast to the cluster approach, which emphasizes inter-firm and collective learning approaches;
- Geographic proximity is necessary to reap the benefits of geographic agglomeration but it is not sufficient. Cognitive, social and cultural proximity are equally necessary for collective learning;
- Firms possess differentiated knowledge bases that cannot logically be diffused to all firms in a cluster; there is considerable asymmetric power and information relationship within clusters;
- Firms do more than produce goods and services, they are repositories of idiosyncratic knowledge, skills and experiences; they are organizations with path-dependent and specific routines and bounded by uncertainty in the pursuit of innovation and production activities (Nelson and Winter, 1982). For this reason, firm-level behaviour is an important factor in understanding the growth of clusters;
- Clustering policy emphasizes collective efficiency through "joint action" by firms and associations to realize productive efficiency while innovation policy emphasizes learning through incremental technical change through capabilities built up within firms and organizations.

and traders. On the other hand, an innovative cluster is more than a geographic phenomenon; it is defined by strong inter-firm interaction and a distinct sectoral specialization (Nadvi, 1994). For the purpose of this book, we identify four factors that distinguish an innovative cluster, or what we suggest is similar to a local system of innovation (LSI). First, this cluster will exhibit high rates of learning and knowledge accumulation within its component firms and institutions, which lead to continual changes to the knowledge base of the cluster. Second, it will be characterized by high levels of collaboration and interaction between key agents and institutions (suppliers, producers and so on). Third, this cluster will begin or has built up a dense network of formal and informal institutions to support production and innovation. On this and the first two issues, the cluster and innovation systems literature tend to share a common notion, although with different emphasis (Becattini, 1990; Saxenian, 1991; Schmitz, 1995). Fourth, successful LSIs will possess a certain optimal skills and knowledge structure in engineering, mathematics and sciences that support industrial development. It is not enough for a country to produce manpower per se, but also the right kinds for its level of development. While general knowledge acquired from formal educational institution forms an important component of a nation's human capital, firm-level training, R&D and production are necessary for the idiosyncratic knowledge bases of firms (Freeman, 2002; Lall, 1992, 2001). Box 1.1 enumerates the stylized facts on clusters and innovation systems.

We now turn our attention to the particular approach to clusters and clustering used in the chapters that follow.

Our approach to clusters

This book adopts the notion of clusters as defined by geography and product specialization. To this end, a cluster is defined as a sectoral and geographical concentration of enterprises (Schmitz, 1995). The starting point of the debate on clusters and clustering is that firms do not innovate and grow in isolation, but rely extensively on external knowledge sources. Firms in dense geographic proximity tend to enjoy certain advantages of agglomeration relative to isolated enterprises. This happens in at least two different ways. First, demand for their goods and services are enhanced as potential customers become aware of the cluster. This is especially true for micro and small enterprises, whose markets tend to be local and dependent on direct sales to traders and individual consumers (McCormick, 1999). Second, a cluster's ability to innovate and supply high quality products also benefits from agglomeration. For these reasons, the main advantage of agglomeration derives from the properties of knowledge, which is that it is largely tacit, uncodified and informal. Therefore, the fundamental system benefit of clustering is knowledge externality. Firms are embedded in a network of users, suppliers, consumers and knowledge producers (Kline and Rosenberg, 1986). These actors are repositories of market, scientific and technical knowledge that potentially provide inputs into a firm's innovation efforts and reduce technical and commercial uncertainty within a spatially bounded environment. Regional clusters are, thus, common and provide a range of advantages to firms locating within them (Ehrnberg and Jacobsson, 1997).

Geographic agglomeration promotes innovative activities and here we take a broader approach to innovation than the conventional view, which is largely focused on R&D. We define innovation as the "process by which firms master and implement the design and production of goods and services that are new to them, irrespective of whether they are new to their competitions, their countries or the world" (Mytelka, 2000: 18). In this framework, innovation has its sources in a wide variety of places and in activities such as R&D, design, production on the shop floor, quality control and marketing. Actors engaged in innovation are embedded within a wide network of agents in a system, or a "system of innovation". A system of innovation is a network of firms and other economic agents that act in concert and govern by formal and informal institutions to foster the generation, absorption and diffusion of new processes and products. The SI framework thus takes policies generated through the formal institutions of government and structures provided by other, less formal institutions as critical in promoting interaction and learning of different actors in the economic system. Studies of systems of innovation have consistently underlined that specialized suppliers and skilled labour are the main sources of continuous innovation. The notion of knowledge externalities and spillovers underlies much of this debate with the conclusion that firms located in clusters and strong in their own industry tend to grow faster and be more innovative than isolated firms.

Clustering supports a diverse range of specialized local input suppliers and intermediate input and service providers at lower cost. The existence of a pool of specialized skills and knowledge – knowledge externalities – promotes different forms of learning: through dissemination of ideas, by continuous dialogue in social networks (learning-by-interaction) and learning-by-doing. Social networking aids knowledge exchange in informal settings (Saxenian, 1994) and promotes the conditions for the emergence of stable relationships over time. In other words, geographic proximity fosters the diffusion of innovation in clusters. Implicit in this statement is another important characteristic of learning: the acquisition of technical skills is an evolutionary process with path-dependent characteristics. This means that an enterprise located in a cluster with a long history of knowledge creation is likely to derive greater benefits from co-location than one in a technologically arid environment.

However, mere co-location is insufficient for achieving high rates of innovative activity, and learning is not an automatic outcome of geographic proximity. In addition, clusters differ widely in their structural characteristics, which have been shaped, as it were, by history and the institutions that govern their actions and interactions. From the foregoing, two weaknesses of the existing framework for analysing clusters emerge. First, much of the current thinking on clusters is implicit on or makes assumptions on the time dimension and analyses clusters through a static framework. As the empirical cases in this book illustrate, clusters are dynamic entities while learning and innovation processes evolve unevenly (Nelson, 2001). For these reasons, innovative activity is more likely to thrive in an environment with a history of continuous invention where there is a fully evolved market to demand and accommodate new technologies and technological change. Insertion into global value chains can be especially important for upgrading (Humphrey and Schmitz, 2002; Schmitz, 2004).

Second, much of the current debate implies a certain degree of homogeneity among clusters but reality speaks to different facts. Clusters differ in structural characteristics such as size and type of product specialization, as well as by the institutions that bind them together and structure them. For example, the presence of supportive formal and informal institutions attenuates communication and market failures. The institutional component of different forms of agglomeration including clusters requires a systemic perspective on innovative activity within clusters. Through this, one can establish the presence of continuous learning, the dynamic combination of technical and organizational innovation, "high quality" interaction among the different actors, including knowledge flows, and continuous investment in competence-building and the social capital of the cluster.

This book draws on evolutionary economics (Nelson and Winter, 1982) and the concept of collective efficiency (Schmitz and Nadvi, 1999) to make two modest contributions. First, we bring together a number of previously unpublished studies of clusters in Africa. Second, we illustrate through a variety of case studies the fruitful use of the cluster concepts, the evolutionary innovation framework and the collective efficiency strand of the literature (see, in particular, the McCormick and Mytelka contributions to this volume). Insights from evolutionary economics call attention to the importance of incremental technical change (minor innovation) rather than the so-called "radical" innovations and, as well, interactive learning, path dependence and the role of formal and informal institutions. Much of the growth and improvements in productivity in dynamic latecomer countries have been due in large part to these kinds of technical change processes that take place on the shop floor rather than in organized formal laboratories (Dahlman and Nelson, 1995), as illustrated in box 1.2.

The studies reported in this book broadly investigate whether firms in clusters collaborate and, if so, why. In so doing, the studies highlight the collective role of formal and informal institutions that foster and hinder cluster growth and innovation. Attention is also paid to the role of external pressures on clusters such as competition and market deregulation. Our working definition of institutions is based on North's (1990) "rules of the game" while the empirical case studies also illustrate the importance of "how the game is played" (Nelson and Sampat, 2001) in studies

Box 1.2 Definition and nature of innovation

There are many definitions of innovation depending either on disciplinary focus (for example, sociological or managerial economics) or perspective (for example, user, producer or seller).[1] In an evolutionary economics perspective, which this book adopts, we take our definition of innovation from Schumpeter (1934: 66). He defines innovation as the "carrying out of new combinations" which he resolves into five different types, namely:

- The introduction of a new good (product);
- The introduction of a new method of production (process);
- The opening of a new market;
- The opening of a new source of supply; and
- The carrying out of a new organization of any industry, like the creation or breach of a monopoly position.

Innovation has several characteristics, prominent among which are uncertainty, interactive learning and a degree of innovativeness, which leads to characterizations such as "minor – major" and "radical – incremental" among others.[2] One might characterize them as follows:

- Radical changes of global significance (radical innovation);
- Small improvements in product design and quality, in production processes or in the way in which production is organized; changes to maintenance routines that collectively modify products and processes, to bring costs down, increase efficiency, enhance welfare and ensure environmental sustainability (incremental innovation); and
- Changes to management and marketing brought about by new technologies (institutional and organizational innovation).

1. In the managerial literature, Tushman and Moore (1982: 132) define innovation "as the synthesis of a market need with the means to achieve and produce a product that meets that need".
2. The Schumpetarian definition tends to address some of the shortcomings of other types of definitions.

of clusters. At the policy level, we examine whether clustering is an appropriate instrument for industrial policymaking in Africa. The readings of the individual chapters clearly show the convergence of the ideas implicit in clusters, collective efficiency and systems of innovation frameworks. If we succeed in advancing the debate on the role of clusters as an important form of industrial organization necessary for fostering industrialization in typically low-technology latecomer environments, then the efforts of the authors will have been richly rewarded. Table 1.1 puts

Table 1.1 Levels of analysis of clusters and system of innovation

Level of analysis	Cluster concept and innovation systems	Focus of analysis: Clusters	Focus of analysis: System of innovation
National level (macro)	Industry group linkages in the economic structure	Specialization patterns of a national/regional economy Need for innovation and upgrading products and processes in mega-clusters	National level actors (organizations and individuals) Knowledge bases and institutions Linkages between actors
Branch or industry level (meso)	Inter- and intra-industry linkages in the different stages of the production chain of similar end product(s)	Benchmark analysis of industries Exploring innovation needs	Sectoral analysis of actors, knowledge bases, linkages and institutions
Firm level (micro)	Specialized suppliers around one or a few core enterprises (inter-firm linkages)	Strategic business development Chain analysis and chain management Development of collaborative innovation projects	Firm level core capabilities for production and innovation Collaboration capabilities

Adapted from Roelandt and Den Hertog (1999)

in perspective the analytical building blocks of systems of innovation and industrial clusters frameworks.

Structure of the book

Dorothy McCormick, in chapter 2, provides three distinguishing features for clusters: geography, sector and/or firm inter-linkages in an increasingly globalized context. These perspectives are based on analyses of institutions, value chains and the collective efficiency of a given cluster. A specific set of formal and informal institutions, or "the institutional environment" according to McCormick, defines the rules by which the cluster and the enterprises within it must and do interact or "play". The institutions most closely associated with a cluster include product markets, firm linkages (including business networks and associations), laws and contracts, state support systems, education system, technology and innovation systems. Value chain analysis determines if clustering results in upward movement by the clustered firms as indicated by increased productivity and revenues, and increased use of sophisticated and complex technologies. Finally, studies of clusters from a collective efficiency perspective examine whether or not clustering helps enterprises, especially the smallest ones, to overcome international and domestic market constraints to expand and grow, thereby improving economic performance. Such constraints include macro institutional lock-in, poor access to technology, inadequate organizational forms and inadequate or insufficient access to market information. Collective efficiency encompasses the two dimensions of local external economies and joint action. The former is passive and may occur simply because of co-location. Joint action, however, requires the active engagement of the clustered enterprises.

In addition to McCormick's three perspectives for cluster studies, the contributors to this book employ the notion of "innovation systems" in their case studies. Lynn Mytelka provides the second theoretical chapter, in which she lays out the elements of a dynamic innovation system. Long used in studies of industrial organization and enterprise agglomeration at different geographical scales in developed economies, an innovation system perspective offers a holistic frame of analysis with a wide breadth. This comes, however, at the expense of in-depth analyses of the various important features of a cluster, or more generally a "system", including the formal and informal institutions as systemic structuring phenomena and policy as an instrument of change. Mytelka applies the innovation system to traditional industries, arguing that although these were previously thought not to require the kind of learning that characterizes high-tech sectors, innovation in industries such as textiles and wine-making can be critical to their success. She further suggests that spontaneous clusters may be more likely to foster new habits and practices of learning, linkage formation and continuous innovation than constructed clusters such as export processing zones or industrial parks.

McCormick and Mary Njeri Kinyanjui report that despite the problems facing clusters in developing countries, they have existed for many years in Africa and, as the other contributors to this volume illustrate, continue to exist and emerge in numerous countries. The authors use the notion of "productive capacity" to draw attention to infrastructure, skill levels, intermediate inputs, technology, joint action and benchmarking as the necessary features for examination in cluster studies. In their study of Kenyan micro and small enterprise clusters, McCormick and Kinyanjui find that many of these features are at best sub-optimal and require intervention through government policy to increase cluster performance through increasing domestic and export market shares based on improved quality and upward movement on the value chain. The authors argue that micro and small enterprise clusters in Kenya lack the productive capacity to take full advantage of the improved market access brought about by liberalization.

Most Kenyan clusters remain locked in low-quality, low-income markets. Weak productive capacity, according to McCormick and Kinyanjui, is at the heart of this problem. Combining insights from the collective efficiency model with those of value chain analysis, the authors examine 17 micro and small enterprise clusters in three sub-sectors. The analysis revolves around the six variables of infrastructure, skills, intermediate inputs, technology, joint action and benchmarking. The chapter concludes that adding issues of governance, benchmarking and upgrading to the original collective efficiency framework greatly enhances the understanding of the potential of these clusters. A key practical conclusion is that encouraging clusters to produce for demanding customers such as supermarkets, hospitals, schools and governments can enhance productive capacity. To achieve this, the clustered enterprises will need the support of government, their own associations, non-government organizations, research institutions and larger private sector actors.

Clusters are not always planned by the participating firms or governments and are sometimes secondary products of exogenous factors. Flora Mndeme Musonda's study of three Tanzanian clusters shows that while two of the clusters somewhat benefited from government assistance, the third cluster emerged and developed independently as a secondary outcome of a government policy to make the main roads in Dar es Salaam aesthetically more pleasant by moving street traders and artisans to a predefined location. However, once this location was populated by the evicted roadside entrepreneurs it acted as a magnet for other traders to move in. This secondary self-organizing feature of agglomeration and clustering by firms is also underlined in Banji Oyelaran-Oyeyinka's chapter on the Otigba information and communication technology cluster in Lagos, Nigeria.

Musonda's chapter tests whether the enterprises in each of the three clusters cooperate, what forms of formal or informal institutions exist to structure and stabilize the clusters, and how these institutions have emerged. The chapter reports on the relationships between cluster performance and the three key variables of the education levels of the entrepreneurs, forms of learning, such as apprenticeship, and competition in the product market. The analysis of the data reveals that entrepreneurs benefit from clustering and are acutely aware of the importance of the external economy. However, contrary to official government pronouncements, this case study finds very little evidence of support from the government and other formal institutions. Support is lacking mostly in finance and technology. Nevertheless, the enterprises feel that they are better off in clusters than those operating alone and especially benefit in having access to tool sharing, tacit knowledge and collective security against damage to or theft of property.

Oyelaran-Oyeyinka's examination of the Otigba computer cluster, dubbed Nigeria's Silicon Valley and located in the heart of Lagos in the "Ikeja Computer Village", shows that it evolved into a sub-regional hub for computer assembly, components sales, repairs and even limited computer-parts manufacturing. From small beginnings in the late 1990s, the Village grew to more than 4,000 computer shops in five years. The mostly young entrepreneurs – graduates of universities and polytechnics – are trained in servicing, repair and assembly of personal computer clones. The chapter weighs the experience of this somewhat unusual agglomeration against the notion of an innovative cluster, how individuals and firms within the cluster learn what they need to know to continue operating in a dynamic sector and how the cluster as a whole maintains stability. A defining feature of the Otigba cluster is the considerable reservoir of tacit knowledge shared by the clustered firms. Despite fierce competition among the clustered firms there are endogenous (to the cluster) and exogenous formal and informal institutions that bring stability to the cluster and promote its long-term interests. The chapter also examines the role of private institutions in fostering innovation and looks at the cluster's potential for process, product and functional upgrading.

Samah El-Shahat's analysis of the Domiatt furniture-making cluster in Egypt begins with a general criticism of the mainstream approaches used in studies of clusters. El-Shahat contends that none of the approaches used by the contributors to this book or by others elsewhere can adequately account for the role of conflict in socio-economic development, including in the development of clusters. The lack of attention to the role of conflict and competing agendas in economic activity implicitly assumes "institutional neutrality" and overlooks the question of power and asymmetries in control and access to knowledge and other resources. Egypt's institutions, like many in the developing world, are not conducive to trust among and virtuous behaviour by the actors in their quest for economic well-being. El-Shahat describes many of Domiatt's institutions as heavily politicized and socially corrupt. What are small firms and micro enterprises, clustered or otherwise, to do insofar as innovation and moving up the value chain are concerned, given this institutional context? El-Shahat's analysis seems to suggest that without direct government action serving as a major structuring factor, complete with a host of incentives and disincentives, firms have few choices within or outside clusters.

The chapters by Rose Kiggundu and Jochen Lorentzen et al. highlight two important issues in the discourse on clusters. They analyse how clusters respond to crises such as changing international trade rules and trade liberalization and underline the importance of joint action through learning in dealing with the crises. Kiggundu presents a detailed empirical study of cluster upgrading by the Ugandan fish-processors. Kiggundu finds that the process and organizational innovation is externally stimulated. The analysis shows a common learning trajectory in developing countries where firms first upgrade their processes before embarking on product upgrading. After the mastery of simple assembly operations, firms then move to "functional upgrading" and value-adding activities. This involves a shift from low-return to high-return activities, consistent with moving upward on the value chain. Eventually, the firms shift to more skill-intensive, technologically complex and profitable business activities.

The evolution of the fish-processing clusters in Uganda demonstrates clearly distinguishable learning characteristics and patterns of joint action to upgrading in processes followed by upgrading in products. The transition from preparation of Nile perch exports to introduction of value-adding technologies had been difficult and required a new form of organizing. While buyers played a minimal role in supporting process-related upgrading following a European Union ban, they have been more important in the second round of upgrading involving the introduction of value-adding technologies. The chapter underlines the clusters' ability to upgrade rapidly in processes to meet new requirements by export markets and the difficulties in introducing product-related change. It also highlights the minimal role of buyers in process upgrading and their more significant role in product upgrading.

Lorentzen, Glen Robbins and Justin Barnes begin from the premise that whether or in what form a cluster exists or defines itself is of less relevance than how it gains competitive advantage and through what means and processes. In their study of the Durban Automotive Cluster the authors focus on the gains to the clustered firms through joint action in the areas of supplier development, human resource development, logistics and benchmarking. They contrast their findings with benefits accrued to firms through increased international competition and technical assistance by foreign partners. As with all other cases reported in this book, the backdrop for the Durban Automotive Cluster case study is the aggressive trade liberalization of the 1990s and its impact on the competitiveness of the domestic automotive sector in South Africa. The foundations of the sector were laid in the post-World War II period by the government of South Africa. Like a number of governments in other developing countries, such as Taiwan and South Korea, the South African government adopted an industrial development policy framework based on import substitution after the war. This policy was bolstered in the last quarter of the twentieth century as the apartheid regime began to suffer the effects of international isolation and sanctions and reacted with greater efforts to become self-sufficient in strategic market areas.

Due to political regime changes and drastically changed external market conditions, the obsession with self-sufficiency gave way to an accelerated programme of liberalization. In its wisdom, the post-apartheid South African government intervened to ensure that the domestic automobile sector could compete under the new market conditions. Benchmarking was used in commissioned studies of the sector, supported by the provincial government and international donor agencies, to examine the gaps between the performance standards of domestic firms and the new performance standards required for meeting the expectations of multinationals. Significant features of the Durban Automotive Cluster include the ability to learn from past experiences, an equitable mode of governance that ensures key actors such as Toyota do not wield excessive procedural control, consistent funding with limited conditions from all levels of government and full engagement of researchers from the academic community. The cluster that has emerged is characterized by a high degree of trust among its member firms. However, Lorentzen et al. caution that the emergence of new formal and informal institutions within the cluster were neither spontaneous nor initiated by concerned firms and that the government played a quite instrumental role in creating the necessary conditions for collaborative initiatives among firms.

McCormick and Winnie Mitullah analyse the institutions charged with managing a fish cluster on the Kenyan side of Lake Victoria. They rightly point out that fisheries management is as much about people as it is about fish and ecosystems. This realization has brought about changes in the institutional framework that are gradually creating a system of co-management. Co-management in this context is a system in which government, the community of fishers, external agents and other stakeholders share the responsibility and authority for making decisions about fishery management. They assert the new direction is positive, but many problems remain. The stickiest of these may be the inequalities of power and economic resources among the different parties who are supposed to cooperate.

Morris and Robbins pay particular attention to the role of government in fostering cluster formation. A synthesis of the evolution of South Africa's post-apartheid industrial policy serves as the basis for highlighting the positive and negative experiences of two successful automotive clusters. The analysis emphasizes the role played by the government at multiple scales and over time in shaping the current state of these clusters. Like other industrial sectors in South Africa, the automotive clusters were protected under the apartheid regime through a policy of import substitution. The post-apartheid era was marked by a less protective government and an industrial policy aimed at a more open domestic market and increased exports. The institutional measures taken by the South African government included the creation of a new Department of Trade and Industry (DTI) with a mandate to open up the economy to competition and to increase exports to global markets. Part of this mandate was to support the growth of micro, small and medium-sized enterprises. Measures taken by DTI in this regard included access to credit and market information, the provision of training and labour market reforms. More broadly, DTI's industrial policies and programmes were based on five pillars: investment support, trade liberalization, a technology policy, human resources development through education and facilitation of collaborative arrangements for information and expertise exchange among firms. Together these measures played a central role in defining the development trajectory of the automotive sector.

Focusing on learning and the spread of information and communication technologies within clusters as a means to increase competencies and collective efficiency, the chapter by Oyelaran-Oyeyinka, Kaushalesh Lal and Catherine Nyaki Adeya examines the uptake of information and communication technologies (ICTs) by the Suame cluster in northern Ghana and the Kamukunji and Kariobangi clusters in Kenya. The authors report that there have been no known policies to introduce ICTs in clusters and collective learning by clustered micro and small enterprises seems to have occurred in response to collective needs. To understand the dynamics of this learning process the authors focus on the role of formal and informal institutions and test a series of hypotheses on the relationships between learning and the sources of information. Two sets of pre-existing conditions are identified for adopting new technologies. The firm-specific conditions are the academic qualification and knowledge of the person in charge of the enterprise, the level of motivation by the leading person to provide the workforce with training on the use of new technologies, skill intensity of the workforce, sales turnover and profit margin. The cluster-specific conditions are the presence of training and collective technological support entities within the cluster and the expectation of the clustered firms to benefit from inter-firm sharing of facilities.

As far as policy measures to induce a higher level of innovation, the authors suggest encouragement through policy for greater private sector participation in setting up training and information service centres within clusters. The authors also suggest that the personnel from leading firms need orientation programmes to build awareness of the potential and actual benefits of adopting new technologies. To support and/or steer moves toward new technology adoption, governments can provide a host of economic incentives including subsidies and financing schemes.

It is clear from the above chapter summaries that to varying degrees the authors in this volume attribute considerable weight to the role of government in industrial development. That governments should play a key role is hardly at the centre of the debates on industrialization. Nevertheless, there continue to be disagreements about the level of government involvement in industrial development, the manner in which government intervenes against it or interacts with it and the dynamics of the global market in relation to the domestic industrial base. From a development policy perspective, Mytelka (in this volume) points out that the emergence of clusters may be nurtured through policy intervention but not manufactured. As she puts it, promotion of clusters with the narrow objective of building up a manufacturing sector rather misses the point about the value of clusters by seeing them as magic bullets for development. The emphasis should be placed on how to create an environment conducive to "continuous learning, capacity building and innovation as needs, opportunities and conditions change". Under these conditions clusters can emerge organically as an integrated part of the economic production system.

Industrial policy aimed at nurturing the growth and sustenance of domestic firms is by no means a straightforward task. There is often a large discrepancy between outcomes and objectives in the industrial policy-making arena, particularly in developing countries. The factors to give rise to this discrepancy are simultaneously endogenous and exogenous and often independent as variables. Some governments have been more successful than others in meeting their industrial policy objectives as the two chapters on South Africa clearly illustrate. But is South Africa's relative success due primarily to government action or are there pre-existing conditions that facilitate and complement government intervention? We invite the readers of this book to consider this two-part question while reading the various chapters. We will attempt to provide our own answers to this important question in the concluding chapter.

Notes

1. Marshall (1890), book V, chapter 4, paragraph 3.
2. In a narrow sense, institutions are seen merely as organizations, such as universities and technological service groups, whereas more broadly the concept includes the political and social context and the rules regulating innovation.
3. Coriat and Dosi (1998) refer to the broad meaning of institutions as having three components: (1) formal organizations (ranging from firms to technical societies, trade unions, universities and state agencies); (2) patterns of behaviour that are collectively shared (from routines to social conventions to ethical codes); and (3) negative norms and constraints (from moral proscriptions to formal laws).

REFERENCES

Becattini, G. (1990) "The Marshallian Industrial District as Socio-economic Notion", in Frank Pyke, Giacomo Becattini and Werner Sengenberger, eds, *Industrial Districts and Inter-firm Co-operation in Italy*, Geneva: International Labour Organisation, 37–51.

Coriat, B. and G. Dosi (1998) "The Institutional Embeddedness of Economic Change: An Appraisal of 'Evolutionary' and 'Regulationist' Research Programmes", in B. Coriat and G. Dosi, *The Institutional Embeddedness of Economic Change: An Appraisal of "Evolutionary" and "Regulationist" Research Programmes*, Cheltenham: Edward Elgar Publishing, 3–31.

Dahlman, C. and R. R. Nelson (1995) "Social Absorption Capability, National Innovation Systems and Development in Long Term Economic Growth", in B. Koo and D. Perkins, eds, *Social Capability and Long-Term Economic Growth*, New York: St Martin's Press, 82–122.

Edquist, Charles (1997) "System of Innovation Approaches – Their Emergence and Characteristics", in Charles Edquist, ed., *Systems of Innovation, Technologies, Institutions and Organisations*, London: Pinter.

Ehrnberg, Ellinor and Staffan Jacobsson (1997) "Technological Discontinuities and Incumbents' Performance: An Analytical Framework", in Charles Edquist, ed., *Systems of Innovation: Technologies, Institutions and Organisations*, London: Pinter.

Freeman, C. (1987) *Technology Policy and Economic Performance: Lessons from Japan*, London: Frances Printer.

Freeman, C. (2002) "Continental National and Sub-National Innovation Systems – Complementary and Economic Growth", *Research Policy* 31: 191–211.

Humphrey, John and Hubert Schmitz (2002) "How Insertion in Global Value Chains Affects Upgrading in Industrial Clusters", *Regional Studies* 36(9): 1017–27.

Kennedy, Loraine (1999) "Cooperating for Survival: Tannery Pollution and Joint Action in the Palar Valley (India)", *World Development* 27(9): 1673–91.

Kline, S. J. and Nathan Rosenberg (1986) "An Overview of Innovation", in R. Landau and N. Rosenberg eds, *The Positive Sum Strategy*, New York: National Academy Press, 275–305.

Lall, Sanjaya (1992) "Structural Problems of African Industry", in F. Stewart, Sanjaya Lall and Sam Wangwe, eds, *Alternative Development Strategies in Subsaharan Africa*, London: Macmillan, 103–44.

Lall, S. (2001) *Competitiveness, Technology and Skills*, Cheltenham, UK, and Northampton, Mass.: Edward Elgar.

Lundvall, Bengt-Åke, ed. (1992) *National Systems of Innovation: Towards a Theory of Innovation and Interactive Learning*, London: Pinter Publishers.

McCormick, Dorothy (1999) "African Enterprise Clusters and Industrialization: Theory and Reality", *World Development*, 27(9): 1531–52.

Marshall, Alfred (1890) *Principles of Economics*, London: Macmillan. See also http://www.Econlib.Org/Library/Marshall/

Marshall, Alfred (1919) *Industry and Trade*, London: Macmillan.

Messner, Dirk (2004) "Regions in the World Economic Triangle", in Hubert Schmitz, ed., *Local Enterprises in the Global Economy: Issues of Governance and Upgrading*, Cheltenham, UK: Edward Elgar.

Mytelka, Lynn (2000) "Local Systems of Innovation in a Globalized World Economy", *Industry and Innovation* 7(1): 15–32.

Mytelka, L. K. and B. Oyelaran-Oyeyinka (2000) "Systems of Innovation, Natural Resources and Competitiveness in Africa", a paper presented to the Working Group on Food Security and Technology, Economic Commission on Africa (ECA), Addis Ababa, Ethiopia, April.

Nadvi, Khalid (1994) "Industrial District Experiences in Developing Countries", in UNCTAD, *Technological Dynamism in Industrial Districts: An Alternative Approach to Industrialisation in Developing Countries?* New York and Geneva: United Nations.

Nelson, R. R. (1987) *Understanding Technical Change as an Evolutionary Process*, Amsterdam: North Holland.

Nelson, Richard R. (2001) "On the Uneven Evolution of Human Know-How", ISERP Working Paper 01–05, New York: Columbia University, Institute for Social and Economic Research Policy.

Nelson, Richard R. and B. Sampat (2001) "Making Sense of Institutions as a Factor in Economic Growth", *Journal of Economic Organisation and Behaviour* 44: 31–54.

Nelson, Richard and Sydney Winter (1982) *An Evolutionary Theory Of Economic Change*, Cambridge, Mass.: Harvard University Press.

North, Douglass (1989) "Institutions and Economic Growth: An Historical Introduction", *World Development* 17(9): 1319–32.

North, Douglass (1990) *Institutions, Institutional Change and Economic Performance*, Cambridge: Cambridge University Press.

Porter, M. E. (1990) *The Competitive Advantage of Nations*, New York: Macmillan.

Porter, Michael (1998) "Clusters and the New Economics of Competition", *Harvard Business Review*, 76: 77–90.

Pyke, F. and W. Sengenberger, eds (1992) *Industrial Districts and Local Economic Regeneration*, Geneva: International Institute for Labour Studies (ILO).

Roelandt, Theo J. A. and Pim Den Hertog (1999) "Cluster Analysis and Cluster-Based Policy in OECD Countries", in OECD, *Boosting Innovation: The Cluster Approach*, Paris.

Saxenian, Annalee (1991) "The Origins and Dynamics of Production Networks in Silicon Valley", *Research Policy* 20(5): 423–47.

Saxenian, Annalee (1994) *Regional Advantage: Culture and Competition in Silicon Valley and Route 128*, Cambridge, Mass.: Harvard University Press.

Schmitz, H. (1995) "Collective Efficiency: Growth Path for Small-Scale Industry", *Journal of Development Studies* 31(4): 529–66.

Schmitz, Hubert, ed. (2004) *Local Enterprises in the Global Economy: Issues of Governance and Upgrading*, Cheltenham, UK: Edward Elgar.

Schmitz, Hubert and Khalid Nadvi (1999) "Clustering and Industrialisation: Introduction", *World Development*, 27(9): 1503–14.

Scott, Allen J. (2002) "Regional Push: Towards a Geography of Development and Growth in Low- and Middle-Income Countries", *Third World Quarterly*, 23(1): 437–161.

Scott, Allen J. and Michael Storper (2003) "Regions, Globalisation, Development", *Regional Studies* 37(6–7): 579–93.

Schumpeter, Joseph A. (1934) *The Theory of Economic Development*, Cambridge, Mass.: Harvard University Press.

Smale, Melinda and Vernon Ruttan (1997) "Social Capital and Technical Change: The *Groupements Naam* of Burkina Faso", in Christopher Clague, ed., *Institutions and Economic Development: Growth and Governance in Less-Developed and Post-Socialist Countries*, Baltimore: The John Hopkins University Press.

Storper, M. (1995) "The Resurgence of Regional Economies Ten Years Later: The Region as a Nexus of Untraded Interdependencies", *European Urban Regional Studies* 2(3): 161–221.

Tushman, Michael and William L. Moore (1982) *Readings in the Management of Innovation*, Boston: Pitman Press.

World Development (1999) "Special Issue: Industrial Clusters in Developing Countries", *World Development* 27(9): 1503–1734.

2

Industrialization through cluster upgrading: Theoretical perspectives

Dorothy McCormick

This chapter starts with the concept of an enterprise cluster as offered by Schmitz (1992): A cluster is a geographic and sectoral agglomeration of enterprises. The definition falls naturally into three parts, each of which suggests a relevant body of theory for our consideration. A cluster is defined geographically. It is, in other words, located in a particular place and embedded in particular institutions that together comprise the national or local business system. A cluster is defined sectorally. It is a group of enterprises engaged in the same or related activities. In recent years, it has become popular to look at sectors in terms of particular value chains, i.e., the chain of production from the conception of a product to its final distribution and even its disposal as waste material. Finally, the definition of a cluster holds within it – though not in all cases evident in reality – the potential for firm linkages and positive or negative externalities. The physical closeness of firms allows them to interact in various ways, both with each other and with those outside of the cluster.

The recognition that clusters are spatially confined and influenced by local conditions should not, however, obscure the fact that they and the firms they encompass are situated in an increasingly globalized world. This means that even those in fairly remote areas are affected by global institutions and are often linked to actors in distant places. The analysis of clusters must increasingly take into account the ways in which global linkages affect local relationships (Meagher, 2005; Schmitz, 2004).

The purpose of this chapter is to explore the main theoretical perspectives taken by cluster studies to set the stage for the empirical analyses

Industrial clusters and innovation systems in Africa: Institutions, markets and policy, Oyelaran-Oyeyinka and McCormick (eds), United Nations University Press, 2007, ISBN 978-92-808-1137-7

presented in the chapters that follow. The chapter is written in five parts. The following section discusses some of the institutions shaping the business systems of African countries. The focus of this book leads us to be selective in this and the following sections, and to place the heaviest emphasis on variables that appear to affect innovation and upgrading. The next section outlines the basics of value chain analysis, focusing particularly on issues such as benchmarking and upgrading potential that are expected to affect the cluster's ability to upgrade. The penultimate section looks at questions around whether and how firms in clusters interact and what happens as a result. The final section attempts to draw the three theoretical perspectives together and to point the way toward a comprehensive frame of analysis.

Cluster upgrading and the business system

Clusters, like individual firms, operate in a particular institutional environment. This environment defines the rules by which the cluster and the enterprises within it must and do play. Business environments are complex, so it is useful to analyse them at two levels: the level of individual institutions and the level of the system formed by those institutions and their interactions.

Institutions of the business system

Using the broad framework of the New Institutional Economics, we define institutions as "humanly devised constraints to human interaction" (North, 1990: 3). Some constraints are formal, in that there are written rules, while others are informal norms or codes of conduct. Institutions operate in different spheres of a society's life, with some being mainly social, others political and still others economic.

We also follow North (1990) in distinguishing institutions from organizations. To use his sports analogy, institutions are the "rules of the game" while organizations are its players.[1] Institutions include rules such as a country's constitution, a community's social norms and the regulations governing the administration of university examinations. Organizations are the embodiment of the institutions; they are, quite simply, the players. Thus, if the state has a constitution, it requires various governmental organizations to implement its provisions. If examination regulations are institutions, they require a complex organization to carry them out.

Whitley's (1992) pioneering study of business systems argues that the basic building blocks of any national system are firms, markets and the

state. Other institutions, ranging from the legal system of laws and contracts to social institutions such as family, ethnicity and gender, also influence businesses and shape their operations in particular ways.

Although one could identify a dozen or more groups of institutions
that affect the way business is conducted in particular contexts,[2] this
chapter concentrates on those believed to be most closely associated
with cluster upgrading: product markets; firm linkages, including business
networks and associations; laws and contracts; systems of state support;
and education, technology and innovation systems. The selection is not
meant to be limiting. Individual chapters bring other institutions into
their analyses to explain particular aspects of cluster behaviour.

Institutions shaping cluster upgrading

Product markets

Studies of business necessarily revolve around markets.[3] Broadly speaking, a market is any context in which the sale or purchase of goods or
services takes place. Taking an institutional perspective, we define a
market as a set of rules for the exchange of goods and/or services
(McCormick and Kimuyu, forthcoming). Markets can be viewed and
categorized in different ways. One of these is the purpose to which the
good or service is to be put. Thus, firms speak of their supply or input
markets and their product markets. Business and industry also find it
useful to describe markets by their geographic reach, speaking of the
local or domestic market, regional markets and the global market. This
designation is important because the characteristics of customers in different places shape the nature, quality and price of the products being offered, the logistics of getting those products to market, and the strategies
that have to be used to compete successfully.

Researchers have argued that global markets are important sources of
firm learning because the intense competition forces firms to improve
their quality and efficiency (see, for example, Gereffi, 2001). Although
this may be true in many cases, not all export markets are quality-
conscious, nor are all domestic markets made up of low-income consumers. The link that seems to be emerging from studies in India and
elsewhere is one between demanding markets – wherever they are
located – and process and/or product upgrading (Knorringa, 1999; Mc-
Cormick, 2004; Tewari, 1999).

Firms and firm linkages

Firms are the basic unit of business activity, the building blocks of the
business system. They occupy a key position between the market and

the state, and both market and state determine their nature and function. In neo-classical economics literature, a firm makes a single product and is defined by that product's production function. Inside the firm, inputs are turned into outputs steadily and smoothly, so that all variations in internal organization can safely be ignored. Real-world firms are more complex. They often make multiple products, either simultaneously or in sequence. Production is subject to delays caused by everything from poor management to unavoidable power failures. They differ in size, form of ownership, internal organization and the ways in which they link with other firms.

Differences in firm size are as likely to be due to the owner's resources or preferences as they are to available economies of scale. An institutional environment that favours larger or smaller firms may be an important determinant of size. Firms also differ in form of ownership and legal status. Although the single-owner firm is most common, partnerships and limited liability companies also exist in most developing countries. Some firms are formally registered with the authorities, while others, for various reasons, operate without such formalities. Firms also differ in their internal organization and management, developing unique sets of firm-level institutions governing such matters as authority relations, worker benefits, working hours and discipline.

Firms often find it advantageous to come together in networks, linkages and subcontracting relationships. Such external relationships enable them to do things that they cannot easily do alone. Business or social networks, for example, can be extremely important in identifying new markets, getting information about suppliers, or deciding whether to offer credit to a new customer. Firms may come together in business associations. Some of these are general, while others are sector- or location-specific. Associations are sometimes vehicles for influencing government to behave in ways favourable to business – what Olson (1971) called "the logic of influence". They may also offer specific services aimed at meeting their members' needs for training, information, technical advice or general consultancy. Olson (1971) has argued that because influence is ultimately a public good that can be enjoyed even by those who choose not to belong to an association, it alone is not enough to draw members into an association.

Laws and contracts

The exchange of goods and services requires a system of laws, including those governing the making and enforcement of contracts. In countries where the legal system is weak, or it is difficult or costly to enforce property rights, doing business is risky. In such situations, businesspersons must often resort to substitutes for the formal legal system. They may be reluctant to start an order without a down payment, or require that all transactions be paid in cash. Alternatively, they may choose to restrict their dealings to persons within their own community or who are personally known to them in order to minimize losses.

While such actions are perfectly reasonable strategies for the individual firm, they tend to reduce the efficiency and reliability of the overall business system and lead to fragmentation of the economy (Faschamps, 1996). Despite wide recognition of this contract problem, little has been done to remedy it in most African countries.

Systems of state support

States differ in their basic orientations. Politically, some are autocratic, while others adopt varying forms of liberal democracy. Their relationship to the economy can, in theory, range from pure laissez faire to centrally planned. African states gained independence at a time when many thought that considerable state intervention was necessary to compensate for the lack of indigenous private capital (Pedersen and Mc-Cormick, 1999). As a result, countries developed large parastatal sectors. By 1980 the World Bank estimated that state-owned enterprises accounted for 17 per cent of gross domestic product in sub-Saharan Africa (Van Dijk, 1994). Structural adjustment and its accompanying privatization policies have changed this somewhat, but many countries continue to have substantial direct involvement in production.

In addition to being directly involved in production, states support business in other ways. The key mechanisms are policies, regulations and infrastructure. Policy, the main support mechanism, sets the broad framework within which production and distribution take place. Both macro-economic policy and specific incentive policies can either facilitate or constrain business development.

Government also affects business by formulating and enforcing specific rules and regulations. These include measures such as business licensing and registration requirements, health and safety regulations, minimum wage regulations, zoning or business location rules and tax regulations. The nature of these regulations and the ways in which they are enforced can have a major impact on business.

Business also depends on government to provide certain basic facilities. Of these, undoubtedly the most important is physical infrastructure, including roads, power, water, sanitation and telecommunications. Whether appropriate facilities exist, as well as their condition, cost and accessibility, all affect the nature and efficient operations of business.

Education, technology and innovation systems

Education, technology and a country's innovation system have direct bearing on the types of businesses formed, the way they are organized and their ability to compete in various markets. Although the level of education in most African countries has increased dramatically since independence, this has not been accompanied by increasing levels of industrial technology and productivity (Biggs et al., 1995; Pedersen and McCormick, 1999). In part, this may be due to education systems that emphasize arts over sciences and academic learning rather than problem solving or practical applications. It also stems from poorly funded technical education that gives students only the most rudimentary skills.

In industrialized countries, new technologies are often diffused through subcontracting relationships. Although subcontracting happens in Africa, there is little evidence of its resulting in technological upgrading. This may be because even large enterprises tend to operate with very low levels of technology (Pedersen and McCormick, 1999).

Business systems

Institutions do not stand alone, but interact to create a business system. The business system is a distinct form of business practice and organization brought about by the interaction of institutions in a particular place (McCormick and Kimuyu, forthcoming; Whitley, 1992). As a cluster is location-specific, its firms share an institutional environment; sometimes they reinforce one another, while at other times they work in opposition. Regardless of how they relate, their interaction creates a system within which business must operate in any given place and time.

Business systems are dynamic. Because the institutions of the business system are interrelated and interactive, the entire system changes whenever there is a significant change in one or more of its institutional components. The change may be immediate or delayed, but it will occur. A change in business registration regulations is likely to have an immediate effect, while changes in other institutions may take longer to register. For example, when the Kenyan government sent one million children to school by proclaiming universal primary education, there were both immediate and long-term effects. Immediately, money that parents might have spent on school fees was freed for spending on other goods or investing in a business, thus boosting business activity. At the same time, the population was growing more educated, which has a long-term effect on the skill base of the labour force.

Business systems include many more groups of institutions than could be described here. It is important for analysts and readers of this book not to confine their thinking to these few, but to see how other institutions also interact and affect the development of the business system under consideration.

Value chains and upgrading

The business system provides the backdrop for business in a particular place. To understand particular businesses, however, it is necessary to know something about the product produced and the various steps it undergoes as it moves from the idea stage to the final consumer. For this, we turn to the useful device of the value chain.

Concept of a value chain

The notion of production involving a "chain" of activities ranging from conceptualizing the product to bringing it to market is not new in industrial thinking. Businesses speak of "supply chains", while the activities of global players have been variously described as international production networks, global commodity chains and *filières* (Gereffi et al., 2001). The concept of a "global value chain" has been seen by many as the most inclusive and most useful. This is because it highlights not only the activities themselves and their interlinkages, but also the value addition that is created at each step. Chains are often diagrammed to show the flow of goods and/or information from the initial design to the final consumers (figure 2.1). More elaborate diagrams show the entrance of particular services into the chain, as well as the providers of machinery and supplies.

Global commodity chains

Although not the first to discuss global commodity chains, Gereffi is credited with developing the concept into an analytical framework that could be applied to various products. Perhaps even more importantly, Gereffi's approach highlights the role played by those who control the chain – what came to be called "chain governance" (Applebaum and Gereffi, 1994; Gereffi, 1994a, 1994b). Gereffi (1994a) observed that contemporary industrialization is the result of an integrated system of global trade and production. In his view, the global commodity chain perspective underscores the need to look both at the geographical spread of transnational production arrangements, and at the linkages between various economic agents in order to understand their sources of both stability and change.

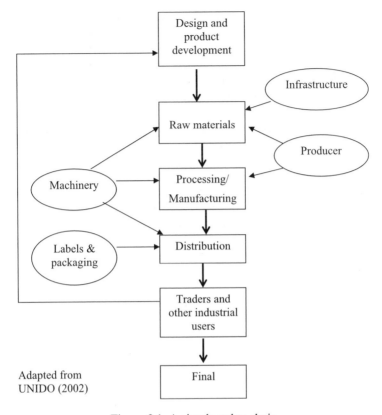

Figure 2.1 A simple value chain

In this model, global commodity chains have three main dimensions: (1) an input-output structure, or a sequence of value-adding economic activities; (2) a territoriality or geographic dimension; and (3) a governance structure. The first two dimensions are fairly straightforward. The sequence of value-adding activities is usually conceptualized as beginning with product design and ending with the sale of that product to its final consumer. Territoriality places the chain on the map. Global chains, with the various stages taking place in different parts of the world, receive the most attention, but the territoriality of regional, national or even subnational chains can also be traced.

The notion of chain governance distinguishes the conceptualization of global commodity chains from other models such as supply chains or filières. A chain's governance structure consists of the authority and power relationships that determine how financial, material and human resources are allocated and flow within a chain (Gereffi, 1994a: 215). Although this definition allows for many forms of chain governance, Gereffi concentrates on only two: producer-driven and buyer-driven commodity chains. Producer-driven commodity chains occur in those industries in which transnational corporations or other large integrated industrial enterprises play the central role in controlling the production system. The automobile industry – at least as it was in the 1980s and 1990s – is the classic illustration of a producer-driven commodity chain. Multinational firms such as Toyota and Ford organized and controlled the production of vehicles bearing their names.

Buyer-driven commodity chains, on the other hand, refer to those industries in which large retailers, brand-name merchandisers, and trading companies are the main actors organizing and controlling production. They do this by setting up decentralized production networks in a variety of exporting countries, mostly in the global South. Buyer-driven commodity chains have become dominant in labour-intensive consumer goods industries such as garments, toys, footwear and consumer electronics. Companies such as Nike, Liz Claiborne and The Gap design, but do not manufacture, the products that carry their labels.

Recent scholarship has taken the notion of chain governance beyond the "buyer-driven – producer-driven" dichotomy. Gereffi (2001) himself introduced a third type, which he called the Internet-oriented chains. Some have refined the categories based on the nature of the networks comprising the chain. McCormick and Schmitz (2002) identify four main types of governance: market, balanced network, directed network and hierarchy. Others have used the analogy of civic governance to develop a more complex analysis. Kaplinsky and Morris (2002: 67) examined a range of issues such as making, implementing and enforcing rules; the types of sanctions used to enforce rules; legitimacy of rule-makers; and the reach and boundaries of rules.

Global value chains

Value chains are essentially the same as commodity chains. The difference between the terms lies in their emphasis on particular issues. Several issues emerge as especially important in the value chain literature. Not surprisingly, the first of these is the measurement of value and the related issue of returns to different actors in the chain.

The literature on global value chains stresses the fact that each activity in a chain adds value to the final product. These value additions can be calculated in order to see how much accrues to each actor along the chain. The calculation requires a methodology that includes mapping the chain and then calculating (or at least estimating) the value additions.

Several handbooks discuss and illustrate these tasks in some detail (see Kaplinsky and Morris, 2002; McCormick and Schmitz, 2002). The data requirements for such calculations are immense and can be very difficult to obtain in places where firms' financial information is not public domain. In these situations, researchers have to either conduct their own surveys or make estimates based on key informant interviews.

The distribution of gains along the chain is related both to skills and competencies and to chain governance. The relative size of the returns to different activities reflects their strength in various competencies. Functions such as design, branding and marketing command high returns. Production activities are less remunerative because they are relatively easy and competition is intense (McCormick and Schmitz, 2002). Remuneration is not only a function of higher-level skills, but also of chain governance. The highest returns generally go to those who control the network.

Benchmarking

Competitiveness – whether internationally or in one's own neighbourhood – implies some sort of comparison with one's competitors. Here the value chain literature has adopted the term "benchmarking" (see Kaplinsky and Morris, 2002). Organizations use benchmarking as a tool for evaluating performance, learning from best practices and understanding how best practices can be achieved (UNIDO, 2002). Benchmarks are needed because for many facets of performance there are no theoretical norms. Are costs low enough? Is quality good or only medium? Is the on-time delivery rate acceptable? The best guide when addressing such questions is the performance of other firms or clusters, especially the industry leaders or direct competitors. For benchmarking to improve productive capacity, the benchmarks must be set high enough to be challenging and certainly higher than current firm, cluster or industry practice.

Benchmarking requires measurement and measurement in turn requires data. For large firms, this requirement is usually not a problem, but micro and small enterprises (MSEs) often operate with a minimum of record keeping. Benchmarking in such situations is likely to be based on rough estimates and, therefore, less effective than it would be if accurate information were available.

Standards and specifications

Observers have begun to recognize the importance of standards and the ability to meet buyer specifications in the upgrading of value chains (Kaplinsky and Readman, 2001). A standard is a rule, normally for measuring capacity, quality or other aspects of production. They include machine capacity standards, labour standards, product quality standards and process quality standards.

For a variety of reasons, there has been a growing demand for both product and process standards. Some of these are legally codified for particular products, while others reflect an agreed set of procedures ratified by national and/or international organizations. The high profile International Standards Organization (ISO) 9000 quality standard and ISO 14000 environmental management system standard are designed to improve product quality (ISO 9000) and minimize the negative environmental impacts of the production process (ISO 14000). Others include health and safety standards, labour standards, content standards and food hygiene.

Firms wishing to export must meet the product standards of the country of destination. For example, firms exporting fish to the European Union must satisfy the EU's hygiene standards. International concern over sweatshops and other social issues has also led some global buyers to monitor their suppliers' adherence to labour standards (McCormick and Schmitz, 2002). Even when a firm or cluster is at the second or third tier of suppliers, the issue of standards can be raised. Many large footwear and apparel buyers have adopted labour codes of conduct designed to guarantee workers reasonable wages and working conditions. These are meant to apply not only to first-tier suppliers, but also to outsourced production.

Specifications are the detailed description of the construction, workmanship, materials and other elements of work to be done. Producers at all levels must be able to make their products according to specifications. The ability to meet specifications is often a determining factor in the entry of a particular firm into a value chain. Prospective buyers will usually provide either a sample of an item to be manufactured or a set of specifications with a request for one or more prototypes. Getting the contract to produce depends on the firm's ability to make exactly what is specified. MSEs have particular difficulty with specifications because they are used to making single items for customers who provide a general idea of what they want rather than exact specifications.

Chain upgrading

The discussion thus far raises a critical issue: What can be done to increase the returns to individuals and firms in poor countries? Attempts to answer this question have generated lengthy discussions of the possibility and probability of upgrading productive activities. Upgrading involves changes in the nature and mix of activities, both within each link in the chain, and in the distribution of intra-chain activities (Kaplinsky and Morris, 2002: 38). The aim is to replace basic, low-paid activities with activities that command higher returns. Four types of upgrading have been identified:

1. Process upgrading, which increases the efficiency of internal processes, thus making the firm more competitive in making existing products;
2. Product upgrading, which involves introducing new products or improving old products faster than rivals;
3. Functional upgrading, which involves increasing value added by changing the mix of activities conducted within the firm, or moving from low-return activities to high-return activities; and
4. Chain upgrading, which, as its name suggests, means moving to a new, more profitable chain.

The literature suggests that the order in which these types have been listed also represents the usual upgrading path (Bair and Gereffi, 2001; Gereffi, 1999; Gereffi and Memedovic, 2003; Kaplinsky and Morris, 2002; Lee and Chen, 2000). Firms first upgrade their processes in order to become competitive, then move into product upgrading. The third step is functional upgrading, in which firms that have become competent in simple assembly operations begin to take on additional functions, such as design, cutting, finishing and marketing. The final upgrading strategy involves changing chains. In electronics, for example, firms may gradually shift from the manufacture of transistor radios to making laptop computers.

Functional upgrading has received considerable attention, probably because it seems to offer producers in poor countries an immediate possibility of higher returns. Bair and Gereffi (2001) follow this aspect of upgrading with a jeans manufacturer located in Torreon, Mexico. In 1993, the producers were subcontracted by US buyers to carry out only a single function – assembly – while US firms undertook the remaining eight activities. Seven years later, in 2000, the Mexican firms were involved in five of the nine activities, leaving only design, marketing and retailing completely in the hands of the US buyers. This represented significant upgrading in a relatively short time. It is important to note that in this case, functional upgrading at industry level was accompanied by improvements in workers' skill levels, wages and working conditions. This suggests that industrial upgrading could form part of a country's overall development strategy and could also be applied to specific clusters.

Clusters and collective efficiency

We turn finally to the theory that derives directly from the study of enterprise clusters. Schmitz (1995) called the set of advantages accruing to clustered firms *collective efficiency*. The advantages come from two benefits that may (but do not always) accompany such grouping: external economies and joint action. The first dimension of collective efficiency is essentially passive and consists of reaping the benefits of the external economies generated by the agglomeration of firms. The second involves active collaboration between firms (Nadvi, 1996).

External economies

An external economy, or positive externality, exists when the actions of one actor create benefits for another actor. An externality, therefore, is the unintended or incidental by-product of economic action. It is, in that sense, the passive side of collective efficiency (Nadvi, 1996). At least four types of external economies are believed to occur in enterprise clusters: market access, labour market pooling, intermediate input effects and technological spillovers (Krugman, 1991; McCormick, 1999; Marshall, 1890; Nadvi and Schmitz, 1994).

Market access is the most common external economy for clustered firms. It results from the fact that clusters of similar enterprises attract buyers from both the immediate vicinity and more distant places. Thus, once a cluster is established, market access is a major benefit of locating within its bounds.

Labour market pooling is the concentration of specialized skills that often develops within manufacturing clusters. The pooling occurs through skills upgrading within the cluster and the attraction to the cluster of persons who already have relevant skills. The importance of labour market pooling varies from one cluster to another, depending on the demands of the production process for specialized skills.

Intermediate input effects are externalities associated with the emergence of specialized suppliers of inputs and services. Suppliers of inputs often arise in clusters. Sometimes this is the result of changes and specialization among existing firms in the cluster or (as in the case of labour) attraction of new firms from outside.

Technological spillovers involve the diffusion of technological knowledge and ideas. Since clustering puts firms in close proximity, they are encouraged to learn from one another and to share ideas. Technological spillovers within a cluster can be crucial to a cluster's upgrading and, ultimately, to a country's industrial development.

It is important to note that the collective efficiency model highlights the positive effects of external economies. This is in sharp contrast to mainstream economics that treats the differences between social and private returns as market failures to be "cured" by policy. Yet not all externalities are beneficial. Some are "disabling" in the sense that they have a perverse effect. For example, when poor technology is replicated and shared, the technological spillover is disabling. The fact that externalities can be either beneficial or costly (enabling or disabling) suggests that they need careful empirical investigation. Furthermore, not everyone benefits equally in successful clusters, as Beerepoot's (2003) study of the impact of cluster dynamics on different groups in the labour force demonstrates.

Joint action

Joint action is the active side of collective efficiency (Nadvi, 1996; Schmitz, 1997). Firms may consciously choose to cooperate and collaborate. The collective efficiency model assumes that it is easier to do this when firms are located near one another. Joint action can be described in terms of the number of firms involved. In bilateral joint action for example, two firms work together when they share an expensive piece of equipment. In multilateral joint action, firms join in groups such as associations or buying groups in order to gain group advantage. Joint action may also be distinguished by the cooperators' relative places in the value chain. When the firms involved are in different stages of the production-distribution chain, joint action is said to be vertical. Thus, cooperation between a supplier and its customers is vertical joint action. When the firms are at the same level, as for example when several producers cooperate to fill a large order, joint action is horizontal.

Empirical studies suggest that the level of joint action varies greatly from one cluster to another, making it clear that proximity of firms does not automatically give rise to cooperation. The cooperation that does exist seems to be mostly horizontal rather than vertical. Studies also suggest that one must look beyond the horizontal-vertical categorization of joint action to its content and purpose. At the level of content, cooperation in production and marketing seems to be more important than, for example, cooperative purchasing of raw materials or supplies (McCormick, 1999). This may be because in liberalized markets production efficiency, improved quality and marketing strategies have gained in importance, while inputs have become both cheaper and easier to obtain. The purpose of collaboration can also be revealing. For example, Barr (1998) showed that the local networks characteristic of small enterprises in Ghana tend to be aimed at reducing uncertainty rather than enhancing enterprise performance. Whether such risk-reducing collaboration has indirect effects on business investment and/or operations remains to be seen.

Collective efficiency, upgrading and industrialization

In this model, collective efficiency is not an end in itself, but a means toward what many African countries are straining to achieve, industrialization. Schmitz and Nadvi (1999) argue that clustering promotes industrialization in two main ways. First, clustering facilitates the mobilization of financial and human resources. It does this by allowing small enterprises to work in clustered settings, where linkages and subcontracting can in many cases substitute for heavy investment in inventories, machinery and human capital, and where specialization is both possible and ultimately profitable. Second, clustering allows ordinary businesspeople to take what Schmitz (1997) has termed "riskable steps". These involve small, incremental investments that over time allow firms to grow and develop.

While clustering facilitates such a two-step industrialization strategy, it is clearly not always successful. At least two additional conditions appear to be necessary for the strategy to work (Schmitz and Nadvi, 1999). The first is the existence of trade networks that enable the products made in clusters to reach appropriate markets. The absence of such networks is believed to account, at least in part, for the weakness of many African clusters. The second condition is the existence of effective sanctions and trust. As discussed earlier, the ability to make and enforce contracts, whether formally or informally, is essential to the conduct of business, especially in clusters that are attempting to develop a productive system based on the specialization and interdependence of firms.

Summary and conclusions

The discussion thus far suggests that questions related to the upgrading of industrial clusters can be addressed from at least three different theoretical perspectives, used singly or in combination.

The business system perspective focuses on the institutional environment of firms and clusters. It lends itself to looking at the impact of institutions at global, national and cluster levels. While not all firms share identical institutions, there is enough overlap to suggest that a core institutional environment exists in most clusters. The choice of institutions to be analysed depends on the focus of the research. This chapter's analysis highlighted five sets of institutions believed relevant to cluster upgrading, while acknowledging the potential importance of many others. The five – product markets; firms and firm linkages; laws and contracts; systems of state support; and education, technology and innovation systems – are expected to impact directly on the nature of clustered businesses, their organization, and the way they can compete in the market.

Some aspects of cluster operations are sector-specific. A garment-producing cluster differs from a vehicle-repair cluster in part because of the nature of the items being produced, the supplies required to make them, the support services needed and the unique features of the sector's distribution system. To understand these and other sectoral issues, we turned to value chain analysis and, in particular, to its typology of up-grading alternatives. One of the tasks in the succeeding chapters will be to examine the types of upgrading that have already been experienced in clusters and to see what would be required to move them further along the upgrading path.

The third theoretical framework examined in this chapter is the one most closely associated with clusters: collective efficiency. The primary focus of this perspective is spatial proximity, which Schmitz (1995) argues offers benefits that encourage firms to change and develop. On the one hand, external economies are the benefits that arise out of the grouping itself. They are passive benefits that may occur simply by virtue of the cluster's existence. Joint action, on the other hand, requires the active en-gagement of clustered firms. Firms must consciously choose to cooperate and collaborate. If they choose not to, there is no joint action and the cluster may fail to upgrade.

It is clear that a cluster exists in a multi-dimensional space. Further-more, the cluster itself and the firms it encompasses may be linked not only locally but also globally. In some cases, the global linkages may be actually stronger than those within the cluster. The cluster and the firms within it are part of a business system of many varied institutions that at once constrain and foster business activity. The cluster is also part of a set of value-adding activities that can be conceptualized as a chain leading from an initial design or idea to the distribution of a product to its final consumers. At the same time, the nature of a cluster as a group of enter-prises in a particular place allows it to be analysed as a collective entity, with collective benefits accruing from both the simple fact of being to-gether and the firms' joint efforts.

The chapters in this book are case studies that attempt to answer a range of questions about African clusters: Why does a particular cluster or group of clusters seem stuck in low technology? What can be done to upgrade a cluster? What policies are likely to encourage industrialization through cluster upgrading? Who benefits when clusters upgrade?

Answering such questions requires examination of the current state of the clusters at the level of the institutional environment, the value chain and the cluster itself. The keys to upgrading may be found at only one level, but if earlier studies are anything to go by, the analysis is likely to be more fruitful if it proceeds at more than one of these levels.

Notes

1. This is not the only possible distinction between institutions and organizations. In the or-ganizational development literature, organizations are technical instruments designed as

means to definite goals. Institutions, whether conceived as groups or practices, are products of interaction and adaptation that hold ideals and values. In this view, organizations may become institutions if they take on value beyond the technical requirements of the task at hand (Selznick, 1966).
2. See, for example, Hollingsworth and Boyer, 1997; McCormick and Kimuyu, forthcoming; Pedersen and McCormick, 1999; Whitley, 1992.
3. This section draws heavily on McCormick and Kimuyu (forthcoming).

REFERENCES

Applebaum, Richard and Gary Gereffi (1994) "Power and Profits in the Apparel Commodity Chain", in Edna Bonacich, Lucie Cheng, Norma Chinchilla, Nora Hamilton and Paul Ong, eds, *Global Production: The Apparel Industry in the Pacific Rim*, Philadelphia: Temple University Press.

Bair, Jennifer and Gary Gereffi (2001) "Local Clusters in Global Chains: The Causes and Consequences of Export Dynamism in Torreon's Blue Jeans Industry", *World Development* 29(11): 1885–1903.

Barr, Abigail (1998) "Enterprise Performance and the Functional Diversity of Social Capital", Centre for the Study of African Economies Working Paper WPS/98-1. Oxford: University of Oxford, CSAE Publishing.

Beerepoot, Niels (2003) "Skilled Workers in Dynamic Clusters: Labour Market Differentiation in the Furniture Cluster in Cebu (the Philippines)", paper presented to European Association of Development Institutes (EADI) Workshop, 17–18 January.

Biggs, T., M. Shah and P. Srivastava (1995) "Technical Capabilities and Learning in African Enterprise", Technical Paper No. 288, Africa Technical Department Series, Washington, D.C.: World Bank.

Fafchamps, Marcel (1996) "The Enforcement of Commercial Contracts in Ghana", *World Development* 24(1): 427–48.

Gereffi, Gary (1994a) "Capitalism, Development, and Global Commodity Chains", in Leslie Sklair, ed., *Capitalism & Development*, London: Routledge, 211–31.

Gereffi, Gary (1994b) "The Organisation of Buyer-Driven Global Commodity Chains: How U.S. Retailers Shape Overseas Production Networks", in Gary Gereffi and Miguel Korzeniewicz, eds, *Commodity Chains and Global Capitalism*, Westport, Conn.: Praeger.

Gereffi, Gary (1999) "International Trade and Industrial Upgrading in the Apparel Commodity Chain", *Journal of International Economics* 48(1): 37–70.

Gereffi, Gary (2001) "Beyond the Producer-driven/Buyer-driven Dichotomy: The Evolution of Global Value Chains in the Internet Era", *IDS Bulletin* 32(3): 30–40.

Gereffi, Gary and Olga Memedovic (2003) *The Global Apparel Value Chain: What Prospects for Upgrading by Developing Countries*, Vienna: UNIDO.

Gereffi, Gary, John Humphrey, Raphael Kaplinsky and Timothy Sturgeon (2001) "Introduction: Globalisation, Value Chains and Development", *IDS Bulletin* 32(3): 1–8.

Hollingsworth, J. and Robert Boyer (1997) *Contemporary Capitalism: The Embeddedness of Institutions*, Cambridge: Cambridge University Press.

Kaplinsky, Raphael and Mike Morris (2002) "A Handbook for Value Chain Research", prepared for the International Development Research Center, available at http://www.ids.ac.uk/Ids/Global/.

Kaplinsky, Raphael and Jeff Readman (2001) "Integrating SMEs in Global Value Chains: Towards Partnership for Development", Vienna: UNIDO.

Knorringa, Peter (1999) "Agra: An Old Cluster Facing the New Competition", *World Development*, 27(9): 1587–1604.

Krugman, Paul (1991) *Geography and Trade*, Cambridge, Mass.: MIT Press.

Lee, J.-R. and J. S. Chen (2000) "Dynamic Synergy Creation with Multiple Business Activities: Toward a Competence-Based Growth Model for Contract Manufacturers", in R. Sanchez and A. Heene, eds, *Research in Competence-Based Research*, Stamford, Conn.: Jai Press.

Marshall, Alfred (1890) *Principles of Economics*. London: Macmillan. See also http://www.Econlib.Org/Library/Marshall/.

McCormick, Dorothy (1999) "African Enterprise Clusters and Industrialization: Theory and Reality", *World Development*, 27(9): 1531–52.

McCormick, Dorothy (2004) "Upgrading MSE Clusters: Theoretical Frameworks and Political Approaches for African Industrialization", paper presented at the Regional Conference on Innovation Systems and Innovative Clusters in Africa, Bagamoyo, Prospective College of Engineering and Technology, University of Dar Es Salaam, Tanzania, 18–20 February.

McCormick, Dorothy and Peter Kimuyu (forthcoming) "Business Systems Theory: An African Perspective", in Dorothy McCormick, Patrick O. Alila and Mary Omosa, eds, *Business in Kenya: Institutions and Interactions*, Nairobi: University of Nairobi Press.

McCormick, Dorothy and Hubert Schmitz (2002) "Manual for Value Chain Research on Homeworkers in the Garment Industry", Sussex: Institute of Development Studies, or http://www.Ids.Ac.Uk/Ids/Global/Wiego.html.

Meagher, Kate (2005) "Social Networks and Economic Ungovernance in African Small Firm Clusters", paper presented for the QEH 50th Birthday Conference, Oxford: Oxford University, Queen Elizabeth House.

Nadvi, Khalid (1996) "Small Firm Industrial Districts in Pakistan", Ph.D. thesis, Brighton: Institute of Development Studies, University Of Sussex.

Nadvi, Khalid and Hubert Schmitz (1994) "Industrial Clusters in Less Developed Countries: Review of Experiences and Research Agenda", IDS Discussion Paper No. 339, Sussex: Institute of Development Studies.

North, Douglass (1990) *Institutions, Institutional Change and Economic Performance*, Cambridge: Cambridge University Press.

Olson, Mancur (1971) *The Logic of Collective Action: Public Goods and the Theory of Groups*, Cambridge, Mass.: Harvard University Press.

Pedersen, Poul Ove and Dorothy McCormick (1999) "African Business Systems in a Globalising World", *Journal of Modern African Studies* 37(1): 109–35.

Schmitz, Hubert (1992) "On the Clustering of Small Firms", *IDS Bulletin* 23(3): 64–69.

Schmitz, H. (1995) "Collective Efficiency: Growth Path for Small-Scale Industry", *Journal of Development Studies* 31(4): 529–66.

Schmitz, Hubert (1997) "Collective Efficiency and Increasing Returns", IDS Working Paper 50, Brighton: Institute of Development Studies, University Of Sussex.

Schmitz, Hubert, ed. (2004) *Local Enterprises in the Global Economy: Issues of Governance and Upgrading*, Cheltenham: Edward Elgar.

Schmitz, Hubert and Khalid Nadvi (1999) "Clustering and Industrialisation: Introduction", *World Development*, 27(9): 1503–14.

Selznick, Philip (1966) "Leadership in Administration", in Robert T. Golembiewski, Frank Gibson and Geoffrey Y. Cornog, eds, *Public Administration: Readings in Institutions, Processes, Behaviour*, Chicago: Rand McNally.

Tewari, Meenu (1999) "Successful Adjustment in Indian Industry: The Case of Ludhiana's Woollen Knitwear Cluster", *World Development*, 27(9): 1651–72.

UNIDO (2002) "Industrial Development Report 2002/2003", Vienna: United Nations Industrial Development Organisation.

Van Dijk, M. P. (1994) "Privatisation in Africa: Experiences from North and West Africa", in M. P. Van Dijk and N. G. Schultz Nordholt, eds, *Privatisation Experiences in African and Asian Countries*, Amsterdam: Siswo.

Whitley, Richard (1992) *Business Systems in East Asia: Firms, Markets and Societies*, London: Sage.

3

From clusters to innovation systems in traditional industries

Lynn K. Mytelka

During the 1980s and 1990s, changes in the pattern of production and competition in the world economy drew the attention of researchers working in the developing world to the process of innovation and its role in competitiveness and sustained economic growth.[1] Two of these stand out in particular: the increased knowledge-intensity of production and the emergence and diffusion of innovation-based competition.

Over the previous two decades production has become increasingly more knowledge-intensive as investments in intangibles such as research and development (R&D), software design, engineering, training, marketing and management came to play a greater role in the production of goods and services. Much of this development involved tacit rather than codified knowledge and mastery required a conscious effort at learning by doing, using and interacting (Mytelka, 1999, 2000).

Gradually the knowledge-intensity of production extended beyond the so-called high technology sectors to reshape a broad spectrum of traditional industries in developed and developing countries – from the shrimp and salmon fisheries in the Philippines, Norway and Chile and the forestry and flower enterprises in Kenya, the Netherlands and Colombia to the furniture, textile and clothing firms of Denmark, Italy, Taiwan and Thailand. Indeed, where linkages have been established to a wider set of knowledge inputs and the local knowledge base was deepened, these traditional industries have shown a remarkable robustness in growth of output and exports.

Industrial clusters and innovation systems in Africa: Institutions, markets and policy, Oyelaran-Oyeyinka and McCormick (eds), United Nations University Press, 2007, ISBN 978-92-808-1137-7

Within the context of more knowledge-intensive industries, firms began to compete on price as well as on their ability to innovate. In information technology, generations of semiconductor chips or software succeed the previous in less than 18 months. In more traditional industries such as textiles and clothing, design changes have turned commodities into diversified goods, while in agriculture, brand names and trademarks have heightened the importance of product innovation in, for example, coffee and flowers.

Over time, an innovation-based mode of competition became entrenched and rapidly diffused around the world through the process of trade liberalization and the deregulation of domestic markets. This raised new issues and new challenges for policymakers and enterprises in the developing world with regard to innovation and competitiveness. In particular, the new mode of competition put into question earlier views of development as a linear process based on low wages and few skilled labourers followed by a slow incremental process of catching up. When the gaps between the northern and southern hemispheres, with rare exceptions, failed to narrow, a stimulus was provided for the emergence of new thinking about the need for learning and innovation as the core of a development strategy.

This chapter draws some elements of the new thinking together, notably those strands rooted in institutional and evolutionary economics, and applies them to an analysis of the role that clustering might play in meeting the new development challenges. In so doing, this chapter provides a note of caution to those who see the promotion of clusters as a magic bullet for development. Instead, it offers a less conventional view of development, one that shifts the focus away from quantitative outputs to a process of continuous learning, capacity-building and innovation as needs, opportunities and conditions change. The chapter is structured as follows. The following section begins by reconceptualizing development in more dynamic terms and discusses the advantages of clustering from this dynamic perspective. The next section provides a complementary framework through the lens of an innovation-systems approach. The penultimate section applies the innovation systems approach to the analysis of a variety of different types of clusters in developing countries. The concluding section offers a number of observations concerning the process of transforming clusters into innovation systems.

Conceptualizing development and the role of clustering

Historically, development processes have been conceptualized more in terms of "production" than of "innovation". The traditional focus on building a system of production lent itself well to a quantitative view of development as the growth of outputs, notably in the manufacturing sector, and the speed with which this could be achieved. Building technological capabilities was not central to this process since the "technology" needed for production was defined narrowly in terms of machinery and equipment. Thus, investment rather than innovation was understood to be the critical factor in building the production system. Foreign direct investment and the licensing of product and process technologies became important vehicles for achieving the rapid growth of productive capacity. However, in most developing countries, licensing became a substitute for learning and innovation within the firm or the linking of a local knowledge base to a process of innovation in the productive sectors more generally (Mytelka, 1978; Mytelka and Barclay, 2004). In this context, trained scientists and engineers were mainly needed to market a product and operate a "technology" or production process as opposed to modifying, adapting, extending or transforming products, processes, management routines or organizational structures. R&D was even less frequently imagined as a task for developing-country enterprises. Where R&D did take place in developing countries, it was mostly limited to resolving short-term problems in the production process.

From the outset, the development literature, using productivity as a criterion, dichotomized the production system into "traditional" and "modern" sectors. Some of the earliest approaches to catching up envisaged development as a process in which labour shifted from the traditional to the modern sectors.[2] These notions have carried over into contemporary distinctions between "low-" and "high-tech" sectors while interest in upgrading the former has progressively declined. Over time, development plans and strategies refocused on the "high-tech" sectors and resources were increasingly allocated to support the infrastructure and plant, equipment and human capital needed for their growth. This widened the differential in productivity growth, learning and innovation across the high-tech/low-tech divide.

Within the context of more knowledge-intensive production and the globalization of innovation-based competition, however, new pressures were felt by local firms in developing countries to engage in a process of continuous innovation for which the production-based paradigm had ill-prepared them. The growing interest in clusters, understood mainly in terms of spatial agglomerations of enterprises and related supplier and service industries, can be traced back to changes in the competitive environment of the firm and the inadequacies of the traditional "production system" approach to dealing with them. The dynamic potential of Italy's industrial districts was at this point rediscovered (Becattini, 1978; Brusco,

1982, 1986) and the search began for similar innovative clusters elsewhere in Europe and in the developing world (Piore and Sabel, 1984; Porter, 1990; Schmitz, 1993).

To a large extent, and for small and medium-sized enterprises (SMEs) in particular, clustering is believed to offer unique opportunities to engage in the wide array of domestic linkages between users and producers, as well as between the knowledge-producing sector (universities and R&D institutes) and the goods- and services-producing sectors. This engagement would create the conditions to stimulate the learning and innovation needed to transform traditional industries (Meyer-Stamer, 1998; Meyer-Stamer et al., 2001; Nadvi, 1995; Nadvi and Schmitz, 1997; UNCTAD, 1998). Stable vertical relationships between users and producers, for example, can reduce the costs related to information and communication, the risks associated with the introduction of new products and the time needed to move an invention from the laboratory or design table to market (Ernst, Ganiatsos and Mytelka, 1998; Lundvall, 1988, 1992; Nelson, 1993). Horizontal relationships between same-sector SMEs can also yield "collective efficiencies" (Schmitz, 1997) in the form of reduced transaction costs, accelerated innovation through more rapid problem-solving and greater market access. Still other studies have pointed to the positive externalities generated by agglomerations – the availability of skilled labour, certain kinds of infrastructure, innovation-generating informal exchanges and learning made possible through the adoption of conventions (Maskell, 1996; Maskell and Malmberg, 1999; Storper, 1995). These studies also stress the supporting role that political and social institutions and policies play in the development of partnering activity and in stimulating the transformation of such networks into broader systems of innovation and production at local, regional and national levels (Best, 1990; Brusco, 1982; Piore and Sable, 1984; Storper, 1998; Wolfe and Gertler, 1998).

Since the 1970s, governments in the industrialized countries have come to believe that locational advantages such as those listed above are critical for development (Best, 1990; Danish Technology Institute, 1993). Governments at all levels – municipal, regional, national and, in the case of the European Union, quasi supra-national – began to foster the creation of science and industrial parks, incubators, export processing zones and technopoles (Mytelka, 1991; Vavakova, 1988, 1995). Clusters, as this brief overview illustrates, come in many forms and each has a unique development trajectory, principles of organization and specific problems. Moreover, not all clusters are innovation systems. Many have emerged only to stagnate as conditions changed. Others were created with limited potential for transformation into innovation systems. How might these differences be explained?

Building an innovation system

As Alfred Marshall first observed, those clusters that survived and prospered did so through a continuous process of technological and organizational change. Subsequent analyses (Boyer, 1988; Freeman, 1988; Piore and Sable, 1984) drew attention to the variety of policies that had helped to orient competition in these clusters in ways that stimulated innovation and encouraged the emergence of new norms, habits and practices supportive of an innovation process. Over time, Schumpeterian, evolutionary and institutional approaches in economics contributed to a rethinking of innovation in more systemic ways. Two innovation-system approaches constitute our point of departure.

First is the recognition that innovation is neither research nor science and technology, but rather the application of knowledge in production. It consists of the "process by which firms master and implement the design and production of goods and services that are new to them, irrespective of whether they are new to their competitors, their countries or the world" (Mytelka, 2000: 18). Innovation thus involves more than research at the frontiers of knowledge. It includes the many large and small improvements in such areas as product design and quality, production organization and management routines, and marketing. It also includes modifications in the production process and techniques that collectively reduce costs, increase efficiency, provide for human welfare and ensure environmental sustainability.

Second is an understanding of innovation as an interactive process involving a network of firms and other economic agents who, together with the institutions and policies that influence their behaviour and performance, bring new products, new processes and new forms of organization into economic use. Underlying the "systems of innovation" approach is the re-conceptualization of firms and other actors as learning organizations embedded within a broad institutional context (Freeman, 1992; Lundvall, 1988; Lundvall et al., 2002; Nelson and Winter, 1982). Institutions in this sense are not only formal structures or organizations but also "sets of common habits, routines, established practices, rules or laws that regulate the relations and interactions between individuals and groups" (Edquist, 1997: 7) and thus "prescribe behavioural roles, constrain activity and shape expectations" (Storper, 1998: 24). In contrast to earlier efforts at mapping the "science and technology" system and its relationship to the "production" system, the innovation system approach draws attention to the need for a "culture of innovation" upon which the efficiency of an innovation system rests.

Figure 3.1 graphically represents a dynamic innovation system. At its core are the flows of knowledge and information that link economic

Innovation Systems

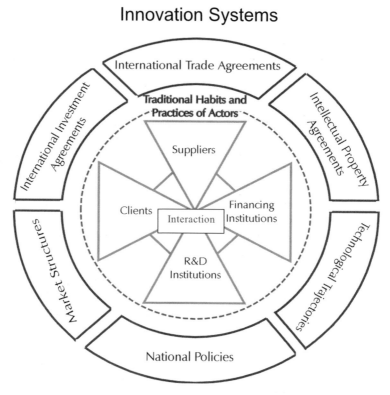

Figure 3.1 A dynamic system framework. Source: Mytelka (2000)

actors and provide a stimulus to innovation. Although such linkages may, on occasion, move along a linear path from the "supply" of research to products in the market, more often they are multidirectional and link a wider set of actors than those located along the standard value chain. Across sectors and time, moreover, different configurations of actors critical to an innovation process will emerge from among the multitude of firms and other organizations. These organizations include industry associations, R&D and productivity centres, universities, vocational training institutes, information gathering and analysis services, engineering services, banking and other financial mechanisms and standard-setting bodies.

That said, simply having potentially critical actors co-located within a national geographic space does not necessarily lead to their interaction or to a process of continuous innovation – the marks of a dynamic innovation system. Actor competences, habits and practices with respect to three of the key elements that underlie an innovation process – learning, linkages and investment – are important in determining the nature and extense of the interactions (Mytelka, 2000: 18). These habits and practices are rooted in the experience of learning to learn and the opportunities to learn provided by practices of transparency and openness that facilitate knowledge flows. They are, moreover, learned behavioural patterns, marked by the historical specificities of a particular system and moment in time. Over time, the relevance of earlier sets of competences, habits and practices with respect to innovation may diminish as conditions change. This is one factor causing stagnation in existing clusters and it is particularly important today as we move away from an understanding of development in quantitative production terms and toward a more innovation-oriented approach to the development process.

Consider two critical actors in the innovation process, SMEs and banks. Most SMEs in traditional industries tend to be risk-averse and lack the linkages needed for learning and the financial means to support a continuous process of innovation. Yet, with rare exceptions, banks have not created the tools or developed the face-to-face relationships that enable them to evaluate SMEs as potential clients or their projects for funding. They prefer to lend to larger firms where transaction costs and risks are lower. Upgrading in traditional sectors is unlikely to take place in this context without policies and other regulatory measures that reduce risks and support innovation. In designing such policies, the specific habits and practices of local actors thus have to be taken into consideration. Continuous monitoring of policy dynamics generated by the interaction between policies and the varied habits and practices of actors in the system will be of importance in fine-tuning policies for maximum impact. Adaptive policymaking is part of what makes an innovation system a learning system.

The innovation system approach thus acknowledges the role of policies, whether tacit or explicit, in setting the parameters within which these actors make decisions, learn and innovate. It recognizes that "innovation" is not the outcome of a unique policy but a set of policies and other factors that collectively shape the behaviour of actors. An overall innovation strategy, priority setting and policy coordination are thus critical in strengthening innovation systems at the national, local or sectoral levels. As situations evolve and competitive conditions change, monitoring the interaction between policies and the traditional habits and practices of actors is a necessary tool for adaptive policymaking. Learning and unlearning by firms as well as policymakers are thus key characteristics of an innovation system, particularly when the system responds to new challenges.

The innovation system approach also has the advantage of bringing demand into the frame of analysis. Demand flows are amongst the signals that shape the focus of research, the decision as to which technologies to develop and the speed of diffusion. Demand is not solely articulated at arms length through the market, but may take place through a variety of non-market mediated collaborative relationships between individual users and producers of innovation (Lundvall, 1988: 35). In still broader systems terms, demand may be intermediated by policies. In the case of pharmaceuticals, for example, policies directed at the local health care system have a powerful impact on the structure of demand and hence the opportunities or constraints in the local supply of research, development and production of pharmaceutical and biopharmaceutical products.

The context for knowledge acquisition today extends well beyond national frontiers. Domestic policies also have a role to play in orienting the behaviour of national actors toward the acquisition of technology and expertise from abroad. The institutional set-up at the global level has become a powerful force in shaping the choices of local actors and the extent of learning that can take place. As figure 3.1 illustrates, these include the shaping effects of transnational corporations on the structure of markets and the pace and direction of technological change as well as the set of international agreements dealing with trade, investment and intellectual property. Here too, domestic policies have a critical role to play in creating the incentives for local learning and innovation as a conscious, continuous and creative process.

From clusters to innovation systems

From a learning and innovation perspective, it is possible to analyze clusters in terms of a set of variables that emphasize the potential for dynamic change within the cluster. According to the innovation systems literature these include five actor-level variables: the configuration of actors in the system; their traditional habits and practices; their competences and the nature and intensity of their interactions; and the degree of change in the cluster over time. The configuration of actors in the system situates critical actors within a dual context: the local and the global. In analyzing the presence of critical actors within the cluster, the concept of "critical" is thus understood to be a function of both the techno-industrial base of the firms within the cluster and the global techno-industrial system in which these firms are embedded. The latter provides a mapping of the knowledge bases required for innovation in a globalized industry. The configuration of critical actors can thus be expected to vary across techno-industrial systems. Table 3.1 characterizes these configurations with reference to the number of critical actors present in a cluster and within this group it emphasizes the size of firms located in the cluster.

Actor competence is broadly defined to include manufacturing and management skills and capabilities as well as technological sophistication.

Table 3.1 Typology of constructed clusters

	Export processing zones	Industrial parks	Science parks/ technopoles
Objective	Promote exports	Promote industry	Promote innovation
Actors	Export-oriented firms, serving as subcontractors to foreign firms	Large anchor firm & suppliers; mixed large & small firms	University anchor; new start ups; mixed large & small firms
Capabilities[1]	Limited to assembly operations	Mainly in engineering and production management	Some design, testing and adaptive capabilities
Linkages[1]	Few within the cluster, as inputs are supplied by contractors	Mainly production-related, e.g., input sourcing, marketing & maintenance	Some to knowledge inputs

[1] For details see Mytelka, 1999: 20.

The higher the level of competence, the greater the probability that re-sources can be found to recombine knowledge bases in new and innova-tive ways. Competence must be tempered, however, by the traditional habits and practices of these actors with respect to learning, investment and linkages. The ability to learn, to invest and to partner increase the likelihood that critical actors in the system will move to assume new roles and develop new institutions in response to changes in competitive con-ditions. In some instances the level of trust is too low to be conducive to cooperative interactions. Policies and programmes can stimulate and sup-port a process of change if their design takes these habits and practices into consideration. Key habits and practices for innovation include learn-ing, creating and sustaining linkages, building trust-based relationships and cooperation.

In the innovation literature, the nature and extensiveness of interac-tions among critical actors in a system take on particular significance. In the context of sector-based clusters built around the value chain, re-lationships between actors have tended to consist mainly in the unidi-rectional transfer of information from a client to its suppliers. Two-way partnerships have been a rarity. In many cases, traditional habits and practices do not predispose actors to a more innovation-oriented form of interaction in which knowledge is shared and learning maximized. The way firms compete is also a critical element in determining the dy-namics of growth in a cluster.[3] Where competition is based on price and wage reductions rather than quality, technological upgrading and product-innovation cooperative relationships are rendered more difficult.

Factors that stimulate change in habits and practices thus deserve further analysis.

Clusters do change but not all of these changes are conducive to innovation. The extensiveness of innovation-oriented changes in a cluster can be assessed in terms of the nature of changes in the configuration of critical actors, the degree to which actor competences are strengthened, the growth of cooperative interactions within the cluster, the extensiveness of changes in the types and sophistication of products produced by the firms in the cluster and the export performance of the cluster over time.

The transformation of clusters into innovation systems is not an easy process and certain forms of clustering appear less likely to make such a transition. Here, a distinction can be drawn between two broad types of clusters: those that originate as *spontaneous* agglomerations of enterprises and other related actors, and those that are induced by public policies. The latter type, the members of which have elsewhere been designated as *constructed* clusters (Mytelka and Farinelli, 2003; UNCTAD, 1998), range from technopoles and industrial parks to incubators and export processing zones (EPZs). Whether in developed or developing countries, few constructed clusters have become innovation systems. The original design of the clusters, the configuration of actors located within them and the habits and practices of the actors in relation to learning, linkages and investment together with the policies that shaped these habits and practices were not conducive to innovation. Table 3.1 provides a schematic overview of constructed clusters and some of the key characteristics.

Industrial parks and EPZs were the earliest forms of constructed clusters. Their focus was on production and exports and the vehicle through which to achieve these objectives was traditionally the attraction of foreign firms. Little attention was paid to learning and technological-capability building. Innovation was not viewed as critical in development goals in either the creation of EPZs or the analysis of their achievements and failures. Although the changing competitive conditions made sustainable export growth problematic, insufficient attention was paid to technological upgrading. It was not until the late 1990s that studies with a focus on learning and innovation began to emerge. In Africa, the best studies from this perspective were based on the EPZ that housed much of the early textile and clothing cluster in Mauritius (Lall and Wignaraja, 1998; Wignaraja and O'Neil, 1999).

Of particular importance in sustaining competitiveness in a traditional sector such as textiles is the ability to develop linkages to a wide set of knowledge inputs and/or build some of these capabilities in-house. Design capabilities, for example, have become pivotal to product upgrading and allow both independent firms and subcontractors to support wage increases by moving toward higher–value-added products. Investment in new imaging, pattern-making and upgrading software is another critical input into a process of continuous innovation that enables the firm to remain competitive in export markets as new low-wage competitors emerge. Figure 3.2 sketches out other linkages that have proven important in supporting innovation in this industry.

Against the historical record of learning through linkages and capacity building that marked a period of sustained export competitiveness in the textile and clothing industries of Korea and Taiwan (Ernst, Ganiatsos and Mytelka, 1998), the experience of Mauritius has been far less successful. Established in 1970, the EPZ had the advantage of being among the first in a developing country. During the 1980s it benefited from considerable Hong Kong and Taiwanese investment in the knitwear sector. Firms in the zone, however, were focused on a narrow range of exports mostly at the low end of the value chain. In a survey of SMEs in the textile and clothing industry, Wignaraja and O'Neil (1999) pointed to the limited capability-building and upgrading as a major factor in the sector's difficulties in sustaining its export success. The authors suggest that SMEs

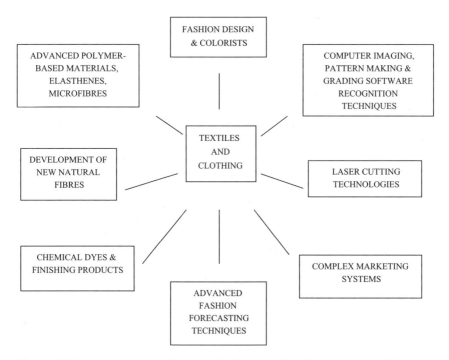

Figure 3.2 Innovation in textiles and clothing requires linkages to a wide set of knowledge inputs

in the textile industry employ mostly obsolete machinery accentuated by lack of investment in new technologies such as computer-aided design and computer-aided manufacturing (CAD/CAM) systems. Firm-level operation is non-automated and the use of electronic technology in management and marketing is at a low level.

Additionally, quality control is mostly ad hoc and dependent on visual checking. Minimal use is made of technical consultants (Wignaraja and O'Neil, 1999: xiii). With regard to clothing, although around half of firms in the apparel industry operate in the low-end segment where price is the major competitive advantage, "relatively high labour costs make this market position untenable. Upgrading into mid-market products is a viable strategy, but is dependent on enhancing design, quality and delivery" (Wignaraja and O'Neil, 1999: 36).

During the 1990s textiles and clothing exports were sustained largely due to a number of privileged market-access opportunities (notably into the European Union through the Lomé Convention and its successors). Other factors supporting this included the existence of quotas under the Multifibre Agreement (MFA), which induced investment in the Mauritian textile and clothing industry by the newly industrializing countries of Asia, and more recently through the American AGOA (African Growth Opportunity Act) initiative. The MFA, however, expired in 2005 and AGOA may not be renewed. Somewhat belatedly, the Mauritian government has begun to reflect on ways to transform this cluster into an innovation system.

Unlike EPZs, science and technology parks are a much more recent creation and were designed from the outset to promote interaction among firms to stimulate innovation. They are built close to university centres to induce proximity spinoffs from the academic and research institutions located in the park and attract foreign firms seeking access to lower-cost knowledge inputs. The process of building the trust and collaborative linkages, however, is a very long one – over 20 years in the case of Sophia Antipolis in France. Besides, few such science and technology parks in the developing world have been successful.[4] Nevertheless, enormous expenditures continue to be made mainly by governments in the hope that a dynamic process of innovation would develop.

Spontaneous clusters have also emerged in many developing countries and have now been "discovered" as their products have become competitive in export markets. Examples include clusters producing surgical instruments in Sialkot, Pakistan (Nadvi, 1998a, 1998b), ceramic tiles in Santa Catarina, Brazil (Meyer-Stamer, Maggi, and Seible, 2001), cotton knitwear in Tirrupur, India (Cawthorne, 1995), auto parts in Nnewi, Nigeria (Oyelaren-Oyeyinka, 1997); the Cape wine cluster in South Africa (Williamson and Wood, 2003); the metal-working cluster in the Suame

Magazine in Kumasi, Ghana (Powell, 1995); and a variety of clusters in Kenya and South Africa (McCormick, 1999). Each of these has shown the emergence of adaptive behaviour by local actors and some organizational coordination in technological upgrading. In the cases of the Brazilian ceramic tiles cluster and the Cape wine cluster, a basis for building an innovation system is slowly being laid. These spontaneous clusters can be classified into three main types: informal, organized and innovative. Table 3.2 provides a summary of the principal characteristics of these clusters.

Informal clusters generally contain micro and small firms whose technology level is low relative to the industry frontier and whose owner-operators generally have weak management capabilities.[5] The skill levels are low and little or no continuous learning takes place for sustained skills upgrading. The low barriers to entry may lead to growth in the number of firms and supporting institutions, but this does not necessarily reflect a positive dynamic as measured by the upgrading of management skills; investment in new process technology, machinery and equipment; improvement in product quality; product diversification; or the development of exports.

Coordination and networking among firms located in informal clusters are low and characterized by a limited growth perspective, cutthroat competition, limited trust and little information sharing. Poor infrastructure; the absence of critical services and support structures such as banking and financial services, productivity centres and training programs; weak backward, horizontal and forward linkages; and a lack of information on foreign markets tend to reinforce this low growth dynamic. There are some exceptions however.

Table 3.2 Spontaneous clusters

Cluster type	Informal	Organized	Innovative
Example	Suame Magazine (Kumasi, Ghana)	Nnewi (Nigeria); Sialkot (Pakistan)	Capetown (South Africa)
Critical actors	Low	Low to medium	High
Size of firms	Micro and small	SMEs	SMEs & large
Innovation	Little	Some	Continuous
Trust	Low	Medium	High
Skills	Low	Medium	High
Technology	Low	Medium	Medium
Linkages	Some	Some	Extensive
Cooperation	Little	Some, not sustained	High
Competition	High	High	Medium to high
Product Change	Little or none	Some	Continuous
Exports	Little or none	Medium to high	High

Adapted from UNCTAD, 1998: 7.

The Suame Magazine cluster in Kumasi, Ghana, consists of nearly 5,000 tradespeople in small garages and workshops making spare automobile parts and offering repair services. Suame Magazine is one example of an informal cluster that began the process of transformation through the establishment of linkages among clients and suppliers and through networking with research institutions such as the Technology Consultancy Center at the University of Science and Technology in Kumasi. Slowly a process of learning and technological upgrading began to take shape. The role of government is of particular interest in the Suame Magazine case. After its initial opposition to the mushrooming of informal workshops, the government moved to support their development through the provision of technology services and training to upgrade technical skills of the mechanics and the management skills (e.g., basic accounting) of the business owners. The government also helped to establish a pilot programme to set up a mechanics' cooperative to purchase and share equipment such as lathes and crankshaft grinders (World Bank, 1989: 121). These developments generated a considerable process-technology capacity-building within the cluster. The process was reinforced during Ghana's long economic crisis, which saw the movement of educated people out of the public sector and into micro- and small-scale enterprises.

It has to be noted, however, that informal clusters such as Suame Magazine are highly fragile. Towards the end of the 1980s when the International Monetary Fund structural adjustment programme liberalized imports, including those of used cars and second-hand parts such as engines, and as foreign currency became more available, the cluster's growth slowed. Hundreds of businesses collapsed and thousands of workers lost their jobs. Businesses that had moved from repair to manufacturing fared better. From this experience, it became clear that "to survive and prosper, fitters must raise their level of technology and many must change their role from that of repairer to that of manufacturers" (Powell, 1995).

Organized clusters are characterized by collective activity supported by infrastructure, services and organizational structures designed to analyze and provide solutions to common problems. Although most firms in these clusters are small, some have grown to medium-size and their competence level has improved through training and apprenticeship. They have also upgraded their technological capability, though few have reached the technological frontier of their industry. Firms in organized clusters also exhibit the capacity to undertake technology adaptations, to design new products and processes and to bring them quickly to market. The Nnewi cluster of automobile parts manufacturers in Nigeria is an example of how firms located in an informal cluster with virtually no infrastructure have been able to grow, export informally and upgrade by grouping together and setting up common utilities.[6]

Since the mid-1970s, local traders in Nnewi have transformed themselves into manufacturers of automobile parts through close linkages to
technology suppliers in Taiwan. Seventeen firms, ranging in size from enterprises with 40 employees to those with 250, supply Nigeria and other
West African markets with switch gears, roller chains for engines, auto
tubes, batteries, engine seats, shock absorbers, foot rests and gaskets for
motorcycles, as well as other parts. Most of these firms have the design
capability to modify products and adapt the production process to the
local market. Firms in Nnewi grew despite major infrastructural and
credit constraints. Electricity, for example, was only supplied through private generators, water was provided through the company's boreholes,
telephone service was poor and tariffs high, land was expensive and
scarce, and banks were reluctant to extend the level of credit required
by companies with high inventory costs. Despite all these limitations,
Nnewi firms succeeded in innovating, growing and exporting to neighbouring countries while other firms in Nigeria were failing.

Much of this success was due to the acquisition of skills by workers,
mainly through learning-by-doing (especially during equipment installation and test run) and through inter-firm linkages with foreign technology
suppliers, notably those from Taiwan. However, as in the Suame Magazine case, vulnerabilities in the production strategy of the cluster have
emerged, especially because firms were not well organized within the
cluster to support a continuous process of improvement. As Banji
Oyelaran-Oyeyinka (1997) points out, "A weak local capital goods capability continues to slow down a full acquisition of major innovation capability". Here is where policies and new support structures, notably credit
facilities are critically needed.

The surgical instruments cluster in Sialkot, Pakistan steadily increased
its exports from the late 1970s to the mid-1990s, with a particularly steep
increase in 1995 and 1996. Over this period exports rose by approximately 10 per cent annually in real terms. Despite a close relationship between exchange rates and export performance, other factors discussed in
the following section appear to explain better the growth of surgical instruments exports, particularly their sharp increase in the mid-1990s (Mytelka and Farinelli, 2003).

By the 1960s, Sialkot had already become an export-oriented cluster,
selling surgical instruments to countries in the region. Today, some 300
manufacturing SMEs (of which 98 per cent have fewer than 20 employees) are surrounded by 1,500 small subcontractors, 200 input suppliers and 800 service providers to produce one-fifth of the world's output of stainless steel surgical instruments generating exports in excess of
US$125 million (Nadvi, 1998a: 14). The exports are mainly to Western
Europe and the United States. In the beginning of the 1990s, after

decades of rising exports, sales fell significantly due to a quality barrier imposed by the United States' Food and Drug Administration (FDA). Of particular relevance to the relationship between clustering and innovation and with regard to SMEs is the speed with which local producers managed to meet the higher standards required by export markets and neutralize the embargo. How this took place provides lessons for the upgrading of clusters elsewhere.

Sialkot had a deeply rooted manufacturing tradition, notably in the steel industry. The knowledge base for the manufacture of surgical instruments began to emerge during World War II when the supply of domestically produced surgical tools in the United Kingdom could not meet the demand of hospitals. As a solution to the shortage of surgical instruments affecting British India, local doctors approached the blacksmiths and artisans of Sialkot, relying on their long-standing ability in manufacturing high quality swords. To assist the local industry, blueprints, drawings and technical experts were brought in from Britain and a technical institute was set up to channel advice (Nadvi, 1998a, 1998b).

Entrepreneurship was also a long-standing characteristic of the local population.[7] Immediately following the imposition of import restrictions by the United States, a delegation of local producers visited Washington in a vain attempt to negotiate a deal with the FDA. The impetus for more positive forms of collective action regarding the upgrading of quality standards was subsequently driven by a combination of local firms, their industry association, the Surgical Instrument Manufacturers Association (SIMA), and government actors. While the local trade association lobbied the Pakistani government for financial and technical support, it also hired a quality-assurance consultancy to train and upgrade local enterprises. Metal-testing laboratories and technical training facilities were set up after federal support was made available. Some firms have been certified and registered as conforming to International Standards Organization (ISO) 9000 quality management system standards while 75 of the 300 manufacturers have been able to meet good manufacturing practices (GMP) standards (Nadvi, 1998b).

Through this process the small firms became more specialized,[8] thus benefiting from economies of scale and scope. Changes in their awareness about the benefits of clustering also developed as the cluster became more visibly organized. In the past, for example, these firms simply benefited passively from the externalities spontaneously produced through clustering. These included the availability of inputs, spare parts, machinery repair units, cargo handling and trade services and skilled labour. In the organizational phase, enterprises engaged actively in the creation of collective efficiencies stemming from a high degree of linkages within and between different sectors, vertical and horizontal ties, a progressive specialization in the various production phases, frequent exchange of information and regular technical discussions among producers and subcontractors. Tacit knowledge flows were facilitated by this conscious, pro-active set of interactions.

Cooperation between the public and private sectors also contributed to meeting the challenges faced by the firms in this cluster. SIMA played a pivotal role in obtaining public support for the creation of a technical training facility, a metal-testing laboratory and a special credit line to provide short-term loans to local manufacturers. A critical role in upgrading quality was played by the publicly funded Metal Diagnostics Development Centre, particularly for heat-treatment technologies and metal testing. Some 90 per cent of the local SMEs are said to have made use of its services (Nadvi, 1998a).

Having successfully weathered one crisis, many of the channels for cooperation, however, began to fall into disuse. The role of SIMA as an interlocutor with the government, for example, had been particularly important in the initial period during which the cluster became more organized. Subsequently this function was of lesser importance for the firms in the cluster and SIMA failed to develop other, more innovation-oriented activities. Sialkot's surgical instruments manufacturers mainly service the low-end market. As technology changes in this industry, keeping up will require a stronger technological base and closer linkages to materials suppliers than in the past.

Although organized clusters by definition have the potential to be *innovative clusters* (as demonstrated in the case of Sialkot), in traditional industries proximity alone is no guarantee that this will take place or that it will be sustained, as the previous section indicated. In the past, traditional industries that were neither science-based nor knowledge-intensive were thought not to require the same level of learning and innovation that have propelled export growth in "high-tech" industries. The low level of R&D expenditure in traditional industries gave further support to this belief. The very locus of change in traditional industries, however, makes the level of R&D expenditure a poor indicator of innovation.

The innovativeness of firms in such industries cannot easily be determined from responses to the now classic question concerning the introduction of new products since this question often fails to capture changes in design or materials that significantly modify products but do not result in the creating of an entirely new product. As competitive conditions continue changing, sustained growth in traditional industries is only possible through a continuous process of innovation. Under these conditions, the trajectory of a cluster's exports over time becomes a useful proxy for innovation. Wine-based clusters are a typical example and the Cape wine cluster illustrates this process.

Winemaking was a classic example of comparative advantage embedded in site-specific characteristics. Soil, grape variety and climatic conditions have traditionally endowed particular regions with advantages in grape growing and many such regions subsequently developed winemaking activities. Because of the close linkage between grape growing and winemaking, wineries have tended to locate close to their suppliers. Over time ancillary supporting organizations and services co-located in these regions formed a geographical agglomeration or cluster. Wine quality and hence price were primarily attributed to these site-specific characteristics. Scarcity and branding in countries like France was then made possible through the location-based appellation system (AOC), contributing to the premium paid for wine from these regions and enhancing opportunities for marketing. Wine exports were thus dominated by a small number of well-known producing regions in a handful of countries.

This would dramatically change in the second half of the twentieth century as production in the sector became increasingly more knowledge-intensive, requiring linkages to a wide range of knowledge inputs (figure 3.3). The clusters that created these linkages and moved toward innovation-based competition saw a sustained pattern of growth in output, enterprises, employment and exports. This included a number of

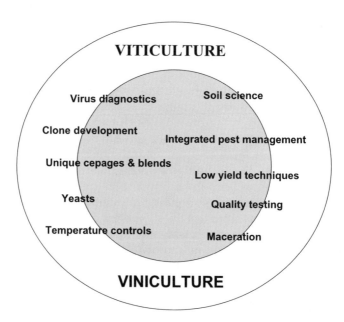

Figure 3.3 Innovation in the wine cluster

developing countries, such as Chile and Argentina, along with new entrants from the developed world – Australia and New Zealand.

Under apartheid, however, South Africa was on a different path. The Koöperatieve Wijnbouwers Vereniging, a vintner's cooperative turned government regulator, controlled prices and surpluses through a quota system that created an incentive for grape growers to focus on maximizing yields and for winemakers to standardize production aiming at a mass market for bulk wines. Those characteristics are no longer selling points in today's rapidly changing global wine sector. With the end of apartheid, the abolition of the quota systems and the lifting of sanctions revealed the negative legacies of apartheid in the poor quality of South African wines when compared to their competitors. South Africa compared unfavourably with its competitors in marketing competency and in intra-industry linkages that formed the basis for the competitors' ability to coordinate and plan strategically. Actors in the Cape wine cluster had the choice of changing the manner in which they conducted business or exiting the industry.

By 1999 a new, three-pronged strategy had been developed to address the need for learning and technological upgrading in viniculture and viticulture marketing. The new strategy was developed and led by the growers and vintners who organized Winetech, the wine industry network for expertise and technology formed in 1996 to conduct research and provide training and technology transfer in the wine sector. Through Winetech, South African grape growers focused on producing higher-quality grapes for wine. Now particular attention was paid to local climatic and soil conditions, which led to the planting of new vines and the practice of low yield viticulture to raise sugar content and heighten flavour. South African wine makers were able to produce uniquely South African grape varieties such as pinotage, a cross between the pinot noir and cinaut grapes. This strategy required the development of a strong knowledge base in soil science and its transfer to growers through the training of farm workers and managers. Linkages that had not existed before thus had to be created, as did the research that underpinned upgrading in the vineyards.

Accompanying the production of higher quality grapes were significant investments in cellar upgrades and the application of new and "softer" viniculture techniques that combined modern technology with tacit knowledge. Once the wine is bottled, WOSA (Wines of South Africa), created in 2000 and funded by a statutory levy of seven cents per litre on all exported wine, takes over. Its mission is to build "brand South Africa" and develop the international distribution channels needed to compete in the global market. Between 1991 and 2001 exports of wine from South Africa rose from 23 million litres to 177 million litres.

Conclusions

As production became more knowledge-intensive across a wide range of traditional industries and innovation-based competition transformed commodities into distinguishable goods, developing countries came under significant pressure to innovate. The emergence of Silicon Valley and the rediscovery of dynamic industrial districts in the northern hemisphere industrial economies led many to view clustering as a critical element in strengthening the innovation process. In the southern hemisphere, however, the focus was more on building a system of production and attention was thus directed toward new plants and equipment, infrastructure building and the supply of human capital. While this may have served to increase output and exports, the presence of such building blocks did not in themselves constitute a dynamic innovation system. The analyses presented have illustrated that the wave of cluster construction that took place in the 1980s and 1990s did not lead automatically to learning, linkages and innovation, despite the co-location of some of the critical actors within EPZs or industrial or science parks.

This chapter has distinguished between constructed clusters induced by public policy and spontaneous clustering that originated in the co-location of firms and farms. As the latter drew users, producers and ancillary services into the cluster over time, opportunities for linkage building and knowledge and information sharing were created. In most clusters based on traditional industries, however, network externalities were not exploited and challenges, even when they stimulated innovative responses, did not lead to innovation-inducing arrangements. Competitive practices remained centred on price-based advantages within a narrow range of standardized, low–value-added products. As a result, the boundaries of the knowledge system were rarely expanded to include a wider set of knowledge inputs, new competences were not consciously acquired and products and markets were not reconceptualized to pursue upgrading, up-scaling or identifying new market niches.

One critical lesson to be learned from these initiatives is that even when output and export growth were positively affected by the creation of a "constructed cluster" or an innovative response to the challenges of market closure or competition, the process of innovation often did not persist. The cases in this chapter show that innovation depends on the extent to which new habits and practices of learning, linkage formation and investment remain in place and use. Innovative clusters develop networks, associations and other forms of organization to facilitate problem-solving research. In the case studies reviewed in this chapter, some of these elements were created through the efforts of actors in the cluster alone. However, it is also clear from the case studies that wider systemic factors are important in supporting the transformation of clusters into innovation systems. Among these are the complementary policies, programmes and financing mechanisms that foster new linkages and create opportunities for sustained innovation. Where these were not established, stagnation and decline in the face of crises and challenges often followed. Policies thus have played an important role in shaping the incentive structure within which actors in an emerging innovation system make decisions about learning, linkages and innovation.

While the emphasis here has been on the need for actors to learn and to unlearn earlier habits and practices, policy learning must also take place to sustain a process of innovation as competitive and technological conditions change. Building the channels for dialogue and feedback will thus be critical for adaptive policymaking over the longer term.

Notes

1. I would like to thank Mike Morris, Jo Lorentzen, Samah El-Shahat and Winnie Mittulah for their helpful comments on this chapter and Banji Oyelaran-Oyeyinka for his encouragement in writing it.
2. See the work of Nobel laureate W. Arthur Lewis in this regard.
3. See Pyke and Sengenberger (1992) for a more extensive discussion of this point.
4. From among the many that have started up, two are generally regarded as most successful: Hsinchu Science-based Industrial Park in Taiwan and the Singapore Science Park. Both were started in the early 1980s and involved massive investment in infrastructure and educational facilities and policies designed to attract foreign firms with an interest in undertaking research in the Parks. Additional incentives were later created to encourage returned scholars and entrepreneurs to locate in the Parks' incubators and a strong enterprise support system was put in place (Lalkaka, 1997: 13).
5. This and the following paragraphs are drawn in part from UNCTAD (1998: 4–8).
6. This case is based on Oyelaran-Oyeyinka (1997).
7. The region is known historically for its development of Basmati rice and more recently for production and export of sporting goods (it is the world's largest producer of hand-stitched leather footballs), musical instruments and leather garments.
8. The surgical instruments manufacturing process consists of eight phases. Most of the SMEs now specialize in only one phase.

REFERENCES

Becattini, G. (1978) "The Development of Light Industry in Tuscany: An Interpretation", *Economic Notes* 2–3: 107–23.

Best, M. H. (1990) *The New Competition: Institutions of Industrial Restructuring*, Cambridge, Mass.: Harvard University Press.

Boyer, R. (1988) "Technical Change and the Theory of Regulation", in G. Dosi, C. Freeman, R. Nelson, G. Silverberg and L. Soete, eds, *Technical Change and Economic Theory*, London: Pinter Publishers, 67–94.

Brusco, S. (1982) "The Emilian Model", *Cambridge Journal of Economics* 6: 167–84.

Brusco, S. (1986) "Small Firms and Industrial Districts: The Experience of Italy", in D. Keeble and E. Wever, eds, *New Firms and Regional Development in Europe*, London: Croom Helm, 184–202.

Cawthorne, P. M. (1995) "Of Networks and Markets: The Rise and Rise of a South Indian Town, The Example of Tiruppur's Cotton Knitwear Industry", *World Development* 23(1).

Danish Technology Institute (DTI) (1993) *Existing Network Programmes in EC-Countries: Encouraging Interfirm Cooperation*, Copenhagen: Danish Technology Institute.

Edquist, Charles (1997) "System of Innovation Approaches – Their Emergence and Characteristics", in Charles Edquist, ed., *Systems of Innovation, Technologies, Institutions and Organisations*, London: Pinter.

Ernst, D., T. Ganiatsos and Lynn Mytelka, eds (1998) *Technological Capabilities and Export Success in Asia*, London: Routledge.

Freeman, C. (1988) "Japan: A New National System of Innovation?" in Giovanni Dosi, Christopher Freeman, Richard Nelson, Gerald Silverberg and Luc Soete, eds, *Technical Change and Economic Theory*, London: Pinter Publishers, 349–69.

Freeman, C. (1992) "Formal Scientific and Technical Institutions in the National Systems of Innovation", in B. A. Lundvall, *National Systems of Innovation: Towards a Theory of Innovation and Interactive Learning*, London: Pinter Publishers.

Lall, Sanjaya and G. Wignaraja (1998) "Mauritius Dynamising Export Competitiveness", Economic Paper 33, London: Commonwealth Secretariat.

Lalkaka, Rustam (1997) "Convergence of Enterprise Support Systems: Emerging Approaches at Asia's Technology Parks & Incubators", paper presented at the 12th Annual International Conference of the Association of University Related Research Parks, Monterey, California, 25–28 June.

Lundvall, Bengt-Åke (1988) "Innovation as an Interactive Process: From User-Producer Interaction to the National System of Innovation", in Giovanni Dosi, Christopher Freeman, Richard R. Nelson, Gerald Silverberg and Luc Soete, eds, *Technical Change and Economic Theory*, London: Pinter Publishers.

Lundvall, Bengt-Åke, ed. (1992) *National Systems of Innovation: Towards a Theory of Innovation and Interactive Learning*, London: Pinter Publishers.

Lundvall, Bengt-Åke, B. Johnson, E. S. Andersen and B. Dalum (2002) "National Systems of Production, Innovation and Competence Building", *Research Policy*, 31(2).

McCormick, Dorothy (1999) "African Enterprise Clusters and Industrialization: Theory and Reality", *World Development*, 27(9): 1531–52.

Maskell, Peter (1996) "Localised Low Tech Learning", paper presented at the 28th International Geographical Congress, the Hague, 4–10 August.

Maskell, Peter and A. Mamberg (1999) "Localized Learning and Industrial Competitiveness", *Cambridge Journal of Economics* 23(2): 167–86.

Meyer-Stamer, J. (1998) "Clustering, Systemic Competitiveness and Commodity Chains: How Firms, Business Associations and Government in Santa Catarina

(Brazil) Respond to Globalization", paper prepared for the International Workshop on Global Production and Local Jobs: New Perspectives on Enterprises, Networks, Employment and Local Development Policy, Geneva: International Labour Organisation, 9–10 March.

Meyer-Stamer, J., C. Maggi and S. Seiber (2001) "Improving upon Nature: Creating Competitive Advantage in Ceramic Tile Clusters in Italy, Spain and Brazil", Inef Report, Heft 54, Duisburg: Gerhard Mercator Universitat.

Mytelka, Lynn K. (1978) "Licensing and Technology Dependence in the Andean Group", *World Development* 6: 447–59.

Mytelka, Lynn K. (1991) "Crisis, Technological Change and the Strategic Alliance", in Lynn K. Mytelka, ed., *Strategic Partnerships and the World Economy*, London: Pinter.

Mytelka, Lynn K. (1999) "Competition, Innovation and Competitiveness: A Framework for Analysis", in Lynn K. Mytelka, ed., *Competition, Innovation and Competitiveness in Developing Countries*, Paris: OECD, 15–27

Mytelka, Lynn (2000) "Local Systems of Innovation in a Globalized World Economy", *Industry and Innovation*, 7(1): 15–32.

Mytelka, Lynn K. and Lou Anne Barclay (2004) "Using Foreign Investment Strategically for Innovation", *European Journal of Development Research* 16(3): 527–55, Autumn.

Mytelka, Lynn K. and Fulvia Farinelli (2003) "From Local Clusters to Innovation Systems", in Cassiolato, Lastres and Maciel, eds, *Systems of Innovation and Development: Evidence from Brazil*, London: Edward Elgar Publishers, 249–72.

Nadvi, Khalid (1995) "Industrial Clusters and Networks: Case Studies of SME Growth and Innovation", Case Studies Prepared for the Small and Medium Industries Branch, UNIDO.

Nadvi, Khalid (1998a) "International Competitiveness and Small Firm Clusters – Evidence from Pakistan", *Small Enterprise Development*, March.

Nadvi, Khalid (1998b), "Knowing Me, Knowing You: Social Networks in the Surgical Instrument Cluster – Sialkot, Pakistan", IDS Discussion Paper No. 364, Brighton: Institute of Development Studies.

Nadvi, Khalid and Hubert Schmitz (1997) "SME Responses to Global Challenges: Case Studies of Private and Public Initiatives", paper presented at the Seminar on New Trends and Challenges in Industrial Policy, UNIDO, Vienna, October.

Nelson, Richard, ed. (1993) *National Innovation Systems: A Comparative Analysis*, Oxford: Oxford University Press.

Nelson, Richard and Sydney Winter (1982) *An Evolutionary Theory of Economic Change*, Cambridge, Mass.: Harvard University Press.

Oyelaran-Oyeyinka, B. (1997) *Nnewi: An Emergent Industrial Cluster in Nigeria*, Ibadan: Technopol Publishers.

Piore, Michael and Charles Sabel (1984) *The Second Industrial Divide: Possibilities for Prosperity*, New York: Basic Books.

Porter, M. E. (1990) *The Competitive Advantage of Nations*, New York: Macmillan.

Powell, J. (1995) *The Survival of the Fitter: Lives of Some African Engineers*, London: Intermediate Technology Publications.

Pyke, F. and W. Sengenberger, eds (1992) *Industrial Districts and Local Economic Regeneration*, Geneva: International Institute for Labour Studies.

Schmitz, H. (1993) "Small Shoemakers and Fordist Giants: Tale of a Supercluster", *World Development* 23(1).

Schmitz, Hubert (1997) "Collective Efficiency and Increasing Returns", IDS Working Paper 50, Brighton: Institute of Development Studies, University of Sussex.

Storper, M. (1995) "Regional Economies as Relational Assets", paper prepared for presentation to the Association Des Sciences Régionales de Langue Française, Toulouse, August–September.

Storper, Michael (1998) "Industrial Policy for Latecomers: Products, Conventions and Learning" in M. Storper, T. Thomadakis and L. Tsipouri, eds, *Latecomers in the Global Economy*, London: Routledge, 13–39.

UNCTAD (1998) "Promoting and Sustaining SME Clusters and Networks for Development", paper prepared for an Expert Meeting on Clustering and Networking for SME Development, Geneva, 2–4 September, Td/B/Com.3/Em.5/2.

Vavakova, Blanka (1988) "Technopole: Des Exigences Techno-industrielles aux Orientations Culturelles", *Culture Technique* 18, Revue de L'Ecole des Mines.

Vavakova, Blanka (1995) "Building 'Research-Industry' Partnerships through European R&D Programs", *International Journal of Technology Management* 10(4/5/6): 567–86.

Wignaraja, G. and S. O'Neil (1999) "SME Exports and Public Policies in Mauritius", Commonwealth Trade and Enterprise Paper No. 1, London: Commonwealth Secretariat.

Williamson, K. and E. Wood (2003) "The Dynamics of the South African Wine Industry Cluster: A Basis for Innovation and Competitiveness?" paper prepared for the Conference on Building Innovation Systems in the Wine Sector, Maastricht, Netherlands: UNU-INTECH.

Wolfe, D. and M. Gertler (1998) "The Dynamics of Regional Innovation in Ontario", in John De La Mothe and Gilles Paquet, eds, *Local and Regional Systems of Innovation*, Amsterdam: Kluwer Academic Publishers.

World Bank (1989) *World Development Report: Financial Systems and Development*, Washington, D.C.: World Bank, and Oxford: Oxford University Press.

4

Industrializing Kenya: Building the productive capacity of micro and small enterprise clusters

Dorothy McCormick and Mary Njeri Kinyanjui

After years of focusing only on individual firms, scholars and policy-makers now recognize the importance of enterprise clusters as productive entities and are trying to understand their potential for contributing to the process of industrialization in countries such as Kenya.[1] What has been observed about the role of clusters is somewhat discouraging, however. Despite the promise of collective efficiency, many clusters, especially those in Africa, have failed to have the desired impact on the national economies. There are at least two reasons for this. One is clearly external to the clusters themselves (McCormick, 1999) and concerns Africa's small markets, overabundance of labour and weak institutional framework, which characterize the operating environment for these clusters and collectively overwhelm the benefits of internal collective efficiency arising from within a given cluster. The second is, we will argue, a problem of weak productive capacity at the firm level. Analysis of the clusters' collective efficiency reveals the problem of productive capacity but is insufficient at providing a solution. Finding a solution requires an understanding of the sector and the specific value chain within which the cluster is or could be inserted.

Productive capacity in micro and small enterprise clusters

An understanding of a particular sector and the specific value chain into which an industrial cluster exists come together in the notion of produc-

Industrial clusters and innovation systems in Africa: Institutions, markets and policy, Oyelaran-Oyeyinka and McCormick (eds), United Nations University Press, 2007, ISBN 978-92-808-1137-7

tive capacity. At its most basic, productive capacity is the ability to produce goods that meet the quality requirements of present markets. This, however, is not sufficient as a definition because it lacks dynamism. Meeting the quality requirements of today's markets is clearly not enough in a rapidly changing world. For a firm, cluster or industry to survive and grow, it must also have the capacity to access new markets successfully. This involves not only technological capability (Bell and Pavitt, 1995; Figueiredo, 2001; Huq, 1999), but also a range of other skills and environmental supports that together give it the potential for upgrading. Figure 4.1 attempts to represent the relationships of the collective efficiency and value-chain variables to productive capacity in diagram form.

Productive capacity, with its two dimensions of present ability and upgrading potential, is at the centre. Feeding into it and influencing it are the skill levels of workers, infrastructure, the availability of intermediate inputs, available technology, actual patterns of joint action and benchmarking practice. The attempt here is simply to show how each directly influences productive capacity. One could, of course, trace feedback effects and inter-linkages among the independent variables, but this is beyond the scope of the current exercise.

The literature examined in chapter 2 suggests first that clusters vary considerably in structure, complexity and technological sophistication. They also have different needs if they are to upgrade. Upgrading some-

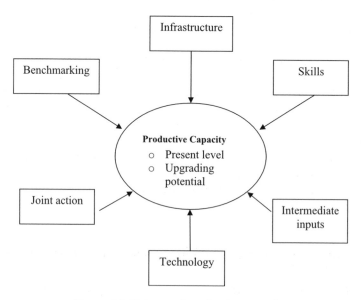

Figure 4.1 Drivers of productive capacity

times requires outside interventions, but ideally these should vary with the developmental level of the cluster (McCormick, 1999). *Groundwork* clusters need help to overcome problems associated with poor infrastructure, insecure property rights, low-level technology and weak inter-firm linkages. *Industrializing* clusters may need higher-level technological assistance, credit facilities and further development of their associations. The micro and small enterprises (MSEs) in *complex industrial clusters* may need help in acquiring the skills to negotiate profitably with larger enterprises both inside and outside the cluster.

Although value-chain research has tended to focus on large enterprises, studies have shown that small producers are often integrated into the chains. Some are small workshops subcontracted by larger producers, while others are individual home-workers (McCormick and Schmitz, 2002). A study of the footwear chains in several European countries documents the various ways in which MSEs, especially home-workers, are involved in production (Tate, 1996). Small producers very often operate in local or national chains. Kinyanjui and McCormick (2001) observe that the value chains of small-scale garment producers in Nairobi are market-driven and tend to be narrow and short, with very few intermediaries. Their work also shows that many of these firms are clustered (McCormick, 1999; McCormick, Kinyanjui and Ongile, 1997).

Economic and institutional context for Kenya's MSE clusters

The clusters examined in this study operate in multiple contexts. At the macro level is the Kenyan economy and institutional framework, while the lower level contains the subsectors or industries within which clusters are embedded. We examine each of these in turn. Kenya is a poor country with a largely rural population. In absolute terms, over half (52%) of the population is poor (Kenya, 1999b). Using the United Nations Development Programme Human Poverty Index as a measure, 37.8 per cent of Kenya's population was poor in the year 2000 (UNDP, 2003a). The Kenyan economy hardly grew at all during the 1990s. In 2000, gross domestic product (GDP) actually declined by 0.2 per cent, then rose in 2001 and 2002 by 1.2 per cent and 1.1 per cent respectively (Kenya, 2003a). Only one-third of Kenya's population of 30 million people lives in cities and towns (Kenya, 2002).

Kenya has most of the problems associated with poverty: low levels of education, poor nutrition, weak health care, poor infrastructure and an overreliance on agriculture. Perhaps unsurprisingly, the country has failed to industrialize. In 2000, manufacturing contributed only 13 per cent to GDP (Kenya, 2003a). Recent development policy has emphasized the importance of micro and small enterprises as a means of countering the failure of large industries to provide employment. However, practical actions to boost the productive capacity of these MSEs have not been forthcoming.

The institutional environment for business activity in African countries is fragmented and weak, with the result that national business systems tend to consist of distinct segments that interact in very limited ways (Pedersen and McCormick, 1999). Kenya is no exception to this general pattern. Markets, legal systems, financial institutions, technology systems and social structures are weak and, to some extent, divided along racial and ethnic lines. The legal framework for commercial and industrial activity is a good example. Many laws have not been updated since the colonial period. The lack of a small-claims court effectively means that only the largest companies have access to the court system. This lack of an institutional mechanism for enforcing commercial contracts leads many small businesses to restrict their dealings to known clients whom they can contact easily in case of default (Kimuyu, 1997).

Informal institutions seem to be emerging, but it is not clear how widespread such arrangements are or how much they can be counted on to replace the missing formal institutions. For example, business-people have developed their own dispute-settlement mechanisms in both vehicle-repair and second-hand-clothes trading clusters (Kinyanjui, 1998; Kinyanjui and Khayesi, 2003; McCormick, 1999). These are informal in the sense that they are not linked to the formal legal system, but they work because of the willingness of the participants to abide by them.

Some recent findings on the textile-, wood- and metal-products sectors are relevant to the clusters under study (Bigsten and Kimuyu, 2002). The first finding is that Kenya's textile sector experienced a dramatic drop of almost 50 per cent in aggregate output during the 1990s because of an inflow of imported used clothes. The second finding relates to the lack of business development services. Overall, approximately one-quarter of all manufacturing firms found lack of business support services to be a problem, but there were significant sectoral differences. Nearly two-thirds of wood and textile businesses saw lack of business services as a moderate-to-severe problem, compared with only one-third of metal firms. The third finding, based on an exhaustive analysis of infrastructure, shows that electricity, security and roads are the most critical concerns to firms in these sectors, with electricity being of greatest import to metal firms. The price of electricity is a moderate-to-severe problem for firms in all three sectors, with wood-sector firms expressing greater concern than either those in textiles or metal.

MSEs in Kenya

In 1999 Kenya had an estimated 1.3 million micro and small enterprises, employing 2.3 million persons.[2] Over a quarter of Kenyan households rely on an MSE for all or part of their income. Women own 48 per cent of all enterprises, but only one-third of those in manufacturing and just under one-third in services. Within manufacturing, women tend to be concentrated in clothing while men are more evenly distributed across a variety of activities. On average, MSEs in Kenya have 1.5 workers including the working owner. One-third of the MSEs are in urban areas. Trade makes up over two-thirds of the enterprises, with manufacturing and services accounting for 13 and 12 per cent respectively. Within manufacturing, the most common activities are textile and leatherwork, production of wood products and food processing. Metal fabrication represents only about 5 per cent of MSE manufacturers.

Many MSEs lack basic infrastructure, which constrains both the quality of their products and their ability to market their products. Kenya's infrastructure is in extremely poor condition. The government's economic recovery plan (Kenya, 2003b) attributes the poor conditions and the deterioration of infrastructure to inadequate allocation of resources for construction, maintenance and rehabilitation of existing facilities; poor contractual work; rapid urbanization; high population growth; and adverse weather conditions.

Of critical importance for technology-driven growth is access to electricity. Yet half of all MSEs lack such access (CBS et al., 1999). Compared to rural enterprises, urban enterprises are twice as likely to have access to electricity. Slightly over one-third of the enterprises reported access to water. Although nearly half of the enterprises are on tarmac roads, only 5 per cent of these roads are in good condition, with the rest described as fair or bad (CBS et al., 1999). Ability to communicate with distant customers and suppliers is important for marketing and for efficient management of supplies. Only one-third of the MSEs had access to a telephone in 1999. However, since the MSE baseline survey was conducted, mobile phones have become widely available in Kenya. Mobile connections rose from 15,000 in 1999 to approximately 3 million by mid-2004 (Waema, 2004). Many mobile users, especially in towns, are businesspeople who previously had very limited access to telephone service. No data on the proportions of clustered and non-clustered firms in Kenya currently exist.[3] Nevertheless, informal observation suggests that clusters of MSE manufacturers and repair businesses are very common, especially in towns. The preparatory work for this study confirmed the existence in nearly every town of at least one agglomeration of motor vehicle mechanics and another of carpenters. Larger towns have multiple clusters, and some have clusters of other manufacturing activities, including textiles and handicrafts. Although the Kenyan Government has not had an explicit policy of clustering MSEs, some of its policies and actions have worked in this direction. Relocation of enterprises, provision of sheds, favourable rents in public markets and specific programmes such as the Kenya Industrial Estates have tended to draw MSEs to common locations.

Billetoft (1996) observed sectoral differences in the location of clusters, specifically that trades that are more dependent on spontaneous contact with customers, such as tailors, dressmakers and shoemakers, usually situate in or near residential areas or major traffic hubs, while others such as metalworkers and woodworkers often concentrate in localities on the outskirts of town. He attributed these location tendencies solely to market factors. It is worth pointing out that location is not always a free choice and may be dictated by government authorities, often in order to rid the town centre of activities considered noisy or dirty (Kinyanjui, 1998; McCormick, 1999). Kenya's manufacturing and repair clusters vary in size, from fewer than twenty enterprises to several thousand. They also vary in their access to basic infrastructure. Given the general lack of information on cluster characteristics in Africa, we can only speculate about whether or not factors such as access to infrastructure for firms in clusters is similar to that for MSEs in general. In other words, without a closer look at how clusters function, one cannot move away from making generalized observations about the role of infrastructure, availability of information, supportive government policy and so forth vis-à-vis the success or failure of clustered firms and their impact on industrialization.

The next section takes a closer look at the textile, furniture-making, woodworking, vehicle repair and metal fabrication clusters in urban and rural settings in Kenya in order to investigate the relationship between cluster formation and industrialization.

Analysis of manufacturing and repair clusters

This study examined seventeen clusters, three in the textile sector, six making furniture and other wood products and eight engaged in vehicle repair and/or metal fabrication. Of these clusters, six were located in the cities of Nairobi and Mombasa, six in smaller towns and five in rural trading centres. The clusters' sizes range from 15 enterprises in the vehicle (including bicycles) repair/metal fabrication cluster in the rural trading centre of Shibale to over 500 enterprises at Majengo in Mombasa.

Methodology

The study used field inquiry as its primary research tool. Kenya's 1999 MSE survey provided important contextual and supplementary information. This survey used the enterprise as the unit of analysis, but identified the enterprises through a household survey that utilized the national sampling frame developed from Kenya's 1989 population and housing survey. The sample was stratified into four groups according to enterprise location: Nairobi and Mombasa, larger towns, smaller towns and rural areas.

To obtain our original sample of twenty-one clusters,[4] we used three-step purposive sampling. Three geographic areas – Nairobi and Central Provinces, Western Province and Mombasa and Coast Provinces – were chosen to represent the populous parts of the country. Within the three areas, places that would, when taken together, cover the four strata of MSEs were selected. The key informants selected for interviews were an association officer, a business owner who had been in the cluster since its inception, three other business owners and other individuals knowledgeable about the cluster's history and development. The number of interviews per cluster ranged from three to ten, with twelve of the seventeen cases based on four or five interviews.

The interviews were semi-structured and focused on nine content areas: the origins of the cluster, its organization, relations with local authorities, links with other enterprises, infrastructure and technology, markets, sources of labour, business services and challenges and advantages of locating in the cluster. We also observed cluster activities and conditions. Some observations became the basis for asking further questions. For example, the presence of an electricity meter prompted our interviewer to probe an earlier response about poor infrastructure. Other observations were helpful in fleshing out case study reports and making comparisons between clusters.

Data analysis consisted of compiling interview reports according to the content areas. The full interview team then discussed the reports and further revised them into full case studies. The cases were later grouped sectorally to allow identification of sectoral patterns.

The clusters

This study examined three clusters in the textile sector, six in furniture making and other wood products and eight engaged in vehicle repair and/or metal fabrication. The three textile clusters are quite different from one another. Uhuru Market in Nairobi has between 400 and 500 enterprises making both knitted and sewn garments. The market is large, but overcrowded. Markets for these products are greatly affected by the availability of second-hand clothing and cheap new goods. Many of the goods made here are destined for other parts of Kenya and/or neighbouring countries. The second cluster, Kariobangi North Market is also in Nairobi and is a successful cluster consisting mostly of custom tailors. The cluster appeals mainly to the local market, but has limited sales to buyers from other parts of the country. The third, Shinyalu, is a small rural textile cluster whose fortunes are closely tied to the local economy. The cluster makes school uniforms and clothing for local residents and also undertakes repairs.

The sample includes six clusters making furniture and other wood products. These clusters are well distributed geographically, with two in the cities of Nairobi and Mombasa, two in smaller towns and two in rural trading centres. Five of these have between nine and fifteen producing enterprises. Only the Changamwe cluster in Mombasa was larger, with over 50 enterprises. Five of the six clusters produce low- to medium-quality furniture whereas the Nairobi cluster makes high-quality furniture. Most enterprises produce for local markets with only the high-quality producers having a somewhat wider reach.

Eight clusters undertake metal fabrication, vehicle and bicycle repair singly or in combination. Although vehicle/bicycle repair falls technically under services, in our study we place them with metal fabrication as a manufacturing activity because they are often located in or near one another in the same or adjacent clusters. In addition, there are often production links between repair and fabrication and the business owners usually belong to the same association. Most importantly, in countries in the early stages of industrialization, repair work often gives rise to simple manufacturing. In this group only one, located in the small town of Kakamega, is a true manufacturing cluster. The other seven engage mainly in repair work. The clusters are well distributed across the size categories (see table 4.1).

Motor vehicle repairers tend to specialize in certain activities. Some firms deal with electrical systems, others with mechanical problems and

Table 4.1 Sampled clusters by sector and size

Size (workers)	Sector			
	Textile	Wood	Vehicle repair/ metal fabrication	Total
Fewer than 50	1	5	3	9
50–99	–	1	2	3
100–499	2	–	2	4
500–999	–	–	1	1
Total	3	6	8	17

still others with bodywork. This is partly due to the complexity of the vehicles and partly because the high cost of some repair equipment makes it difficult for very small firms to have the full range of skills and equipment. As a result, vehicle repair clusters tend to have a good deal of subcontracting and inter-linkages among firms.

Collective efficiency

The clusters show very little evidence of collective efficiency. Apart from market access, external economies were limited. Nearly all of the clusters visited reported that a major advantage of locating within the cluster is access and visibility to customers. Most of the clusters sell to local farmers, town residents, civil servants and factory employees. In most cases, especially in rural areas and small towns, cluster performance is clearly tied to the status of the local economy. Clustering provides opportunities for learning, sharing ideas and ultimately for technological upgrading. Artisans in several clusters spoke favourably of the positive atmosphere that encouraged continual learning. However, there were very few cases where the adoption of new technologies constituted a significant part of this learning process.

Labour market pooling was observed to be weak or disabling in most of the clusters. The clusters do not attract skilled labour. Most draw untrained school-leavers who become trainees or apprentices and then go on to establish their own businesses in competition with those already in the cluster. This was especially noticeable in the vehicle repair clusters in Nairobi and Mombasa, but it no doubt affects others as well.

Intermediate input effects are mostly in the form of traders or service providers. The two textile clusters in Nairobi had the most extensive range of input suppliers. Several of the vehicle repair clusters also had spare parts dealers located within them. None of these clusters, however, manufactured their own inputs. In many cases, especially in the metal and vehicle repair clusters, manufacturing would require infrastructure and machines not presently available.

The respondents named other external economies not generally mentioned in the literature. For example, interviewees were in favour of clustering as a means for the clustered firms to benefit from collective security. This is very important because tools, machines, stocks and work in process must be protected, yet hiring security guards individually would be prohibitively expensive. Clustering was also said to provide a certain measure of protection from official harassment so often experienced by micro and small enterprises. Finally, respondents mentioned the positive working environment, unity and support of other business owners, ease of communication, quality of training and availability of transport as benefits of clustering.

Clustering makes joint action easier by encouraging various types of bilateral and multilateral linkages. Most of the bilateral linkages observed were fairly weak. Operators borrowed one another's tools, trained each other's trainees and shared ideas about how to tackle difficult production problems. Two vehicle repair clusters had significant linkages between larger, more technologically advanced enterprises and small firms. The relationships appeared to be mutually beneficial and could be a model for others elsewhere. Even though the bilateral linkages were not very strong, we noted that they helped firms to make good use of relatively scarce resources.

Most clusters have multilateral linkages and some have multiple sets of membership groups. The most common form of multilateral linkage is the *jua kali* association.[5] Although many clusters have registered jua kali associations, the status of those associations varies considerably. Some seem to be functioning well while others have collapsed. In some cases, the artisans claimed that they were not aware of a jua kali association to which they could belong. Although jua kali associations are technically open to all micro and small enterprises in a given area, men and male-dominated activities predominate.

Several of the clusters have other types of multilateral linkages. There was only one cooperative, which was small and informal. We also found various types of savings and credit groups, including a few registered savings and credit cooperatives, several credit guarantee groups attached to micro-finance institutions and many informal merry-go-rounds. Merry-go-rounds, which are rotating savings and credit groups, are especially popular among the women business operators, but a few men also reported participating in them.

Business development services, however, were almost entirely lacking. None of the associations, non-governmental organizations or private businesses provided bookkeeping, marketing or consultancy services to the clustered enterprises. A number of respondents expressed hope that the development of the World Bank Voucher Training Scheme would give rise to new training services in these areas. Some service businesses, such as accounting firms, exist even in fairly small towns but appear to cater to somewhat larger businesses.

In sum, application of the collective efficiency model to the sampled clusters reveals that most are at a low level. Without a doubt, the clusters have the potential of contributing to the industrialization process by improving market access and thus enabling firms to produce more; however, most need help to upgrade. Since the specifics of upgrading tend to differ between sectors, we now examine the sectoral dimensions of these clusters.

Sectoral patterns in enterprise clusters

As can be seen from table 4.2, the main markets for all of the clusters are local. Only three of the seventeen clusters have gone beyond the local market to other towns and, in the case of Uhuru Market, to neighbouring countries. The only furniture maker with a wider market is the one making higher-quality products.

The other potential external economies are weak or missing in many of the clusters. The numbers, however, do not tell the full story. For example, the textile clusters experience moderately positive labour market pooling, while in the vehicle repair sector the labour market pooling is inadequate. In all sectors where they occur, intermediate input effects tend to be positive in the sense that producers have inputs readily available to them. But these inputs are not made in the cluster. Many are imports and therefore do not contribute to industrialization, either of the cluster or of the wider economy. Technological spillovers occur only in the metal clusters. In three of the four clusters, they are fairly weak, but in one case there are positive spillovers between a Kenya Industrial Estates workshop and the local jua kali vehicle repair cluster.

Bilateral joint action is common across all sectors, though its form varies from sector to sector. For example, in textiles, borrowing and lending of tools is most common, while vehicle repair has extensive subcontracting. Multilateral joint action varies greatly by sector. Both textile

Table 4.2 Markets, external economies and joint action by sector

	Sector		
	Textile (n = 3)	Wood (n = 6)	Metal (n = 8)
Main markets			
Local	3	6	8
Wider domestic	2	1	0
External economies			
Market access	3	6	8
Labour market pooling	2	0	1
Intermediate input effects	2	1	3
Technological spillovers	0	0	4
Joint action			
Bilateral	2	6	8
Multilateral	2	4	3
Vertical	0	0	0
Horizontal	2	6	8

clusters reported membership in merry-go-rounds, credit groups and a market association, but not in a jua kali association. Only one of the woodworking clusters has a well-organized jua kali association. Two other clusters reported a mix of welfare associations and merry-go-rounds. One cluster was a church project that served to bring members together, while two others reported no multilateral linkages. In contrast, all three metal and vehicle-repair clusters that reported multilateral joint action had active jua kali associations.

In all sectors, reported joint action was horizontal, involving producer-to-producer relations. Vertical relationships appear to be based on the market, with little interaction beyond the basic supply or customer relations.

Value chains and productive capacity

Reinterpreting these findings in the language of value chains and productive capacity provides additional insights into what might be done to facilitate the upgrading of MSE clusters. Although the available data does not permit a full value chain analysis, we can strengthen our findings by looking at the key issues of governance, benchmarking and upgrading from a value-chain perspective.

The analysis of joint action suggests that all of these clusters are market-driven. There is little or no evidence of anything resembling a lead firm in these chains. In all three sectors, the firms operate as equals, competing with one another for the limited market for their products. Even the two cases where there were linkages to larger firms, the firms neither controlled the chain nor attempted to upgrade it.

Despite the importance of benchmarking in upgrading industrial performance, there is little evidence of it in these MSE clusters. Formal benchmarking, in the sense of measuring firm or cluster performance against specific product quality or productivity targets, was not mentioned by the interviewees. One could argue that there is a certain amount of informal benchmarking, but that this appears to be relative to local competitors only. Garment and furniture makers, for example, readily copy others' designs and seem to match each other's quality. Producers are also sensitive to their customers' quality standards. Garment producers in Nairobi know that their rural customers have lower quality expectations and they adjust their own standards to fit that market.

Much more research is needed to do justice to the issue of upgrading. We can, however, make some observations that may help to set the parameters for further study. The first is that, although studies of larger firms suggest that process upgrading usually comes first, we saw little evidence of firms focusing on increasing the efficiency of their internal processes. Rather, the observed upgrading appears to be concentrated on the introduction of new products or new designs of existing products. This was particularly so in the case of the textile and furniture clusters. This may be because the environment in most clusters does not lend itself to improvements in efficiency. The inadequate and inconsistent electricity supply in some clusters militates against efficient furniture production, for example. The overcrowding in markets like the Uhuru textile cluster also makes such improvements difficult. Firms may then try to stay competitive by attracting customers with new products rather than by becoming more efficient.

The second observation concerns the link between benchmarking and upgrading. Lead firms in global value chains provide benchmarks for their suppliers. Producers in MSE clusters do not have the necessary linkages to global value chains and thus do not face such challenges. As long as benchmarking remains relative to the mass of comparable small producers, there is likely to be little or no upgrading. Small producers in all three sectors need information about best practices, efficient costs and reasonable production times, as well as incentives to meet or exceed these benchmarks.

The third observation is that learning to adhere to norms, standards and specifications is crucial to the building of productive capacity. If MSE clusters are not assisted in doing this, then they will remain low-income producers of low quality products.

The final observation concerns technology and the related issues of infrastructure and workers' skills. Process upgrading, which should be the first step in upgrading each of the value chains, depends on the ability to make internal processes more efficient. In other words, it requires adopting improved technologies. The constraints of electricity and space have already been discussed, but their importance cannot be overemphasized. The conditions of some MSE clusters simply cannot support efficient production. Technology is also closely related to workers' skills. Many of the workers in these clusters have obtained their skills either in the cluster itself or from local training institutions, such as village polytechnics. A commitment to upgrade such clusters requires a serious review of the content of training programmes to ensure that workers have appropriate and adequate training in quality production techniques.

Conclusions

Our discussion of MSE clusters in Kenya has theoretical and practical implications. At the level of theory, we have seen that the collective-efficiency model continues to be useful for understanding the internal workings of enterprise clusters. It can, however, fruitfully be supplemented by examining additional issues related to the value chain in which the clusters operate. Three of these issues – governance, benchmarking and upgrading – seem especially important for enhancing productive capacity.

The qualitative data from our relatively small number of cases need to be complemented with a larger survey. What is actually needed is an update of the 1999 National MSE Survey that includes a few additional questions to capture key clustering and productive capacity variables. In addition, it would be useful to carry out follow-up studies of those clusters that appear to have the potential for upgrading to identify the changes that have occurred. Value chain studies – in the sense of specific products for specific markets – are also needed to complement existing sectoral analyses. The discussion of these clusters has also highlighted the need for practical actions by government, support organizations and the clusters themselves. Some of these apply equally to all of the clusters, while others are specific to one or another of the sectors.

Our first conclusion is that all of the clusters studied rely mainly on the local market. Present market conditions were rated at poor or fair for all of the clusters. All interviewees indicated that lack of demand was a problem. All, therefore, indicated that they would benefit greatly from an improved local economy. The Government of Kenya needs to revive the country's economy, particularly agriculture and other activities affecting the rural areas since most Kenyan clusters are located in rural areas and small towns and a strong rural economy is likely to increase demand for their products. Even city clusters "export" goods and services to distant market centres and thus stand to benefit from improvements in rural household incomes. While this may seem too obvious to be worth mentioning, the experience of years of steady economic decline suggests that government cannot be reminded too often of the need to take action to strengthen the rural economy.

The second conclusion is related to the issue of productive capacity. One way to build clusters' productive capacity is to have them fully engaged in producing for demanding customers. Since the analysis of global value chains emphasizes the benefits that can accrue to local producers from interacting with global buyers, it is logical to propose that these MSE clusters should try to enter the export market. Very few enterprises are ready to make that leap, however. For most, considerations of capital, information, scale of production and the ability to cope with the export bureaucracy make an export strategy unrealistic.

As already suggested, the domestic market has one important group of demanding customers: high-volume buyers such as supermarkets, hospitals, schools and government. To reach this market MSE clusters need support. Individual traders and MSE support organizations can serve as brokers, bringing potential buyers and sellers together and providing the services producers require to compete successfully for orders. This strategy is most likely to succeed if the seller is an organized group such as a cluster or a subset of a cluster; the broker receives a commission for services provided; and the buyer is willing to tailor contracting and payment arrangements to the requirements of supply by a group of firms (see Tendler and Amorin, 1996).

The third related conclusion concerns "remote preparation" for supplying to high-volume buyers. MSE associations can help their members to prepare for high-volume contracts by encouraging them to develop cluster-wide quality and delivery standards and by assisting them to access the training needed to implement such standards. Government, through its small-enterprise department, can inform the public and other government organs of the possibilities for purchasing from MSE producer groups. Government can also help by reviewing the technical training programmes offered in government institutions to ensure that they adequately meet the needs of the MSEs.

The remaining conclusions pertain to the three sectors. The situation of the textile clusters depends on their location. Rural textile clusters mainly serve individual rural consumers. The clusters tend to be small and many have no access to electricity. The present upgrading potential of such clusters is very limited. Some, especially those served by electricity, may be able to appeal to bulk customers, such as local schools and hospitals.

Urban textile clusters, on the other hand, could, with proper support, upgrade significantly. One possibility would be for these clusters to continue as first-tier suppliers to the domestic and regional markets. In this case, they would need direct access to bulk buyers. Some firms already have this, but for significant cluster upgrading, associations and individual firms need to better promote their products and services. Furthermore, to produce competitively, the clusters need adequate space to enable them to organize production efficiently. Many also need specialized machines as well as the training to use them. A second strategy would be for some clusters to become second-tier suppliers to global value chains. This means that the cluster would supply or be subcontracted by larger exporting firms. For this to take place, government would either have to review the present restrictive regulations concerning movement of goods in and out of export processing zones (EPZs) or allow small producers to form a cluster within the boundaries of an EPZ.

The furniture clusters studied are all small and mostly oriented toward local markets. Some may have the potential to appeal to bulk buyers, especially buyers such as schools, which may be more concerned with price rather than with obtaining the highest quality. None of these clusters could be incorporated into global value chains without serious upgrading efforts.

In the metal-fabrication and vehicle- and bicycle-repair clusters it may be feasible to meet upgrading needs through linkages to larger firms or by securing contracts with high volume buyers of goods and services. Before that can be done, however, metal clusters need improved premises and access to electricity.

It is clear that MSE clusters will need support if they are to play their part in industrialization. That support can come from the government, associations, NGOs, research institutions, brokers and larger private-sector actors. Each has a role to play in transforming both attitudes and physical attributes. Tapping into the potential of the MSE clusters as engines of industrialization requires commitment and innovative policymaking to bring together, coordinate and steer diverse private and public interests toward the common good of industrializing Kenya.

Notes

1. We acknowledge with gratitude all who contributed to this work. The International Centre for Economic Growth (ICEG) provided research funding. David Mwangangi and Michael Marita assisted with the interviewing. Crispin Bokea offered helpful comments on the original research report. Participants at the German Academic Exchange Service African Studies Workshop in Leipzig, in October 2003, raised insightful questions on an earlier draft of this chapter, as did participants in the authors' workshop for this volume held at the United Nations University Institute for New Technologies, in July 2004. We are responsible for any remaining errors or omissions.
2. Data in this section are taken from Kenya's National MSE Baseline Survey (CBS et al., 1999).
3. A question in the 1999 MSE Survey that attempted to gather this information proved to be unreliable because some enumerators confused enterprise clusters with census clusters.
4. The study included four additional cases that are not reported here. Three were not clusters but mixed agglomerations, and the fourth was a handicraft cluster that was excluded because there were no others in its sector.
5. *Jua kali* is the Swahili phrase meaning literally "hot sun". It is commonly used in Kenya to describe micro enterprises, especially those operating outdoors or with minimal shelter.

REFERENCES

Bell, Martin and Keith Pavitt (1995) "The Development of Technological Capabilities", in I. ul Haque, ed., *Trade, Technology and International Competitiveness*, Washington, D.C.: World Bank.

Bigsten, Arne and Peter Kimuyu, eds (2002) *Structure and Performance of Manufacturing in Kenya*, Oxford: Palgrave.

Billetoft, Jorgen (1996) *Between Industrialisation and Income Generation: The Dilemma of Support for Micro Activities: A Policy Study of Kenya and Bangladesh*, Copenhagen: Centre for Development Research.

Central Bureau of Statistics (CBS), International Center for Economic Growth (ICEG) and K-Rep Holdings Ltd. (1999) *National Micro and Small Enterprise Baseline Survey 1999: Survey Results*, Nairobi, Kenya: Central Bureau of Statistics (CBS), International Center for Economic Growth (ICEG) and K-Rep Holdings Ltd.

Figueiredo, Paulo N. (2001) "Technological Capability-Accumulation Paths and the Underlying Learning Processes: A Review of Empirical Studies", *Journal of International Business Studies*, May.

Huq, M. M. (1999) "Technological Capability Building in Low-Income Developing Countries: Towards Understanding the Nature of the Problem", paper presented at the Development Studies Association Annual Conference, University of Bath, 11–14 September.

Kenya, Republic of (1999) "National Poverty Eradication Plan, 1999–2015", Nairobi: Government Printer.

Kenya, Republic of (2002) "National Development Plan, 2002–2008", Nairobi: Government Printer.

Kenya, Republic of (2003a) "Economic Survey 2003", Nairobi: Government Printer.

Kenya, Republic of (2003b) "Economic Recovery Strategy for Wealth and Employment Creation, 2003–2007", Nairobi: Government Printer.

Kimuyu, Peter (1997) "Enterprise Attributes and Corporate Disputes in Kenya", Discussion Paper No. 001/97, Nairobi: Institute for Policy Analysis and Research.

Kinyanjui, Mary Njeri (1998) "Vehicle Repair Clusters in Kenya: Alternative Strategies for Slowly Industrialising Countries", report prepared for research project on Collective Efficiency and Small Enterprise in Kenya, Nairobi: University of Nairobi, Institute for Development Studies.

Kinyanjui, Mary Njeri and M. Khayesi (2003) "Building Social Capital in Micro and Small Enterprises: Implications for Poverty Alleviation", research report submitted to Organisation for Social Science Research in Eastern and Southern Africa (OSSREA), Addis Ababa.

Kinyanjui, Mary Njeri and Dorothy McCormick (2001) "Value Chains in Small-scale Garment Producers in Nairobi: Challenges in Shifting from the Old Global Regime of Import Substitution to a More Liberalized Global Regime", paper presented at the 44th African Studies Association Meeting, Houston, Texas, 15–18 November.

McCormick, Dorothy (1999) "African Enterprise Clusters and Industrialization: Theory and Reality", *World Development*, 27(9): 1531–52.

McCormick, Dorothy, Mary N. Kinyanjui and Grace Ongile (1997) "Growth and Barriers to Growth among Nairobi's Small and Medium-Sized Garment Producers", *World Development* 25(7): 1095–1110.

McCormick, Dorothy and Hubert Schmitz (2002) "Manual for Value Chain Research on Homeworkers in the Garment Industry", Sussex: Institute of Development Studies, or http://www.Ids.Ac.Uk/Ids/Global/Wiego.html.

Pedersen, Poul Ove and Dorothy McCormick (1999) "African Business Systems in a Globalising World", *Journal of Modern African Studies* 37(1): 109–35.

Tate, Jane (1996) "Every Pair Tells a Story: Report on a Survey of Homeworking and Subcontracting Chains in Six Countries of the European Union", Brussels: European Commission, mimeo.

Tendler, Judith and Monica Alves Amorim (1996) "Small Firms and Their Helpers: Lessons on Demand", *World Development*, 24(3): 407–26.

UNDP (2003) "Human Development Report 2003", New York: United Nations Development Programme.

Waema, Timothy (2004) "Universal Access to Communication Services in Rural Kenya: Project Inception Report", Nairobi: Communications Commission of Kenya.

5

Small and micro enterprise clusters in Tanzania: Can they generate industrial dynamism?

Flora Mndeme Musonda

The role played by micro and small enterprises (MSEs) in job creation and income generation, and therefore poverty alleviation, has been widely recognized.[1] Liedholm (2002) indicates that small firms involved in non-primary activities in some developing African and Latin American countries employ about 17 to 27 per cent of the working group population. Berry et al. (2002) report that micro and small manufacturing enterprises in Indonesia employ 67 per cent of total workers in manufacturing establishments. Apart from sustaining employment, manufacturing MSEs are likely to offer strong grounds for linkages-creation among firms in the manufacturing sector (Ranis and Stewart, 1999) and between local primary activities and manufacturing subsectors since they utilize high percentages of local inputs (Ishengoma, 2004). However, although micro, small and medium-sized firms offer employment and income to the majority of people in the developing countries, their performance has been characterized by low contribution to output (Berry et al., 2002), low growth rate and an inability to move into higher size categories (Liedholm, 2002).

MSEs have become the dominant actors in the economy of many developing countries as they accommodate a workforce characterized by low education and workers displaced by restructuring programmes within these countries. Furthermore, the sector traits also include very low productivity, lack of capital accumulation, low capital intensity and labour-intensive and capital-saving production. In addition, actors in this sector ensure survival through risk-minimizing strategies that compromise

Industrial clusters and innovation systems in Africa: Institutions, markets and policy, Oyelaran-Oyeyinka and McCormick (eds), United Nations University Press, 2007, ISBN 978-92-808-1137-7

productivity and innovative capacities, such as employing family members or paying workers poorly.

However, recent studies have shown that even with the above-mentioned constraints there are significant differentiations within and among MSEs. Some informal firms are innovative, use modern technology and satisfy the growing demand in urban agglomerations. Innovative MSEs are therefore able to occupy a growing market segment. Ranis and Stewart (1999) argue that small enterprises have their inherent advantages. They can use production opportunities better and can grow through links to the modern sector (large enterprises) through subcontracting. MSEs provide a direct benefit by linking the formal and informal sectors, as in many cases the informal sector cannot or is unwilling to develop endogenously.

Like many other developing countries, Tanzania has grappled with achieving rapid industrialization using different models. Since independence in 1961, economic development policymakers have experimented with capital intensive and large-scale industrialization as well as an industrial strategy based on nurturing small-scale production. Despite these efforts, industrial development has been slow. In 2003, the manufacturing sector's contribution was only about 8 per cent of gross domestic product (GDP). It is only recently that the government openly recognized the potential socio-economic contribution of MSEs and the informal sector. This recognition is based on estimates that one-third of Tanzania's GDP originates from the informal sector and the MSEs. According to the Informal Sector Survey of 1991, 1.7 million businesses were operating in the informal sector employing about 3 million people or 20 per cent of the Tanzanian labour force.

Despite the importance of the informal sector and MSEs in Tanzania and other developing countries, studies have shown that it is confronted with many problems, many of them acute. These problems include heavy costs of compliance to government regulations including taxation, inadequate working environments, limited access to finance, lack of entrepreneurial skills, lack of marketing expertise and business training, low rates of technology adoption and lack of information. These problems are reflected in the low quality of products. The institutional structures and business associations that support the informal sector are weak, fragmented and uncoordinated. The sector also lacks clear guidance and policy from government authorities. We find, however, that in Tanzania some informal MSEs have managed to survive over time and at times even produce relatively high-quality products despite the intensified competition after import liberalization. What then has been the source of the relative success of MSEs?

This chapter presents our position that the key to success and production of high-quality products lies in industrial organization, and, in the case of Tanzania, clustering. The manner in which industrial activity is organized plays a very important role in economic development and in alleviating the problems inherent with MSEs such as those identified in the previous paragraph. Clustering refers to the agglomeration of enterprises in one location (geographical dimension) and enterprises producing the same types of commodities (sectoral dimension). Much of the earlier empirical work on clusters has been in developed countries such as Germany and Italy; however, studies are now available of developing countries' clusters. We now know that clusters of MSEs have a strong presence in Africa and that they have a potentially instrumental role in industrialization and economic growth (McCormick, 2004; Oyelaran-Oyeyinka, 1997).

This chapter examines three clusters in Dar es Salaam, Tanzania, namely Mwenge, Gerezani and Keko clusters, to establish whether they possess the potential for industrial development. The viability and potential for industrialization through clustering is tested using field observations and field data obtained through questionnaires. The chapter tests the attributes of clusters, including collective efficiency, externalities and joint action. It also tests the issues of flexible specialization, cooperation and competition in the clusters. The chapter further looks at how knowledge is shared and examines the roles of formal and informal institutions.

The survey questionnaire raised a query to determine if the observed agglomeration of micro, small and medium-sized enterprises in one location (geographic definition) that were producing the same types of commodities (sector definition) qualified to be called clusters. The survey further checked whether Tanzania's MSE clusters possess agglomeration advantages such as collective efficiency and flexible specialization and whether these inherent advantages of clusters were the forces behind the survival of these MSEs in a difficult and very competitive market.

This chapter is organized as follows. The next section provides a historical overview of the development of the three Tanzanian clusters surveyed. The following section deals with analysis of the data collected and the final section discusses the findings and offers some policy implications.

Potential contribution of MSE clusters in Tanzanian manufacturing

Performance of manufacturing in the 1990s

From the available data for the period 1997–2000, we observe a trend of mixed performance in Tanzania's manufacturing sector (table 5.1). One major problem with the manufacturing sector in Tanzania is its

Table 5.1 Manufacturing value in Tanzania (1997–2000)

	All firms	Food & beverages	Textiles & garments	Wood & furniture	Metal & machinery
Real output	13.8%	−4.2%	27.9%	29.8%	2.0%
Real value added	22.6%	−22.2%	33.6%	38.2%	20.8%
Employment	1.9%	−1.2%	6.5%	−7.0%	7.6%
Real capital stock	4.8%	8.6%	4.2%	1.5%	5.4%

Source: Survey Data (May 2004)

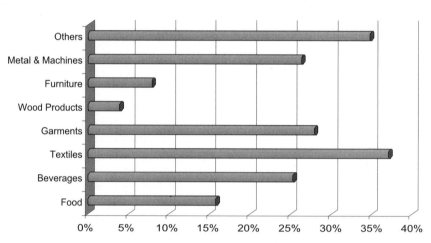

Figure 5.1 Raw material import intensity in selected sectors. Source: Harding et al. (2002)

dependence on imported raw materials, especially in the beverages, textiles, garments and metal-working sectors (figure 5.1). This dependency makes the sectors highly vulnerable to exchange-rate fluctuations.

The vulnerability of large, formal enterprises to external pressures has provided a niche for MSEs as they are generally less vulnerable to raw material price fluctuations, at least in the short term. The MSEs have thus played a significant role in meeting short-term demand shortfalls. The MSEs have also provided employment opportunities for the less-skilled segments of the workforce, especially after market liberalization. MSEs have increasingly played an important role as a source of income for people who cannot find employment in other sectors and for those employed in the formal sector who need to supplement their meagre wages. Wangwe et al. (1998) cite a study by SIDO-GTZ that estimates the number of micro enterprises in the period following economic restructuring to have increased at least three-fold compared to the period before restructuring.

Analysis of Tanzanian clusters

Studies of clustered MSEs in Tanzania are minimal. Lwoga (1995) conducted a study on informal-sector clusters in Dar es Salaam with the objective of understanding how operators could be assisted to improve their productivity and work environment. The findings of the study show that most of the surveyed clusters were operating in the informal sector and generally lacked government support. Most of these clusters were engaged in small-scale trading activities that involved simple buying and selling, with little value-added initiatives. They were constantly in fear of eviction from their business premises since the incidence of agglomeration was spontaneous and formal and legal arrangements such as the possession of title deeds of business premises were rare. Grassroots organizations play a significant role in these clusters and act as intermediaries between the authorities and the MSEs.

Tanzania's clusters have a relatively long history behind their establishment. After independence, there were experiments with many development and industrialization strategies to determine the most appropriate path toward transforming the economy. Although emphasis was placed on the development of the large-scale sector, some initiatives were taken to stimulate enterprise at the small-scale level. In the late 1960s the National Small Industries Cooperation was established. But the first serious step in this direction was in 1973 with the formation of the Small Industry Development Organisation (SIDO) and an Act of the Parliament to empower it. The objective of SIDO was to promote and establish small-scale enterprises in the private sector by providing training, advice, credit, technology and industrial estates.

However, the 1967 Arusha Declaration overshadowed these developments. The declaration spelled out the government commitment to socialism, self-reliance and rural development. One major consequence of the Arusha Declaration was the focus on large-scale enterprise and industrial development at the expense of micro and small enterprises. The nationalization of industrial activity, the substantial increase in state intervention in the economy, and the Africanization of the economy did not take place through the transfer of ownership to the indigenous business class but through the state takeover and the establishment of a public-sector enterprise. The focus on public enterprise in effect suppressed the entrepreneurial impetus. Within the framework of socialism and self-reliance, which were linked to a strategy of import substitution, the government opted for the development of large-scale, monopolistic and mostly state-owned enterprises. The policy environment had a strong bias against small private enterprises.

At the end of the 1970s the economic performance of Tanzania deteriorated considerably. External factors, including a worsening of the terms of trade and increased oil prices, provide a partial explanation for the crisis, but there were also internal factors. Large-scale state enterprises, which were capital- and import-intensive, became unsustainable due to a lack of technological and management knowledge and scarcity of foreign investment. The severity of the economic crisis and pressures from the World Bank and the International Monetary Fund (IMF) forced the government to change its economic policy. The objective of the Economic Recovery Program, as the structural adjustment program adopted in 1986 was called, was to halt economic stagnation and to transform the state-run economy into a market-oriented economy. Market deregulation occurred through trade liberalization, the elimination of government price controls and the privatization of the state-owned enterprises. Now the private sector was encouraged but the base for its growth remained very small and limited. During the rule of President Mwinyi, starting in 1985 and coinciding with the reforms, the private sector was mostly engaged in trading activities and not production.

The structural adjustment programmes had both positive and negative impacts on small enterprises. The external sector reform consisted of the devaluation of the currency and the liberalization of the foreign exchange market that resulted in an increased availability of imports, but also a rise in import prices. The increase in imports made it possible for some firms to diversify into new products and to upgrade their product quality. The diversification was, however, limited because of technological weaknesses. The increased price of imports allowed some businesses to compete with imported goods while freer trade increased competition from foreign firms. The inflow of cheap second-hand clothing and shoes, for example, had a negative impact on the production of these goods domestically. The price increases also had a negative effect on large-scale, import-dependent enterprises.

The restructuring resulted in a decrease of the purchasing power of low-income groups and public-sector workers. Small enterprises that depended on the demand of these groups or of public institutions were negatively affected, while those that developed links with the growing sectors of the economy benefited. The number of private firms, especially micro and small enterprises, increased due to the reforms. Although the reforms had some positive effects, the overall impact on the MSE sector was lower than expected. The RPED surveys[2] show that sales and the employment of permanent, full-time employees declined in all size classes of manufacturing firms in the 1990s (RPED, 1993). The likely cause for this development was that the reforms were only partially implemented and, consequently, there was only a partial removal of the policy bias against MSEs. The considerable structural and institutional obstacles of the Tanzanian economy tend to limit the capacity of the small enterprises sector to develop to its full potential. Structural characteristics, such as market imperfections, low education level, lack of adequate infrastructure and inadequate support and incentives are equally important factors.

The third government, under President Mkapa, started in 1995 and reinforced the reforms and put more emphasis on removing some of the obstacles uncovered under the second government. The reform's imperative was to create an enabling environment to encourage private-sector activity through macro-economic stability and tax and regulatory systems. Many of these initiatives are still in their infancy but the policies and strategies seem to be pointed in a direction that nurtures the long-term development of the private sector with expected benefits for MSEs. The combination of historical development in the policy dynamics of Tanzania and external intervention by international financial agencies such as the IMF and World Bank appear to have initiated an upsurge of informal MSEs. Some clusters were deliberately created as a result of the policy to create industrial parks, coupled with structural reforms. The informal sector and MSEs have in effect filled a vacuum created by the collapse of large industries following deregulation.

Historical development of the individual clusters

The Mwenge handcrafts cluster

The Mwenge handcrafts cluster is located in the capital Dar es Salaam at Mwenge in the Kinondoni district. According to author's estimates, the cluster had 2,200 members in 1995. The cluster is well organized and has its own informal organizations with elected officials such as chairpersons, secretaries and treasurers. This cluster is governed by two registered groups: the Mwenge Arts and Crafts Dealers Association and Chama cha Wachonga Sanaa na Wauzaji Tanzania (CHAWASAWATA), which represents carvers.

The history of this cluster shows that it has both formal and informal origins. In the past, the arts and carving activities were widespread along the main roads of Dar es Salaam and they operated informally. Because the enterprises were not formally registered, city authorities subjected them to continuous harassment and eventually the artisans were evicted and relocated to the current area in an operation designed to "keep the city clean". The forced relocation resulted in considerable difficulties for the entrepreneurs within the clusters as they moved to an area unfamiliar to their customers. However, gradually the area developed and gained considerable popularity in carving and art businesses. The area occupied by the Mwenge cluster has expanded significantly since then and currently is recognized (protected by the law) by the Dar es Salaam city council. In the future, the area has been proposed as the primary location for all handcrafts dealers, particularly carving and similar businesses.

The cluster is highly organized with well-kept shops showing diverse displays of merchandise. The key actors are the carvers and their apprentices who perform both production and marketing and interact closely with sellers who also run shops within the cluster. In order to gain greater share of the tourist market for carvings, the carvers tried to gain the status as sole manufacturers and sellers of Makonde carvings but without success. The cluster has attracted the attention of international bodies such as the International Labour Organization through SIDO. Marketing activities by the cluster enterprises are carried out individually rather than through associations. Some enterprises seek footholds in external markets including South Africa and Europe, but prospects are limited by lack of marketing capabilities. Without the appropriate collective marketing and export support, enterprises will find it difficult to compete outside the national border in the short term. To build skills and capacity of enterprises, the government has established a college for handcrafts at Bagamoyo in recognition of the commercial and cultural importance of this art and cluster. It is expected that this initiative will promote higher skills acquisition leading to better product quality.

The Gerezani metalworks cluster

The Gerezani cluster is largely a concentration of informal-sector operators, but it also has both formal and informal origins. Before the emergence of this cluster, the post-independence government of President J. K. Nyerere had established a complex of metalworking firms and had mobilized people with technical knowledge to join the cluster as part of the "self-reliance and independence" policy. Many technicians came together under this programme and received government aid to acquire capital equipment. As more personnel arrived, the area dedicated to metalworks needed expansion. The expansion, combined with the structural effects of liberalization, led to the emergence of the current cluster, characterized by its largely informal operators. The informal operators perform a variety of activities including manufacturing, selling spares and hawking, among others.

The area has gained a reputation for offering a variety of goods and services including welding, car-board construction, metal fabrication, engine maintenance, car-seat manufacturing and repairing locally made spare parts. Despite its potential, some of the interviewees complained that the government is not doing enough to use this cluster as the foundation for a higher-value metal industry.

The Keko furniture-making cluster

The Keko furniture-making cluster is located near Chang'ombe Road and has its origins in the 1970s with the evolution of five key firms, namely Matharu Wood Works, Pan African Enterprises, Palray Limited, Jaffery Industry Limited and Kilimanjaro Furniture. The firms had machinery and equipment for timber cutting and cleaning and sold manufactured furniture including chairs, beds and tables. In the same vicinity were many individual timber sellers who also made furniture. In addition, there were individuals who made furniture of varying quality and whose production depended on the availability of cheap timber. Increased demand forced this latter group of entrepreneurs to integrate into the activities of the large firms and the timber sellers. This also drew individuals from outside the cluster who had carpentry skills and were looking for employment.

The Keko cluster, unlike the others, is not formally protected and does not occupy space provided by the government. The cluster has developed a reputation for producing a wide range of quality furniture at reasonable prices. Although space limitations and the search for new markets has led some entrepreneurs to take their products to other parts of town such as Ilala, Namanga, Kinondoni and Mwenge, furniture makers from other areas are drawn to the cluster because of its concentrated market and potentials for collective efficiency gains. We visited the cluster in 1997 and 2004 and observed that although the cluster seemed more orderly and organized in 1997, there had been a significant increase in the number of firms over this time and some of the founding firms had left the cluster.

Fieldwork and analysis of data

Approach to the study

A survey questionnaire was used to collect the study data. This chapter reports and compares surveys conducted in 1997 and 2004 that were intended to capture the basic firm and owner characteristics; the production and marketing performance, technological capabilities and networking and linkages by the firms; and the views of the firm owners on the existence and development of the cluster. The surveys questionnaire contained open- and closed-ended questions. The survey sample consisted of 60 firms from the three clusters interviewed in 1997 and in 2004. A sample of 20 firms on average was selected from each of the three clusters. All attempts were made to interview the same people in 2004 as were interviewed in 1997. In two clusters it was possible to interview the same firms but this was not possible in the Keko cluster, as some firms no longer exist there.

Analysis of survey data

In general, clusters are attractive because they hold the possibilities of collective efficiency through positive externalities and joint action. Other attributes include flexible specialization and expanded market access. We tested Tanzania's surveyed clusters for some of these attributes to establish if the clusters have potential for industrial development. Proxies are constructed for externalities through market access, labour market pooling, intermediate input effects and technological spillovers. Investigating the development of the firms in the clusters and gauging the extent to which some of the factors have changed in those firms requires a historical perspective. The firms in the surveyed clusters used similar capital inputs, raw materials and technology and there was little variation or differences in the quality of their products. However, while some firms joined the cluster recently, others had been part of it for a long time. At Mwenge cluster 67 per cent of the firms were established between 1980 and 1985, while 86 per cent of the firms in the Gerezani and Keko clusters were formed between 1970 and 1980.

Advantages of being in clusters

One of the objectives of this survey was to find out whether the firms recognize the existence of their clusters and if there are benefits identifiable with being part of a cluster. Geographic proximity tends to foster greater inter-firm collaboration. Ninety-eight per cent of the firms surveyed regarded their location as being in a cluster. In all three clusters, inter-firm relationships and linkages were found to be common. The entrepreneurs also indicated that operating in clusters gave the firms many advantages, including shared marketing information, joint display of goods and common use of tools. All responses by entrepreneurs show that firms are aware they are operating in a cluster and consciously find it advantageous. Collaboration through different inter-firm exchanges was identified as a benefit of geographic agglomeration.

Qualities important for development of small firms

Level of education

The level of education of entrepreneurs has a positive relationship to their performance, as it increases the possibility of knowledge-based

Table 5.2 Level of education of entrepreneurs

Level of education	Mwenge	Gerezani	Keko
Primary school (7 years and below)	38.9%	90.5%	25%
Secondary school and other post-primary school (7–11 years)	22.2%	9.5%	50%
Advanced secondary school and post-secondary diplomas (11–14 years)	16.7%	0%	25%
University degree or advanced diploma (14 years and above)	22.2%	0%	0%
Did not respond	0%	0%	0%
Total	100%	100%	100%

Source: Survey Data (May 2004)

production, innovation and the ability to adapt to changes in the business environment. Table 5.2 shows the percentages of different educational levels among the firms.

A significant number of the entrepreneurs are primary-school leavers (38.9 per cent for Mwenge, 90.5 per cent for Gerezani and 25 per cent for Keko). However, in Mwenge, 22.2 per cent had university degrees and advanced diplomas. Two of the clusters have a relatively high percentage of secondary-school leavers. Compared across the clusters, Keko has relatively more-educated workers, but as the nature of work demands innovativeness, this might well be reflected in the distribution of education levels.

However, it is unclear why this cluster has such a sizeable number of educated individuals. Even more curious is the considerable proportion of university or advanced diploma holders in the Mwenge cluster. This phenomenon is explainable by the migration of unemployed labour from paid to self-employment. In the specific case of Keko, a plausible explanation could be that furniture making, which was originally craft-based, has become more and more quality-based and tends to attract educated workforces.

Motives for starting a business
All entrepreneurs have different motives for starting a business and those interviewed demonstrated various rationales for starting a particular enterprise. Some had been motivated by the opportunities created by economic liberalization, while others lost a job elsewhere and so sought new opportunities. Table 5.3 underscores the need for more explicit investment in training and points to why training and apprenticeship should be an important activity to realize dynamic development of MSEs in Tanzania.

The majority of the firms interviewed in the three sectors were motivated to start their businesses by a lack of opportunity for business activity elsewhere in the country. Given the severe labour dislocation

Table 5.3 Motives for starting a business

Motive	Mwenge	Gerezani	Keko
Opportunities of reform policies	5.6%	0%	0%
Relative in business	11.1%	5.0%	25.0%
Training and apprenticeship	0%	0%	0%
Few opportunities elsewhere	66.6%	81.0%	50.0%
Lost other jobs	11.1%	14.0%	0%
Other motives	5.6%	0%	25.0%
Total	100%	100%	100%

Source: Survey Data (May 2004)

resulting from adjustment programmes, this is not surprising. Previous training and apprenticeship are shown to be another significant reason for entrepreneurialism. The table underscores the absence of training and why training and apprenticeship should be an important activity to realize dynamic development of MSEs in Tanzania.

However, much of the migration to the small-scale sector is mostly low-level skills, which presents a threat to the clusters. Long-term growth of clusters embedded in this sort of milieu is stifled and clusters fall further behind in such a globally competitive environment. Furthermore, the lack of adequate formal institutions to support informal clusters tends to exacerbate the poor skills situation, a point stressed repeatedly by respondents.

Firms have relied largely on learning-by-doing, but a "closed" cluster where knowledge flow is scarce would be in a disadvantaged position in the long-term. Most enterprise owners have experience in production and trading activities on specific products, which provides an added advantage for growth and development. Although respondents identified this experience as an important asset that they brought to the cluster, it is only a starting point for potential firm expansion. About 79 per cent of the firms showed that their entrepreneurs had experience in production and trading activities related to the current production line, 16 per cent had no experience at all and 4 per cent had other kinds of professional experience not related to present activities.

Product range
The product range of a firm is an important indicator of its specialization and technical capability. The survey data showed that product range also depends on the nature of specialization. In general, it seems the product range has increased over time. The increase and improvements in product range can invariably be linked to the flexible specialization concept. To meet rising customer demands, the more capable firms change design

and adjust quality levels frequently. Given the flexible specialization argument, what matters in the product range is the ever-changing quality and designs of the product rather than the number of the types of the products in the cluster.

The Keko cluster in particular has grown significantly in the number of designs, as well as in the variation and quality of products, while keeping production costs low and remaining competitive. Mwenge cluster has also been able to meet a growing customer demand.

While Makonde carvings have spiritual connotations rooted in the long history of the Makonde tribe of southern Tanzania, there is now widespread imitation and redesigning that targets foreign tourists and external markets. Although this increases carver revenues, it may threaten the industry in the long-term. Makonde carvings are made from ebony and, despite legal restrictions designed to maintain the species, the expanding carving market could jeopardize the future of this resource.

The external efficiency of clusters

Some of the positive attributes of clustering include collective efficiency via externalities and joint action. We investigated these points by asking questions related to marketing, inputs (raw materials) and technology. The firms sell their products in local town markets, other cities and for export.

Table 5.4 shows that local markets and townships neighbouring the cluster are the major market for the firms' principal products. This accounts for 55.6 per cent of the market at Mwenge, 90.5 per cent for Gerezani and 75.0 per cent for Keko. Other big cities take a small portion of the market (22.2 per cent and 9.5 per cent for Mwenge and Gerezani respectively). Firms from Mwenge and Keko clusters earn significant revenues from exports, mostly to Comoros. This is a new development: The 1997 survey indicated that none of the firms in Keko were exporting outside the country. Nevertheless, the MSEs find it difficult to extend their market frontiers in terms of the number of customers and geographical coverage. Most of the marketing activity continues to take place within the cluster.

Table 5.4 Market destination for major products

Market destination	Mwenge	Gerezani	Keko
Local and neighbouring townships	55.6%	90.5%	75.0%
Other (big) cities	22.2%	9.5%	0%
Export	22.2%	0%	25.0%
Total	100%	100%	100%

Source: Survey Data (May 2004)

Through the surveys we found that firms collaborate in marketing by displaying their merchandise together. This collective display of goods provides a sense of choice for the customer and thus draws many potential customers to the area.

Subcontracting, networking and linkages

Networking and firm linkages are some of the attributes of clustering. In this section we report on our findings on subcontracting relationships and information sharing.

Subcontracting relationships

The 2004 survey indicated that 96 per cent of firms had engaged in subcontracting arrangements. As well, 75 per cent reported subcontracting arrangements with other enterprises within the cluster, while 20 per cent of the firms reported subcontracting with enterprises outside the cluster. Most subcontracting arrangements took the form of input procurement and marketing activities. Others included production of intermediate products and final output.

An important feature of subcontracting arrangements is the mechanism for making and enforcing agreements and contracts. Although some firms in the clusters are subcontracted through formal arrangements, many firms have resorted to using informal agreements and methods of enforcement because the legal framework in Tanzania remains inadequate to enforce the rules of commercial contracts.

In addition to subcontracting, most firms (80 per cent) report that they engaged in one or more forms of technical relationships. Enterprises routinely lend tools and equipment to one another. This is another location-driven benefit that builds trust, as there is no financial transaction in these sharing arrangements.

Reasons given for the cluster firms to subcontract were joint marketing, increased capacity to accommodate fluctuations in demand, greater efficiency potential, lower costs of production and higher quality (due to specialization) of products. Seventy-two per cent of the firms felt that being in a cluster enhanced their exposure to different and useful ideas and provided them with opportunities to seek common solutions and strategies for common problems. Other significant ways that firm performance is improved is through entrepreneurship, innovation and imitation of others' products in the clusters.

Information sharing

Clustering tends to foster formal and informal regular contacts and information sharing among firms in a cluster. One of the benefits is the reduction in transaction costs because of proximity. Surveyed firms indicated that firms tend to visit each other's site, which is an important way of learning and a significant benefit of clustering's collective efficiency and flexible specialization. Data on Mwenge shows that only 16.7 per cent of the sample visited other firms' sites occasionally, and the majority (83.3 per cent) visited often. A similar picture emerged in the case of other firms coming to the sites of the firm interviewed. For Gerezani, 14 per cent were occasional visits and 86 per cent were often. The above shows the informal nature of cooperative learning and the non-adversarial competition among enterprises in the cluster.

However, few firms engage in explicit learning through visits to training centres, technology centres and small business service centres. Visits by firms between themselves facilitate information sharing but it is mainly on marketing and procurement topics. Sharing information on technology matters is possible but not very widespread in the clusters. This could be a result of low levels of technologies used and lack of capital to access advanced technologies.

Innovation and sources of new ideas

Firms indicated differing sources of new ideas and innovation. Ideas on new designs, for example, came through a number of sources, as listed in table 5.5. From the statistics shown, clients are the significant source of innovation and new designs in the cluster. This underlies the role of buyers in a user-producer interaction framework. Of the sample firms, 85 per cent reported that product quality had improved moderately while 2 per cent said that it had improved significantly. A new development found in 2004 is that many firms are now producing sophisticated catalogues for their products and indicating cell phone contacts and e-mail addresses. This development is a significant marketing innovation in the region.

Awareness of quality-control systems

Quality-control systems are important to ensure continuous product-quality improvement, but over 70 per cent of the firms surveyed had ei-

Table 5.5 Sources of new ideas

Source	%
Specification by the clients	45
Catalogues and magazines	24
Visiting trade fairs domestically	15
Hired designer	10
Visiting trade fairs abroad	4
Others	2

Source: Survey Data (May 2004)

ther not heard of quality-control systems or felt the need to learn about them. As noted earlier, customers induce most of the product innovations and improvement in product quality.

Procurement of inputs

In the Mwenge and Gerezani clusters, most of the sample firms procure inputs by subcontracting (74 per cent), while others procure inputs from other MSEs (8 per cent), joint activities with other firms (10 per cent) or by other means (8 per cent). For the Keko furniture traders, 75 per cent of the firms procure inputs by subcontracting and 25 per cent procure inputs from other MSEs, joint activities with other firms or through other means. We also observed many interrelationships in input procurements as the firms used similar sources.

Technology and capability in the cluster

Source of technology
The firms in the clusters rely mostly on manual tools rather than machinery in their production, which may explain why sharing tools is very common. Firms also shared information, especially regarding the appropriateness of the equipment and machinery purchased within the cluster. The 2004 survey shows that 70 per cent of the firms exchange information with enterprises in the cluster regarding the sources and appropriateness of technology. Only 5 per cent of the surveyed firms showed that they got information from government bodies or organizations.

Technology use and major innovations by firms
Most of the innovations relate to two major production areas, the use of different types of raw materials at competitive prices for better quality products and modifications to produce designs that match changing consumer tastes and preferences. The absence of significant innovative activity can be attributed to the small size of the majority of firms in each cluster. Small firm size and lack of adequate access to finance have a direct impact on firm capacity to finance research and development. We also note that the skill level among a majority of the firms surveyed was generally low.

The special skills considered in the surveyed firms included skills to handle sophisticated equipment. Most employees (80 per cent) obtained their skills in the firm (on-the-job) or through in-house training and learning, however the proportion of employees with above-average skills is rather low and some firms do not have any employees with such skill levels.

In-house training facilities
In-house training facilities are considered to provide significant opportunities for cluster firms to raise their skills base. When asked, over 90 per

cent of the surveyed firms indicated that apprenticeship is the most significant training facility/opportunity for the cluster firms. The remaining 10 per cent acquire skills through a combination of learning mechanisms such as organized workshops and apprenticeship as a form of in-house training. The average duration of apprenticeship training ranges from 3 to 36 months, although this period varies considerably between clusters and depending on the type of skills required.

Institutions and organizations

Availability of general services
Some of the clusters are provided selective services by SIDO, although this service has not been sustained. Electricity services are available in all three clusters, although not in every individual store. In the handicrafts village, service lines are available to everyone and over half have already connected to the grid. However, most business is done during daytime. Water is available through communal standpipes and mobile telephones are widely used.

Informal association
While formal institutions are necessary for the formation and sustenance of clusters, informal institutions also play a significant role. Informal institutions may manifest as loosely defined associations that act as forums for firms to air their concerns. The survey results showed that almost all firms are involved in one or more cluster-based associations. The associations also act as valuable source of information and the more formal associations are often instrumental in offering technological advice.

The surveys attempted to find out what motivates firms to join these associations and found that 60 per cent of the firms stated access to relevant or useful information on marketing and government policy as the reason for joining. About 30 per cent engage in association activities because of tribal or kinship links.

Similarities and differences between clusters

The three clusters emerged under different historical circumstances. Mwenge and Gerezani were assisted through government policy while Keko emerged as a result of initiatives taken by a group of individuals. Yet government involvement continues to have a significant role in the characteristics of the clusters. In terms of water services and housing, Mwenge has better infrastructural support than Keko, where vendors have to leave their goods in makeshift structures or outside the stores.

Although firms in two clusters export about a quarter of their goods while firms in one did no export business, we do not find significant differences in performance of these firms. It thus seems that MSEs in clusters possess evident agglomeration advantages from being in a cluster, but the advantages are rather static in nature and have not provided the impetus for dynamic growth. There are other barriers to growth, such as poor public-goods and real-services support, which could be alleviated with proper state support.

A positive dimension noted in the comparison of surveys is that the three clusters all witnessed significant growth between the survey periods. Many new firms have entered the clusters, indicating that through their success the clusters continue to draw new entrants. The clusters' products now cover a wider range and show improvements in quality.

Conclusion and policy implications

This chapter examined three MSE clusters in Tanzania to determine whether small enterprise clusters could play an important role in the industrial development of less-developed countries. Despite making many attempts, Tanzania has not been able to develop its manufacturing sector rapidly. The analysis suggests that the unique characteristics of MSE clusters, including collective efficiency and flexible specialization, offer a significant potential for industrial development in Tanzania.

Most of the firms studied regard the cluster setting as ideal for the promotion of collective efficiency. In all three clusters inter-firm relationships and linkages were present among the older firms and the new entrants. These linkages manifest as subcontracting, collaboration and mechanisms for information exchange and dissemination. Lower production costs and higher quality products provide the motivation for firms to subcontract.

One policy implication of these findings is that cluster development should be considered as an instrumental policy option for generating industrial development and sustained economic activity. Key to successful implementation of this policy is the pre-existence or establishment of enabling institutions. In Tanzania the formal institutions created by the government to support the growth of MSEs have been inadequate and ineffective. Clusters increase the possibility of success particularly when combined with selective intervention through government policy.

To sustain economic growth and the expansion of clusters, it is imperative to provide businesses with the necessary facilities, infrastructure and utilities (electricity, telecommunication, water services and housing). Government should assist research and development initiatives that enhance the technological and production capabilities of MSEs. In addition, the MSEs should have access to flexible finance and credit arrangements, such as financing based on collective collateral.

Notes

1. Dorothy McCormick, Banji Oyelaran-Oyeyinka and Saeed Parto contributed to significant revisions of earlier drafts of this chapter.
2. The Regional Programme on Enterprise Development (RPED) is a programme of the World Bank that focuses on enterprise behaviour and performance in sub-Saharan Africa.

REFERENCES

Berry, A., E. Rodriguez and H. Sandee (2002) "Firm and Group Dynamics in the Small and Medium Enterprise Sector in Indonesia, *Small Business Economics* 18: 163–75.

Harding, Alan, Mans Soderborn and Francis Teal (2002) "Survival and Success among African Manufacturing Firms", Working Paper, Oxford: Centre for the Study of African Economies.

Ishengoma, E. K. (2004) "Firm's Resources as Determinants of Manufacturing Efficiency in Tanzania: Managerial and Econometric Approach", Ph.D. thesis, Institute of African Studies, University of Leipzig, mimeo.

Liedholm, C. (2002) "Small Firm Dynamics: Evidence from Africa and Latin America", *Small Business Economics* 181: 227–42.

Lwoga, C. M. F. (1995) "Report on Informal Sector Clusters in Dar Es Salaam", I.L.O. Interdep Project, Dar Es Salaam: Economic and Social Research Foundation.

McCormick, Dorothy (2004) "Upgrading MSE Clusters: Theoretical Frameworks and Political Approaches for African Industrialization", paper presented at the Regional Conference on Innovation Systems and Innovative Clusters in Africa, Bagamoyo, Prospective College of Engineering and Technology, University of Dar Es Salaam, Tanzania, 18–20 February.

Oyelaran-Oyeyinka, B. (1997) *Nnewi: An Emergent Industrial Cluster in Nigeria*, Ibadan: Technopol Publishers.

Ranis, G. and F. Stewart (1999) "V-Goods and the Role of the Urban Informal Sector in Development", *Economic Development and Cultural Change* 47(2): 259–88.

Wangwe, Sam, Flora Musonda and J. P. Kweka (1998) "Policies for Manufacturing Competitiveness: The Case of Tanzania", Discussion Paper No. 18, Dar es Salaam: Economic and Social Research Foundation.

6

Learning in local systems and global links: The Otigba computer hardware cluster in Nigeria

Banji Oyelaran-Oyeyinka

This chapter examines an unusual phenomenon of industrial organization in an African setting, the emergence of an information technology hardware cluster. Conventional wisdom suggests that poor countries are unlikely to host high-technology enterprises, let alone do so within the organization of small and medium enterprises. Significantly, the evolution of the Otigba Computer Hardware Village (OCV) in Lagos, Nigeria has proceeded largely without direct support from the state and indeed within a decidedly hostile institutional and arid infrastructural environment.

The OCV exhibits two features of a cluster that could potentially transform into a local innovation system[1] producing high-value products. The first is the emerging firm-level capabilities for assembling computer hardware (a "complex" product[2]), the second is the growing inter-firm interaction needed to build a knowledge-based cluster. More significantly, it exhibits a development associated with progress in local economies that made successful transitions to modern production. The major activity at the cluster is the assembly and trade of computers and peripherals, a path that offers a relatively lower-risk approach to rapid technological advance for two reasons (Kash, Auger and Li, 2004).[3] First, this approach thrives on incremental innovation because the basic technological design has been established and the uncertainty attending innovations in flux has been largely eliminated. Second, the technological infrastructure required is also equally established and could be further developed to support greater autonomous domestic innovation efforts beyond the initial products.

Industrial clusters and innovation systems in Africa: Institutions, markets and policy, Oyelaran-Oyeyinka and McCormick (eds), United Nations University Press, 2007, ISBN 978-92-808-1137-7

The early emergence of a network organization of suppliers, buyers, clone builders and parts and components traders at Otigba cluster has generated an intense competitive environment and a local milieu that provides a significant knowledge base with potential as a computer hardware (CH) cluster. Network organization represented in a cluster provides the learning capacity necessary for continuous technical innovation. A local system of innovation differs from a static cluster (specified only by geography and specialization) in the sense that it is a network of individuals, firms and organizations whose interactions foster continuous technical innovation. The capacity for continuous learning is a required characteristic of such a local innovation system (a dynamic cluster) in order to import, absorb and diffuse innovation. Transforming a cluster into a local innovation system (LIS) requires a change of focus from production to building a knowledge system with equal emphasis on enhancing intra-firm technological capability. We call attention to this phenomenon in our analysis.

This chapter is organized as follows: The next section presents a brief account of the evolution and market structure of the cluster. It is followed by the study's methodology, an analysis of the findings and a concluding section.

The context and evolution of the cluster

Otigba Computer Hardware Village, otherwise known as the Ikeja Computer Village, evolved from trading in imported information and communications technology (ICT) equipment, components and products over twelve years ago. Located within a former residential area of Ikeja, the industrial capital of Lagos State, the cluster has grown to become a beehive of computer hardware and software trade and production. Two broad phases can be identified in the evolution of the OCV.

The phase of stationeries and office equipment sales

In the early 1990s, the location along Otigba and Pepple streets featured just a few sales and repair outlets that specialized in stationeries, printers, photocopiers, branded computers and office equipment. However, the quiet neighbourhood quickly turned into a major business district. As the demand for computers grew in Nigeria, Otigba Street, which is the longest in the district, quickly assumed the agglomerative character of a cluster. By 1998, most of the residential buildings had been converted to new high-rise shopping complexes. Moreover, the increased activities in the computer and information technology (IT) business in Otigba and its environs led to increased awareness in the knowledge-based cluster that not only encouraged the entry of new enterprises but also generated employment for unemployed university graduates.

Once the potential of the new IT business was recognized, space became scarce and business buildings were constructed largely through private efforts.[4] This singular act brought the less-popular computer components and accessories business in Lagos State to the national limelight, but was still insufficient to elicit positive support action from the local and state governments. This market, characterized by a wide range of computer hardware and allied products on display, ushered in a new dispensation – the era of computer-hardware assembling and allied IT business in Nigeria.

The phase of computer assembly

By 2003 the Otigba ICT cluster had about 2,500 sale and repair outlets spread throughout it. With the new era in full operation, the cluster started attracting new sets of actors and the ecology of the environment changed significantly. The new actors included retailers, importers of computers and, notably, builders of computer clones. The retail market activities changed to involve activities such as direct importation of computer parts (previously limited to a few privileged firms), components and accessories for direct sales, as well as repairs and servicing of computers and all sorts of office equipment. The popular *tokunbo*[5] business is a development that cuts across every sector of the country's economy while the Otigba cluster has become a hub for the computer imports. The sales of used imported computers and the refurbishment of old models by system upgrading is as common as the sales of brand new products.

By the end of 2003, the cluster had grown in market size and undergone a major structural change increasing the number of computer shopping malls and street software vendors and subsequently the pedestrian and traffic congestion along the major streets that lead into the market. The cluster was now attracting buyers and traders from neighbouring African countries as well, thereby serving as a hub for ICT transactions in Africa.

In the current study, the Otigba cluster showed that the major business activities and elements of productive capacity are computer cloning, reprocessing (upgrading) technology and sales of branded ICT products. The vendors and operators within the cluster are mainly graduates of computer science, computer engineering and business administration. Remarkably, 55 per cent of respondents are university graduates, 15 per cent are graduates of the polytechnic, 20 per cent are technicians and only 10 per cent are unskilled traders.

The main trade association records collected show a continuous stream of self-employed entrepreneurs entering the cluster. Over 5,000 enterprises (employing more than 10,000 workers) were recorded as operating by the end of 2004; measured in terms of employee size, they were mostly micro and small enterprises (MSEs). This is a huge increase (42 per cent) from 2003; then an estimated 3,500 MSEs directly employed over 6,000 people. The cluster has started to witness the arrival of bigger players from the formal sector.[6] The cluster's distinguishing feature is the uncommonly high number of skilled graduates educated in electronics and computer sciences and related disciplines. There is considerable learning and diffusion of tacit knowledge through apprenticeship in the cluster, which has led to an observable trend. Trained personnel either set up new businesses within the cluster or outside the cluster with linkages to the cluster for technical support. The competition is keen and price-driven as can easily be gleaned from the advertisements of diverse products and services in the national dailies by firms in the cluster. However, what has emerged in the face of fierce competition, poor state support and sometime hostile municipal government posture is cooperative competition mediated by the Computer and Allied Products Dealers Association of Nigeria (CAPDAN).

The formation of CAPDAN in 2003 is one of the most significant outputs of inter-firm collaboration at the Otigba cluster. This umbrella association gained legitimacy by addressing the considerable institutional constraints confronting its membership in the cluster, namely security and infrastructure. CAPDAN has and continues to serve as a protective umbrella to address the problems of the cluster in the areas of technology support, market support, security and infrastructure maintenance.[7]

A notable organizational difference when compared with traditional clusters in Africa is the level of inter-firm cooperation in evolving joint action to foster cluster growth. This is attributed largely to the preponderance of educated entrepreneurs facing common threats of fierce competition and poor state support. There is a surprising level of cooperation between small emerging enterprises and bigger IT players all operating within the cluster. A major impetus for cooperation alongside market competition is the threat posed by imports from China, Malaysia and Dubai. Entrepreneurs have responded to this in novel ways. One is by establishing technical and production channels with firms in these countries. This has led to greatly encouraged informal exportation and importation (trans-border trade) with price as the major competitive factor. Other local market strategies deployed by the operators include weekly advertisements and promotions in daily newspapers, enhanced distribution networks and developing strong customer services. Unlike in Taiwan, in Nigeria the state has only recently recognized the sectoral value.

Within the last five years, through individual efforts by vendors and operators, Otigba computer cluster has transformed into an international ICT market that serves not just the Nigerian demand, but also countries in the West African sub-region and other African nations. With the growth of the businesses in the cluster, more financial institutions and banks have locations in and around Otigba to take advantage of the high volume of money resulting from the rapid economic development of the area.

The enterprises have progressively deepened their knowledge of the core technical activity of this cluster, computer-assembling process technology. The key learning mechanism has been apprenticeship and flow of tacit knowledge. There is a preponderance of knowledge and skill of trading, servicing and repairing computers and intricate allied products. Collective action within the cluster is in the form of inter-firm credit facilities, technical support in the form of knowledge sharing, joint warehousing of goods and active membership in CAPDAN.

Methodology

Study area and research process

The study was conducted at the computer village located in Ikeja, Lagos. It comprises eight streets with Otigba Street being the most popular because of its size and daily volume of business activities. The activities in the cluster involve the sales, servicing and repair of information and communication technology products and components with a core group producing cloned systems from imported components.[8] Lagos, the former capital of Nigeria, is a sprawling combination of towns with a total population in excess of seven million people.[9]

The study was carried out to evaluate the enterprises in terms of size, capacity development, modes of operation, performance and sustainability, as well as constraints to the growth of the cluster. Both primary and secondary data were collected. The primary data were obtained through questionnaires while the secondary data were obtained through participatory research appraisal using a structured interview guide. The information retrieved includes input sources; sources of technology (process and product technology); availability of infrastructure; and levels of technical support, financial support, market access and cluster collaboration.

Exactly 450 questionnaires were administered to enterprises within the cluster. There are over 4,500 enterprises registered with the umbrella association CAPDAN and an additional 1,500 street operators. Questionnaires were administered randomly, ensuring that owners of multiple outlets within the cluster were not interviewed twice. The involvement of CAPDAN officers was crucial to the success of the survey, particularly in encouraging its members to accept and respond, which was an initial obstacle encountered by the researchers.

The second phase of the study was the case study of 10 enterprises purposively selected from the initial 450 respondents. Selected in order to achieve a more complete picture of the operations within the cluster, these firms were all within the micro, small and medium category of enterprises ensuring thereby that the operations, limitations and constraints of each were captured by the study. Four micro enterprises were selected while the small and medium enterprises are each represented by three firms. To understand the dynamics of the cluster, its competitiveness and constraints, some secondary data were obtained through enterprise records and we also used an earlier report prepared by Bamiro (2003) as a guide.

Basic demographics

The Otigba Computer Hardware Village (OCV) is an example of self-starting and self-sustaining small enterprises (SSEs) that are in some cases family-owned. The SSEs have operated on the classic advantages of flexibility, compact management structure and low transaction costs. They rely largely on their own savings and tend to access required product and service information through informal social networks in- and outside the cluster. The long-term sustainability of this sort of organizational arrangement is still unclear but for now it is a strong advantage for the cluster enterprises. The cluster entrepreneurs tend to specialize in different aspects of computer production, repairs, maintenance and sales. The recent increased awareness of computer use has led to high demand from all sectors of the economy and provided growth impetus for the cluster. This has thus provided a mass market for various types of computer hardware and accessories. The cluster therefore generates locational externalities that also led to forms of inter-firm collaboration, which in turn increase the cluster's collective competitiveness.

The composition of the cluster is presented in table 6.1. The sample surveyed comprises 379 enterprises employing 3,260 workers. There are nine main types of activities involving 71 per cent of the SMEs. While 24.9 per cent of the enterprises are regarded as micro enterprises, 73.8 per cent and 1.3 per cent are small enterprises and medium enterprises, respectively.[10] Most of the enterprises were only recently established, largely in response to the global trend of developing countries in computer hardware trade and assembling. About 95 per cent of the enterprises in the cluster were established after 1995, making them all less

Table 6.1 Composition of the Otigba Computer Hardware Village

Type of hardware	Number of firms	Number of employees
Peripherals	7	379
Computer accessories	269	2014
Typewriters; mobile phones; camera components, parts and accessories	26	191
Maintenance and repairs	3	22
Services and marketing	17	141
Sales	16	129
Branded computers and equipment	33	313
Production and installation	2	16
Networking	6	55
Total	379	3260

Source: Author's field survey (2005)

Table 6.2 Trends in total employees

	2000	2001	2002	2003	2004
Management staff	2.5	2.7	2.8	2.8	2.8
Local technical staff	2.5	2.5	2.5	2.7	2.8
Foreign technical staff	1.0	0.9	0.9	0.7	0.9
Other unskilled	2.5	2.6	2.8	3.1	3.2
Average total	6.1	6.4	6.9	7.6	7.6

Source: Author's field survey (2005)

than 10 years old. Their growth and performance over this period is impressive. The cluster had an average employee size of six persons in 2000 and had increased to eight by 2003 (table 6.2). However, the story of the Otigba cluster is not just about employment generation.

The literature on the development and activities in clusters suggests that enterprises in clusters tend to exhibit dynamic growth and productivity. Table 6.3 shows this to be the case as reflected in the turnover and profitability profile of the enterprises. Both indices have increased in the past years and average profitability in the cluster, which was 39.5 per cent in 1999, increased to 44.4 per cent in 2004. This is also reflected in the proportion of outputs exported, which maintained an upward trend in those years. While only 24.5 per cent of output was exported in 1999, more than 38 per cent was exported in 2004. When examined by size, larger enterprises tend to be more active in the export market. For example, 40.7 per cent of small-scale enterprises engage in exports compared to 53.6 per cent of medium-scale enterprises.

The performance of the enterprises also reflects the entrepreneurial skills of the largely Nigerian owners. Our findings reveal that 88 per cent

Table 6.3 Trend in profitability turnover and exports

	Profitability	Turnover (%)	Output exported (%)
1999	39.48	107.50	24.51
2000	34.75	82.14	23.98
2001	36.63	64.83	27.41
2002	39.24	192.50	33.37
2003	41.85	87.25	35.48
2004	44.37	58.00	38.99

Source: Author's field survey (2005)

Table 6.4 Structural composition of the computer hardware cluster

Type of hardware	Description	Manufacturer
Foreign-branded computers	New and second-hand desktops and laptops	IBM, Dell, Toshiba, Compaq
Locally branded computers	New	Zinox, Omatek, Nigerian companies
Locally made unbranded	PC clones, assembled to order	Otigba enterprises
Computer components	CPU casings, motherboards, processors, CD-ROM drives, hard disk drives, floppy disk drives, flash drives, high-density disk drives, mice, keyboards, random access memory (RAM) chips, monitors	

Source: Author's field survey (2005)

are wholly owned Nigerian enterprises while 10 per cent have foreign ownership. The remaining 2 per cent are international joint ventures with Nigerians. Entrepreneurship tends to reflect in the level of education attained by the entrepreneurs. More than 90 per cent of the entrepreneurs have formal schooling beyond secondary school level. While 62 per cent of these owners have competed secondary education, an additional 30 per cent have technical education beyond secondary education. This is an important factor given the technical nature of the computer business and contributes to the success of the firms in the sector.

Structure of the market in the cluster

The cluster demonstrates a classic feature of a market in flux, where products of different types and manufacturing origins are found (table 6.4). The market comprises three broad product types grouped according to manufacturing origin, namely: foreign branded products, local branded products and the unbranded or clone products.

Foreign-branded systems

The foreign branded computer products market is dominated by IBM, Compaq, Dell, Toshiba, Sun Microsystems and Gateway. They are imported into the country by three main sources:

- direct import by end-users (especially the multinational companies through their international network);
- direct importation of new or second-hand (tokunbo) systems by individuals for their own use and for sale by operators in the cluster; and
- local vendors (there is a considerable number with several years of experience) appointed by foreign brand manufacturers and given responsibility for marketing, sales and technical support services.

Second-hand branded systems, most especially notebooks, are becoming increasingly popular due to their relatively low cost and reasonable period of good service. The importance of second-hand computers is an important starting point for a large number of entrepreneurs who import these systems to be serviced and sold. The business is sustained largely due to the comparatively low cost of such systems, which are sought by those who either cannot afford new systems or do not necessarily look for the latest brand in the market.[11]

Locally branded systems

Zinox Computers Ltd. (jointly owned by Stan Tech, of Nigeria; Mustek, of South Africa; and Alhena, of France) led the way in the local production of what can be regarded as locally branded computers. The firm has the Windows Hardware Quality Lab (WHQL) certificate, the globally recognized hardware standard, for its range of products – desktops, notebooks, servers – launched in October 2000. The Zinox Computers assembly plant, located in Lagos, has at present (2005) a daily operational capacity of 200 to 350 computers with plans to increase capacity in response to market demand. The firm's computers have a number of components and parts – power circuits, casing, keyboard and packaging – fabricated abroad to the company's design.[12] Zinox plans to expand its market beyond Nigeria into the significant export market in the West African sub-region. To this end, the firm is planning additional investment aimed at digitizing its current technology in order to increase production capacity and raise productivity and product quality.

The Federal Government of Nigeria has enacted an explicit policy support to the efforts of locally branded systems. Immediately after the launching of the Zinox series of locally branded computers in Nigeria in 2002, the Federal Government directed all its ministries, agencies and parastatals to purchase the firm's products. Following Zinox's pioneering efforts other actors such as the United Information Technologies (UNI-TEC), Omatek Computers and Beta Computers have entered the Nigerian market with different branded products. The products of these new entrants were also recently endorsed by the federal government. The support given by the government was based on the positive employment effect of the industry on science and engineering graduates. The second rationale was the desire of Nigeria to acquire capability in the manufacturing process of the computers and other computer-related products that were being assembled in these firms. It seems now that a number of other actors will soon join. Omatek, a fully Nigerian-owned firm, has developed and launched an innovative keyboard that is local currency (naira)-enabled and capable of handling three major Nigerian languages. UNI-TEC was founded by nine highly successful computer vendors who have brought their experience in handling foreign brands over the years to bear on the establishment of a joint local assembly plant.

The local brands compete against established foreign brands largely on price. However, the strategy of the local brand manufacturers is predicated on matching the foreign brands in terms of quality, and by adapting the systems to the local environment particularly to cope with the incessant power outages and excessive humidity.

Unbranded/cloned computers

The Otigba cluster dominates the clone market in the country. The major attributes of such clones are their relatively low cost compared to all other brands. Commenting on local clones, a major assembler remarked as follows: "Although the quality of branded systems are better, both clones and branded products are in high demand. Multinational companies prefer branded systems while 85 per cent of Nigerians prefer cloned systems due to the price differential.... The computer market will thrive if government regulates the quality of computer components being imported into the country."

The present market competition seems to be between the local branded and unbranded cloned products and the foreign brands. Clones have started penetrating big corporations, the traditional turf of branded desktop systems, and banks are now patronizing Otigba for desktop clones, components and accessories. IT consultants readily recommend clones in areas such as simple workstations. The competition in clone assembling is very fierce, leading to some operators switching to other IT-based areas.[13]

Learning path: Capability for production and assembly at the Otigba cluster

The analysis of the productivity capacity of the cluster involves a brief assessment of the following factors impacting production capacity: origin of the entrepreneurs, the skill levels of workers, the availability of intermediate inputs, available technology, actual patterns of joint action, benchmarking practice and physical infrastructure. In what follows, each of these factors is examined in turn.

Origin of the entrepreneurs

A major reason for the migration of highly skilled workers to this knowledge-based cluster was high unemployment among graduates coupled with the unprecedented growth in IT usage in Nigeria and countries along the West African coast. Graduates and undergraduates with different backgrounds came to the cluster determined to make the most of the opportunities of an increasingly growing IT business and in turn contributed to its success. The most experienced seem to be former employees of large IT firms who have acquired considerable IT capabilities. Entrepreneurs often start as a small, family-based business with self-financing or money from friends and relatives. Some operate as street vendors until they accumulate sufficient funds to rent shop space because of institutional bias against lending to small businesses. There are three sets of systemic institutional biases against small businesses identified in this cluster. First, government policy had long favoured the establishment of large, state-owned enterprises in which the government invested considerable efforts and resources but with little return. Second, while the Nigerian government has formulated many industrial/sectoral policies over the years, there has been no explicit differentiating mechanism across size and product groups. For instance, while there is now an ICT policy, it is not specific on product groups and ways in which to foster their growth. Support from the state has been reactive in nature. Third, there are no initiatives to facilitate firm entry, the reason for the pervasive smallness of the enterprises in terms of starting capital. Box 6.1 illustrates the typical path of an entrepreneur into the cluster.

Types of technology in use

The core technology at this stage of development of the cluster is the computer hardware-assembly process technology. It is pertinent to note that the components and parts merchandise in the cluster is geared toward providing inputs into computer system assembling, repairs, servicing,

Box 6.1 Entrepreneurship trajectory at the OCV

The case of Victor, the managing director of Rofem Cybernetics, illustrates the typical trajectory and entrepreneurial spirit of owners of some of the highly innovative enterprises in the cluster. Victor had his first degree in Business Administration from the Ahmadu Bello University, Zaria, Nigeria, in 1999. He purchased his first computer when he was an undergraduate student. Dissatisfied with the performance of his 286-architecture laptop and curious about the technology, he started pulling the system apart and re-assembling it based on readings from computer manuals and publications. He gained confidence and became an expert of some sort. Having upgraded his laptop, he persuaded one of his lecturers to buy it. This singular sale unexpectedly started him on his journey to computer business as the news of the sale made him popular with other lecturers who approached him to supply them with similar systems. To satisfy this initial demand, he travelled to Lagos (a distance of about 800 kilometres from Zaria) to shop for serviceable laptops. According to Victor, "With the unexpected increase in demand for computers in the university, I had no alternative but to establish a computer sale and service shop in Zaria and hire a few people to help me in its operation, since I was still an undergraduate. The shop still exists and has grown."

After graduation Victor moved to Lagos and enrolled for a short course in e-Technology at NIIT, an international IT training school. This sharpened his technical skills in computer software, hardware repairs and servicing, particularly in the more intricate laptops and notebooks: "At this point I faced the dilemma of either accepting the fairly good job offer by a bank or launching fully into the computer business. I chose the latter and came to the Otigba cluster to establish Rofem Cybernetics as a computer sales and service enterprise with specialization in notebooks and laptops of all brands – Compaq, Toshiba, Dell, IBM and even the less-known brands."

Along with his staff of ten, Victor has been closely following the developments in computer technology. He has been actively engaged with moving from notebook sales and services operation to assembling his own brand of notebooks using imported parts and components but with casings and keyboards based on his own design to be manufactured for him by a company in Asia. His company has several clients from Nigeria and from outside Nigeria, including Benin Republic, Senegal, Kenya and the Republic of the Congo.

Source: First field survey (2004).

networking and the like by enterprises not only in the cluster but also for computer practitioners spread over the country and beyond. Thus, the computer-assembling operation is central to the discussion of technology as the driver of the businesses in the cluster while also providing a useful framework for the discussion of other elements of productive capacity, the environment created by the product market, government policy, institutions and business associations.

Learning to build capability in the computer-assembly process

The basic computer-assembly process flow is encapsulated in figure 6.1. There are two basic routes for capturing user requirements – either by direct specification from the purchaser or by using regular market surveys to determine the requirements and capabilities required to meet the perceived needs of a broad spectrum of potential buyers. The first route is typical of the computer clone business as it operates in the cluster while the latter is the mode of operation of firms producing branded systems in the formal sector.

The user requirements – defined by the user or by the producer – form the basis of the system design to meet the requirements. The system design involves the specification of the hardware components (motherboard, processor, amount of RAM, number of various drives, hard disk capacity, casing and so on) and software configuration to satisfy both compatibility and system functional requirements. This is a critical step as there are diverse makes of components with different capacities, operational characteristics, durability and price and some are incompatible with others.

For example, the HP RAM may not be compatible with the GIGA-PRO motherboard. This is where the clone assemblers in the cluster depend on tacit knowledge from past successful system configuration. There is an element of trial and error in the use of non-standardized components. This distinguishes a brand manufacturer from a clone manufacturer. The former has standardized components and parts for the assembly process based on established system design while the latter, in order to satisfy varying customer requirements, sometimes juggles with various available components to produce a functional system at minimal cost.

The system design leads to the specification of parts and components for the assembly process. One of the advantages of the cluster is the clone assemblers' ready access to a variety of components available in the cluster. Apart from ease of sourcing components within the cluster, the assembler can easily return malfunctioning or inappropriate parts at the assembly stage. The hardware assembly involves the coupling of the various components, basically a skillful manual operation to ensure proper fit. This is followed by the installation of the operating system

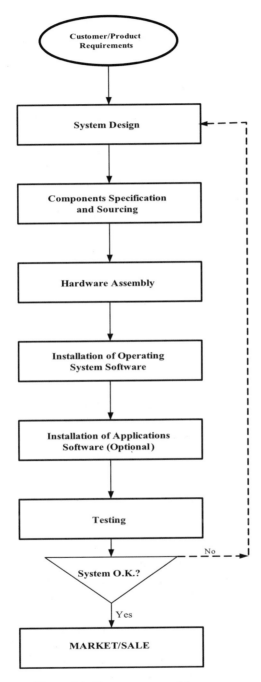

Figure 6.1 Computer assembly process

software to drive the various hardware units. In clone assembling, low-cost "trial" versions of a variety of applications software (e.g., Microsoft Office suite, CorelDraw, Photoshop) are usually installed to save cost. Cloned systems from the cluster are usually Internet-ready. This is in contrast to most branded systems, which leave the assembly line without pre-installed application software except the Microsoft Office suite. Users of branded systems often have to purchase separately any additional applications software needed for their systems.

The final stage is the testing of the assembled system. If the system works as designed, it is packed and ready for delivery. If there is any problem, the assembler may have to revisit the system design. According to Biodun Marquis, chief executive officer of Pragmatic Technology, the company that unveiled Nigeria's first branded notebook,

> It is important that products are of the highest standards and quality because nothing can damage a brand name more than inferiority or unreliability affect perception. A good product will always sell itself. In developing new products, it is important that comprehensive tests, especially with regards to our local environment, are carried out before introduction to the public. Our products are tested for a minimum of six months before going public.

Capabilities to learn: The role of skills and knowledge in the cluster

Every aspect of computer business – trading or production – requires, in varying degree, technical knowledge of computer hardware and software. This point was buttressed by one of the respondents who noted that "many businesses owned by computer-illiterate managers have since gone under due to their inability to meet up with the constant demanding and dynamic trends in the global computer industry". So, what skills or competencies are required?

There is no gainsaying the fact that basic computer knowledge is *sine qua non* to entering any of the ICT-driven businesses in this cluster. The prerequisite can then be further refined according to area of interest, including trading in components and parts, hardware assembling, hardware servicing, hardware repairs and software.

Trading in computers and allied products requires a reasonable level of marketing skills matched with astute business acumen. Trading requires close monitoring of the technology market due to the rapid rate of obsolescence of equipment and processes characteristic of the IT sector. Obinna of IT World advocated what he called "Technology Watch" to ensure that the trader keeps pace with the continual changes as they unfold in the computer industry. While some leaders in the cluster tend to share their knowledge of the market trends with the smaller players, a few rely on "spying" on what the leader is currently stocking to determine what components to import. Although the leaders are relied upon to bring in bulk items such as casings, keyboards, mice, speakers and monitors for sale to the small players, nearly 70 per cent of the operators travel abroad to purchase fast-moving and relatively compact items like RAM, hard disks, processors and motherboards. Such components are usually air-freighted to the Murtala International Airport, which is a few kilometres from the Otigba cluster. Close to 800 different suppliers from China, Dubai, Taipei, Singapore, Japan, the United States and some additional Asian countries are involved. Most operators closely guard their supply sources in an attempt to gain market advantage.

A trader must be able to determine when to buy, sell and clear inventory. Information is critical to the success of the business so it is small wonder that most traders in the cluster have been using the Internet for information and business transactions. Most operators have sophisticated mobile telephones "to connect the world". Equally important is a close monitoring of the Nigerian foreign exchange market due to heavy dependence on importation and the sensitivity of buyers to prices. The market is also seasonal, with the month of December recording the lowest sales. Consequently, most shops declare clearance sales toward the end of the year to clear stocks in preparation for the New Year because, according to one of the operators, "We are all waiting for the New Year and what the government's budget for the coming year will bring. We must analyse the budget, particularly what the budget has to say about duties, projected foreign exchange, IT projects ...". Thus, close monitoring of trends in computer technology and strategic planning of purchases are critical to computer trade.

Computer hardware assembling consists mainly of fitting and screwing operations due to the present high level of standardization of parts and components in the industry. It involves a number of technical tasks that are based largely on tacit knowledge and learning.[14]

In the past, characterized by less standardization, assemblers did a bit of cutting and soldering to get parts to fit. Nowadays, critical components are standardized and come with manuals to guide installation so assembling capability is now relatively easier to acquire. A number of enterprise owners and individuals (including undergraduate students in Nigerian tertiary institutions) acquired such capability through apprenticeship in the cluster. As noted by Stan Ekeh, the chairman of Zinox Computers Ltd., the first manufacturer of branded systems in the country, "People start as clone assemblers until they become branded. You learn the cloning process before you start talking about branding. Even our partners in South Africa started to clone before branding." Thus, cloning-capability acquisition is usually the first step in the journey toward upgrading to brand manufacturing in the computer production business. For a firm's product to be regarded as branded, it is normally issued with the WHQL certificate for the product. WHQL is more a certification of product than process by Microsoft. Four firms – Zinox Computers, Omatek Computers, UNITEC and Beta Computers – have entered the Nigerian market with different branded computer systems. Branding is therefore achievable in Nigeria but it is still too early to say whether firms in the cluster should be encouraged to pull resources together to upgrade from cloning to branding. The competition between locally branded systems and foreign brands (e.g., Compaq/HP, Dell, IBM, Toshiba) is still keen in the volume-driven computer market as discussed further in this chapter.

Hardware servicing involves cleaning operations using blowers and suction pumps to get rid of accumulated dust. It may also comprehensively involve disassembly and replacement of components to upgrade the system. Thus, servicing involves some elements of system design and assembling. Service technicians generally acquire the necessary skills through apprenticeships at experienced firms in the cluster.

Hardware repair involves a good knowledge of software and hardware relationship, good diagnostic capability to establish the state of the system and knowledge of components and their compatibility characteristics. Most operators in the cluster depend on tacit knowledge to undertake repairs. Some problems are not easily identifiable as software-related or as a hardware malfunction. This often results in extra work, lost time and expensive repairs. The hardware repairs capability varies considerably in the cluster with the successful operators being mainly those with a strong technical background. It is also an area that involves wide consultation among operators when repairs become problematic. Computer repairs are relatively easier than repairs to printers and monitors. Only a few enterprises engage in the latter due to the specialized nature of such highly standardized and technology-intensive accessories. Some of the operators involved in printer and monitor repairs trained in the formal sector before establishing in the cluster. Maya Enterprises has a well-equipped printer repair shop and is the source of many apprentices.

Software installation is quite easy since all an installer has to do is follow closely the installation procedure provided by the developer. What is critically absent in the cluster is software development capability, most especially the applications software. It is a knowledge-intensive activity requiring a relatively small capital investment, but is a non-existent activity in the cluster despite the growing demand for application software in the country. It is therefore not surprising that some of the respondents to the questionnaires felt that acquisition of applications software development capability was the direction to go to upgrade the cluster to "total ICT solutions provider". As indicated earlier, most clone assemblers use "trial" versions of proprietary software. These are cheap to use but have been a source of serious discord between the clone assemblers and software giants such as Microsoft, as well as the Nigerian Copyright Commission (NCC), which classifies it as pirated software. CAPDAN, the cluster's umbrella association, stepped in to demand a considerable reduction in the high price of original software from Microsoft. Suffice to note that NCC has arranged for a meeting between CAPDAN and Microsoft to resolve the matter.

Overall, the cluster has both attracted and generated diverse skills. Some of the operators have upgraded their skills through apprenticeship training in the cluster, while others have taken advantage of training provided by the training schools located in and around the cluster. Some operators have even attended a few function-specific courses conducted by the popular Lagos Business School to upgrade their management skills.

Availability of intermediate inputs

As indicated above, intermediate inputs for the assembling, repairs and servicing of computers and accessories, either in the cluster or outside of it, are imported mainly by a few firms in the cluster. The cluster has become the IT hub for the country, known for its diversity of computer components and accessories. Enterprises in the cluster enjoy the following advantages: easy sourcing of components due to close geographical location to the suppliers; competitive prices arising from stiff competition between suppliers, with pricing as its main tool; and special financing of purchases due to good relationships between sellers and buyers in the cluster. The undeclared "price war" between sellers in the cluster can easily be gleaned from newspapers advertisements of ICT components, parts and accessories. As well as advertisements, the *Guardian* newspaper devotes several pages to ICT issues every Tuesday. The dominance of firms in the Otigba cluster in the advertisement columns is always apparent from the addresses, while the varying advertised prices and conditions of sales for identical components underscores the competition. Prices were found to vary by as much as 10 to 15 per cent for identical products.

It is pertinent to note the emergence of backward integration through local production of some computer parts and accessories in the country. Omatek Computers, one of the new producers of branded PCs in the country, has launched into the local production of casings and speakers. Now 70 per cent of the casings and speakers produced by the firm are used internally on its PC assembly line while the rest enter the Nigerian market. The company is planning to expand production to capture the Nigerian market.

It is also pertinent to note that some of the firms in the formal sector have redesigned some critical components in response to local realities. Zinox redesigned the power unit of its branded systems to withstand the erratic power supply and low voltage in the country. The keyboard has also been modified to incorporate the local currency symbol, N. These redesigned components are, however, manufactured abroad and brought to the country.

Benchmarking

Benchmarking is mainly at the level of the few formal firms producing branded computer products. The WQHL certificate, as mentioned earlier, is the industry standard for assembled computers, but assembled clones in the cluster are not subject to any standardization either of process or product. Branded systems are more expensive than clones but tend to last longer. The cost of maintenance is also much higher due to standardization of parts. Such parts are usually more expensive when available but are often unavailable in the local market, thereby complicating servicing and repairs. The advantages of clones are derived from their cheap purchase price, flexibility in assembling, and ease of maintenance. The components of clones are readily available and cheaper. Some have observed that inasmuch as users protect their systems with uninterruptible power supplies (UPS) and stabilizers, cloned systems can last as long as branded. The observed tendency in most networked organizations in the country is to use branded systems as servers to safeguard the database while using clones as workstations. Most, if not all, cybercafés in the country use such a configuration.

Inter-firm learning and collaboration

The strength of clusters lies in the quantity and quality of inter-firm learning and collaboration between members. This is because these collaborations generate positive externalities that reduce the average transaction costs, externalities which individual enterprises may not be able to generate internally by themselves. In the same vein, lack of cohesiveness can limit the capacity of SSEs to defend their collective interests and effectiveness. The type of linkages, whether horizontal or vertical, determines the overall performance in the cluster and can ultimately make them more competitive and better. Our findings from the Otigba cluster reveal that there is a high prevalence of cooperation existing within the cluster. More than 97 per cent of the enterprises indicate that they cooperate with other firms within the clusters while 78 per cent and 99 per cent of the enterprises collaborate on subcontracting and use of industrial associations, respectively.

We further examined the changing horizontal and vertical linkages among the enterprises. Firms reported that there has been a tremendous increase in the level of cooperation among firms (horizontal linkages) and no firm indicated a strong decrease in this relationship. The relationships also translated to more use of industrial associations. The industrial associations are formed in order to foster unity and embed social capital that can be tapped into by the members. Although 19 per cent of the firms indicated that there was no change in this relationship over the past five years, 76 per cent of the firms indicated that there has been an increase in the use of industrial associations (table 6.5). Most of the horizontal linkages identified are in joint marketing, quality improvement and information exchange, where 87 per cent, 83 per cent and 80 per cent of the enterprises, respectively, indicated relationships with other firms have increased over the past five years. However, a significant proportion of the enterprises have not increased collaboration with other firms. For example, in the case of joint labour training, 26.9 per cent of the enterprises indicated that the relationship remained the same over the last five years.

There is evidence of considerable vertical linkages. There are two main types of vertical linkages, forward linkage and backward linkage. We find that firms in the cluster engage in two types of backward linkages, collaboration and cooperation with suppliers and contractors. There is considerable cooperation between the firms and the suppliers and contractors in all areas of operation including information exchange, quality improvement and others.

The same is true for the collaboration that exists between domestic and foreign buyers. More than 80 per cent of the firms indicated that cooperation in the past five years has increased tremendously between them and buyers of their products. The lowest cooperation exists in the case of joint labour training for foreign buyers and even in that situation cooperation has increased in more than 53 per cent of the firms.

The role of private institution: Supplanting the state

Firms build linkages on four broad types of relationships: family and ethnic cohesion, buyer-supplier relations, geographical proximity and, finally, ownership, investment or organizational membership (Perry, 1999). Cooperative relationships may be created through trading ties, personal connections and links with collective institutions or a combination of these sources. Links have roots in business opportunities and external

Table 6.5 Perceptions of firms on changing horizontal and vertical linkages

	Horizontal linkage between SSEs					
	Strong increase (%)	Increase (%)	Remain the same (%)	Decrease (%)	Strong decrease (%)	Total (%)
Cooperation with other firms	41.61	50.67	7.38	0.34	–	100
Usage of industrial association	19.73	56.12	19.73	3.74	0.68	100
Horizontal linkage						
Exchange of info & experiences	31.37	49.02	16.99	2.61	–	100
Quality improvement	29.09	54.18	14.55	2.18	–	100
Joint labour training	18.65	43.65	26.98	8.73	1.98	100
Joint marketing	35.49	51.54	11.73	0.93	0.31	100
Backward linkage with supplier of input						
Exchange of info & experiences	32.48	53.70	13.83	–	–	100
Quality improvement	24.14	67.24	8.28	–	0.34	100
Speeding up delivery	30.69	51.38	14.83	3.10	–	100
Joint labour training	17.04	38.52	31.48	10.74	2.22	100
Joint marketing	40.26	44.73	10.86	3.83	0.32	100
Backward linkage with sub-contractors						
Exchange of info & experiences	22.63	60.95	15.69	0.73	–	100
Technological upgrading	22.09	58.53	18.99	0.39	–	100
Quality improvement	20.77	59.62	18.46	0.77	0.38	100
Labour training	16.47	40.96	31.33	10.04	1.20	100
Joint marketing	35.23	46.26	13.52	2.14	2.85	100
Forward linkage with main buyers						
Exchange of info & experiences	53.27	42.68	4.05	–	–	100
Quality improvement	38.13	48.44	13.44	–	–	100
Setting up of product specification	36.24	50	10.4	3.36	–	100
Organization of production	23.16	46.67	26.67	3.16	0.35	100
Forward linkage with foreign buyers						
Exchange of info & experiences	31.03	58.62	10.00	0.34	–	100
Quality improvement	21.45	60.73	16.73	1.09	–	100
Joint labour training	23.11	30.28	33.86	8.37	4.38	100
Joint marketing	26.64	50.19	20.08	2.32	0.77	100

Source: Author's field survey (2005)

pressures and function "through time-space economies, not sustained solely by historical forces alone" (Perry, 1999: 27). In developed export clusters, local networks are increasingly being integrated into global systems, creating new forms of industrial governance (Schmitz, 1998; Vargas, 2000). Ethnic and family ties are prominent in African clusters (Brautigam, 1997; Dijkam and Van Dijk, 1997; Forrest, 1995; Pedersen, 1997). According to McCormick (1997), Asian business success in Kenya owes much to the formal and informal use of extensive family networks that are exploited to resolve a diverse range of managerial, technical, marketing and financial problems. Perpetuation of kinship and ethnic dominance in business is sometimes overt. In south-eastern Nigeria, Igbo businessmen reduce transportation and other costs through cooperation in trading by pooling resources to send a member of the group to make purchases in Asia (Oyelaran-Oyeyinka, 1997).

An important horizontal collaboration of increasing importance is with industry or business associations (Perry, 1999; Schmitz, 1998). An industry association is a network of firms coordinated by a third party association or federation. They are established independently of the firms, but have vested in them powers to guide, cajole and aid participating firms. This kind of network is influential and active in a variety of ways in developed and developing countries. Romijn (2001) cites the role of associations in mediating contractual problems between firms and clients, and their role in acting as intermediaries between large clients and small manufacturers. Manufacturers' associations also act as contractual guarantors by enforcing group, rather than individual, responsibility in contract performance.

There are several IT-based associations in the country including the Computer Association of Nigeria, the Institute of Software Practitioners of Nigeria, the Internet Service Providers Association of Nigeria, CAPDAN and the Association of Telecommunications Companies of Nigeria. While they all originated under different historical circumstances, a number of events suggested the need for the groups to pursue a larger vision beyond narrow group interest. The need for umbrella associations was expressed by individuals, corporate bodies and some institutions of government who wanted to create synergy among the disparate groups within the IT industry. This led to the formation of the Nigerian Computer Society (NCS) as an all-embracing IT body for Nigeria. All IT professionals – individual and corporate – have registered with NCS while operating in their various interest groups. Some members of CAPDAN at the Otigba cluster are registered with NCS, which uses its political leverage to pursue diverse issues of relevance to IT development in the country. NCS has lobbied successfully for significant reduction of duties on certain categories of computer and allied products. Since 2002, there has also been further reduction. The locally branded computer assemblers and NCS now advocate zero duty on computer hardware components for computer assembly, repairs and servicing on the one hand and on the other hand increased duty on imported computer systems. Such joint action outside of the cluster has impacted positively on Otigba.

However, the cluster faces other problems such as lack of space as the quantity of goods far exceeds the available space. This necessitates two or more enterprises coming together to rent spaces close to the cluster to store their goods, resulting in significant cost reduction. CAPDAN has been negotiating with government to address the space problem through the allocation of a new space tailor-made to the requirements of the cluster. Only government can help solve this problem, which has been limiting the growth of the cluster.

Joint action in this cluster takes four main forms: inter-firm credit facilities, technical support, joint warehousing of goods and participation in CAPDAN, the cluster's umbrella association.

Often an operator runs out of components either to sell to customers or for internal use to meet an order. This is not a problem though as components are readily available to purchase on credit from other shops in the cluster through inter-enterprise credit facilities. This practice operates based on mutual trust.

Technical capabilities vary widely among enterprises in this cluster. There are recognized experts in this cluster in some key areas who are freely consulted when problems in their areas of expertise arise. It is not unusual for a technician to seek free consultations from experienced colleagues in the cluster to solve problems. The collective technical capability of the cluster in computer servicing, repairs and system design is at such a level that people believe that any problem that cannot be solved in the cluster can probably not be solved anywhere else in the country. This contributes to the wide patronage of the cluster from far and near. It is worth noting that the collective IT capabilities that exist in this cluster are at a much higher level than those found in most IT-based faculties in Nigerian universities and polytechnics.

The rapid growth of the cluster ushered in problems of security and unwholesome practices that gave the cluster a bad image. A number of potential clients stayed away out of fear while those who patronized the cluster were usually safety-conscious. According to Victor of Rofem Cybernetics, "We realized that things were getting out of hand and already hurting business. This led to the formation of CAPDAN to sanitize the system and clean up the bad image of the cluster as a haven for hoodlums." The initial one or two associations formed in the cluster attracted only a few members and were rather ineffective until problems threatening the existence of the entire cluster surfaced. Upon its formation a few years ago, CAPDAN embarked on the registration of all the business units in the cluster. As of 2002, close to 1,500 business units were registered. This excluded those engaged in street trading. CAPDAN tackled security by working closely with the police and other security agents. For proper street surveillance, electronic cameras were installed in key locations and monitored by security personnel ready to respond quickly to any criminal activities or distress calls. This has reduced considerably cases of theft or disturbances in the cluster.

CAPDAN has also taken up some critical issues such as software piracy, street trading and infrastructure affecting the cluster. As indicated earlier, CAPDAN has started negotiations with Microsoft on the issue of software piracy.[15] Also, through the intervention of CAPDAN, the Ikeja Local Government has now provided space in a new location for the street traders in the cluster. The elimination of street trading will reduce the usual vehicular traffic problems in the area and enhance security.

CAPDAN has also applied for land allocation at Abuja, the capital city of Nigeria. The Association planned to develop such land into another ICT cluster to meet the growing government-driven demand for ICT products and services.

Conclusions and implications for policy

From a few shops selling imported computer systems and allied products in the late 1990s along Pepple Street, the Otigba ICT cluster has grown to 2,000 shops spread over six streets. The development of the cluster is a salute to the courage and entrepreneurial spirit of the operators as government intervention was, and still is, minimal. The cluster is characterized by the display of a wide array of computer hardware and allied products, computer shopping malls, street software vendors and bustling traffic along its streets. This attests to the growing market for ICT products in the country, which is estimated at several billion naira per year. Customers of the cluster are drawn from all over Nigeria and, most significantly, from across the West African coast – from Benin Republic to Senegal. Otigba has become the IT hub for the Economic Commission of West African States (ECOWAS) region while attracting the attention of big component manufacturers such as Intel, the world's largest chipmaker. The cluster, often referred to as the Ikeja Computer Village, though dominated by merchandise of imported products and with limited production activities, is now perceived (based on media reports and several casual government pronouncements) as Nigeria's Silicon Valley.

Analysis of the productive capacity of the cluster showed that the core technology driving the various ICT activities and other elements of productive capacity was computer-assembling process technology. This has been easily acquired by the operators through apprenticeship and tacit knowledge. The cluster, providing direct employment for more than 6,000 people, also possessed the skill set to handle trading in computers, servicing and repairs of computers and intricate allied products. Joint action within the cluster was in the form of inter-firm credit facilities, technical support in the form of knowledge sharing, joint warehousing of goods and active membership in the Computer and Allied Products Dealers Association of Nigeria (CAPDAN), the cluster's association.

The cluster has great potential for process, product and functional upgrading which is expected to be greatly enhanced through institutional support in the following forms: government provision of infrastructural support, stable macroeconomic policy (stable foreign exchange and favourable import duty regimes), financial institutions attuned to the requirements of micro and small enterprises for long-term financing and educational and training institutions supporting the development of the requisite technical and managerial capability.

Impact of the cluster

The impact of this cluster cannot be easily measured as it manifests in employment generation (direct and indirect), practical IT knowledge acquisition and diffusion into the economy and international trade. The direct employment in this cluster at enterprise level varied from 2 to 20 employees with most enterprises having about 10 staff members. The total direct employment has been estimated between 15,000 and 20,000. Added to this is the army of apprentices and street operators freely operating in the cluster as contact men with impressive knowledge of the IT business – software sales, minor repairs and market information. This category of indirect employment is also in the thousands. Undergraduates and unemployed graduates have been trained in the hundreds in this cluster through apprenticeship, with most setting up in other parts of the country. The availability of cheap computers and computer components has also been a source of support for consultants, individual clone assemblers and computer technicians spread over the country. It is not an exaggeration to say that this cluster accounts for the highest employment in the IT industry in the country.

The cluster is also playing a vital role in the transmission of practical IT knowledge in addition to nurturing potential entrepreneurs. This is through the involvement of a number of enterprises in the cluster with the Students Industrial Work Experience Scheme (SIWES), operated by the country's universities and polytechnics. Under SIWES, science and technology students are sent to industry for practical exposure in their areas of study. The cluster has become a popular place for student placements and they have been making positive impacts on the development of technical skills and imbibing the entrepreneurial spirit freely exhibited in the cluster. Some of the present operators in this cluster had their first contact with IT through this route.

The cluster has also attracted cross-border trading between Nigeria and countries along the West Africa sub-region. This is a positive development for ECOWAS in its drive toward the economic integration of the sub-region.

Prospects for cluster upgrading

How can this dynamic cluster upgrade? Three areas of strategic upgrading that hold great promise have been identified in this study: process upgrading, product upgrading and functional upgrading.

Process upgrading would involve finding ways to improve on the clone-assembling process, which has been effected by the lack of standardization of some components. In the process of becoming cost leaders in the highly competitive computer-system production market, most enterprises have shown less concern for the quality of parts and components used in the assembly process. The assembly process is highly informal, there are no standards kept, no record of the components used for the finished product, no serialization or record-keeping of the product; consequently, the assembled product is faceless.

We posit that it is still possible to satisfy the varying requirements of customers by using standardized components whose performance characteristics are well established. This will lead to the production of more durable and still relatively cheap systems. It is noteworthy that De-Goal Ltd., one of the leading firms in the cluster, is already moving in this direction with standardized components from specific sources. Other operators need to be exposed to the inherent advantages of standardization on product quality and long-term cost advantage. Fortunately, the emergence of "combo" casings will help increase component standardization. A combo casing comprises integrated casing, mouse, keyboard and speakers. A combo casing is even cheaper than purchasing the individual components in the casing. Pcgreen, a computer components manufacturer, has started to produce such casings, which are already in the Otigba cluster.

So far, the operators in this cluster have relied entirely on individual efforts in the acquisition of computer technical capability. There is as yet no government intervention in this respect in the cluster. The nearest government institution that could help is the Industrial Training Fund

(ITF), with its mandate targeted at industrial skills upgrading. As a matter of fact, ITF has over the years been funding industrial training of undergraduates under SIWES, the undergraduate industrial training programme referred to earlier. ITF can initiate and fund appropriate industry-based training targeted at the operators in the cluster.

The second possible upgrading strategy is product upgrading, where there are already some positive indicators. The operators in the cluster have so far concentrated on cloning desktops, the simplest in the computer product line including notebooks, minicomputers, mainframes and supercomputers, as reflected in figure 6.1. Cloning a notebook is more complex due largely to a high degree of non-standardization of designs and parts such as motherboard, keyboard, mouse, casing and monitor. Added to this is the relatively "micro-level" of operation, which taxes the skill of the assembler. Fortunately, there is a firm in the country, Pragmatic Technology, established by Biodun Marquis, which has been assembling notebooks based on what he referred to as "garage start-up". In respect to the term, Marquis had this to say: "Apple and Dell Computers, both leading brands today, started from the 'garage' concept to their present large production capacity. Rather than the traditional brick-and-mortar infrastructure of most business start-ups – these acorns grew to the proverbial oak, due to an unyielding entrepreneurial spirit and being customer oriented. The same scenario can unfold in Nigeria." The same scenario is set to unfold in this cluster if the on-going strategic plan by Victor of Rofem Cybernetics revealed during the interview for this study is anything to go by. According to Victor, he has acquired enough experience in servicing and repairing different branded notebooks to launch into assembling his own brand of notebooks. Toward this end, he has secured an agreement with a computer component manufacturer in China to produce non-standard components such as casing, motherboard, keyboard, monitor and mouse based on his own design. He can then source for the remaining, largely standardized, components. He expects to hit the market before the end of 2006 buoyed by a standing order for 400 units by a tertiary institution committed to encouraging him in the venture. It is anticipated some other operators in the cluster will embark, if they have not already started, on similar product upgrades. The market for notebooks is large, as evidenced by the considerable sales of both new and second-hand products in the cluster and in the country in general. Its portability makes it a favourable product for most traders in Nigeria and the ECOWAS sub-region. Such new lines of assembled products will generate additional employment opportunities for IT graduates and technicians in the country.

Functional upgrading, which involves increasing value added by changing the mix of activities conducted within the cluster, is indeed possible.

Possible areas of market growth identified by some operators in this cluster are backward integration to produce some of the less technology-intensive computer components, acquisition of the VSAT satellite-communications technology, repairs of mobile sets and applications software development.

Some operators, particularly the big computer component traders, feel that the country stands to gain from investment in local production of components such as casings, speakers, mice and keyboards. Increasing the local content of locally assembled PCs to improve ICT diffusion in Nigeria was one of the themes at the 2004 national conference of the Nigerian Computer Society, the umbrella organization for all IT associations in the country. The Conference, attended by close to 1,000 participants drawn from the public and private sectors as well as Nigerian IT professionals from around the country, also emphasized the need for government intervention.

Omatek, a local branded-computer assembler has started to produce casings and speakers locally. Given the highly competitive nature of computer components production, it stands to reason that any entity entering this field must be profitable and able to stand up to established international producers in terms of cost and quality. In the IT world, only a few component makers have specialized in the manufacture of specific components worldwide. For example, RAM is produced by only two or three companies (SpekTek, Kingston) in the world; motherboards by American Megatrends and Gigabytes; Intel and AMD produce microprocessors; Seagate and Fujitsu, hard disks; and so on. These component makers have developed research-based specialty in their products and have achieved production and cost efficiency. Furthermore, the computer business is a volume business requiring sales of components in the millions to be cost-effective. As desirable as local production of components is to the economy, it is a venture that must be handled with extreme caution.

The telecommunications sector is growing rapidly in the country with the introduction of the GSM mobile-phone technology. Internet connectivity is also growing with companies, banks, Internet service providers (ISPs), educational institutions and so on installing VSAT satellite systems (estimated to be some thousands in the country) to improve connectivity. The operators in this cluster are mainly involved in the sale of imported mobile sets and there is no single enterprise involved with VSAT installation and maintenance. Some operators feel that the cluster should acquire VSAT technology to participate not only in its installation, but also in its maintenance, which has been identified as a major problem in the country. Fortunately, there are a few schools in Lagos, such as Cyberschuul, for training people on VSAT technology. The country already has over 6 million mobile sets and the numbers are expected to continue growing as the three licensed GSM operators increase coverage and competition drives down service cost. Seriously lacking, however, is the capability for maintenance of mobile sets, leading people to replace faulty sets in most cases. There were only a few operators in the cluster specializing in the repairs of mobile sets. Noteworthy was a graduate of electronics from one of the Nigerian universities involved with repairs of mobile sets at a street corner in the cluster. But of particular interest was an operator who went to Ghana and Côte d'Ivoire to train on the repairs of different makes of mobile sets and has also attended two training programmes abroad. It is anticipated that more such actors will evolve and become big players in the cluster.

The software industry, most especially application software, is a growing sector in the country. The study by Bamiro (2003) identified several areas of opportunities for application software in virtually all sectors of the economy. Software solutions account for close to 40 per cent of the investment in IT in the banking and finance sector. There are no software firms in the cluster despite the widespread handling of software by those involved with the assembling, repairs and servicing of computers and some classes of computer problems being software related. This is a major weakness of most of the operators in the cluster. The observation is that the cluster does not offer any particular attraction for developers who are to be found mainly in other parts of the city. This may soon change.

Potential for cluster upgrading

The potential for the upgrading of the productive capacity of a cluster is central to the theoretical model adopted in this project. The following three potentially viable routes to upgrading the Otigba cluster have been identified:

1. Upgrading the clone assembling process is possible through training assemblers in the use of standardized components whose performance characteristics are well established. The emergence of "combo" casings, integrating otherwise separated components such as casing, mouse, keyboard and speakers, will help in this direction. This will lead to the production of more durable and relatively cheap systems and the possible convergence to branding.
2. Product upgrading is expected by the upgrading from cloning desktops to the more intricate process of assembling cloned laptops/notebooks.
3. Functional upgrading, which involves increasing value added by changing the mix of activities conducted within the cluster, is indeed possible in the following areas: backward integration to produce some

of the less technology-intensive computer components, acquisition of the VSAT technology, repairs of mobile sets and software development. These activities are geared toward the development of the cluster into a one-stop provider of ICT solutions. Backward integration will require strong financial support due to its capital-intensity. VSAT technology is already in the country and knowledge of it is possible to acquire through training in some of the existing specialized training outfits. Some repair capability for mobile phones already exists, but it will have to be built upon to capture the growing market for such services. Software development is knowledge-intensive but fortunately there are several schools around the cluster providing training.

Notes

1. I apply the concept of a "local system of innovation" drawing inspiration from the approaches by Lundvall (1992) and Nelson (1993) but delimited in term of a locality the same way in which, say, a sectoral system of innovation is delimited by a sectoral boundary (Malerba, 2004). The notion of a "local system" has been applied to series of case studies in Brazil (Cassiolato et al., 2003).
2. A good is categorized as complex if either the product itself or the process of manufacturing it is complex. A complex technology, unlike a simple technology such as making furniture or footwear, requires organizational forms, whereas the latter can be understood by an individual. Complex goods are different from "high-tech" in that the latter is measured by the ratio of research and development expenditure to output. See the United Nations *Statistical Yearbook*.
3. Building a local system of production and innovation is a path followed by arguably the most successful personal-computer industry in the developing world based on clustering of small and medium-sized enterprises. The Taiwanese PC industry has relied on extensive imports from Japan progressively.
4. Notable among these is the Police Women Association (POWA) Shopping Complex with 100 office spaces at 30/31 Otigba Street. This initiative stimulated the entrepreneurial spirit of the computer and allied products vendors and operators considerably.
5. *Tokunbo* is an ethnic Yoruba word meaning "imported". This term assumed a specific business meaning to denote the importation of second-hand electronic goods, components, and parts, and motor vehicle parts. Second-hand consumer goods, appliances as well as industrial machinery and replacement parts, has become a multi-billion dollar business in Nigeria although precise figures are difficult to come by.
6. "It is the place to be now or you go under", noted an IT hardware company executive locating to the cluster from the highbrow part of Lagos city.
7. According to the present president of CAPDAN, Mr. Ibrahim Tunji Balogun of Baloq Technologies Ltd., the number of registered enterprises in the cluster under the Association is over 3,500 with the employees numbering between 8,000 and 10,000 excluding their employers, with an estimated minimum turnover on an individual's investment of over 5m naira per annum (US$30,000). This of course is the mean for much of the small operators. There are instances where some of the enterprises realize this figure in a week.

8. The cluster is located at the heart of Ikeja and bordered by Unity Road, Awolowo Road and Oba Akran Avenue. It has been variously described as the ICT hub of West Africa, potentially the biggest ICT market in Africa and the Silicon Valley of the West African sub-region. According to the report by Bamiro (2003), the cluster covers an area of 325 square kilometres.

9. Lagos is the commercial centre of the nation and home to many industries, government agencies, the head offices of most financial institutions, embassies of other countries and many commercial institutions. It has the country's major seaport and the busiest international airport in Nigeria.

10. We define large firms as being those with 100 workers and above, medium firms as those with 20 to 99 workers, small firms as those with 5 to 19 workers, and micro firms as those with fewer than 5 workers. See Oyelaran-Oyeyinka (2006).

11. For example, second-hand notebooks currently sell for ₦90,000 to ₦120,000 while prices for new ones from such manufacturers as Dell, HP/Compaq, IBM and Toshiba range between ₦170,000 and ₦300,000. 1 US$ = ₦170 on the open market (mid-2005) at the time of this survey.

12. According to Mr. Stan Ekeh, the managing director and chief executive officer of Zinox: "Regarding competition, we made it clear from the onset that our competitors are the world market leaders – Compaq, HP and Dell. That is the class we fall into.... Those companies are still holding most of the major accounts that we are gradually cutting into. With time, we'll be there."

13. The chief executive of IT World noted, "This business of cloning is no longer as profitable with customers not wanting to buy original software.... If we sell components we only give one month guarantee but if you proceed to make systems you have to provide a one year warranty liability all for an additional ₦300. On a risk-reward basis it is not worth it.... Thus, as a strategic shift we are moving away activities to non-PC areas such as video-editing products, ID cards, photo printing, CD/multimedia specialty printer machines ..."

14. Fixing the processor with its cooling fan onto the motherboard; adjusting the necessary jumper settings on the motherboard; attaching the drives (CD-ROM, floppy disk, hard disk, high-density disk, etc.) to the appropriate parts of the casing; fastening the motherboard to the casing; connecting the drives to the motherboard with the controllers; connecting the appropriate interface cards (e.g., video card, modem, sound card) to their appropriate slots on the motherboard; starting up the computer and installing the desired operating system; installation of the required application software.

15. This step was not unconnected with the following observation of Prof Nwauche, director of the Nigerian Copyright Commission, in a recent interview: "I am going to have a meeting with the Otigba people to talk to them; to encourage them to come as a group to Microsoft and negotiate with them so that their jobs are not destroyed, so that the market itself is not closed.... If they reach an agreement, it means the Otigba people must only sell the original given to them by Microsoft to sell."

REFERENCES

Bamiro, O. A. (2003) "The Otigba ICT Cluster: The Making of a Local 'Silicon Valley' in Nigeria", Maastricht: UNU-INTECH.

Brautigam, D. (1997) "Substituting for the State: Institutions and Industrial Development in Eastern Nigeria", *World Development* 25(7): 1063–80.

Cassiolato, J., H. M. M. Lastres and M. L. Maciel (2003) *Systems of Innovation and Development Evidence from Brazil*, Cheltenham: Edward Elgar.

Dykam, H. and P. Van Dijk (1997) "Opportunities for Women in Qugadougou's Informal Sector: An Analysis Based on the Flexible Specialization Concept", in M. P. Van Dijk and R. Rabelotti, *Enterprise Clusters and Networks in Developing Countries*, London: Frank Cass.

Forrest, T. (1995) *The Makers and Making of Nigerian Private Enterprises*, Ibadan: Spectrum Books.

Kash, D. E., R. N. Auger and N. Li (2004) "An Exceptional Development Pattern", *Technological Forecasting and Social Change* 71: 777–97.

Lundvall, Bengt-Åke, ed. (1992) *National Systems of Innovation: Towards a Theory of Innovation and Interactive Learning*, London: Pinter Publishers.

McCormick, Dorothy (1997) "Industrial Districts or Garment Ghetto? Nairobi's Mini-Manufacturers", in Dorothy McCormick, ed., *Industrial Districts or Garment Ghetto? Nairobi's Mini-Manufacturers*, Nairobi: Institute for Development Studies.

Malerba, Franco (2004) *Sectoral Systems of Innovation*, Cambridge: Cambridge University Press.

Nelson, Richard, ed. (1993) *National Innovation Systems: A Comparative Analysis*, London: Oxford University Press.

Oyelaran-Oyeyinka, B. (2006) *Learning to Compete: Institutions, Technology and Enterprise in African Development*, Aldershot: Ashgate Publishing Limited.

Pedersen, Poul Ove (1997) "Clusters of Enterprises within Systems of Production and Distribution: Collective Efficiency and Transaction Costs" in M. P. Van Dijk and R. Rabelotti, *Enterprise Clusters and Networks in Developing Countries*, London: Frank Cass, 11–30.

Perry, Martin (1999) *Small Firms and Network Economies*, London: Routledge.

Romijn, H. (2001) "Technology Support for Small-Scale Industry in Developing Countries: A Review of Concepts and Project Practices", *Oxford Economic Papers* 29(1).

Schmitz, H. (1998) "Responding to Global Competitive Pressure: Local Cooperation and Upgrading in the Silicon Valley, Brazil", IDS Working Paper No. 82, Brighton: University of Sussex.

Vargas, Marco Antonio (2000) "Local Systems of Innovation in Developing Countries: A Study of Technological Learning in Local Productive Arrangements in Brazil", paper prepared for the Druid's Winter Conference on Industrial Dynamics.

7

Power and firms' learning in the Egyptian furniture cluster of Domiatt

Samah El-Shahat

The furniture cluster of Domiatt is characterized by economic and power asymmetries between the actors involved in both its domestic and exporting value chains. This status quo is mirrored in the institutional environment underpinning firm interaction. Due to the scope of the chapter, we will only analyse the domestic value chain that has been pursuing an unproductive growth trajectory characterised by firms' de-skilling rather than learning. We will delineate how the institution-interlinking factor markets, in particular that of combining credit with other factor markets such as the selling of the furniture and the purchasing of timber, effects firms' learning. This case study draws on political economy constructs and specifically the work of the institutionalist economist, Douglas C. North.

Reinserting political economy into the analysis has two consequences. First, it reintroduces complexity and conflict into the analysis, challenging the traditional focus in cluster studies on mutual gains, unitarist unified firms and organizational trust and social capital between firms. This is of most importance due to the relative absence of the notion of conflict in the national systems of innovation framework. Second, in conceptualizing knowledge as a social process where institutions are path-dependent, it focuses our attention on questions of power in understanding how firms learn and, more precisely, in understanding the sources, actions and effects of unequal socio-economic power in the relations between firms of unequal assets. This differentiation includes not only the conventional differences provided by the cluster, value-chain and national systems of

Industrial clusters and innovation systems in Africa: Institutions, markets and policy, Oyelaran-Oyeyinka and McCormick (eds), United Nations University Press, 2007, ISBN 978-92-808-1137-7

innovation (NSI) frameworks between users and producers of knowledge, or governors of the chain, and those firms who are governed, but also social differentiation due to class and differential access to resources in the national systems of innovation itself.

Chapters 2 and 3 in this book provide the theoretical backdrop on which the analysis of the Domiatt case study is based. The focus is on one of the cluster's value chains, the showroom (buyer)-led domestic value chain. This shows how the institution of interlinking factor markets as used by Domiatt's powerful actors, namely, the showroom owners as well as the wood sellers, has crippled the small workshops' scope for upgrading by limiting their research and development process. This has led to a situation of knowledge- and learning-stagnation for the workshops in the showroom-led value chain and will lead in the long-term to the demise and de-skilling of the artisan. The Domiatt case will show that institutions reflect power relations and have been opportunistically used by certain dominant actors to further their interests. This might mean that institutions are not created to be socially efficient for interactive learning as implicitly implied within the NSI framework. In fact, in this cluster they often tend to serve the interest of the most powerful.

The chapter is organized as follows. The next section provides the methodology for this research and the following section provides an introduction to Domiatt, its history and its institutions. It gives a detailed empirical treatment of the showroom-led chain and identifies the sources of knowledge and scope for small-workshop upgrading. This will be followed by an analysis of the effect of the interlinking of factor markets on the small-workshop research and development process and the workshops' potential for learning and upgrading.

Methodology

Data collection in Domiatt followed two stages. First, snowball sampling was used to trace all actors in the showroom-led value chain; this included the workshops, the wood sellers and the showroom owners themselves. Using the sample identified by the snowballing method, a series of both quantitative and qualitative research methods, which included semi-structured questionnaires and open-ended interviews, were then applied on a research sample of 80 workshops, 10 wood sellers and 6 showrooms. These individuals were interviewed regularly over a period of two and a half years from June 2000 to November 2002.

Snowball sampling may simply be defined as a technique for finding research subjects. One subject gives the researcher the name of another subject, who in turn provides the name of a third, and so on (Vogt, 1999).

This strategy can be viewed as a response to overcoming the problems associated with sampling weaker and more vulnerable actors involved in power and exploitative relationships (Faugier and Sargeant, 1997). Snowball sampling can be placed within a wider set of link-tracing methodologies (Spreen, 1992), which seek to take advantage of the social networks of identified respondents to provide a researcher with an ever-expanding set of potential contacts (Thomson, 1997). This process is based on the assumption that a "bond" or "link" exists between the initial sample and others in the same target population, allowing a series of referrals to be made within a circle of acquaintance (Berg, 1988).

This was of most importance for this research as many small workshops, due to their vulnerable social standing, felt incredible fear of the interview due to the exploitative relations they had with showroom owners and wood sellers. Moreover, many producers and showroom owners refuse to admit to an existing relationship with small workshop owners, and/or also refuse to specify whom they contract to work. This methodology was also found to be useful in identifying the power bases of control in Domiatt. While many have considered snowball strategies primarily as an aid to accessing the vulnerable, some studies have used them to engage with the "hard to reach" among urban elites. Saunders's (1979) study of urban politics is an example where a "reputational" method was used. Respondents were asked who held power in the local arena. This led to a series of contacts and the establishment of a subjective indication of the relative local power bases. This suggests that snowball sampling has a wider applicability in economic research than has hitherto been realized. It is this dual aspect of snowball sampling, the fact that it can assist the researcher to locate both vulnerable as well as more powerful social actors, which lent itself to the research. This allowed the researcher to identify the powerful actors in Domiatt, such as the showroom owners and wood sellers, and to determine how their power manifests itself negatively on the small workshops' scope for upgrading.

The combination of snowball sampling and quantitative and qualitative data collection methods enabled the researcher to delineate and map out the knowledge flows and stocks in the showroom-led value chain. This was achieved by evaluating and tracing the knowledge flows between the different actors in the chain. This was useful in assessing the knowledge stock of each actor in every stage of the chain as well as determining how much of their knowledge base was communicated to other actors in the chain. Moreover, it enabled the development of a map of the dynamics and sources of power in the cluster, and how this affected firms' learning and acquiring knowledge from the different actors in the chain.

The section that follows will analyse the showroom-led value chain and the acquiring of technological capability by those workshops in the chain.

It starts with a description of the workings of the chain, followed by a detailed analysis of small workshops' technological capability and their sources for acquiring knowledge on production and innovation. The section also focuses on the effect of the interlinking of factor markets in Domiatt on small workshops' learning and research and development process. In so doing it shows how the socio-economic power of the showroom owner and the wood seller manifests itself by limiting the workshops' growth and leading to the de-skilling of this industry.

Domiatt: Furniture cluster

This first part of the case study provides a detailed analysis of Domiatt. This section looks at the unique characteristics of both furniture-making and the prevalence of interlinked factor markets in Domiatt, which lend themselves to the application of our conceptual framework. It will also highlight Domiatt's unique indigenous knowledge base and extensive division of labour, which makes it stand out vis-à-vis other Egyptian clusters, and introduces Domiatt's disparate value chains. This first part of the case study ends with a detailed history of industrial relationships between the major protagonists of the value chain, namely the workshop owners and the showroom owners. It will be shown that the power disparities that impact firms' learning and development today followed path-dependent social and technological trajectories shaped by history decades ago.

General introduction to Domiatt

Domiatt provides us with an interesting testing ground for the interaction between technological change and institutions. This results from the prevalence of the institution of interlocked or interlinked markets, which dictate the quality, nature and scope of interaction between the actors involved. Interlinkage, or the practice of offering contracts that combine transactions across multiple markets, is a phenomenon that prevailed in the Italian Industrial Districts (Dei Ottati, 1993). One further issue for investigation is determining the effects on firms' learning when key agents operate in two or more stages.

Moreover, the furniture industry provides an ideal theoretical simulated environment to apply some of the salient points of the NSI framework as well as the technological-capability literature findings. The Egyptian case is highly relevant from an NSI perspective, as Egypt has no natural wood resource of its own. The industry imports all the intermediate factors of production; paint and varnishes, metal fittings et cetera are imported

Table 7.1 Size composition of furniture enterprises by number of employees in Domiatt

Number of employees	Enterprises (%)
1–4	92.39
5–14	7.51
15–49	0.09
>50	0.01

Source: CAPMAS (2003)

from overseas. This makes it an ideal example for testing NSI's assertions, which focus on skill-acquisition as the root of competitive advantage, as opposed to traditional advantages associated with comparative-advantage theories. Despite Egypt's relatively low labour costs, the existence of high tariffs placed on all intermediate products as well as on export mitigates its cheap labour advantage. This gives us an early indication that the "high road" to competition, characterized by firms pursuing strategies of continuous innovation and creating flexible learning networks that focus on a range of issues besides price, might prove to be the most preferable strategy for Domiatt. In sum, Domiatt's success will lie on the institutions, both formal and informal, underlining learning via interacting.

Domiatt, like other furniture clusters internationally, consists predominantly of micro and small enterprises. Large firms, defined as those employing more than 50 workers, make up the remaining 0.01 per cent as can be seen from table 7.1.

The data on Domiatt and on furniture production in Egypt in general is riddled with many inconsistencies and is highly inaccurate, which severely constricts the ability to diagnose and design effective policies to help this cluster and industry as a whole. The common statistical consensus is that this industry as a whole was facing a major economic downturn with imports overtaking exports from 1999–2002. Statistics obtained from the Ministry of Foreign Trade indicate that exports increased from US$2.4 million in 1999 to reach US$3.6 million in 2000 and US$7.8 million in 2003. Imports on the other hand rose slower, increasing from US$6.1 million in 1999 to US$9 million in 2002. In the last three years exports have rocketed to a yearly sales figure of US$100 million.

There are said to be 35,000 furniture workshops in Domiatt made up of 24,000 formal workshops and 11,000 informal ones.[1] Yet, recent research indicates a higher level of at least 50,000 (El-Shahat, 2002). The industry employs over 100,000 people, which is approximately 10 per cent of the local populace. There is no official estimate of how much Domiatt produces, only three rough and highly inconsistent figures provided by the chamber of trade and commerce and by the office of the Governor of Domiatt. The first figure, the yearly turnover from furniture making, stands at 400 million Egyptian pounds (approx. US$570,000)[2] and the second is that Domiatt produces one million bedrooms a year. The third figure provided by the office of the Governor estimates that Domiatt's exports have rocketed to US$100 million dollars yearly since 2003. Estimates of Domiatt's share of total Egyptian furniture production range from 15 per cent to 75 per cent, according to Domiatt's governorate. It is estimated that Domiatt exports between 3 and 10 per cent of all its furniture production.

Domiatt stands out from all the other clusters in Egypt due to its high skill content and rare indigenous knowledge of the artisans. Theirs is a highly complex and tacit skill that is only acquired after a lengthy and arduous learning process rooted in master-apprentice relationships. Artisans require 10 years of apprenticeship before being elevated to journeyman and then another 15 years before qualifying as a master-artisan. Due to the physical as well as tacit intensity of interaction required to master the skill, this learning process lends itself to fathers teaching their sons their skills. So the skills until quite recently were bequeathed from generation to generation. There has been a marked change in that though in the last decade in particular, with children of the artisans preferring to go into the state or private sector due to the difficulty in earning a living in this craft.

This elevated skill content and complexity is uniform across many different specializations within this cluster. This ranges from carvers and veneerers, to marquitrirers (those who carry out inlaid work) and gold-leaf appliers. There are those who solely specialize in making chairs; others, sofas; others, beds. Artisanal furniture workshops produce white wood (wooden frames), furniture still needing paint and upholstery. These latter stages are directly controlled and overseen by the governors of the value chains.

We will now look at these value chains in closer detail. In which of the value chains the small workshop is involved will determine the scope for learning and upgrading.

Domiatt's value chains

There are two variants of the value chain in Domiatt involving small workshops as figure 7.1 shows.

Of the two variants in the Domiatt value chain, one feeds into the domestic market and is governed by the showroom owner, who is the furniture buyer/retailer, while the other feeds into the export market. In this chapter, we look at the showroom-led value chain that feeds into the domestic market.[3]

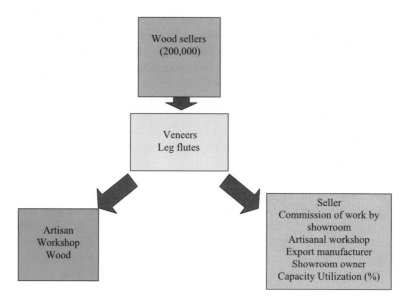

Figure 7.1 Domiatt's value chains

It is estimated that 60 per cent of Domiatt's small and medium-sized enterprises (SMEs) are involved in a showroom-governed chain, while only 40 to 70 firms are involved in the exporting-manufacturer value chain. In part, the latter's small number is because these SMEs act as subcontractors to manufacturing exporters, that is, firms that already have a manufacturing capacity. Additionally, these export manufacturers resort to the SMEs as a last measure due to ignorance of global manufacturing practices such as just-in-time manufacturing. Thus they resort to these SMEs due to organizational and management failure.

Despite the fact that this chapter will not be analysing the export value chain, it is important to situate the local showroom-governed value chain against that of the export chain. These two value chains are driven by completely different if not opposing markets. The local value chain is price-driven and caters to a "bulk-buy mentality" of its final users. In Egypt, furniture is no ordinary commodity; it has important cultural significance. The purchase of furniture is a fundamental step toward marriage for both the prospective bride and groom, but more so for the bride's family as the onus is on them to furnish every room in their daughter's marital abode. Moreover, Egyptians still like to have multiple salon sets in their living rooms and salons. Furniture-buying becomes even more highly prohibitive if the families have more than one daughter. Hence, families start saving early for the costs of their daughter's marital expenses, particularly her furniture, what is called *el gehaz*. Considering that over half of Egypt's 70 million inhabitants are poor, with 26 per cent living below the poverty line, buying furniture for marriage is burdensome. Domiatt caters for this poorer half of the population. That is why it has been coined the "marriage capital of Egypt". Given these factors, it is clear that the protocols driving most of this chain favour price and quantity over quality.

The exporting value chain feeds into a completely different chain where classical reproduction furniture of the Rococo and Louis XIV and XV styles command high prices and sell as high-value-added niche products in top boutiques and under exclusive brand names across Europe and America. Its clients are highly discerning and wealthy and appreciate the quality craftsmanship of the elaborate and sinuous carvings. Furniture produced for this exporting chain is looked upon more as artwork and is appreciated as family heirlooms. Prices commanded by these pieces are quite high. The protocols driving this chain are quality and high craftsmanship.

One can argue that these two opposite final markets can provide disparate learning trajectories: one marked by stagnation and limited scope for upgrading and the other by learning and innovation. In a sense this is correct, yet as we shall see this only goes part way toward explaining the stagnation and de-skilling that exists in the local showroom-led value chain. Moreover, even within the exporting value chain it was clear that learning was taking place, but small firms were unable to access higher-income knowledge associated with working with medium-density fibreboards and paint application and methods.[4] The reasons for both outcomes lay in their respective governance structures. Due to the scope of this chapter and space limitations brought about by the complexity of the institutional arrangements governing the showroom chain, we present only an analysis of this.

Yet before we do so we first briefly look at Domiatt's industrial history, as it provides interesting insights into the status quo and the path-dependency of today's production relationship between showroom owners and the artisanal workshops.

Historical path-dependent trajectories

Furniture-making has always existed in Domiatt, but it was not until the two World Wars that the industry truly flourished. Furniture production existed on a small scale prior to the onset of the First World War. For a country without its own wood resources, it was natural that a furniture cluster would locate close to a port that shipped in timber for the industry. Both wars had brought about a crippling increase in tariffs on furniture imports, which were mostly imported from Italy and France. This increased demand for locally manufactured products by both Egyptians and the foreign population. This demand started Domiatt's sophisticated division of labour that has become a feature of its organizational landscape to this day.

Estimates are that by 1949, Domiatt had 400 enterprises employing over 4,000 people in this industry and produced 80,000 bedroom sets a year. The largest factories had a minimum of 20 workers and a maximum of 50. During this period, names such as Hamed Hashem and Sons, Ahmed El Atribi, El Far and Hassan Atai El Alfi and Sons were established. These families still hold great prominence in Domiatt today, stemming from the quality of their workmanship, particularly Ahmed El Atribi and Sons.

Mechanization was also introduced in Domiatt during this golden era of high demand.

The bringing together of workers in factories also brought an awakening of worker rights and demands for consequent unionization. Scare publications of the time point to strike action taken by workers demanding a reduction of daily working hours to 9 hours from the stipulated 12 to 15, improved working conditions, more holiday time and extra pay. Unfortunately these articles do not provide detailed information as to the specifics of the amount paid to the workers at the time. Yet it was clear that between 1946 and 1952 there were significant strikes that made household names of the union leaders such as Abdullah El-Badri and Mohamed Farana. Furthermore, there are indications that the workers' movement colluded with the student movement, with students demanding fairer rights for workers. The situation had reached such a head that capitalists felt that their own workers were holding them for ransom. Their reaction was furious and unrepentant: They fired the strike leaders and most of their adherent followers. An immediate mechanization of production to make up for the drop in worker numbers followed. Some capitalists invested heavily in equipment imported from Italy and Germany. A majority of the capitalists though preferred to move down the value chain and become showroom owners to avoid further labour dissent. Often in those cases, the factory owners had closed down all their factories and fired all their workers. Finding themselves unemployed, the artisans began working from home or started small workshops.

There was a sudden shift in the degree of power yielded by the capitalist owners. Before, workers had some degree of power through collusion and had a voice through their union leaders, who could present their arguments directly to their employers. They had a weekly wage and safeguards to protect them. Yet now they were independent autonomous actors whose bargaining power had dissipated. At the same time the capitalists were now showroom owners with the final say on whether they

would commission or purchase pieces of furniture made by the small artisanal workshops. The workers' bargaining power had diminished and
their ex-bosses' had soared. There were no contractual obligations bind-
ing the showroom owner to adhere to standards of pay or anything else
for that matter. Although enthralled with their absolute power, the showroom owners still needed workers of outstanding skill and quality to
adorn the shop windows to create a reputation for high-quality craftsmanship and excellence. Highly skilled master-artisans were initially able
to bargain on almost equal footing with the showroom owner. Knowledge was the equal to capital as long as market demand necessitated and
required high quality. When this disappeared, so did the workers' bargaining power.[5] The power of the showroom was assisted by the poverty
that has gripped Egypt, and the associated need for cheaper furniture,
which in turn was further magnified by the cultural significance of furniture buying, which ranked quality second to price.

Before we will look at the final part of the case study that analyses the
showroom-led value chain, we need to situate the workshops within their
wider institutional environment linked to government policy, government
associations and training infrastructure.

The institutional environment

The furniture sector is a policy sector neglected by the government. For
a sector that relies chiefly on imports,[6] it is plagued by an incredibly hostile policy and business environment. Tariffs on materials and inputs used
in furniture production are extremely high, ranging from 25 to 35 per
cent on intermediate products and 40 per cent on whole-piece exported
furniture.

Taxing workshops is also highly destructive to the workshop's potential
for expansion. This is due to a tax on the number of different artisanal
specializations located in-house. For example, assemblers pay additional
taxes if they have a permanent in-house sculptor or veneerer. This means
that any development or expansion activities aimed at housing more than
one specialization under one roof is thwarted by a "specialization" tax
that is levied on the workshops. This is a huge impediment for small
workshops seeking to benefit from process innovation, for example, or
from immediate interactive feedback between the different specializations.

Domiatt's major furniture association is the Chamber for Trade and
Commerce, which has 12 board members who are mostly either traders
or wood sellers. There is very little representation on the board by either
manufacturers or exporters. The association, despite its rhetorical claims
that it is a voice of all those involved in furniture, appears to have

missed out producers and, more fundamentally, the small and medium-sized workshops. It does arrange trips overseas to visit international fairs; however those are mostly geared toward traders not manufacturers. Furthermore, upon further investigation, it was blatantly clear that many of these trips were less didactic and educational than assumed. Far too often, it was a way for leading traders to travel together for recreational holidaying purposes. Even traders who had travelled on these trips were unable to identify a leading furniture design that they had seen on these trips. If anything, this organization acts as an "old boys' network" which strengthen the ties between traders and wood sellers and reinforces the existing network of power and patronage. Membership is so expensive that it acts as a deterrent for any outsiders that might want to perturb the status quo. Furthermore, the lack of representation of SMEs, despite the fact that they make up the majority of all furniture establishments, makes it clear that this is a trade body that acts solely on behalf of the men of capital in Domiatt. The chamber of commerce is the first port of call for any company, local or foreign, seeking orders for manufacture. These orders that it receives are passed on to its members only. That is, it acts on the behalf of its board, and not on the behalf of all furniture makers. It is by all accounts a private club.

The degree of neglect to the furniture industry is clearly apparent when one identifies that three of the five technical furniture training schools in Domiatt are closed. Upon first-hand visits at these schools, it was clear that they were underfunded and the quality of teaching staff was poor. Most teachers had not been able to find employment in the workshops due to their own poor skill levels and had sought employment as teachers. Domiatt does have a technology centre, which has been set up by the social development fund,[7] yet due to Egypt's recession and the freezing of development capital by the social fund, it has been unable to expand and deliver some of the proposed training and testing programs.

We will now look at the final part of the case study. This is divided into three sections. The first section provides an overview of the methodology applied in this research. This is followed by a detailed description and analysis of the showroom-led value chain that also identifies the sources of knowledge for the workshops. The final section shows the effects of the interlinking of factor markets on firms' scope for upgrading and investment in search activities.

The showroom-led value chain

The value chain involving the showroom shows the buyer dominance in Domiatt. It is depicted in figure 7.2.

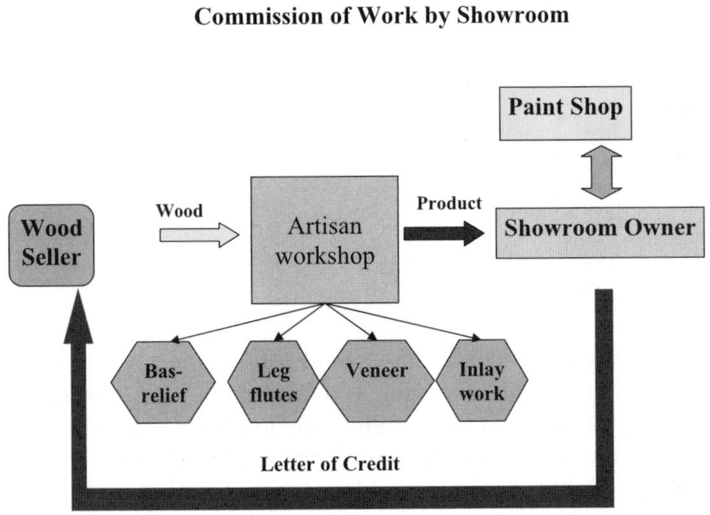

Commission of Work by Showroom

Figure 7.2 The showroom value chain

The showroom owner often determines the design of the furniture to be made by the small workshop. He provides the artisan with a letter of credit to use for the purchase of timber from the wood seller. The artisan then works on the respective order and gives them to the showroom owners as "white wood", still in need of paint and upholstery, a process directly overseen by the showroom owner.

The showroom owner provides the artisan a small advance payment (around 15 per cent of total cost of the order) so he can hire his base unit collaborators.

The base unit consists of a number of small artisanal workshops with different specializations including leg cutters, sculptors and veneerers (see Figure 7.2). These are independently owned entities each headed by its owner. As discussed before, the intense specialization is a feature of this furniture cluster. The process of wood cuts, tracing the pattern, basic cutting, pattern design, sanding and profiling and final assembly are all carried out in the artisanal assembling workshop. Other activities such as engraving, veneering, leg cutting and fluting are subcontracted to a faithful network of collaborators. The relationship between these autonomous workshops is rooted in trust developed over many years.

In earlier work, El-Shahat (2002) showed that the artisans' high skills also extended to modifying and designing machinery used in production. Table 7.2 shows the extent of their capabilities. I have given particular weight to activities that require a great deal of problem-solving, and hence learning-by-searching. Search is seen within the evolutionary

Table 7.2 Base unit's technological capabilities

Capability	Firms (%)
Construct own machinery	58
Construct own flexible machinery	43
Modify imported machinery	87
Number of product varieties > 25	85
Research and development	11
Internal design skills	9

Author's sample of 80 firms

school as a continuum that leads toward innovation, as it requires constant learning and problem-solving to overcome new challenges.

The paucity of design skills as well as the low level of firm research and
development into new prototypes is clearly represented in table 7.2. The
lack of design ability is a huge problem facing Domiatt, in that it has no
designers. The 9 per cent in the table above that identified themselves as
having internal design skills are not formally trained as designers, but are
good at drawing. Further questions relating to internal design skills identified that no one in Domiatt could read technical drawings. This also included the top three leading exporters. Firms could make drawings, yet
in a correlation exercise between different capability variables, making
drawings and reading drawings were highly insignificant. The weakness
of Domiatt's design skills indicates the importance of the showroom
owner in transmitting information and knowledge on current design
trends in furniture by virtue of his position and role in the chain.

The lack of scientific knowledge on ergonomics and on the different
proportions of different French, Italian and American styles was very
clear. In fact, an aspect of firm research and development in creating a
prototype involves sitting on the chair to determine the proportions that
would suit the "average person". This seemed quite astonishing given
the fact that this is basic codified knowledge in furniture making. Yet it
clearly highlighted the lack of institutional structures to assist firms with
even the most basic information. Furthermore, it was clear that the showroom owners themselves, who, as commissioners of the work, should be
providing these pieces of information, are themselves ignorant of them.
The workshops' major and significant source of design information was
photographs in catalogues. In fact, this is how the showroom owner commissioned work. Given the one dimensionality of photographs in non-
specialized furniture catalogues, where no dimensions are given, it became clear why the artisans had no idea of which proportions tally with
the different styles and trends.

Table 7.3 Sources for the acquiring of knowledge on production and innovation

	Often (%)	Occasionally (%)	Never (%)
Catalogues (>5 years old)	87	13	0
Catalogues (<2 years old)	5	20	75
Timber suppliers	7	2	91
Machine suppliers	0	5	95
Showroom owners	35	14	51
Paint/lacquer appliers	18	25	57
End users	67	28	5
Product fairs	9	14	77
Specialized publications	0	0	100
Technology centre	0	0	100
Network (base unit)	88	12	0
Other network	4	10	86
Export agents	0	21	79
Libraries or information services	0	0	100
Spillovers	63	28	9

Author's sample of 80 firms

Table 7.3 highlights the importance of catalogues relative to other sources of external knowledge. It also shows that the artisans rely on old designs found in catalogues over five years old, meaning that they are not keeping up to date with new furniture styles.

Table 7.3 also highlights how knowledge acquisition is a very insular activity, where firms relied chiefly on their base unit colleagues for ideas. They learn very little from interactions with other specializations and actors along the chain and surprisingly little from the governor of the chain, the showroom owner. Upon further questioning, the 34 per cent who often acquired knowledge on production from the showroom only got information relating to product-design specification, such as the intensity of the engraving, and no feedback on product performance improvements. The interaction with showroom owners did not act as a mechanism for them to acquire new information on market trends and fashions.

Horizontal cooperation between different base units was very low. In fact that 10 per cent who occasionally consulted with other networks were always related by family ties to those other base units. This lack of cooperation is attributed to the levels of deep mistrust that permeate all relationships in Domiatt, but is even more pronounced between horizontally related firms. It will be shown how the showroom owner has played a pivotal role in the creation of severe mistrust between workshops.

What table 7.3 also shows is the surprising lack of interaction between artisans and any of the suppliers of intermediate products such as machinery, wood or paint, given that in this industry innovation is "supplier-driven". Upon further investigation it was clear that the machinery suppliers, of which there were only two, preferred to interact with the larger firms. Yet what was completely inexplicable was that despite the presence of 130 wood sellers in Domiatt, there was very little knowledge feedback between them and the artisans. This in part explained why workshops in this sample wasted a great deal of time trying to discover the workability of new wood species. This is information one would expect to be an aspect of the knowledge flow between the wood seller and artisan. Yet, early in the fieldwork, it was still not clear why firms were wasting valuable time overcoming and mitigating the problems found in very low-quality wood. This leads to high levels of wood waste, which is estimated at 15 to 20 per cent per metre. Part of this is because the imperial measures used by the mills supplying timber differs from the metric measures used in furniture manufacturing in Domiatt. Additionally, the grading and quality of wood bought was of the lowest in the market; at grade 6, it was not suitable for furniture production. These two problems conflated and had dire effects for the whole value chain. Firstly, the raw material supplied created lower wood-recovery rates as indicated earlier; it also affected production, and resulted in manufacturers trying to design according to the wood supplied rather than producing the most optimal designs. Secondly, the very high humidity rates in the wood purchased made the wood very difficult to work with and required kiln drying, which was too expensive for any of the workshops and the majority of large manufacturers to afford. Some 56 per cent of firms reported that trying to overcome problems associated with the wood reduces time spent on research and development processes, as well as the time spent teaching apprentices and journeymen.

Many of the answers as to why the industry had reached such deterioration are due to the interlinking of factor markets. We now turn to this.

The impact of interlinkage on workshop upgrading

As the fieldwork continued, it became clear that the showroom owner dictated to the workshop where they should purchase their timber. In fact this was part of the type of "interlinkage" contractual relationship that tied the artisan to the showroom owner. Here the showroom owner and the workshop owner enter into several transactions linked to trade credit including the purchasing and marketing of the output. This is the interlinking of factor markets. By providing the artisan with letters of credit so that the artisan can purchase wood, they dictate from whom the artisan should purchase the wood. So the choice of wood seller with whom the artisan interacts and gains information on wood characteristics and design trends is not self-determined. This is of utmost importance as this industry lends itself to supplier-led innovation (Pavitt, 1984). This indicates that the choice of wood seller has a direct impact on the artisan's knowledge stock.

The interlinking of contracts based on working capital is a partial institutional response to inadequacies and imperfections in other markets, particularly that of an inadequately developed credit market. The showroom owner has the incentive to supply working capital since he shares the outcome of its use and is in the best position to enforce repayment. Furthermore, the artisan has few if any assets acceptable in the formal credit market. In the case of informal workshops, he would have no assets acceptable to the workshop. The situation is further exacerbated in Muslim countries where money lending as an alternative source of credit is explicitly banned.

The power of the showroom owner is further strengthened by their easier access to formal credit at relatively cheaper rates. Due to political connections and dominance in these formal credit markets, owners have managed to postpone repayments for quite substantial periods. Of the showroom owners, 32 per cent had access to formal credit at relatively cheaper rates with their repayments postponed by over five years. This is a truly iniquitous situation, given that SMEs are frozen out of the credit market. In fact, over 96 per cent of all SMEs do not have access to formal bank credit in Domiatt due to fear of default. Yet the political governance structure accepts huge defaults by its more powerful actors.

The showroom owner often dictates the amount owed to the artisan, as well as when and how that payment amount is received. The spread of payments strongly correlates to the purchasing of new machinery as well as firm-search activity. The less spread-out the payments, the greater the amounts provided per tranche, and the less discounted the payments, the greater research and development carried out by the firms.

One further noteworthy feature is the rollover arrangement that comes into force when the showroom owner refuses to pay the balance owing to the artisan. We find a perverse situation whereby the richer party, and consequently the party more able to bear risk, is indebted to the poorer, less powerful artisan. The money owed seems to roll over to the next order consignment, and so a cycle of reverse debt begins. Moreover, the showroom might return unsold pieces produced by the artisan and subtract it from the money owed to the artisan. These circumstances tell us about the fragility of furniture making and of the livelihood it provides. The artisans become dependent employees for subsistence wages despite having their own workshop. Moreover, with the shift of risk onto the weaker party, the artisan assumes the role of risk-bearer for the selling of the product, as well as sharing, if not paying for, most of the production cost. In this sense, there is a perverted risk transfer. The tendency of traders not to pay the balance owed is a powerful proxy for the dominance yielded by the showroom owner.

Moreover, the nature of the trade credit agreement in Domiatt is such that it prevents artisans from exercising choice and deprives them of market prices in both the capital and the commodity markets. When buying timber, the trade credit agreement makes the artisan purchase wood at above-market prices. It is estimated that trade credit inflates the average metre of wood by 7.5 per cent (El-Shahat, forthcoming). Additionally, the price the showroom owner provides for the furniture is usually 25 per cent below market prices. Furthermore, interlinked contracts are underpinned by the condition that the artisan sells all his production to the showroom owner. Hence, the artisan's option to exploit any price increases for similar products in the market is removed. Those artisans who try selling furniture to other buyers risk severe consequences if discovered; they are frozen out of the market and prevented from buying timber anywhere in Domiatt. This is called triadic interlinkage. The closing of options limits the ability of the weaker party to recover from such dependency situations, especially when there are no alternative means of livelihood. The purchasing of new equipment or even furniture catalogues is limited. These constraints on the artisans have direct effect on their incremental technical change and skill-deepening.

The effect this has on firm research and development activities is extreme. This manifests itself in the low level of prototyping activities that embody most of the artisanal workshops' research and development (R&D). From table 7.2 one can see that only 11 per cent of the sample carried out R&D. Firms that carried out search activities had to limit the time they spent on it and the number of people dedicated to it. Hence, the typical two-month process to bring an idea from conception to prototype is reduced to only three weeks. Moreover the level of interaction and feedback within the network is minimized so as to involve an average of two or three persons instead of the required fourteen people as identified by El-Shahat (forthcoming).

Searching becomes a cost-prohibitive endeavour. Over 67 per cent of the 80 firms sampled have reported that as a result of their crippling financial situation, they have cancelled their apprenticeship schemes as they are unable to afford to pay the apprentices their daily rate. Considering this skill is passed on through master-apprentice relations, this is a powerful proxy for de-skilling within this cluster. Furthermore, 43 per cent of the sample has reduced the number of journeyman due to their dire financial situation. This has resulted in a situation where journeymen leave artisanal workshops lacking the adequate experience and training to become master-artisans. They have very limited opportunity for employment by other workshops and must either accept piecework, start their own workshops or leave the industry completely.

In addition, 53 per cent of the sample reported that their first prototype was stolen by the showroom owner. It is commonplace for the showroom owner to steal the artisan's prototypes under the pretext of taking it back to his showroom and then going to another network to mass-produce the prototype for less. This has acted as a disincentive for artisans to invest heavily in "prototyping" activities. This is one of the chief reasons behind the intense levels of mistrust between horizontal networks and explains the lack of cooperation between them. It acts as disincentive for collective action between them. This takes on much importance given that the cluster literature has shown that small firms in developing country clusters were able to conquer distant markets through horizontal joint action.

The showroom owner, due to business interests in other sectors, chooses to invest little in the furniture chain, further adding to the problems of the artisan. Showroom owners and wood sellers often diversify into other activities, bearing witness to the limited value they place on their specialization and any incentive to invest in their respective knowledge stock. A large number of traders are involved in real estate and use their furniture operations to buttress their central real estate trade. Hence, furniture-making is not their central focus. This has dire repercussion on the artisans involved in the chain as their potential to acquire new knowledge on design and market trends is limited. All the information which should directly flow from the showroom owner is absent due to his involvement elsewhere. This shows the systemic weakness in the chain provoked by weak investment by those who can most afford it.

The other critical actor in this chain is the wood seller (see figure 7.2). The wood selling business appears to be highly profitable, as within the span of 10 years the number of wood sellers increased from 10 in 1990 to 133 by 2000. The new entrants to this field come from varied backgrounds; a number of them are financial speculators and use the wood-selling business as a way to circulate money. They are responsible for purchasing the low-quality-graded timber (grade 6 and below) that is highly unsuitable for furniture production. Most wood entering Egyptian harbours has a moisture level exceeding 40 per cent and there have been frequent cases of rotting wood. The overall effect this has had is on product quality, with furniture cracking either during final production or when it reaches the clients' homes. With a no-returns policy pursued by most showroom owners in Domiatt, this does not seem to be causing much concern.

Ten wood sellers were interviewed to gauge the quality, scope and depth of their knowledge stock. Upon interview, it was identified that only one regularly read specialized wood-technology publications. Moreover, when asked about the characteristics of different wood species, only 2 out of 10 were able to answer questions on shrinkage, working and durability. Questions on wood storage and layout to overcome the humidity levels, a basic fact that any wood seller should know, were not even understood. The wood sellers impoverished knowledge of the industry did not appear to cause them much hindrance, as they were soon able to set up credit links with the showroom owner and overcharge on each metre. This means that the artisan cannot rely on the wood seller for any technical advice on workings of the wood. This became a serious problem for the artisans, particularly with wood species they had not worked with before.

In this value chain, the small workshop owner finds himself in the most unenviable of positions, caught in a pincer by two actors who invest little in their own knowledge stock. Due to interlinked contracts, timber merchants join the showroom owners as the power elite who rule and dominate despite their ignorance and inefficiency. This has a direct effect on the artisan – he is denied quality wood and the knowledge of market trends from upstream and downstream in his chain. Moreover, this relationship results in exploitative surplus extraction that cripples the enterprise to the point of destruction. In this variant of the value-chain credit, learning and power are inextricably tied together.

Conclusion

The Domiatt furniture cluster has shown the critical role of power in determining the scope of firms' upgrading. Fundamentally, it has also clearly identified how institutions, such as interlinkage, affect the propensity of firms to invest in their own skill base. Power in this case clearly underpins learning, linkage and investment. This uncovers two important points. Firstly, from a theoretical perspective it shows that these interinstitutional approaches of the cluster, value-chain and NSI frameworks need to incorporate power and its asymmetries within their make up. Additionally, that co-location and the existence of certain actors do not necessarily mean that learning and innovation will take place due to the institutional setting underpinning these actors' interaction. Secondly, from a policy sphere, it shows the limitations of grafting best practices from external contexts and clusters that have different institutions. This emphasizes the need for effective policy design to understand the way in which innovation processes are contextually specific (Mytelka and Farinelli, 2003).

Let us turn now and analyze the implications of the Domiatt case study for the NSI framework as well as the cluster and value-chains frameworks. We shall look in turn at the theoretical contribution and policy implications that the Domiatt case study has revealed and by doing so identify future research avenues.

Despite the usefulness of the cluster approach, its major weakness has been its assumption of homogenized relationships between the different-sized firms in its locale. That is, all firms are equal in the status and power they yield in the cluster. This has underplayed any confrontation, friction or domination by any powerful group of firms vis-à-vis the rest and has encouraged the framework to be optimistically naive about its handling of collective learning with an implicit assumption that all actors in the cluster benefit from interactions. This is underpinned by the overwhelmingly unrealistic assumption that actors will be unified in interest and behaviour, putting the collective above the individual, despite joint action being blatantly selective by nature, hence making its applicability to all actors uneven (Kennedy, 1999). This was markedly buoyed in the literature by the abundant use of the concept that learning is "social embeddeness". Yet as was revealed earlier, the Domiatt case has shown that there are differentiated relationships between firms and this reflects in confrontations over power, knowledge and income. Moreover, that not all interaction, where firms supposedly cooperate over the creation of new knowledge, is beneficial to all actors but that in fact interaction can lead to de-skilling.

When concepts of power and segmentation between large and small firms are introduced in the value-chain literature, they have always been external to the cluster. This literature has neglected the local institutional environment. This applies equally to the dual meanings of institutions in the literature, as organizations and as "rules of the game" mediated by habits and norms (North, 1990; Williamson, 1985). The local institutional environment does matter as the Domiatt case has shown. This manifests itself in the framework predominantly in two ways. Firstly, a disregard for the national systems of innovation surrounding the value chain in the cluster, such as technology and research centres as well as other horizontal firm associations that could assist firms upgrading in the chain. In turn, this has meant that it has been unable to extend its political economy and power analysis to local organizations and institutions, so the nature of these institutions in this framework is a black box. Secondly, it has distanced itself from the effects of local socio-economic institutions such as class and ethnicity on local firms' governance in the value chain. This has also meant that despite its handling of power, it has tended only to see power in association with the lead governors in the chain and their protocols. Therefore, governance has always been analysed from the side of the global buyers located in developed countries with little, if any, attention paid to local governance and how this interacts with global governance. Moreover, it is explicitly suggested that global buyers would be the sole controllers over SMEs' profit margins, insinuating that no one in their own domestic environment might already be controlling and even exploiting them as in Domiatt.

This internally deterministic approach has led to quite mechanistic policy prescriptions. Kaplinsky, Morris and Readman (2002) and Posthuma (2003), for example, identified taxonomy of the different types of capabilities that can be acquired through different governance structures with their respective buyers. This assumes a direct link between "local capability" and governance structure. Yet the work in Domiatt shows that the local environment can spoil any such direct link. The value-chain literature has ignored the local governance rules, which might overwhelm or even mitigate any benefits or capabilities acquired from participating in these chains. This lacuna has opened the potential for interesting future research that could analyse the competition between local culture and habits and the different governance modes. In the case of Domiatt, future research could study how and if the institution of interlinkage changes depending on the different governance modes in different value chains as an example.

The national systems of innovation framework has included all actors and institutions that the value-chain and cluster literature have incorporated and also ignored. One would assume that its fallibility as a framework would be more limited due to its rectification of the omissions from the other two frameworks. Yet it, too, like the value-chain literature, was able to rectify one limitation, to step forward once, yet still also manage to go two steps backwards simultaneously. In this case, the NSI framework has replicated the weakness within the cluster approach by disregarding concepts relating to power and political economy that were partly mitigated in the value-chain literature. Yet it shares with the value-chain literature the disregard for and ignoring of unequal political and economic power in the local context. This consequently also leads it to disregard how these power asymmetries reflect themselves in institutions and how these institutions represent the interests of the powerful. This in particular unhinges its methodological underpinnings given the institutional centrality of this framework. The fallacy here is that the NSI has built a whole framework around one extreme nature of institutions. It looks at institutions through the vista of institutional neutrality. In this framework they are there to promote virtuous behaviour between actors and reduce the uncertainty associated with innovation for *all* actors. The NSI has preferred to focus on the "good side" of institutions, which not only limits the incidence of opportunism but creates the best platform for firms to interact and acquire knowledge. After all, opportunism cannot lead to knowledge sharing and learning (Lundvall, 2002).

Yet, as the Domiatt case has shown, institutions reflect power relations and have been opportunistically used by certain dominant actors to further their interests. The chamber of trade and commerce, as well as the banking and credit sectors have been instrumental in advancing and buttressing the showroom owners and wood sellers' power nexus. This has enforced their position vis-à-vis the artisanal workshops by allowing them to act as the only source of working capital for the workshops. This has conferred upon them greater power and has allowed them to exploit the institutional relationship of "interlinkage" to their advantage, indicating that institutions are not created to be the most socially efficient for learning as implicitly implied within NSI. In fact they are there to serve the interest of those in power. This is ascertained by the new-institutionalist economist Douglas C. North. Furthermore, it has also been forwarded by North (1995) that institutions that serve self-interest groups can continue on a path of economic stagnation due to the nature of their own path-dependence.

This indicates that the matching and co-evolution of institutions and technological trajectories can no longer be a certainty; it is not difficult to imagine a situation where institutions would support perverted learning if it were economically successful. The case study of Domiatt supports a stagnant knowledge trajectory pursued by its more powerful actors, the showroom owners. Due to their social power, they have been able to appropriate the profits associated with the artisans' new designs, which embody all the artisans' research and development process. Moreover, the showroom owner has been able to take artisan work and not pay fully for it. Despite the huge profits that he makes, the showroom owner does not invest any of it into the artisanal workshops or even in his own knowledge stock by learning about new design and trends in furniture. Consequently, he cannot be a source of knowledge for the artisan, advising on new trends, designs and market standards and protocols. The showroom owner has chosen a path that is learning-poor because the immediate perceived pay-offs do not favour technological deepening but rather learning stagnation. In this sense, there is a mismatch between the desired technological and learning trajectory that would be conducive to firm growth and the institutional set-up.

This is a classic example of institutional and technological mismatching with the effect of knowledge not being passed on to the people who need it most. This will have very negative effects on economic growth, as Barr (2000: 23) highlights: "The degree to which the structure of the network of relationships within society allows for knowledge to flow to those who can make most of it is an important aspect of the society's capability with respect to the generation of growth." It is this inherent tension between the two forces of institutions and technological change that needs recognition, and necessitates further research into their dynamics.

This highlights a further point that inasmuch as the literature speaks of technological path-dependency it must also do the same for institutional path-dependency, as it appears that the two influence each other profoundly. Institutional path-dependency requires a much clearer understanding of a cluster's social and institutional history. While the NSI emphasizes the historical path-dependent evolution of regionally organized production systems, there is a tendency in the applied work on clusters in the policy sphere to adopt a more static framework. Yet what is required for both innovation theory and public policy is a dynamic framework that emphasizes the formation and historical evolution of the cluster to the present day. Ahistorical research, which captures the social fabric of a culture or society in a static real time framework, has little to contribute to questions relating to the dynamics of power and its effects on learning and future economic growth. It cannot capture the conflicts and shifts in power over time or provide explanation of how the status quo came into being or how it will change. Confrontations over knowledge and power between people of yesteryear manifest themselves in the status quo and power networks of today. Domiatt is a case in point. The ramification of the struggle between the workers and the capitalists is still being played out to devastating effect on the small enterprise whose indigenous knowledge now is dying. This has highlighted that a firm/class/ group's previous investment in their enterprise will either constrain or facilitate its future growth trajectory. In turn, this investment is largely shaped by other actors and external influences on the firm or class under study. Bygones are rarely ever bygones when institutional path-dependency exists.

Furthermore, any policy or donor project aimed at assisting Domiatt's artisans has to have a clear understanding that interlinked contracts bias the operation of financial markets as well as the firms' search endeavours and knowledge sharing. Due to these being privately established market institutions, without effective state and legal intervention they are unlikely to be affected by donor programs aimed at providing business development services, credit, technology centres and other components. Hence, the uneven distribution of local power, as well as the uneven distribution of knowledge will inhibit any policy prescription or program that does not account for these political economy factors.

In closing, the problem with the NIS approach is the vague way in which institutions have been defined (Edquist, 1997). The preference for this framework's proponents to assume institutional neutrality stops them from delineating how institutions can facilitate or retard learning and innovation. Hence, despite this approach's hypothesized institutional underpinnings, it does not provide us with new insights as to how institutions affect economic performance. This has allowed the NSI approach to relapse into technological determinism where economic growth, as well as most social institutions, derives from technologistical matters (Boyer, 1988). Yet, as we have seen, the social institution of "interlinkage" is not only derived from technological matters, the unequal economic and social powers of dominant actors have shaped it to suit their purposes. Historical struggles between these groups also played an important role in determining this. The Domiatt case study has emphasized the omissions within the frameworks reviewed. The problems in Domiatt's furniture industry are systemic and exist due to tainted institutions that have been hijacked by Domiatt's more powerful actors, namely the showroom owner and wood seller. These are self-serving, self-interested institutions, which exclude artisans from accessing both knowledge and credit, leading to the exploitation and de-skilling of the artisans.

Notes

1. An enterprise in Egypt is defined as informal if it has not complied with a vast number of government requirements necessitating the obtaining of a plethora of separate licences. Due to the time, cost and, often, bribing required to facilitate the obtaining of these licences, as well as the arbitrary tax levied, some firms prefer to be informal.
2. This figure in particular is highly questionable, given that in my own fieldwork, I have come across large exporting firms in Domiatt whose end-of-year sales from exports were twice the size of this amount.
3. For a full analysis and comparison of the two discrete value chains see El-Shahat (forthcoming). Moreover, the domestic showroom-led value chain also has another variant, whereby the workshop acts as a subcontractor to a larger manufacturer, who in turns sells the pieces to the showroom owner. The small workshop in this case has no direct interaction with the showroom owner. Further detail and empirical measurements for small workshops' scope for upgrade in all the chains mentioned are also to be found in the above-referenced paper.
4. For more information on the export-led value chain, please see El-Shahat (forthcoming).
5. For further discussion on additional factors that weakened the workers' position vis-à-vis that of the showroom owner see El-Shahat (forthcoming).
6. Producers are highly dependant on imported wood for raw material, as well as a number of intermediate products that include paints and varnishes, glues, metal fittings, electrical and non-electrical woodworking equipment, upholstery material and plastics.
7. Since the establishment of the social development fund in 1991, it has played different roles at the development arenas of Egypt. Initially, it was designed as a social safety net associated with the Egyptian government's agreement to undertake its extensive Economic Reform and Structural Adjustment Program.

REFERENCES

Barr, Abigail (2000) "Social Capital and Technical Information Flows in the Ghanaian Manufacturing Sector", *Oxford Economic Papers* 52(3): 539–59.

Berg, S. (1988) "Snowball Sampling", in S. Kotz and N. L. Johnson, eds, *Encyclopaedia of Statistical Sciences* 8.

Boyer, R. (1988) "Technical Change and the Theory of Regulation", in G. Dosi, C. Freeman, R. Nelson, G. Silverberg and L. Soete, eds, *Technical Change and Economic Theory*, London: Pinter Publishers, 67–94.

Dei Ottati, G. (1993) "Trust, Interlink Transaction and Credit in Industrial District", *Cambridge Journal of Economics*.

Edquist, Charles (1997) "System of Innovation Approaches – Their Emergence and Characteristics", in Charles Edquist, ed., *Systems of Innovation, Technologies, Institutions and Organisations*, London: Pinter.

El-Shahat, Samah (2002) "Literature Review on Egyptian SMEs", Ottawa: International Development Research Centre.

El-Shahat, Samah (forthcoming) "Learning and Power: The Tale of Three Chains", Economics Working Paper, London: School of Oriental and African Studies.

Faugier, J. and M. Sargeant (1997) "Sampling Hard to Reach Populations", *Journal of Advanced Nursing* 26: 790–97.

Kaplinsky, R., M. Morris and J. Readman (2002) "The Globalisation of Product Markets and Immiserising Growth: Lessons from the South African Furniture Industry", *World Development*, 30(7): 1159–78.

Kennedy, Loraine (1999) "Cooperating for Survival: Tannery Pollution and Joint Action in the Palar Valley (India)", *World Development* 27(9): 1673–91.

Lundvall, Bengt-Åke (2002) *Innovation, Growth and Social Cohesion*, Cheltenham: Edward Elgar.

Mytelka, Lynn K. and Fulvia Farinelli (2003) "From Local Clusters to Innovation Systems" in Cassiolato, Lastres and Maciel, eds, *Systems of Innovation and Development: Evidence from Brazil*, London: Edward Elgar Publishers, 249–72.

North, Douglass (1990) *Institutions, Institutional Change and Economic Performance*, Cambridge: Cambridge University Press.

North, Douglass (1995) "The New Institutional Economics and Third World Development", in John Harriss, Janet Hunter and Colin M. Lewis, eds, *The New Institutional Economics and Third World Development*, London and New York: Routledge, 17–26.

Pavitt, K. (1984) "Sectoral Patterns of Technical Change: Towards a Taxonomy and a Theory", *Research Policy* 13: 343–73.

Posthuma, A. C. (2003) "Taking a Seat in the Global Market Place: Opportunities or 'High Road' Upgrading in the Indonesian Wood Furniture Sector?" Mimeo, Geneva: Infocus Programme on Boosting Employment through Small Enterprise Development, International Labour Organisation.

Saunders, P. (1979) *Urban Politics: A Sociological Interpretation*, London: Hutchinson.

Spreen, M. (1992) "Rare Populations, Hidden Populations and Link-Tracing Designs: What and Why?" *Bulletin Methodologie Sociologique* 36: 34–58.

Thomson, S. (1997) "Adaptive Sampling in Behavioural Surveys", *NIDA Research Monograph*, 296–319.

Vogt, W. P. (1999) *Dictionary of Statistics and Methodology: A Nontechnical Guide for the Social Sciences*, London: Sage.

Williamson, O. E. (1985) *The Economic Institutions of Capitalism*, New York: The Free Press.

8

Learning to change: Why the fish processing clusters in Uganda learned to upgrade

Rose Kiggundu

In the cluster literature, several empirical studies point to the important role played by the clustering of firms for growth and competitiveness. The argument is that "collective efficiency" affords clustered firms, especially smaller ones, growth and export capabilities that they could not acquire individually. Some analysts, however, caution that a mere geographical clustering of firms does not necessarily predict their development into systems of learning and innovation. This seems to be exactly where clusters in many African developing countries find themselves, for, as we shall shortly elaborate upon, the literature indicates that many clusters in Africa are not only weak in collective efficiency but are often unable to innovate or, more broadly, to upgrade in a dynamic sense. The central question for this chapter is: Why and how did the fish processing and exporting clusters in Uganda learn to upgrade?

Conceptually, the notion of upgrading occupies an important place in the analytical framework of at least two strands of economic-development literature: value-chain analysis (Dolan, Humphrey and Harris-Pascal, 1999; Gereffi, 1994b; Humphrey and Schmitz, 2000; Schmitz and Knorringa, 1999; and many others) and innovation systems (Freeman, 1987; Lundvall 1988, 1992). However, as a concept, upgrading sometimes denotes different meanings, hence the importance of clarifying the context in which we use it. According to the value-chain literature, firms tend to functionally upgrade after mastery of simple assembly operations.[1] This involves a shift from low- to high-return activities such as design, marketing and branding. If successful, they shift to more skill

---

Industrial clusters and innovation systems in Africa: Institutions, markets and policy, Oyelaran-Oyeyinka and McCormick (eds), United Nations University Press, 2007, ISBN 978-92-808-1137-7

intensive and profitable lines of activity. Indeed, the value-chain literature provides insights into the concept of upgrading, especially the range
of activities that are most profitable, in addition to the barriers of entry
into such activities. However, it does not sufficiently explain what knowledge inputs and actors are critical at different upgrading stages and why.
Neither does it explain whether or not each upgrading stage dictates a
different form of learning and pattern of "joint action". From a technological learning and innovation perspective, the concept of upgrading is
in the main a matter of technological learning to introduce minor and
major improvements in products, processes and the way production is organized. This is also the sense in which we use the concept here.

Technological learning may be defined as a process of acquiring, applying, adapting and transforming knowledge that manifests in changes in
products, processes and organizational forms. Applied to the study of
clusters, one might then raise the question: what facilitates or holds back
the transition from one upgrading stage to the next within an African
cluster? Broadly speaking, both the value-chain and innovation-systems
strands of research are lacking in empirical examples that illustrate what
is essentially required for the African cluster to upgrade fully. This chapter contributes to filling this gap by examining the factors that drove the
fish-processing clusters in Uganda to move from upgraded processes to
product-upgrading.

Process upgrading in fish processing refers to the introduction of and/
or improvement in handling, cold chain management, basic factory flow
procedures, product flow and the entire set of food safety and sanitary
and phytosanitary (SPS) measures with which firms are required to comply. Product upgrading refers to a shift from preparation and export of
whole and semi-processed fish products (portions, fillets) to the export
of further processed products such as crumbed fish products, perfectly
portioned fillets and loins, barbecue sticks or differently packaged fresh
and frozen products.

The main point of this chapter is that fish-processing clusters in Uganda
have shown clear and distinguishable learning requirements as well as
patterns of joint action to upgrade processes and then, later, products.
Overall, upgrading in products has involved coordination, knowledge inputs and inter-firm relationships markedly different from those that characterize process upgrading. For instance, while overseas buyers played
only a minimal role in assisting Uganda's fish exporters to deal with their
first major challenge of upgrading in process, the support of buyers has
since become critical to the ability of fish exporters to deal with their second challenge, to upgrade in products. To upgrade in process, the clusters
previously sought and obtained joint solutions through their fish processors association but have worked less cohesively to upgrade in

products. Moreover, only a few other actors within Uganda have come together so far to jointly search and respond to the new product-upgrading challenge and, perhaps not surprisingly, the firms that managed to invest in product-upgrading were also those that were relatively more successful in establishing closer ties with their overseas buyers. In this context, the chapter addresses two sets of questions:

- How can we explain the clusters' ability to upgrade so rapidly in processes demanded by export markets compared to their difficulties in introducing product-related change?
- Why at was the role of buyers in process-upgrading following the imposition of the EU ban and what was their role in the second round of product upgrading?

In seeking answers to these questions, we shall draw on insights from three literatures: clustering, value chains and innovation systems. The empirical illustrations are based on field interviews conducted in 2002 with fish exporters in Uganda and in 2004 with the European buyers of Uganda's fish.

The chapter is structured as follows. The next section calls attention to some insights in the literature relevant to the analysis of this cluster. We then describe the structure of the fish processing clusters in Uganda and examine the scope for deriving agglomeration advantages. Changes in international conditions that triggered the first round of upgrading are discussed next. This is followed by an examination of joint efforts that emerged, and those that failed to emerge, in response to the challenges faced by the clusters. The role of policy to reverse some of the more ill-adapted "institutions" and create an enabling environment for upgrading is discussed next. The connection with global trading conditions – particularly the influence of buyers in both rounds of upgrading – is then examined. The last section concludes and outlines broad directions for policy.

Insights from the literature

One of the most influential contributions to the clustering literature was by Hubert Schmitz (1997) who attributed the growth and competitiveness of exporting clusters to collective efficiency, which he defined as the "competitive advantage derived from local external economies and joint action" (Schmitz, 1997: 3). In the African context, the work by McCormick (1998) called attention to the limited impact of clustering in Africa. The author found some clusters in Africa to be no more than mere agglomerations of small enterprises that helped to build "a productive environment" and prepare "the ground for industrialization ... (by) helping to reduce growth constraints associated with independent operation of

small-scale enterprises" (McCormick, 1998: 11). Some technological upgrading was observed across emerging clusters such as the Nnewi auto
parts cluster in Nigeria (Oyelaran-Oyeyinka, 1997, 2000). However, weak
division of labour arrangements, specialization and a lack of systemic
support hampered further growth and innovation. In Kenya's Lake Victoria Nile Perch fish cluster, Mitullah (1999) highlighted the absence of
"institutions" to facilitate effective joint action. In the Nnewi cluster in
Nigeria, "learning at a distance" from Taiwanese suppliers was crucial
for the Nnewi firms to upgrade (Oyelaran-Oyeyinka, 1997, 2000). Similarly, external knowledge inputs from European public-sector agencies
and private firms enhanced the learning process across fish-processing
clusters in Uganda (Kiggundu, forthcoming). It should be mentioned,
however, that while available research on clustering provides useful insights, this kind of connectedness between the local and the global is not
adequately captured by clustering theories. Within the specific context of
the questions addressed here, available works on clusters in Africa –
particularly the few that have included technological upgrading in their
analysis – provide only limited insight on the notion of "joint action".
Hence, we still know very little about the critical nature of joint action
at the different stages of upgrading. This chapter makes a distinction between types of upgrading. It focuses on the pattern, nature and intensity
of joint efforts as key determining factors in the attempts by clusters to
upgrade processes and products. The fish-processing clusters in Uganda
provide good case material for this exercise because the first challenge
of upgrading in the clusters was predominantly process-related while the
second main challenge involved upgrading in products.

Value-chain literature[2] makes an interesting observation of relevance
to the questions we address in this chapter. It observes that the more
powerful firms along the value chain tend to control how far other firms
on the chain can go in their upgrading activities. This literature underlines the influence of global buyers on upgrading developing country
exports especially in buyer-driven value chains (Dolan, Humphrey and
Harris-Pascal, 1999; Gereffi, 1994; Humphrey and Schmitz, 2000; Kaplinsky, 2000; Sandee, 1995; Schmitz and Knorringa, 1999; Schneider, 1999).
Crucially, the work by John Humphrey and Hubert Schmitz (2000) provides a conceptual link between clustering and value-chain literatures.
First, they define "governance" as "co-ordination of economic activities
through non-market relationships" (Humphrey and Schmitz, 2000: 4) or
the pattern of direct and indirect control over a value chain (McCormick
and Schmitz, 2002). Humphrey and Schmitz (2000) also make a distinction between different types of upgrading and argue that some forms
of governance favour some types and not others. "Quasi-hierarchical
chains" help local export producers to pursue rapid product and process

upgrading but often make moving into design and marketing difficult. In contrast, both "network relationships" and "market-based" arms-length relationships between export producers and buyers – the non-hierarchical chains – are not likely to undermine upgrading in design and marketing.

In discussing the upgrading role of buyers, the question for Schmitz and Knorringa (1999) is not whether buyers help producers to upgrade, but what are the circumstances under which they might or might not provide support? To address this question, the authors propose a framework that examines four aspects. The first is whether or not buyers are at an incipient or advanced stage, while the second is whether producers operate in price-driven or quality-driven chains. The third is whether upgrading is limited to production or if it extends to guarded competences of design and marketing. Whether buyers engage in indirect or direct sourcing of supplies is the fourth consideration. Undoubtedly, this work is very useful and particularly inspirational for a study of how clusters learn to upgrade, especially in Africa where research on the subject is in its infancy.

Despite the usefulness of such insights, there are still a number of questions about the role of buyers that need further exploration. For instance, if overseas buyers tend to make a greater contribution to product upgrading (under certain circumstances), what facilitates the initial step of process upgrading? In the case of Uganda's fish-processing clusters, why was the role of buyers in process upgrading minimal following the imposition of the EU ban and what is their role in the second round of product upgrading? Besides links with buyers, what other critical actors, joint action and knowledge flows for product upgrading should be supported in African clusters? Value-chain literature provides some but not all the answers.

The realization is that producer upgrading is not only buyers and their subsequent influence or even simply joint action and external economies. Cluster upgrading in Africa is a key starting point of our discussion. We recognize that buyers matter. Joint action and external economies derived from clustering, where they exist, also matter. However, historical habits and practices also play a significant role. Thus, exploring how policy can help reverse sub-optimal historical habits that hold back upgrading is critical. A focus on how policy overcomes sub-optimal historical institutions (routines and habits) can help us identify the incentives and triggers relevant for process and product upgrading. Processes that permit knowledge flow between clusters and the knowledge-generation sector – both local and foreign – are also important. Availability of relevant financing and support agencies in the public and private sectors are also crucial. In other words, numerous relationships and actors matter in upgrading processes. How well these relationships and actors interact to create an environment conducive to learning and investment in technological upgrading is a centrepiece of research undertaken within the innovation systems approach.

Hence, in this chapter we apply the innovation systems framework to examine how well certain elements interacted or failed to interact in the first round of (process) upgrading. Elements of relevance to the fisheries sector in Uganda include firm agglomeration, joint efforts, role of various support organizations, historical patterns, local policymaking, global buyers and international standards-setting bodies. We then explore how well these elements interacted within the second round of (product) upgrading. Using the same approach, we also examine the reconfiguration of critical actors and the organization and knowledge inputs observed in the clusters. Innovation-systems literature provides only limited insights into why the buyers' role and their interaction with other actors was more important during product upgrading, compared to their minimal involvement during process upgrading. Value-chain literature offers more insights on this particular question. Therefore, the analysis in this chapter is broadly anchored by the innovation-systems conceptual framework, but also draws on some aspects of value-chain literature in regards to the buyers' involvement. The central point in our approach is that the three sets of literature complement one other in our attempt to address the two questions we raised in the beginning of this chapter.

Clustering and technological upgrading in Uganda's fish processing and exporting industry

Going by this book's definition of a cluster, fish processing and exporting firms in Uganda are not all clustered in a particular geographical "city" or sub-region. Table 8.1 shows that in Uganda, these firms have agglomerated in several cities surrounding Lake Victoria. However, the table also shows that 10 out of 17 plants are located around two major cities: Kampala and Jinja (Jinja is about 80 kilometres east of Kampala). Thus, one could talk of a clustering of five plants in Jinja and another five around Kampala City. But there are important locational differences between the Jinja and Kampala clusters.

While plants within the Jinja cluster are relatively close together, three out of the five firms in the Kampala cluster are located in different suburbs or parts of the city covering a total cluster area exceeding one square kilometre. It may be possible to talk about agglomeration in the Kampala–Entebbe and Masaka–Kyotera sub-regions.[3] Both of these sub-regions fall under a broader geographical zone known as the central

Table 8.1 Geographical location of fish-processing plants by nearest "city" in Uganda (as of March 2004)

Number of plants in same city	Plants located in same suburb within city	Suburb where plants are located	District
5 (Kampala)	Plant 1	Nakawa Industrial area	Kampala
	Plant 2	Nakawa Industrial area	Kampala
	Plant 3	Old Kampala	Kampala
	Plant 4	Kanyanya	Kampala
	Plant 5	Luzira	Kampala
5 (Jinja)	Plant 6	Jinja	Jinja
	Plant 7	Jinja	Jinja
	Plant 8	Jinja	Jinja
	Plant 9	Jinja	Jinja
	Plant 10	Jinja	Jinja
3 (Entebbe)	Plant 11	Entebbe Municipality	Wakiso
	Plant 12	Entebbe Municipality	Wakiso
	Plant 13	Kisubi	Wakiso
1 (Kalisizo)	Plant 14	Kalisizo	Rakai
1 (Kyotera)	Plant 15	Kasensero	Rakai
1 (Masaka)	Plant 16	Masaka	Masaka
1 (Busia)	Plant 17	Busia	Busia

region. However, the idea of a central region cluster is inappropriate given the long distances and notable differences in the state of infrastructure, utilities and general state of development in the two sub-regions. Masaka City, for instance, lies about 120 kilometres from Kampala City, making it difficult for firms to benefit from economies of agglomeration.

Let us now consider the kind of agglomeration economies derived by these clusters. In the literature, clustering is often associated with four key advantages for member firms, namely market access, labour market pooling, intermediate input effects and technological spillovers. Currently, the fish processing industry depends on Lake Victoria, a freshwater lake shared by Tanzania, Kenya and Uganda, as its natural resource base. This resource is used to produce fresh export products but because fish is a highly perishable product, the ability of the firms to handle, prepare and export their product under a functional "cold" chain is critical to their operations. For a majority of firms, access to supplies and infrastructure must thus have provided greater locational advantages than market access alone.

All fish-processing firms in the various clusters have had to provide intensive training for their workers to create a new local skills pool in factory-based fish preparation. This skill base has benefited both new and old firms in the clusters through labour mobility and the diffusion of ideas often associated with the routine interaction of workers. However, the clusters are marked by an acute absence of highly skilled workers in the more sophisticated aspects of fish processing. This is largely because Uganda still suffers from a shortage of skilled food technologists, industrial scientists, engineers, technicians and other workers (MFPED, 2000; Reinikka and Svensson, 1999; Stamp, 1993; UNCTAD, 2001; and others). Our fieldwork revealed that a majority of owners had up to university-level education but they did not have formal technical qualifications in food or fish processing. Most workers do not possess formal qualifications. Three-quarters of plant workers we reviewed had either primary-level schooling or lower-secondary-school education (11 years of schooling or less). The firms faced difficulties finding local technicians for repairs and maintenance let alone finding personnel with industrial food-processing expertise and experience.

The formal technical or vocational education institute in Uganda has failed to provide adequate numbers of graduates qualified for industrial food processing. For their personnel needs, therefore, firms tended to rely more on in-house training of persons with only a few years of formal schooling but, occasionally, also of graduates of the few local institutes available. For more complex tasks such as product development, some firms obtained technical expertise from buyers and other experts outside Uganda as such skills were unavailable locally (Kiggundu, forthcoming). Thus, inasmuch as improved skills in the labour pool might have contributed to mastery of the familiar, skills available in the pool were insufficient for further upgrading.

According to the literature, clustered enterprises often induce the emergence of suppliers who benefit from their customers' close proximity. Some of the suppliers often receive support from their customers. Both phenomena were observed within Uganda's fish-processing clusters but we should emphasize that the situation with raw-material supplies was very complex. Not so long ago in the development of these clusters, a registered supplier was assisted by processing plants in keeping the fish under a cold chain, including transportation to the plant in an insulated truck. This support clearly enhanced the abilities of suppliers to procure and compete for fish supplies. From 2002 onwards, fish-processing firms have increasingly relied on suppliers with insulated trucks for their procurement requirements. Although the clusters have benefited from the emergence of this type of supplier,[4] they have not yet mastered a production system that can resolve the problem of reliance of a limited natural resource.

There were also difficulties with linkages within clusters. For example, given the close proximity of the Jinja cluster and the two strong research institutes, Fisheries Research Institute (FIRI) under the National Agricultural Research Organization (NARO) and the Lake Victoria Fisheries

Research Project of the EU, we expected to find stronger research-industry linkages. However, field interviews indicated that this close proximity did not necessarily result in industry commissioning research to solve specific industry problems, let alone generate basic data required for developing new product lines. While the focus of research at these institutes was on several subjects important to the country, their research program was not necessarily influenced or designed to address industry requirements. Judging by the lists of publications and research themes obtained from these institutes, academic and non-academic research rarely addressed technological upgrading in the fish industry.

Overall, agglomeration of fish-processing firms in several locations provided only limited advantages. In particular, the clusters in Uganda seem to have benefited less from the four types of agglomeration economies than has been the case with clusters elsewhere. Instead, early indications suggest that the clearest advantage derived from clustering has had to do with the relatively low transaction costs afforded by the clusters to actors that provided services to these firms. Clustered firms enabled government service providers, international development agencies and private providers to minimize transaction costs and enhance outreach. This notion of easier access to services by clustered firms needs more attention and further exploration.

Trigger for technological upgrading in processes

Upgrading in process was driven by external developments in the international trading environment, particularly the new European Union legislation known as Council Directive 91/493/EEC (Kiggundu, forthcoming). Briefly, the legislation required the government to appoint a competent local authority to oversee and manage the inspection process across the fisheries sector. Secondly, testing laboratories were to be designated and approved by the EU to ensure produce quality and safety. Third, infrastructure at landing sites was to be upgraded to improve sanitary conditions. Fourth, government had to ensure better hygiene and handling of fish throughout the supply chain – by fishermen, fish collectors and other transporters in addition to a whole host of improvements at industrial fish-processing plants. More specifically, fish-processing plants would only be certified compliant if they fulfilled requirements in the broad areas of plant layout, operations, application of HACCP (Hazard Analysis and Critical Control Point) systems and inspection. The list of compulsory requirements was long, complex and required major restructuring.

However, almost six years after the passing of Directive 91/493/EEC the relevant agency from the EU had not visited Uganda to monitor compliance. Uganda, in the meantime, had made little effort to comply with the directive. In February 1997 Spain discovered salmonella bacteria in fish exports from Uganda. Consequently, Spain and Italy imposed a bilateral ban on fish exports from Uganda.[5] In April 1997, the EU made a decision requiring fresh and frozen Nile perch exports from all three countries sharing Lake Victoria to be systematically checked for salmonella bacteria as it entered the EU market. As Uganda started to learn new ways of dealing with changed exporting conditions, a cholera outbreak hit the country in December 1997. On 23 December, 1997, the EU placed a ban on fresh fish imports from Uganda, Kenya, Tanzania and Mozambique due to insufficient measures to control the outbreak of cholera (Nathan Associates, 2000). Shortly after the November 1998 EU Inspection Mission, anecdotal evidence pointed to a possible use of agricultural chemicals, particularly pesticides, to poison fish as a method of fish capture. A self-imposed export ban (March 1999) was announced by Ugandan authorities until the safety of fishery products could be guaranteed. One month later, the EU suspended imports of fish products from Uganda, Kenya and Tanzania. This series of bans created a hard-hitting and prolonged fish export crisis in all three countries.

Given the importance of the fish sector to Uganda's economy, there was a sense of urgency within government and development agencies to support compliance with the EU-imposed sanitary and phytosanitary (SPS) measures from 1997 to 2000. Due to the demanding but highly remunerative nature of the EU market, firms invested in process upgrading well beyond what was compulsory. For example, some introduced computer-aided devices for critical procedures such as tracking yield and storage temperature. Some introduced automated methods and non-basic mechanized equipment, which opened up a further process of technological learning. All firms upgraded their in-house laboratory capabilities too. Their working knowledge of HACCP procedures, plant layout and industrial fish-preparation and exporting improved at the same time. In other words, there was a great deal of process-related learning across these clusters. However, our findings also show that fish-processing firms had not yet learnt sufficiently to export fully processed products at this point.

Joint efforts in process upgrading

According to Schmitz (1997), "joint action" is an important element of a cluster's collective efficiency. Joint action can take two forms, bilateral and multilateral. Bilateral (and horizontal) joint action occurs when individual enterprises cooperate to share equipment, for example. Bilateral cooperation between individual enterprises could also be vertical when firms and their suppliers come together to improve components. Similarly, multilateral cooperation could be horizontal or vertical. Business associations are conceptualized as examples of horizontal multilateral cooperation (Schmitz, 1997).

Joint efforts were critical in enabling Uganda's fish-processing clusters to upgrade their processes. Most were horizontal and took three forms:

- Joint efforts between firms in the clusters. These were largely multilateral through the national-level fish-processors association and their purpose was to search for joint solutions to the process-upgrading challenge. The association was not a one-off forum for cooperation. It became an organization serving its members on a continuous basis. In addition, there were limited vertical interactions between a few buyers and some firms in the clusters.
- Joint efforts between buyers outside the cluster. These were largely multilateral through a buyers' business association, created as a one-off forum in Europe to deal with the EU fish ban.
- Joint efforts between public and private actors supporting the clusters. These were horizontal and consisted of various actors coming together to collectively deliver services to the clusters. In other instances organizations worked closely with some fish-processing firms to upgrade input providers.

In the following section we explore some examples of these three forms of joint effort.

Joint efforts between firms in the clusters

Fish processing firms jointly explored solutions through the fish-processors association (the Uganda Fish Processors and Exporters Association, UFPEA). Exploiting the international networks already established by some members of the association, UFPEA approached CDI (the Centre for the Development of Industry), a Brussels-based organization working within the EU's Africa, Caribbean and Pacific (ACP-EU) framework for technical assistance. CDI assisted the Ugandan firms in implementing the required improvements to product flow and layout (forward motion principle). Experts accessed through CDI also made practical demonstrations at the plants, ranging from hygiene control to chemical and microbiological tests, optimal arrangement of premises, waste treatment, movement of products and application. Following the initial training provided to all the firms in the business association, CDI arranged a consultancy mission through which two French companies (IDMER and LPIA) assisted local firms to reorganize plant layout. Another consultancy mission was implemented for the "internal refitting of the production line ... with the objective of reorganizing the flow of products during processing, in accordance with the forward motion principle" (CDI, 1996: 15). In a third intervention, CDI provided start-up assistance to a local firm producing polystyrene boxes used in the packaging of fresh fish exports.

Joint efforts between buyer firms outside the clusters

European buyers formed an association to serve as an information broker between the fish processors in Uganda and the European Commission in Brussels. Interviews across buyers in Europe indicated that the European Nile Perch Importers Association (ENPIA) played a major advocacy role during the export crisis. It served to update EU officials in Brussels on improvements made by fish-processing firms in Uganda. It also exerted pressure on relevant EU officials to schedule progress-assessment missions to Uganda. ENPIA disbanded after the EU had lifted the ban on fish exports from Lake Victoria. According to interviews, individual buyers provided only limited assistance to enable producers to comply with the new EU regulations. However, the exchange of information between the buyers association (ENPIA) and the producers association (UFPEA) was viewed as useful.

Joint efforts between public and private actors supporting the clusters

To undertake process-related upgrading, the government, donor agencies, the fish-processors association and private firms all worked very closely and swiftly to support the clusters. Through UNIDO-UIP, the Uganda Integrated Program of the United Nations Industrial Development Organization and the fish-processors association (UFPEA), standard operating procedures were devised for inspectors and a voluntary code of conduct on good manufacturing principles for fish processing firms was established. UIP provided technical assistance to the government in preparing timely and effective communication with the European Commission. It identified and paid private consulting firms (based in Europe) to strengthen HACCP audit systems of the government's Department for Fisheries Resources (DFR) and to train fisheries inspectors as well as quality assurance managers across all fish processing and exporting firms. Lake Victoria Environmental Management Program (LVEMP), a project supported by the World Bank, also provided duty allowances, transportation and other logistical support critical for effective implementation of a revitalized inspection and law enforcement system.

There was another joint effort between the government, donor agencies, fish-processing firms and boat builders to upgrade the state of fish collection boats and fishing canoes. With financial support from UNIDO-UIP and the World Bank's LVEMP, traditional boat builders were trained at the Fisheries Training Institute (FTI), a government training institute that conducts formal courses in boat building. Out of this training process, two pilot boats designed to fulfil food safety and SPS conditions were handed over to UFPEA for trials and further assessment.[6]

In the meantime, university departments combined efforts to develop and jointly deliver a new training course in fisheries and aquaculture. Donor agencies participated in this effort. Government departments and other providers of technical assistance introduced joint mechanisms for delivering services to fish processing firms. For example, the DFR, the Uganda National Bureau of Standards and NARO-FOSRI[7] conducted joint evaluation visits. Such efforts enhanced interactivity and cross learning.

In summary, joint efforts accounted for an important part of the success achieved by Uganda's fish processing firms to upgrade in process. Both bilateral and multilateral joint efforts were present but they were mostly horizontal. Vertical efforts were most common between clusters and their suppliers. Some buyers engaged in bilateral efforts with a few processor firms to pursue process-related improvements. Importantly, we found that the joint search for solutions extended well beyond producers in fish-processing clusters, their suppliers and buyers. Many more actors embarked on a variety of joint efforts in support of process upgrading. Foreign providers of knowledge played a vital role partly because local research institutes provided insufficient support to the clusters. Using Lundvall's (1988) terminology, we found that some form of "interactivity" emerged across the clusters, buyers, suppliers, policy makers, inspectors and regulators in the government, development agencies and firms outside the country in a manner that facilitated Uganda's fish-processing clusters to rapidly upgrade in process. However, critical linkages with the knowledge-generation sector failed to develop, a subject worth further inquiry.

Government policy and process upgrading in Uganda's fish-processing clusters

According to the innovation-systems literature, policies do influence innovative behaviour as they set the parameters within which economic agents can learn and innovate. Policies ensure the presence of critical actors for learning and innovation. They can also ensure the development of a number of competences, building upon these to meet changing con-

ditions (Mytelka, 2003). When the enforcement of Council Directive 91/
493/EEC began to take effect in 1997, the state had to take a number of
difficult policy decisions and steps whose accomplishment required clear
vision, leadership and a readiness to institute change. For example, national standards were formed and the government put in place all the conditions that would allow private firms to invest in technological change.
The state promptly created a legal framework that effectively delegated
government authority to the Fisheries Department to handle and rectify
the fish export crisis. The process of updating laws and regulations in the
fisheries sector was accelerated and the new legal framework granted
powers of surveillance and enforcement to the inspectorate of fish processing standards. In addition, the state played a very central role to sustain pressure on firms to maintain new process-related standards achieved.

Before we move on to a comparison of process upgrading with product
upgrading, we need to make one point of clarification. Elsewhere (Kiggundu, forthcoming), we have emphasized that the enactment and enforcement of standards played a vital role in triggering process-related
upgrading and, in structuring specific technical assistance, required fish-
processing firms to upgrade. Crucially, enforcement of these standards
was facilitated by good local policy. In a recent paper, McCormick (2004)
has noted that standards and specifications can have positive or negative
effects on micro, small and medium-sized enterprise clusters in the form
of barriers to markets and exit from the industry. Referencing earlier
works on the Kenyan side of Lake Victoria (McCormick, 1999; McCormick and Mitullah, 2002; Mitullah, 1999), McCormick (2004) notes that
standards can produce negative effects as revealed by the examination
of the Lake Victoria fish cluster in Kenya. The negative effects observed
on the Kenyan side do not necessarily lie at odds with the positive effects
we have observed on the Ugandan side of Lake Victoria. In relation to
developing country trade, a large strand of the literature on standards[8]
draws attention to their possible use as a protectionist tool, providing scientific justifications for prohibiting imports of certain products or discrim-
inating against imports by applying higher standards or more rigorous
regulatory oversight than on domestic suppliers. Given that many developing countries lack the administrative, technical and scientific capacities
to comply with the emerging requirements, and because the investment
and recurrent costs of compliance can serve to compress the profitability
of high-value food exports, the competitive position of developing countries can be undermined, thereby contributing to the further marginalization of the weaker economic players.

However, while the emerging view of "standards as catalysts" certainly offers a
more balanced view, highlighting both the concerns and potential opportunities

provided by the rapidly changing standards environment, the emphasis still seems to be on the informational role of standards, in "providing a common language within the supply chain" or in promoting the "confidence for consumers in food product safety" for example.... Standards are not just a matter of addressing the market's inability to effectively facilitate information flows or merely a question of non-tariff trade barriers although they have and could be used to serve trade protectionist objectives.... While noting their possible role in retarding the innovation process, we take the view that standards can, in addition, be innovation-enhancing. (Kiggundu, forthcoming: 226)

Our contention is that negative and positive effects of standards on clusters in Africa (or unclustered firms for that matter) do not necessarily exclude each other. On the Ugandan side of Lake Victoria, we took a technological development approach to explore whether or not sanitary and phytosanitary standards imposed by the EU on Uganda's fish exports had triggered technological upgrading. The available evidence suggests that these standards triggered vast technological learning and process-related upgrading and, by extension, further upgrading in products that would succeed the initial step of upgrading in process.

Upgrading in products

Considerable process-related upgrading enabled the fish processing clusters in Uganda to redirect fish exports back to the European Union, where they had been previously banned. However, changes were predominantly process-related adaptations and improvements in production organization as opposed to product-related changes. Three to four years later, after the clusters had completed the first round of critical process upgrading that occurred between 1997 and 2000, many firms in the Nile perch-processing industry had not yet embarked on product upgrading. But the situation would soon change, given the rising problem of diminishing Nile perch stock in Lake Victoria. The clusters increasingly came under pressure to invest in product-upgrading activities such as the introduction of better packaging and processing Nile perch into ready-to-eat products for different customers and seasons. Other possibilities for upgrading and innovation include processing fish juices, salted or in-brine products, fish pellets, flours, fishmeal, fish-skin leather, fishmeal for non-human consumption, fish eggs and glue.

What are some of the factors that might explain the clusters' difficulties to introduce product-related change? The hypothesis is that these relate to market incentives and the nature of triggers for product upgrading, degree of state effort, level of joint efforts undertaken, range of accessible finance, knowledge inputs and technical assistance. The discussion that follows draws on empirical examples from case-study material collected from Uganda's fish-processing clusters, support organizations and European buyers to discuss these factors.

Market incentives and triggers for product upgrading

Process upgrading in Uganda's fish-processing and exporting clusters was triggered by an import ban of Uganda's fish into the EU resulting from enforcement of Directive 91/493/EEC. Since this was a conditional ban, the incentive for compliance was connected to the premium profits that producers in Uganda expected to appropriate in return for meeting high technological standards. Once these standards had been attained, producers sought to retain their market share. However, they faced growing difficulties with raw material (fish). In 2002, the government ban on harvesting juvenile Nile perch began to be strictly enforced, a move that further complicated the supply situation since juvenile Nile perch provided better fish products to the European customer. While some firms in the clusters were already considering investments into product-upgrading technologies, they did not have pressure from their export markets to do so partly because many buyers in Europe preferred fresh, unprocessed or semi-processed fish products in various forms (fillets, portions and the like). As the shortage of raw material worsened and capacity under-utilization reached record lows, more firms began to take the product-upgrading challenge more seriously.

From the government's perspective, introducing product-upgrading activities would help to contain fishing pressure and thus conserve the natural resource while allowing private processing activity in the fisheries sector to thrive at the same time. The main problem was the lack of markets for upgraded fish products. Who would buy these new products? How would their marketing be organized in potential export markets, especially if existing buyers had a strategic interest in holding onto unprocessed or semi-processed fish imports, and retaining control of the marketing function? Inasmuch as the clustered firms increasingly felt pressure to upgrade in products, incentives to stimulate private investment in product upgrading were still weak.

Efforts by the state and horizontal joint efforts

The state played a more direct role in providing leadership and coordination to develop local standards and, through its fisheries inspection service, regular monitoring. It also sustained pressure on the clusters to keep up with improved process-related standards. The state's involvement in the process-upgrading effort following the EU ban was much greater and swifter mainly because of the compelling need to rescue an industry that was important to Uganda's economy. Product upgrading was supported and desired by the state, but the state's response to this new challenge was less decisive than was the case at the time of process upgrading. For instance, laws to restrict fishing pressure on the Nile perch were being enforced while the state was also licensing new plants to commence operations, before resolving the question of raw material conservation and diversification.

Country-level documentation on the fisheries sectors in Uganda, Kenya and Tanzania indicates that public research (including by universities) in Uganda has undertaken far fewer efforts to experiment with product development activities than in Kenya and Tanzania.[9] On the Ugandan side of Lake Victoria, the product upgrading challenge seems to have attracted greater attention toward a search for sub-regional solutions than national-level search and learning solutions. For example, the government department responsible for fisheries in Uganda was found to be actively involved in a publicly financed sub-regional joint effort designed to supply research and marketing information necessary for product upgrading of the fish harvested from Lake Victoria. Anchored by two sub-regional intermediaries, the Common Market for Eastern and Southern Africa (COMESA) and the Lake Victoria Fisheries Organization (LVFO),[10] the sub-regional joint effort included international development agencies, notably the Food and Agriculture Organization (FAO) of the United Nations, the CFC (Common Fund for Commodities) based in the Netherlands and the three governments of Uganda, Kenya and Tanzania. Seeking to encourage the close involvement of industry in market research and product development, the CFC/FAO/COMESA/LVFO project involving Uganda, Kenya and Tanzania carefully selected a few fish-processing firms as champions for product development. In Uganda, two firms were selected for these trial efforts.

While inclusion of research and market information inputs to support the clusters represents an important shift in conventional government thinking, the effort was project-based rather than a systemic government investment to establish a sustainable fisheries sector based on effective linkages and research jointly conducted by private and public interests. Local university departments and research institutes in Uganda such as Makerere Food Science and Technology, Kyambogo Food Technology Department and the Fisheries Research Institute (FIRI/NARO) did not appear to play a direct role in this joint effort. Overall, only a few actors within Uganda came together to jointly search and respond to the product-upgrading challenge.

This is where government policy in Uganda might have played a more direct role in forging links between the research sector and industry. Additionally, the government might have directed resources toward public research institutes in the food sector to enable new ideas and product development possibilities. The government might also have financed studies for specialists from foreign universities or research centres to work with local industry in mapping and identifying possibilities while sustaining pressure on industry to keep searching for innovative solutions to facilitate upgrading.

Similarly, the processors business association (UFPEA) played a lesser role in the product-upgrading effort than it did with process-related upgrading. This was probably because clusters perceived the introduction of product upgrading more as a competitive strategy requiring creation of firm-level investment solutions and vertical joint efforts and less as a challenge requiring joint solutions of the horizontal multilateral type. Processors rapidly searched and accessed critical external knowledge inputs for upgrading in process because they faced a common difficulty – a lack of knowledge inputs to introduce improvements demanded by the EU. In response to the product-upgrading challenge, the clusters still faced a common challenge. However, the knowledge inputs required were exactly those that were better provided through bilateral linkages of the vertical type where producers and proprietors of this knowledge would minimize free-riding and supplier disloyalty.

Product development in food products and other upgrading activities requires knowledge in design and a scientific base. It requires familiarity with market tastes and marketing abilities. Introducing better packaging, for example, requires design and manufacturing capabilities. Thus, because the introduction of product upgrading technologies was more knowledge-intensive, it dictated a new form of organizing to search and access solutions. The horizontal joint efforts of the multilateral type, as previously pursued, would offer only limited solutions to the more knowledge-intensive challenge the clusters faced in product upgrading. In other words, the fish-processing clusters in Uganda had to reconfigure their joint efforts to suit different steps of upgrading. Some firms seem to have been less successful than others in embarking on new forms of organization to access the knowledge inputs required.

Financing and knowledge inputs for product upgrading

To upgrade in process, many firms in the clusters sought financial services in the form of loans and leases for the importation of equipment, machinery, vehicles and working capital. Product upgrading, however, required financial resources to import equipment as well as expertise to train staff. In other words, the requirements for product upgrading were not consistent with the conventional criteria used by Ugandan banks to advance funds. These criteria associated a higher level of risk to product upgrading loans than to process upgrading loans. It is no coincidence that the leading firms in product upgrading were also those that had access to a financial support beyond what could be accessed inside Uganda. Such possibilities included financing from parent firms, buyers or other sources outside Uganda.

Critical knowledge inputs absent for product upgrading included advanced knowledge in breeding and farming Nile perch to supplement the natural supply. There was an absence of research and development firms, organizations, research-oriented universities and technology centres with knowledge, resources and competencies to undertake this kind of work. Absent too were knowledge inputs for increased productivity and product development technologies. There were no technology and productivity centres to provide technical assistance or to demonstrate possibilities. Similarly, few efforts had been made to establish links with sources of technological knowledge for further processing of by-products. Overall, the policy in Uganda had done little to ensure the emergence of systemic linkages between actors and their competencies to facilitate product upgrading.

In the next section we describe the role of buyers in the Ugandan fish processing clusters and examine the possible causes of their minimal role in process upgrading, but more instrumental roles in product upgrading.

Buyers and technological upgrading

An important difference between the first and second rounds of upgrading has to do with the involvement of buyers in the upgrading process. What role did buyers play in product upgrading and why was their involvement greater? Before addressing this question, it is useful to start with a broad description of the buyers.

The buyers are not a homogeneous group. Some are importers and wholesalers while others are only importers. Some of the importers have factories to reprocess imports while others do not. Some buyers have negotiated shelf space for their branded products with the large supermarket chains. Of the importers that reprocess, some have only managed deals with discount supermarket chains while others have succeeded in obtaining shelf space at the non-discount supermarket chains as well. Some firms that reprocess do not import. They obtain Victoria perch supplies from other importers. Some small importers unable to meet supermarket requirements simply sell to other importers and wholesalers. Among these wholesalers there is further variety. Given their strong distribution infrastructure, networks and resources, the larger wholesalers dominate supplies to supermarket retail chains and operate differently from the smaller wholesalers.

Only a few buyers seem to buy from one single producer in Uganda. Others source from various producers in the clusters, offering different prices to different producers, a practice that has forced producer firms to compete on price. Interviews indicated that price stability of the Victoria perch was one of its strengths in the European market. For example, some buyers were dissatisfied with the quality of filleting and skinning undertaken in the producer countries but they preferred to import directly from the three East African countries of origin in order to qualify for zero-duty rating. For buyers that supplied large supermarkets, price considerations were even greater. Supermarkets tended to drive prices down through end-of-month promotional events, a routine that obliged European suppliers (of supermarkets) to regularly cut prices to that of fish substitutes "on promotion" (at the supermarkets). Inevitably, this persistent pressure on price was passed down to the producers of the fish in East Africa.

In figure 8.1, we see that the flow of fish imports from Uganda into the EU market is quite complex. A key point of distinction among Victoria perch buyers is whether or not a buyer reprocesses and brands or is a mere commodity trader in minimally prepared and/or semi-processed fresh and frozen products. As one buyer observed, "moving from commodity trading to full line value-added options permits one to net more of the benefits of the final consumer price" where value-added options include product design and branding.

Within the commodity segment of the market, there are the larger importers who simply import and sell to wholesalers and re-export to Eastern Europe or Scandinavian countries. The commodity is delivered by the importer to a collector. Smaller importers also sell to other importers and wholesalers. For clarity, we have referred to all importers as first-tier buyers. In the buyers' jargon, the collector is often referred to as a wholesaler but because some importers are also wholesalers, we have referred to this collector as a second-tier buyer because they do not import directly. The strength of the second-tier buyers (especially the larger ones) rests in their ability to efficiently manage logistics of transporting the purchased commodity to a central platform, splitting up bulk packaging and organizing the rapid delivery of the right specifications and volumes to the next level of buyers. Key requirements of commodity suppliers to the large second-tier buyers (wholesalers) are a good price, regular and prompt delivery and suitable packaging such as small, waterproof and reusable cartons. Besides supermarkets, the commodity is also distributed to restaurants. The smaller buyer at the second-tier focuses on distribution to these restaurants in addition to fish mongers at weekly outdoor food markets and other small retail outlets.

One second-tier respondent described his firm as operating 24 warehouses in their main country of operation while managing a fleet of

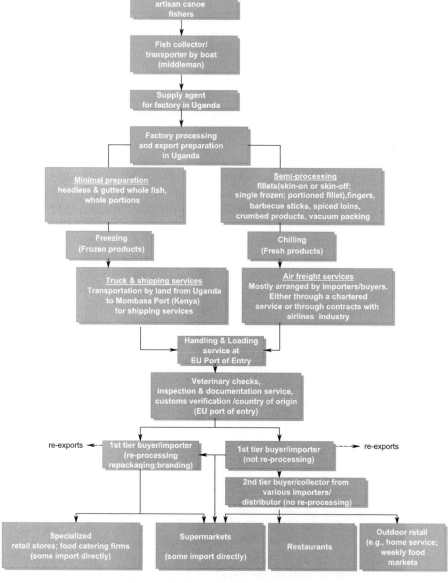

Figure 8.1 Flow of Victoria perch (*Lates niloticus*) imports from Uganda to European markets. Source: Author

1,500 refrigerated trucks. The trucks move the commodity from the two main collection points (located in two different EU countries) to a national distribution platform for direct delivery to retail chains – such as supermarkets – in a matter of hours. According to the respondent, "It takes about 1 to 2 days (48 hours) for fresh fish to reach the retail store in Europe from the time it is caught in Africa", which resonates well with the lead time indicated in Morris (2003). As we might expect, the larger second-tier collector and distributor is better placed to manage the delivery-time logistics for the fresh commodity. Key requirements of commodity suppliers to third-tier buyers (such as supermarkets) include the right price, volumes, regular and prompt deliveries and non-bulky packaging.

Where Victoria perch imports are reprocessed, the situation is different. Firms that reprocess can be direct importers or might simply procure from importers. Re-processing, including re-packing, is either at the firm's European factory or out-sourced to another firm.[11] Reprocessed material enters the EU market as minimally prepared or even semi-processed imports as shown in figure 8.1. Repacking is by weight – into small convenience packs of 250 grams, for example. Reprocessing also involves transformation of chemical properties of the commodity into crumbed or coated ready-to-eat fish fingers, for example. Reprocessed products are distributed to retail stores, discount or non-discount supermarket chains or other specialized retail stores. Whether the imported commodity is simply re-packed by weight into specially manufactured "retail packs" and branded, or further processed, reprocessing adds immense value to these imports. Crucially, the reprocessing market segment also opens up wider upgrading possibilities for Victoria perch producers in East Africa. For instance, policy and actors in Uganda's fisheries sectoral system might consider supporting a process of upgrading to produce and meet buyers' specifications for retail packaging.[12]

The commodity segment seems to be price-driven while the reprocessing segment is quality-driven. However, the reprocessing segment is as concerned about price as the price-driven segment is about product freshness and quality. Interviews also indicated that the core competences of buyers in the commodity segment are logistics and marketing while buyers in the reprocessing segment tend to combine logistics competency, product design and innovation with marketing competencies.

Buyers' role in process and product upgrading

Schmitz and Knorringa (1999) identify three sets of circumstances that might explain buyers' role in upgrading. First, whether the producers are at an early or advanced stage of operations. Second, whether the producers operate in price-driven or quality-driven chains. Third, whether upgrading is limited to production or whether it extends to design and marketing and whether buyers source directly or indirectly. We do need to clarify that in their framework, these authors focus on buyers' involvement and do not necessarily apply this framework to the analysis of the circumstances under which buyers' involvement might be greater in product upgrading than in process upgrading as we do here. More specifically, the discussion in this section seeks to explain the circumstances that might have led to the buyers' minimal involvement in process upgrading and their greater involvement in product-related upgrading.

New producers are said to require more technical help than well-established ones. This was also our finding in Uganda. Some buyers, especially importers, indicated that they had supported their suppliers around Lake Victoria with technical assistance to help set up production. Some provided pre-shipment finance against export shipments while others provided both finance and technical assistance. This was confirmed by recent interviews with a few producers. Some of the suppliers had been weaned off pre-shipment finance because they could self-finance and had less need for this. Others continued to receive pre-shipment finance as demonstrated by one case where the buyer, who acquired some strategic interest (ownership) in the firm, continued to provide pre-shipment finance and maintained a resident staff member with technical expertise. Visits from buyers to suppliers have continued. Through such visits, buyers often undertake factory audits and provide advice on basic factory-floor operations such as advice on bulk packing or management of supply logistics.

Were buyers minimally involved in process upgrading because producers had already reached an advanced stage of operations in the Schmitz and Knorringa (1999) sense? Yes, to some extent. Interviews indicated that the more established producer firms did not ask for buyers' financial support because their parent and sister firms could deal with the requirements for process upgrading internally. However, we do need to explore another line of observation emerging from our interviews.

The fish processing industry in Uganda is dominated by a certain type of internationalized firm and not necessarily the multi-national foreign firms often associated with superior technology. Other foreign firms in the industry are also not global. It is these types of firms that initially demonstrated possibilities for industrial fish preparation and export. However, the "processing" technology that was widely diffused at the time was relatively "low-tech" and certainly did not meet international standards. In the fisheries case in Uganda, we found that foreign internationalized firms required assistance for technology adoption and upgrading as much as local firms. The key point here is that, at the time the entire industry in Uganda was compelled to process-upgrade, none of the producer firms had reached an advanced stage in terms of mastering production skills let alone attaining structural standards internationally acceptable in the food industry. There were problems related to plant layout and firms still relied on low-tech methods to handle and prepare fish exports. Some of these producers received buyers' support to set up production. We might have expected that because these firms had mastered the improper competencies they were still incipient producers requiring help to upgrade.

Our fieldwork indicates that the buyers' capabilities or area of competence might be an important factor. Flowing from the line of reasoning we have stated above, these were incipient and not advanced producers. Buyers were minimally involved in helping incipient producers to meet new process-related standards set by the EU because these standards were quite complex, requiring specialist knowledge inputs outside the area of competence of most buyers. While buyers had accumulated other areas of competence, the specific knowledge required for process upgrading was unavailable among existing buyers at the time. According to one of the buyers, the rules imposed by the EU "were very complicated" while one producer stated, "Buyers were heavily impacted by the new EU rules, which is why they formed a buyers association, ENPIA. However, the EU requirements were very complex and most buyers did not know much more than we did" (author's interviews, 2004).

There is a major difference between what we might call science-intensive advice and generalist production advice. As far as basic factory-floor skills and process-related upgrading was concerned, the advice that most buyers provided tended to be of a generalist production nature. More advice flowed at the beginning of the process than later, as suppliers mastered the initial technology adopted industry-wide. Yet science-intensive advice was a critical ingredient of what producers needed to deal with process upgrading, for instance, in applying the HACCP principles. Producers and the organizations that supported them sought such knowledge inputs from specialist firms and organizations overseas, such as a firm in Scotland that specialized in dealing with issues related to HACCP. Other specialist firms were accessed by UFPEA through the CDI.

The second set of circumstances that might influence buyers' involvement is if they operate in a price-driven or quality-driven chain. As observed by Schmitz and Knorringa (1999), the line between price-driven chains and quality-driven chains cannot be firmly drawn. Part of the overview of buyers presented earlier indicates that the commodity segment of the chain might be price-driven but is also concerned with quality in the form of product freshness as well as food safety. Similarly, the reprocessing segment of the chain might be quality-driven but price is also important. The overview further showed that most importers dealt with a number of producers and did not have long, stable relationships. But there are exceptions – we found one buyer had maintained staff and supported its supplier for over seven years. Nonetheless, we did find that operating in a price-driven chain was one of the factors that might explain why buyers provided only minimal support for process upgrading. This might have been true for two sets of reasons. First, adoption of improved sanitary and phytosanitary (SPS) measures imposed by the EU was not likely, at least directly, to lower transaction costs of buyers and thus help to improve rents. The second, related reason is that buyers that dealt in fresh fish products had only limited spaces and flexibility to recover costs in process upgrading, especially under the commodity segment that is largely controlled by supermarket chains.

The situation with product upgrading was different for two reasons. First, producers were truly incipient in the area of product upgrading. They required help from buyers who already had product-development competencies. Second, for branded importers with the requisite competence, introduction of product upgrading activities would open up more possibilities for product differentiation and more effective marketing of fish products. Across Uganda's fish processing clusters, product-upgrading activities were still in their infancy and seemed to be quality-driven. Both buyers and producers confirmed that buyers that had ventured to support producers in the product upgrading effort were not only knowledgeable in product development, but also had research capacity and well-established global networks required for the development and marketing of value added products. These buyers had the cumulative competency and knowledge inputs relevant to the product-upgrading process. Therefore, in addition to existing theory on circumstances under which buyers are most likely to support developing-country producers' upgrade efforts, we find that technological capabilities and competencies of buyers matter too.

Our interviews indicate that it is the labour-intensive, non-knowledge-intensive tasks in product upgrading that are being undertaken and tried out in Uganda. Drawing upon their accumulated competencies, including knowledge of the market, buyers come up with ideas for product upgrading. To a certain degree, producers are involved in idea development and further specification given their familiarity with characteristics of the product. As one buyer put it, "(The producers) are involved in the development of our ideas." However, buyers often provide intensive advice at this stage to guide and direct the entire process of idea development. Buyers also arrange any required research inputs and specialist knowledge and coordinate the process of sending samples to retailers. In other words, buyers play a leading role in idea development and product specification. Some had engaged in joint idea development with their supplier firms while others insisted that "Product development is and will remain our own work" (author's interviews, 2004). Similarly, buyers were key players in marketing, which was another guarded area of competence. For example, some considered the innovation process around retail packaging strictly as their own territory. This directly counters the ambition of producers and organizations supporting these East African producers to explore possibilities for direct marketing of the upgraded products. Indeed, the journey from process upgrading to product upgrading has exposed signs of what value chain researchers would call quasi-hierarchy. Buyers have responded to the product upgrading challenge by helping local export producers to pursue labour-intensive tasks in product upgrading but the move into design and direct marketing is not likely to be easy.

Conclusion

The fish-processing clusters we studied in Uganda learned to upgrade in process, and did so quite rapidly, over a period of four years. This chapter has sought to contribute to a better understanding of the source of learning across these clusters. More specifically, we sought answers to two questions:
• How can we explain the clusters' ability to upgrade so rapidly in processes demanded by export markets and their difficulties in introducing product-related change?
• Why was the role of buyers in process-upgrading minimal following the imposition of the EU ban and what was their role in the second round of upgrading involving product upgrading?
The learning process was driven and facilitated by a number of factors. Crucial drivers were export-orientation to demanding markets, sound government policy and the high degree of effort by the state, the nature and intensity of joint efforts undertaken, access to required knowledge inputs through public and private intermediaries or agencies and the range of accessible finance. All these factors interacted to cause tremendous process upgrading across the clusters. Joint efforts were critical for process upgrading. The chapter has provided additional examples of joint efforts important for cluster upgrading. Besides joint efforts through the business association, joint efforts between organizations that support the clusters and joint efforts between buyers (multilateral) were also important.

Geographical agglomeration helped only minimally. This chapter has shown that fish-processing firms in Uganda are not all located in one single cluster. They are geographically located around two main cities and, even then, we found clustered firms to have enjoyed only weak agglomeration economies. Market access was not a major benefit for locating in the various clusters. Improved skills in the labour market pool might have contributed to the adoption of common operations but available skills in the pool were collectively insufficient for further upgrading. The clusters benefited from the emergence of specialized suppliers but had not yet learned how to resolve the rising problem with fish supplies. The situation with knowledge spillovers within clusters was also difficult. The greatest observable benefit derived from agglomeration in various locations was the lower transaction costs obtained by organizations that supported these clusters, thereby enhancing the clusters' access to services. This angle might require further exploration for policymaking in Africa where services to firms are often problematic.

Enactment and enforcement of EU market standards played a vital role in triggering learning- and process-related upgrading. Standards provided performance benchmarks and guidelines for structuring specific technical assistance that would flow to the clusters. In Uganda, the state played a central role in sustaining the pressure on firms to maintain the new process-related standards. The implication is that clusters in Africa (or non-clustered firms) might need a trigger to upgrade since other forms of pressure might fail to stimulate upgrading. Collective efficiency (external economies and joint action) is important but might be insufficient to enhance learning and technological upgrading. In the case of Uganda's fish processing clusters, demanding export markets (the EU), standards and local policy on their enforcement played a vital role. The hallmark of the upgrading process was the speed and decisiveness with which local actors and policymakers successfully coordinated joint efforts to learn and acquire new knowledge inputs and other resources crucial to the upgrading process.

Similarly, policy was critical for the emergence of product upgrading. The trigger for product upgrading in the fish-processing clusters was the change in local policy associated with the rising problem of fish supplies. This confirms that triggers for technological upgrading do not necessarily come from international pressures alone. It is possible for the state to stimulate upgrading through local policy and its enforcement. However, the market situation was still too unpredictable to stimulate private investment in product upgrading, at least as of early 2004. The state played a direct role in providing leadership and coordination, developing local standards and, through its fisheries inspection service, monitoring and sustaining the pressure on the clusters to keep up with improved process-related standards. However, the state's involvement in product upgrading has been less decisive and, importantly, key knowledge inputs were still absent for product-related upgrading. Yet policy in Uganda had done little to ensure the emergence of systemic linkages, actors and the delivery of competencies needed to upgrade in products.

Tapping into knowledge bases through linkages with external actors overseas seems to be an important element for upgrading clusters in Africa. Across Uganda's fish processing clusters, learning from foreign specialists was important for upgrading in process and later in products. However, the clusters have had to reconfigure their learning strategies to suit different forms of upgrading. They have had to learn and access a different set of abilities to upgrade in products well beyond what it took to upgrade in process. The kind of horizontal joint efforts of the multilateral type, as previously pursued, would offer only limited solutions to the product upgrading challenge. To seek appropriate solutions, the clusters showed a tendency toward vertical joint efforts to learn from, and partner with, their buyers.

In addressing the second question of buyers' minimal involvement in process upgrading and greater involvement in product upgrading, our main conclusions are as follows. Process upgrading in Uganda's fish processing clusters is closely related to sanitary and phytosanitary (SPS) measures imposed and enforced by the EU through a ban of fish imports into the EU. Buyers were minimally involved in helping incipient producers meet new process-related standards set by the EU because these standards were quite complex and knowledge-intensive, requiring specialist knowledge outside the area of competence of most buyers. While buyers had accumulated other areas of competence, the specific science-intensive advice and support required for process upgrading were unavailable among buyers. But why did these buyers not arrange to pay for acquisition of such specialist knowledge? This might have been so for two reasons. First, adoption of improved SPS measures was not likely, at least directly, to lower transaction costs of buyers and thus improve profits. The second reason, which relates to the first, is that buyers that dealt in fresh fish products had only limited space and flexibility to recover costs in process upgrading given the powerful influence of supermarkets on the activities and decisions of their European suppliers.

The situation with product upgrading was different. Firstly, producers were truly incipient in the area of product upgrading, and product upgrading still remains a work-in-progress in these clusters. The producers needed the help provided by their buyers. Buyers had the cumulative competence and knowledge inputs relevant to the product-upgrading process. Secondly, the introduction of product-upgrading activities opened possibilities for branded importers to increase their profit. Buyers have helped local export producers to embark on labour-intensive aspects of product upgrading but design and direct marketing are closely guarded areas of competence. Hence, learning from buyers in these two areas is not likely to be easy but, as was previously observed, possibilities do exist for upgrading, especially in the reprocessed product segment of the market. How well the existing or evolving sectoral innovation system is able to deal with the difficulty of minimal local learning in fish product design, innovation and marketing of upgraded fish products would therefore be an interesting area for further inquiry.

Notes

1. Kaplinsky and Morris (2003) define functional upgrading as the changing of functional positions by adjusting activities within a particular stage of the chain or by moving to activities taking place in other stages of the chain.
2. In an extensive "how to" handbook for conducting value-chain research, Kaplinsky and Morris (2003) define a number of value-chain concepts as well as the entire methodological approach to value-chain analysis.
3. Kyotera is about 40 kilometres from Masaka city.
4. Specialized suppliers of Styrofoam packaging and insulated panels also emerged.
5. The chronology of events during the EU export ban was first documented in Nathan Associates (2000).
6. Based on interviews with FTI and UNIDO-UIP in 2001 and 2002.
7. This is the Food Science and Research Institute (FOSRI) under the National Agricultural Research Organization (NARO).
8. See section on trials for value-added products (Nile perch) and organizations involved, in country reports by Fisheries Departments of all 3 countries (2002) under the CFC/FAO/COMESA/LVFO/Uganda–Kenya–Tanzania Project at LVFO, Jinja, Uganda.
9. Jaffee and Henson (2004) not only provide a recent and critical review but also discuss an alternative perspective.
10. The Lake Victoria Fisheries Organization (LVFO) is a sub-regional organization headquartered in Jinja, Uganda.
11. Manufacture of retail pack boxes, for example, was out-sourced by one of the buyers from a firm in Europe with manufacturing capabilities.
12. For a more detailed characterization of the fish-processing industry in Uganda, see Kiggundu (forthcoming).

REFERENCES

Center for the Development of Industry (CDI) "Lake Fishing in Uganda: The Nile Perch Dossier Nr. 1", Brussels: CDI.

Dolan, Catherine, John Humphrey and Carla Harris-Pascal (1999) "Horticulture Commodity Chains: The Impact of the UK Market on the African Fresh Vegetable Industry", IDS Working Paper 96, Brighton: Institute of Development Studies, University of Sussex.

Freeman, C. (1987) *Technology Policy and Economic Performance: Lessons from Japan*, London: Frances Printer.

Gereffi, Gary (1994a) "Capitalism, Development, and Global Commodity Chains", in Leslie Sklair, ed., *Capitalism & Development*, London: Routledge, 211–31.

Gereffi, Gary (1994b) "The Organisation of Buyer-Driven Global Commodity Chains: How U.S. Retailers Shape Overseas Production Networks", in Gary Gereffi and Miguel Korzeniewicz, eds, *Commodity Chains and Global Capitalism*, Westport, Conn.: Praeger.

Humphrey, John and Hubert Schmitz (2000) "Governance and Upgrading: Linking Industrial Cluster and Global Value Chain Research", IDS Working Paper 120, Brighton: Institute of Development Studies, University of Sussex.

Jaffee, Steven and Spencer Henson (2004) "Standards and Agro-Food Exports from Developing Countries, Rebalancing the Debate", Policy Research Working Paper 3348, Washington, D.C.: World Bank.

Kaplinsky, R. (2000) "Globalization and Unequalisation: What Can Be Learned From Value Chain Analysis?" *Journal of Development Studies* 37(2), December.

Kaplinsky, R. and M. Morris (2003) "A Handbook for Value Chain Research", report prepared for the International Development Research Centre (IDRC). Available through www.ids.ac.uk/ids/global.

Kiggundu, Rose (forthcoming) "Technological Upgrading in Developing Country Firms: The Fish Processing and Export Industry in Uganda," Ph.D. dissertation, Maastricht, the Netherlands: United Nations University, Institute for New Technologies.

Lundvall, Bengt-Åke (1988) "Innovation as an Interactive Process: From User-Producer Interaction to the National System of Innovation", in Giovanni Dosi, Christopher Freeman, Richard R. Nelson, Gerald Silverberg and Luc Soete, eds, *Technical Change and Economic Theory*, London: Pinter Publishers.

Lundvall, Bengt-Åke, ed. (1992) *National Systems of Innovation: Towards a Theory of Innovation and Interactive Learning*, London: Pinter Publishers.

McCormick, Dorothy (1998) "Enterprise Clusters in Africa: On the Way to Industrialization", IDS Discussion Paper 366, Nairobi, Kenya: University of Nairobi.

McCormick, Dorothy (1999) "African Enterprise Clusters and Industrialization: Theory and Reality", *World Development* 27(9): 1531–52.

McCormick, Dorothy (2004) "Upgrading MSE Clusters: Theoretical Frameworks and Political Approaches for African Industrialization", paper presented at the Regional Conference on Innovation Systems and Innovative Clusters in Africa, Bagamoyo, Prospective College of Engineering and Technology, University of Dar Es Salaam, Tanzania, 18–20 February.

McCormick, Dorothy and Winnie V. Mitullah (2002) "Institutional Response to Global Perch Markets: The Case of Lake Victoria Fish Cluster", paper presented at a Conference on Systèmes Agroalimentaires Localisés, Montpellier, France, 16–18 October.

McCormick, Dorothy and Hubert Schmitz (2002) "Manual for Value Chain Research on Homeworkers in the Garment Industry", Sussex: Institute of Development Studies, or http://www.Ids.Ac.Uk/Ids/Global/Wiego.Html.

MFPED (2000) "Medium-Term Competitiveness Strategy for the Private Sector 2000–2005", Ministry of Finance, Planning and Economic Development (MFPED), Republic of Uganda.

Mitullah, Winnie (1999a) "Lake Victoria's Nile Perch Fish Cluster: Institutions, Politics and Joint Action", IDS Working Paper 87, Brighton: Institute of Development Studies, University Of Sussex.

Mitullah, Winnie (1999b) "Fishing and Fish Processing Cluster at Lake Victoria, Kenya", Nairobi: University of Nairobi, Institute for Development Studies.

Morris, Mike (2003) "Using Value Chain Analysis as a Policy and Strategy Intervention Tool", Background Contribution to the Third Conference of the Global Value Chain (GVC) Initiative at the Rockefeller Conference Center, Bellagio, Italy, 8–12 April.

Mytelka, Lynn (2003) "The Dynamics of Catching Up, the Relevance of an Innovation System Approach in Africa", in Mammo Muchie, Peter Gammeltoft and Bengt-Åke Lundvall, eds, *Putting Africa First: The Making of African Innovation Systems*, Aalborg, Denmark: Aalborg University Press.

Nathan Associates (2000) "Restrictions on Uganda's Fish Exports to the European Union (EU)", United States Agency for International Development (USAID), Private Sector Foundation (PSF), Trade Policy Capacity Building Project, Uganda.

Oyelaran-Oyeyinka, B. (1997) *Nnewi: An Emergent Industrial Cluster*, Ibadan: Technopol Publishers.

Oyelaran-Oyeyinka, Banji (1997) "Technological Learning in African Industry: A Study of Engineering Firms in Nigeria", *Science and Public Policy* 24(5): 309–18.

Oyelaran-Oyeyinka, Banji (2000) "Technology and Institutions for Private Small and Medium Firms: The Engineering Industry in Nigeria", ATPS Working Paper 15, Nairobi: African Technology Policy Studies.

Reinikka, Ritva and Jakob Svensson (1999) "Confronting Competition: Investment Response and Constraints in Uganda", Policy Research Working Paper 2245, Washington, D.C.: World Bank.

Sandee, Henry (1995) "Innovation Adoption in Rural Industry: Technological Change in Roof Tile Clusters in Central Java", Ph.D. thesis, Vrije Universiteit, Amsterdam, the Netherlands.

Schmitz, Hubert (1997) "Collective Efficiency and Increasing Returns", IDS Working Paper 50, Brighton: Institute of Development Studies, University Of Sussex.

Schmitz, Hubert and Peter Knorringa (1999) "Learning From Global Buyers," IDS Working Paper 100, Brighton: Institute of Development Studies, University of Sussex.

Schneider, Denise (1999) "The Role of Buyers in the Development of the Hotel Furniture Industry in Kenya", IDS Working Paper 93, Brighton: Institute of Development Studies, University of Sussex.

Stamp, Maxwell (1993) "Study of the Effectiveness of Policies, Facilities and Incentives for Investment Promotion in Uganda", Uganda Investment Authority.

UNCTAD (2001) "Transfer of Technology Policies: Case Studies on Ghana, Kenya, Tanzania and Uganda", Geneva: United Nations.

9

The Durban Auto Cluster: Global competition, collective efficiency and local development

Jochen Lorentzen, Glen Robbins and Justin Barnes

Our tale begins as follows: Once upon a time, in far-away lands where the lion and the bushbuck meet, there was a bunch of automotive component suppliers. A high wall fenced off their territory against foreign marauders, and the bunch gaily went about their business of manufacturing substandard parts for vehicles produced in such small batches that consumers in this strange nation paid among the highest prices in the world for their cars. One day our suppliers woke up and to their astonishment realized that the wall was gone. Worse, before they could finish breakfast, heavily ekwippt suppliers and kar assemblers schpeeking with strange akzents had taken over half zee nation's territory. Word on the street was that fifth columns in the country had helped the outside forces prepare their assault. The future looked dim for our terrified and demoralized bunch! And the end of our tale goes like this: ... and thus, our bunch lived happily ever after, sort of.

The tale's missing mid-section requires some elaboration.[1] The following section of this chapter describes the historical evolution of the Durban Automotive Cluster (DAC) in the context of the impact of aggressive trade liberalization and expanding global automotive supply chains on the South African automobile industry. Next is the analytical core of the chapter. It first presents our data and lays out our methodology. It then discusses the performance of the cluster over time, benchmarked against international competitors. Next, it develops a composite cooperation index to measure joint action, a key hypothesized determinant of cluster performance. Finally, it verifies the reasons behind the growth of the

Industrial clusters and innovation systems in Africa: Institutions, markets and policy, Oyelaran-Oyeyinka and McCormick (eds), United Nations University Press, 2007, ISBN 978-92-808-1137-7

cluster through a survey of its members. The final section concludes with some remarks about the significance of our tale for both understanding and influencing cluster development in an advanced latecomer economy.

From import substitution to global value chains: The automotive industry in KwaZulu-Natal

The principal purpose of this section is to describe *what* happened, rather than *why*. A considerable body of work on clusters is guilty of giving extremely detailed accounts of specific instances of agglomeration without showing the relative weight of the multitude of variables employed to explain their growth. Description in many cases substitutes for analysis and stands in the way of theoretical understanding rather than helping to advance it. The historical account that follows is uncontroversial. But our contention that the elevation of a mere agglomeration to a vibrant cluster was critically due to joint action may well not be. That is why we construct this argument more carefully in the next section.

This section outlines the evolution of the South African automobile sector with particular emphasis on the policy environment. It shows how the rapidly changing competitive environment since the early 1990s affected automotive supplier firms based in the KwaZulu-Natal Province (KZN). To provide the context for the formation of the Durban Automotive Cluster we examine how the supplier firms adjusted to change.

The South African automobile-related sector is relatively insignificant compared to total global automotive production but it has captured the attention of policymakers in the country for many decades.[2] Through government intervention, South Africa made considerable efforts in the post-World War II period to create the conditions for the development of a solid automobile manufacturing sector. The involvement of state entities in concessional financing regimes, the presence of subsidized state enterprises in the defence industry, the imposition of import quotas and tariffs and the repression of labour unions all played their part in the development of a sector that supplied, almost exclusively and in a highly protected manner, to the domestic market. This policy regime was part of an industrial development framework based on import substitution that was central to the apartheid-era economic policy (Joffe et al., 1995). The policy was reinforced in the last quarter of the twentieth century as the apartheid regime reacted to the effects of international isolation and sanctions with a growing obsession for national self-sufficiency in strategic market areas.[3]

Automotive (and other) firms operated at levels of productivity, quality and innovation well below international best practice (Joffe et al.,

1995). For a relatively small passenger and commercial vehicle market, there was a proliferation of domestically manufactured model varieties, produced and sold at costs well above those in more liberalized markets. In this sense, South Africa up until the early 1990s resembled the Mexico of the 1970s. Component firms supplying to this market were characterized by low volumes and short-run production cycles. It is no wonder that benchmarking exercises showed them to be uncompetitive in pricing and international operational standards (Kaplinski and Morris, 1997).

The political changes of the early 1990s heralded a new era of economic policies. In line with multilateral orthodoxies of the time, the country embraced an accelerated trade-liberalization programme and began systematically to remove demand-oriented industrial policies. Within a relatively short period the government abolished quotas and agreed to tariff adjustments in the Uruguay Round of the General Agreement on Tariffs and Trade. Duty levels on "completely built up" vehicles fell from 115 per cent in 1995 to 40 per cent in 2002 and are scheduled to reach 25 per cent by 2012. Tariffs on "completely knocked down" components are lower yet. However, despite an unambiguous commitment to trade liberalization in general, the Department of Trade and Industry (DTI) also pursued a policy agenda specific to the automobile sector. It did so in an effort to manage a shift toward greater export orientation. Policymakers did not want to run the risk of de-industrialization – with disastrous effects on export prospects – that they knew global competition had rained on more or less unsuspecting emerging markets elsewhere. In 1995 this motivation led to the Motor Industry Development Programme (MIDP).

The objective behind the initial form of the MIDP was to secure the investment commitment of the major original equipment manufacturers (OEMs) with an existing manufacturing presence in South Africa. The MIDP was largely negotiated with these key-role players, and the government pursued it despite concerns from trading partners that it contravened World Trade Organization commitments. The MIDP sought to encourage the domestic-based OEMs to reduce the range of models produced domestically. To this end, it allowed the OEMs to earn import credits by expanding exports of the reduced range of models with significant local content. Thanks to the "Import Rebate Credit Certificates" OEMs could bring in a fuller range of vehicles from foreign plants to sell in South Africa at a reduced duty level. Volkswagen, BMW and Daimler (later DaimlerChrysler) were the first to respond by injecting significant capital into their South African operations for the production of a limited range of vehicles, the bulk of which would be destined for export markets. Responses by other OEMs were slower, in part because of more complicated ownership arrangements where international brands were being produced under licence by domestic firms, but soon all major

OEMs signed up. The impact on South African vehicle output and exports was significant (see figure 9.1). Exports have grown substantially since 1995, and between 1998 and 2002, when early OEM investments had realized production potential, unit exports rose 383.9 per cent.[4] Import levels have also grown under the more liberal trade arrangements. Imported units made up 23.1% of total domestic sales in 2002 compared to 6.5% in 1995.

The MIDP, together with the depreciation of the Rand in the mid-1990s, turned South Africa into a relatively competitive producer of both components and completed vehicles. The contribution of the auto sector to total manufacturing sales grew from 9.7 per cent in 1994 to 12.8 per cent in 2003. Component sales during this period also grew from around R6 billion in 1994 to almost R15 billion in 2000. The performance of the component firms during the 1990s was largely driven by the MIDP. Prominent exports were, for example, catalytic converters and leather seat covers. However, the growth in capacity utilization demanded by these changes and the increasingly stringent requirements on suppliers joining global supply chains placed considerable pressure on these firms. Local industry consolidated and subsidiaries of multinational component manufacturers entered the country. Stagnant domestic demand exacerbated the competitive pressure. Insofar as the initial design of the MIDP focused on the OEMs, the policy environment was less conducive to facilitating the adaptation of component firms. Subsequent adjustments to the MIDP addressed this shortcoming to avoid a hollowing-out of the manufacturing base in which South Africa would merely be an assembly location. Figure 9.2 shows that the growth rate of component output increased after 1999.

The overall impact of these policies was in line with expectations. Production of export vehicles has increased considerably since the late 1990s, and global OEMs expanded investments in their South Africa-based plants. However, the period has also witnessed much greater import penetration, with firms taking advantage of the possibility of exchanging credits earned from exports with local content for imported models and components.

It was this changing environment that confronted firms in the KwaZulu-Natal region. KZN is the country's third centre in the hierarchy of automotive sector activity (see figure 9.3). The Gauteng area around Pretoria and Johannesburg is both the largest market and has the largest concentration of OEMs (BMW, Ford, Nissan, Fiat) and component firms. The Eastern Cape, with its three major OEMs (DaimlerChrysler in East London, Volkswagen in Port Elizabeth, and Delta Motor Corporation in Uitenhage) is the next most significant car-manufacturing centre. Production activity in KZN is dominated by the Toyota plant, which had for

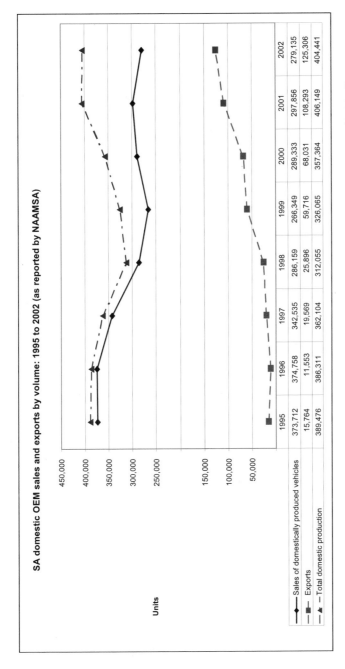

Figure 9.1 Domestic OEM sales and exports by volume. Source: Barnes and Johnson (2004: 6)

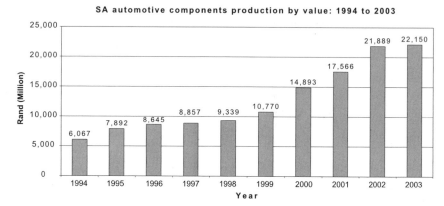

Figure 9.2 South African automotive component output by value. Source: Barnes and Johnson (2004: 8)

many years been the operation with the most significant domestic output. Although many component firms also supplied other OEMs in the country, traditionally Toyota was their most important customer. The Toyota plant used a mixture of first-tier supplies from in-house operations and local component firms, and imported the rest.

Most automotive firms based in KZN, including Toyota, are based in or around Durban. Pietermaritzburg, the provincial capital, hosts the second most numerous contingent. These firms are closely integrated with supply and logistics activities in Durban some 90 kilometres away. The firms in Ladysmith, Stanger and Richards Bay rely less or not at all on sourcing arrangements generated in Durban directly or indirectly by Toyota. In KZN 10 firms are first-tier suppliers, 20 are second- or third-tier, 10 supply the aftermarket and a dozen more marginal firms straddle the latter categories. Figure 9.4 shows their product profile. Some second- and third-tier suppliers are not exclusive auto component firms and produce for other sectors but count the auto sector as a significant customer.

The performance of these firms during the period of adjustment has been highly uneven. Toyota, which until early 2002 operated in South Africa under licence from Toyota Manufacturing Corporation of Japan, initially failed to respond to the changing trade environment fostered by the MIDP. Licence conditions imposed major limits on exporting and the firm continued to focus on producing a range of vehicles for the domestic market. However, in view of contracting global markets, Toyota (Japan) sought more competitive platforms worldwide and the attractive offer through the MIDP led it to take a majority stake in the Durban-based operations. The plants in KZN subsequently moved rapidly toward

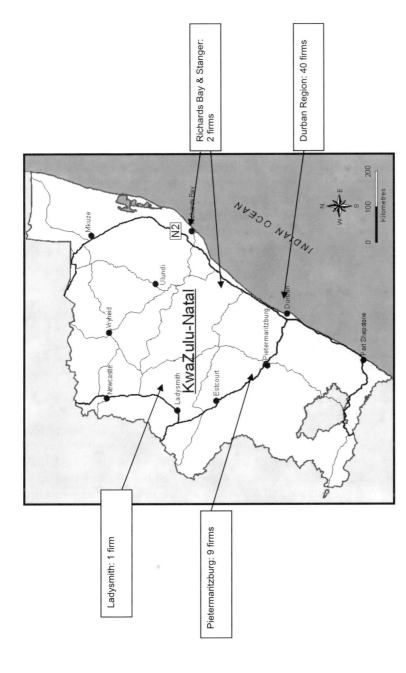

Figure 9.3 Distribution of automotive component firms in KZN (2004). Source: Unpublished map by F. Sokolic, UKZN, B&M Analysts

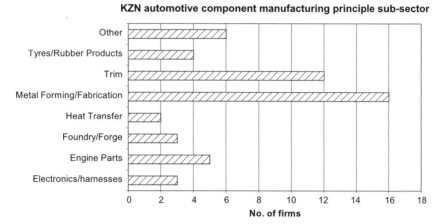

Figure 9.4 Profile of KZN component producers by product type. Source: Barnes and Johnson (2004: 16)

greater specialization in production and improving performance levels in order to secure export contracts into Toyota's global supply system. At present Toyota exports the Toyota RunX to Australasia and is in the process of meeting requirements to export new generation Corolla and Hilux models to a range of markets, most notably the European Union. Toyota has also managed to retain a quarter of the domestic market making it the dominant assembler in South Africa.

The impact of this new strategic orientation was very significant for many local Toyota suppliers. Delivery specifications became more oner-ous and relationships in the supply network had to move to approved systems. The price for non-compliance was the prospect of losing local Toyota business to other global suppliers. Some firms struggled to adjust, while others were willingly or unwillingly drawn into becoming local plants of multinational component firms. A number of firms that either did not supply Toyota or had Toyota as only one of a number of OEM customers faced a barrage of adjustment requirements to specialize, in-crease volumes of output and improve product and process standards. A few new entrants also appeared in response to the new policy environ-ment. These included manufacturers of catalytic converters, seat cover manufacturers and electronics assemblers.

Although most firms survived these changes, more than a handful admit to doing so by the barest of margins. The combined pressures over a lim-ited period generated almost continual upheaval. It was in this context that studies first examined the gaps between the firms' performance stan-dards and what was to be expected of them in the future. Researchers from the Institute of Development Studies at the University of Sussex and the School of Development Studies at the then-University of Natal (today the University of KwaZulu-Natal) investigated endogenous factors that affected the competitiveness of firms, using performance-benchmarking techniques. With a combination of provincial government and international donor funding – notably from the UK's Department for International Development – the KwaZulu-Natal Industrial Restructuring Project (KZN IRP) initiated detailed benchmarks in sectors active in the region, including the automotive components sector, furniture, clothing and textiles. The results of the studies were presented to managers in a series of participatory workshops. A number of automotive components producers showed considerable interest. In response, the research team and the firms made a series of applications to DTI's new supply-side funds for financial support to sustain the benchmarking work and expand the activities of the researchers into more active facilitation.

In January 1998 the KwaZulu-Natal Benchmarking Club was formally constituted with participation from eleven automotive component firms, Toyota SA, and facilitators from the KZN IRP. The Club had as its focus the following activities from which each member would benefit:

- Confidential scheduled diagnostic reports of firm operational performance and customer and supplier perceptions;
- Confidential benchmarks against a similar international competitor;
- Monthly newsletters outlining aggregated benchmark findings;
- Quarterly workshops to examine generic issues and tackle specific problems, and sharing of information between the participants.

Research reports that resulted from the project attracted attention from the metropolitan government of the Durban region. Problems of long lead times with DTI funding mechanisms and unwieldy bureaucratic application processes encouraged the KZN Benchmarking Club facilitators to explore links with local government officials. In 1999 the then-Durban Metropolitan Council's Economic Development Department, motivated by a series of independent research reports it had commissioned into cluster potentials within the automotive, chemicals and textiles sectors, agreed to provide seed funding toward an investigation into the potential of broadening participation by auto-sector firms in cooperative processes. The company that had been formed to carry out the facilitation and research functions related to the KZN Benchmarking Club explored the potential of expanding both the participation and the agenda of the Club. A series of workshops with KZN-based automotive-components and OEM firms confirmed interest from over 20 firms in participating in information sharing and joint action activities. An additional funding commitment from the Durban Metropolitan Council enabled the Deputy Mayor to formally launch the DAC in 2002.

The DAC differed in a number of ways from the KZN Benchmarking

Club. The Club's main activity was to benchmark confidentially each member firm against domestic and international competitors once a year. The Club also shared information on how member firms responded to the key challenges arising from the benchmarks. This required a considerable commitment of time and resources on the part of the firms, and – insofar as they revealed sensitive information – could obviously only function with a high degree of trust amongst them. What the Club did not do was to focus on identifying competitive challenges facing its firms and organize a collective response to them. By contrast, the DAC did both. The DAC facilitated horizontal and vertical information sharing among its members and made arrangements to involve a variety of firms from different tiers of the supply chain to work toward establishing a functioning and growing local supplier infrastructure. Membership in the DAC was open to any automotive firm in KZN. Many DAC members also belonged to the Benchmarking Club. The DAC's operational structure is depicted in figure 9.5.

DAC programmes are governed by a nominated Technical Steering Committee (TSC) to ensure the successful implementation of the business plans. Each TSC comprises senior managers from DAC participants, interested government officials and a facilitator from the cluster's service provider. The four TSCs are in turn directly answerable to a DAC Executive, comprising the four chairs of the Technical Steering Committees and three further automotive component manufacturer representatives from an SME and a PDI (previously disadvantaged individual)-owned firm. Additional executive members include a representative of each government tier providing DAC funding, a representative of Toyota SA and two senior facilitators from the service provider.

Crucial to the early funding of the DAC was an agreement with officials from the local government that a firm-driven governance structure was essential to secure the confidence of the participants and the sustainability of the initiative. Early participants voiced reservations related to

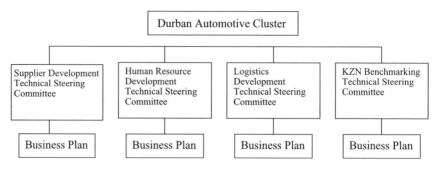

Figure 9.5 Operational structure of the DAC

their experiences with impractical national-level cluster initiatives driven by government officials in conjunction with industry associations (who reportedly delighted in scheduling frequent meetings in Johannesburg at such inopportune times that no one from out of town could attend). These initiatives typically showed little interest in micro-level or shop-floor operations that firms often felt deserved priority. While both local government and provincial counterparts expressed a desire for the DAC to take on matters such as black economic empowerment and investment attraction, initial funding was not made conditional on these objectives. The DAC Executive was in a relatively strong position in these discussions partly because the participating firms provided its funding and the early successes in its activities improved its credibility as a sound partner. Presently the DAC, having diversified its income sources and nurtured the maturing of its programme areas, has begun cautiously to move beyond its initial focus points onto partnering with government on strategic initiatives such as facilitating the entrance of black-owned components firms into the sector.

It is worthwhile to reflect on the roles of the specific players that led to the formation of the DAC. The DAC was not a creation of direct orchestrated government intervention as was the case elsewhere (for example, the Eastern Cape Auto Cluster which was formed out of DTI national cluster initiatives in 1997/98). However, it would also be incorrect to describe the DAC as a pure "bottom-up" creation of the firms that had originally participated in the formation of the KZN Benchmarking Club. Prior to the formation of the Club, most firms would have been rather sceptical about the benefits of interacting with either government or academic audiences. However, the role played by the researchers in the formation of the DAC ensured that contact with the government – through DTI – was mediated. Hence government appeared as a benign, if perhaps at times frustratingly quirky, partner. The research team, acting as facilitator, ensured that the more messy aspects of the interaction with the DTI did not affect the day-to-day operating of the Club. It was aided in this process by the nature of the funding mechanism that left the recipients relatively free to allocate resources where they felt they would be most useful. The Club experience for the firms therefore left them more open to future engagement with the government than they might have had had government officials been carried away with asserting their own agendas of what *they* believed were the priorities for sustainable firm growth.

With regard to the formation of the DAC, the Benchmarking Club facilitators and participating firms had been discussing for some time the possibility of involving additional firms and extending their activities. Their cautious response to local government requests for a future partnership showed that they felt they were in a position carefully to consider the merits of any proposal and were not solely reliant on sourcing lucrative government grants for their survival. While the local government, and to a lesser degree its provincial counterparts, saw an opportunity to invest in a process that was already showing returns – and therefore had a good chance of future success – the firms saw an opportunity to reduce their risks in expanding their level of cooperation without the added threat of becoming dependent on (often unreliable) government attention and support.

It is also worth noting that Toyota generally has taken a keen interest in the workings and activities of the cluster but has been very careful not to dominate processes. A member of its management team has been involved in the governance structure at the request of the other DAC members, but it recognized that the company must not dominate the workings of the DAC. Many DAC members supply other OEMs, but with Toyota as a dominant regional customer, they have been cautious not to rely too heavily for funding or operational support on the assembler. In this regard the DAC is an entity focused on component firms, whereas the cluster process in the Eastern Cape was for a long time dominated by OEMs seeking to improve relationships with their suppliers. Toyota participants in DAC processes have indicated that the projected growth in unit exports from the Durban plant (anticipated to almost double from 100,000 annually to over 180,000) will require ongoing and perhaps more intensive relationships between the OEMs and the DAC as time progresses.

In the South African context, and perhaps on the continent more generally, the formation of the DAC was unique. It is clear that from the beginning there has been early and sustained "buy-in" by the participating firms of the notion of networking and sharing information for individual and collective benefit. In its initial form as the KZN Benchmarking Club (which continues to operate as a programme within the DAC), firms essentially managed a self-government process. Increasing firm contributions have reinforced the notion of a process that firms feel they are able to direct to meet their own needs. Such self-reliance, combined with demonstrated success, has enabled the firms to negotiate the terms of funding from various government entities. In sum, the DAC and the Benchmarking Club have placed the concerns of the components sector at the heart of their activities instead of seeking primarily to serve the interests of the OEMs.

The DAC process is also noteworthy for the role of its facilitators. The academic team and later the service company spun out of the academic research programme were always neutral providers of information and facilitation services. The service provider has not engaged itself as a consultancy providing strategic or other advice to firms, other than benchmarks and information on sector dynamics. This enabled it to play the role of a trusted agent without having its agenda clouded by providing or needing to market specific services. Firms were thus more than usually willing to share information and insights. This arrangement has also minimized the DAC's overhead – firms are not expected to cover the costs of a large consulting operation or invest in elaborate value-adding business development services as part of the deal. This has enabled broader participation, especially from smaller firms.

Finally, government played a significant role in the formation and evolution of the DAC. Although this role has not always translated into direct participation, consistent funding with limited conditions has enabled the DAC to expand its activities and involve more marginal firms. The recognition by municipal authorities that funding with excessively onerous conditions would limit the ability of firms to give direction to the process and compromise flexibility was an important element in the funding-operational dynamic. By focusing its funding mandates on outcomes such as employment creation, output and export growth and improved sustainability of firms, especially emerging black-owned enterprises, the municipality enabled the DAC to establish its own path to work toward the outcomes. A similar sensitivity to the stresses, strains and trust issues involved in formalizing a network into an action-oriented collective has not always been apparent to other spheres of government. Reduced reliance on such sources for funding was clearly beneficial.

In sum, an existing spatial agglomeration where buyers and suppliers interacted and made use of the labour pool around the city of Durban, but which historically did not exhibit cluster-like network externalities, gave rise to the benchmarking and then the DAC initiative. Since membership was open to all automotive firms in KZN regardless of their distance to Durban, the cluster was inclusive and did not impose locational restrictions. In practice, the cluster is a spatial agglomeration with two relatively distant subscribers whose activities relate, at least in part, to the supply relationships in the core of the cluster in Durban. Neither the Benchmarking Club nor the DAC evolved spontaneously or even primarily as initiatives by concerned firms. Instead, the principal protagonists were associated with the municipal government and a local university. Hence, in the face of its peculiar evolution and its partially dispersed structure, the preliminary empirical answer to the theoretical question posed at the beginning of the previous section – How do you know a cluster when you see one? – is that in this case its member firms chose to call themselves just that. This turns attention to the question of the degree to which this self-styled cluster generates activities that allow it to improve collective performance.

Cluster performance and inter-firm cooperation

Our contention is that joint action made a noticeable difference to the performance of those automotive suppliers in KZN that joined the DAC and its forerunner, the Benchmarking Club. Put differently, while the longstanding agglomeration of firms in KZN is likely to have given rise to externalities even prior to the formation of the Club and the DAC, they cannot account for the improvement in firm performance since the latter part of the 1990s. By contrast, joint action can.

The remainder of this section underlines three aspects of the cluster. First, we show the improvement in operational competitiveness over time based on the data collected by the Benchmarking Club. The Club evaluates members once a year against international competitors in both advanced and latecomer countries. This allows gauging performance in relative and absolute terms. Second, we make a plausible (but refutable) case that joint action is an important element behind the improved performance. *Ceteris paribus*, increased inter-firm cooperation should yield better results. The challenge is to operationalize this. Third, we test this contention through a survey of DAC members. Many other factors may be responsible, individually or jointly, for the generally positive performance of the DAC. Notably this would include increased international competition and other forms of inter- or intra-firm cooperation, for example between licence partners or subsidiaries and multinational principals.

Performance improvement in the DAC

It is easy to demonstrate that member firms have become better in a range of activities. Indeed, firm-level data confirm that operationally much has been happening since the late 1990s (see table 9.1). The infor-

Table 9.1 Average competitiveness improvements recorded at Benchmarking Club members

Indicator	Unit	1999	2002	Improvement (%)
Total inventory holding	Days	51.14	40.19	21.41
Customer return rate	Ppm	4,269	1,034	75.78
On time & in full delivery	%	91.73	92.17	0.48
Absenteeism	%	4.20	3.59	14.52

Source: KZN/Eastern Cape/Gauteng Benchmarking Club database
Note: Total inventory holdings = ratio of operating days over stock turns per annum; customer return rate = parts per million units of production delivered to customers returned due to defects; on time and in full delivery = percentage of total deliveries supplied to customers on time and in full; absenteeism = percentage of man days lost due to employees not being at work except for holiday leave

Table 9.2 Relative performance of Benchmarking Club members

Indicator	Club member average	Club member upper quartile	Developing/ transition economy average	Developed economy average
Total inventory holding	40.19	23.00	32.81	37.30
Customer return rate	1,034	23	529.71	785.22
On time & in full delivery	92.17	98.00	96.38	91.91
Absenteeism	3.59	2.00	4.35	5.67

Source: KZN/Eastern Cape/Gauteng Benchmarking Club database

mation comprises competitiveness and financial performance data from over 40 automotive component manufacturers, including DAC members, which belong to one of three regional Benchmarking Clubs in KwaZulu-Natal, Eastern Cape and Gauteng provinces. In 2002, their employment ranged from under 50 to over 2000, and turnover from R11 million (US$1 million) to R1.1 billion (US$116 million). They represent roughly 25 per cent of the national automotive-components industry by value.

Each member is benchmarked against an international competitor based in either Western or Eastern Europe, Malaysia or Australia. Thus the database includes information on international firms that broadly match the product profile of their South African counterparts (see table 9.2). South Africa-based firms generally lag behind their competitors. Only the top performers match and indeed sometimes outperform their international peers.

The gains from joint action: A plausible but refutable case

The indicators in tables 9.1 and 9.2 measure how successfully DAC and other Benchmarking Club firms implement lean management practices. Not all DAC members are also members of the Benchmarking Club. Due to the relatively recent vintage of the DAC and its growing membership, not all of those that are members have been benchmarked twice, making it impossible to evaluate performance over time. Technically the correct procedure would have been for us to report performance indicators only for DAC firms, but this would have reduced our sample, making it more vulnerable to outliers while not changing the underlying positive trend. Hence, our analysis of joint action is conservative in that it suggests that DAC firms are as least as good as Benchmarking Club members. This is not a heroic assumption. In future work and as our database expands both in terms of membership and over time, we aim to look for differences across the three provinces and, within KZN, between ordinary Benchmarking Club members and those that are also members of the DAC.

The data do not show what the improvement results from, although one possibility is joint action. The DAC runs programmes in the areas of supplier development, human resource development, logistics and benchmarking to advance these practices. Committees staffed by managers of member firms, supported by facilitators from the service provider, meet regularly to identify problems, discuss how to address them, disseminate their deliberations and ultimately develop solutions. These are incidences of cooperation. In other words, the firms engage in joint action.

In an attempt to systematize this notion we separated it into two components, commitment and frequency. Regarding the former, it would be different for managers merely to attend a workshop and (passively) absorb information as opposed to actively seek and provide data to share with their peers. Low commitment by a firm means that it underwrites the (partial) cost of an activity but devotes no management time to it. For example, in the DAC's case the service provider surveys trends in the world car industry and summarizes their implications for the regional automotive economy. This intelligence is distributed regularly to member firms. It creates awareness and potentially informs their strategic thinking, but firms have no direct input. High commitment means the investment of comprehensive management time across functions, such as the participation of senior staff in specialized work groups (e.g., on purchasing skills) that report to a technical steering committee that oversees the supplier development programme within the cluster. Frequency concerns how often activities or meetings take place. This goes from low (once in five months to once a year) to medium (once every two to four months) to high (more than once a month).

In table 9.3 these two parameters are combined into a composite cooperation index. The index weighs commitment more heavily than frequency. This is because a high-commitment exercise that happens once a year is worth more than a largely passive exercise that happens once a month. The expectation is that a relatively high-value joint action would lead to more solid gains. The last column in table 9.3 illustrates that this is indeed generally the case. For example, in the area of supplier development, a high-powered technical steering committee with a busy meeting schedule, assisted by a specialized work group, identified purchasing skills as a key weakness and ultimately succeeded in instituting a dedicated course aimed at training the requisite skills at the local technical university. Likewise, joint action, albeit with a low cooperation score – as with pretty much all activities in the DAC's Logistics Programme – did yield a tangible result, namely reduced shipping rates for DAC members, but this was a smaller feat than re-organizing the training

Table 9.3 Joint action in the DAC: Incidence and gains

Incidence of cooperation		CCI	Gains
Commitment (a)	Frequency (b)		
	Supplier development		
Dissemination of locally relevant global industry trends (LC)	N/A	1.19	Launch of automotive purchasing course at Durban Institute of Technology (DIT) (with 13 enrolled students in first year)
Workshops on topical supplier development issues (MC)	Once every 5 weeks (HF)	2.38	
Technical steering committee of supplier development business plan (HC)	Once every 6 weeks (HF)	4.00	Launch of PDI supplier development programme with KZN Manufacturing Advisory Centre (with 6 firms in first run)
Specialized work groups (purchasing skills, supplier-development best practices, vertical information sharing, PDI/BEE) (HC)	More than once every 6 weeks (HF)	4.00	
Special interest groups (inventory and quality mgmt) (HC)	Up to fortnightly (HF)	4.00	Launch of Web-based, globally marketed supplier data base
	Human resource development		
Workshops on information sharing and capacity building (MC)	Once every 8 weeks (MF)	2.00	Launch of in-service training programme with DIT and Mangosuthu Technikon (with 20 enrolled students in first run)
Investigation of joint training opportunities (MC)	Once a month (HF)	2.38	
	Logistics		
Dissemination of logistics-benchmarking survey (LC)	Annual (LF)	1.00	Negotiation of joint in- and outbound shipping and air freight rates
Survey of road freight movements in and out of cluster (MC)	Once (LF)	1.68	
Workshops on information sharing (variable)	Semiannual (LF)	1.00–2.83	
	Benchmarking		
Dissemination of Benchmarking Club newsletters (MC)	Monthly (HF)	2.38	Improvement in average operational competitiveness
Workshops on HRD, change management, FX management and product development (MC)	Once every 4 months (MF)	2.00	Increase in profitability, sales and employment

Table 9.3 (cont.)
Note:
- CCI = composite cooperation index. The formula used is $c = 2^{\alpha f + (1-\alpha)i}$. The weight α is set equal to 0.75. This is somewhat arbitrary but reflects the greater importance of commitment relative to intensity. Choosing 0.66, for example, would yield similar values, only less dispersed. The nice feature of this exponential function is that the minimum possible value is 1, the maximum 4, hence making for easy comparisons.
- LC, MC, HC = low, medium and high commitment
  - LC = firm only underwrites (partial) cost of activity (= 0)
  - MC = firm dedicates select management time to activity (= 1)
  - HC = firm dedicates comprehensive management time across functions and layers to activity (= 2)
- LF, MF, HF = low, medium and high frequency
  - LF = once every 5–12 months (= 0)
  - MF = once every 2–4 months (= 1)
  - HF = more than once every 2 months (= 2)
- PDI = previously disadvantaged individuals
- BEE = black economic empowerment

programme in a school. Hence across the four cluster programmes it appears that a higher incidence of cooperation leads to more impressive results – it is plausible that joint action matters. However, the case is not solid yet.

Joint action, competition and non-co-located inter-firm cooperation

Schmitz and his team based their work on collective efficiency on the proposition that shocks like trade liberalization would catalyze joint action (Schmitz, 2000). Consequently they looked at whether or not the exchange of information and experiences, cooperation in improving product quality and in speeding-up delivery and so forth increased in the wake of an external shock. Our approach is clearly in the tradition of Schmitz's work. But in our case the link between trade liberalization and inter-firm cooperation is obvious, as is the increase in the latter. Our question is whether this increase has made a difference in terms of improving cluster performance. More formally, was the DAC instrumental in the acquisition, assimilation, adaptation and exploitation of information?

Of course, the answer could be negative. Increased competition might have motivated firms to become more efficient. In this case the market matters the most, externalities to some extent, and joint action little to nothing. Likewise, inter-firm cooperation may well be important but in a different sense, namely between licence partners. In addition, knowledge transfer that ultimately manifests itself in more capable local adoption of lean management techniques may be primarily intra-firm, especially from foreign multinational corporations to their subsidiaries. Of course, global competition and DAC activities are different types of variables. Competition is the driver that propels firms to undertake (or not) some form of adjustment, and cluster activities are its manifestations. Joint action is unlikely in the absence of increased competition because there is no challenge that would justify the required commitment of resources. At the same time, however, a firm can adjust primarily because of increased competition – and because it can draw on internal resources that allow it to do so even in the absence of joint action – or primarily because, given this competition, it can draw on collective resources. Smaller and under-resourced firms may not even be aware of the more dynamic aspects of competition that can affect them in the mid-term more so than in the short run, unless an external agency explains market trends to them. For this reason, it makes sense to compare the relative weight of the rather different factors influencing firm adjustment.

We explored the relative weight of these different variables in a survey of the managers of the DAC member firms. The questionnaire inquired about the importance of intelligence member firms receive from the business-service provider, the gains they get from participating in DAC workshops and if members would be able to substitute these services if the DAC did not exist. It also asked about the relative importance of a number of variables that individually or collectively could conceivably influence the performance of individual firms. Of the 26 member firms targeted, 19 responded.[5]

The results are revealing (see table 9.4). On average a minimum of one in three managers attaches a high value to the acquisition and assimilation (questions 1, 3 and 4) and to the exploitation (question 2) of knowledge made possible by DAC activities, and practically the entire respondent group assigns this at least medium significance. Interestingly, fewer managers benefit strategically from workshops (question 5) than from surveys. In other words, external knowledge is possibly more important to dealing with the challenges of global supply chains than intra-cluster intelligence. The efficiency of joint action is not in doubt; more than nine out of ten respondents report that substituting cluster activities would be expensive or not an option at all (question 6). Likewise, the same number of respondents is convinced of the effectiveness of cluster activities in generating performance improvements (question 7).

The latter point can be disaggregated further (see table 9.5). The single most important factor for achieving internationally required performance standards is global competition. This underlines the essential role of the DAC in facilitating learning about global competition reported above. In other words, inter-firm competition in global supply chains exerts

Table 9.4 Survey results (questions 1–7): Significance of learning

Question/importance	Low (%)	Medium (%)	High (%)
1. Importance of intelligence by DAC service provider for own understanding of global auto industry	0	68	32
2. Importance of intelligence by DAC service provider for strategy	5	53	42
3. Importance of DAC workshops for understanding global best practices	0	47	53
4. Importance of DAC workshops for understanding cluster dynamics	5	42	53
5. Importance of DAC workshops for strategy	5	74	21
6. Ease of substitutability of DAC workshops	37	58	5
7. Importance of DAC activities for improvement of operational competitiveness	10	16	74

Note: For question 7, low = only own competitiveness; medium = only that of other DAC members; high = both.

Table 9.5 Survey results (question 8): Determinants of required performance levels (mean)

	Quality	Cost	Flexibility	Delivery
DAC activities	4.6	4.4	4.8	4.6
Competition from DAC members	3.7	3.3	3.7	3.5
Competition from non-DAC suppliers in KZN	2.8	2.7	2.9	3.0
Competition from suppliers elsewhere in SA	3.5	3.9	3.7	4.1
Competition from suppliers outside SA	5.4	5.5	4.9	4.9
Technical assistance from foreign partners	4.6	4.7	3.6	3.5
Consultants	3.1	2.8	2.8	2.7

Note: 1 = least important; 7 = most important

pressure on firms within the cluster and the cluster helps its members understand the nature of this challenge. A key factor for the "hard" performance criteria of quality and cost is technical assistance from foreign partners; this includes licensors as well as multinational investors. It is in these two areas that South African firms are most burdened by the legacy of import substitution and where their competence was most in question. It appears that DAC activities, the joint second and third most important factor, respectively, helped them rise to the challenge.

The situation is somewhat different with respect to the two "soft" criteria of flexibility and delivery. In these areas, cluster activities are almost as important as global competition while technical assistance, on average, is not particularly important at all. Table 9.3 showed that on-time and in full delivery, especially of the Club's top performers, was on par with international standards. South African firms had always had to employ flexibility to compensate for the cost disadvantages associated with small production runs. The managers' responses suggest that joint action has been instrumental in turning these "make-do" attitudes into internationally acceptable competences. Small and PDI-owned firms evaluate the importance of joint action more positively than larger firms. On balance, small firms say that the DAC is essential while larger firms consider it merely useful.

The information in table 9.5 also shows that inside the cluster cooperation is more important than competition. By contrast, competition is more important than inter- or intra-firm cooperation outside the cluster. This raises the question of the relative significance of alliance capitalism in developing countries or, more specifically, the extent to which individual subsidiaries act as conduits for knowledge that lends to technological upgrading of domestic firms. It would be interesting to address the nature and quality of technology-relevant extra-cluster links in future research.

Conclusions

Joint action matters for firm performance, at least in the case at hand. Joint action lowers the costs of information provision about markets, product standards, process requirements and other variables that determine the competence with which firms confront global value chains. Joint action also helps firms gear up for what is, not just in the global automotive industry, a tough fight for a place in the sun. Cooperation-vs-competition is a meaningless dichotomy. If global competition is the challenge, local cooperation is the efficient answer for firms that would stand little chance of understanding what this competition is really about, let alone facing up to what it asks of them. This applies to all firms in the cluster, but especially so to those relatively disadvantaged by small size and lack of experience in supplying to global value chains.

The success of the DAC is due to a fortuitous combination of impartial analysis by academics-turned-consultants whose competence and motivation – unlike that of most pure-bred consultants – was beyond doubt; the realization by firms of their own limitations along with a commitment to overcoming them; and a policy framework conducive to the strategies of multinational assemblers and component suppliers that incorporated South Africa into their worldwide production networks.

It is not easy to draw lessons from this success story for the rest of Africa. Perhaps the key insight from this experience is that firms in latecomer – and even more so in developing – countries need to learn the rules of the game before they get a realistic chance to play. Hence, knowledge is key, and collective efficiencies are perhaps most effective when marshaled to provoke, promote and verify learning.

Notes

1. We are grateful to Peter Møllgard, Kaushalesh Lal, Mike Morris and Lynn Mytelka for helpful suggestions.
2. The industry comprises eight light vehicle original equipment manufacturers (OEMs), a number of medium and heavy commercial vehicle OEMs, and some 250 dedicated component manufacturers, many of which are multinational corporation subsidiaries.
3. For an overview of policy in that period, see Black (2001).
4. Data in this section are from Barnes and Johnson (2004).
5. In mid-2004 the DAC had more than forty member firms. We approached only those firms that have been members since the beginning of the Cluster in 2002 in order to elicit more informed responses.

REFERENCES

Barnes, Justin and Julia Johnson (2004) "Sectoral Overview of the Automotive Industry in the eThekwini Municipality and Broader KZN province", unpublished research note produced for eThekwini Municipality by B&M Analysts (www.bmanalysts.com).

Black, Anthony (2001) "Globalisation and Restructuring in the South African Automotive Industry", *Journal of International Development* 13.

Joffe, Avril, David Kaplan, Raphie Kaplinsky and David Lewis (1995) *Improving Manufacturing Performance in South Africa: Report of the Industrial Strategy Project*, Cape Town: UCT Press.

Kaplinsky, Raphie and Mike Morris (1997) "The Formulation of Industrial Policy in South Africa: A View from the Edge", Working Paper 15, Durban: School of Development Studies, University of Natal.

Schmitz, Hubert (2000) "Does Local Co-Operation Matter? Evidence from Industrial Clusters in South Asia and Latin America", *Oxford Development Studies*, 28(3).

10

Global markets and local responses: The changing institutions in the Lake Victoria fish cluster

Dorothy McCormick and Winnie V. Mitullah

Globalization of the world food economy has created commodity chains that require adequate rules, regulations and sustainable management by the actors involved. Lake Victoria fisheries made their entry into the chain in the beginning of the 1970s. Participation of actors in the chain has had both advantages and problems. By the end of the 1990s, a central problem of the Lake Victoria cluster was the conflict between providing current livelihoods to the fisherfolk and ensuring the sustainability of the fisheries. The problem is a classic example of a potential "tragedy of the commons" (Hardin, 1968). Resolving it will require a fresh look at the management of the fisheries.

"Community participation" or "co-management" are increasingly being suggested as essential to natural resource management, both in Kenya and elsewhere (Berkes, 2001; Jansen et al., 1999; Kenya, 2002), yet such proposals often leave many questions unanswered. Who, for example, is the community that should be participating? Does it include only the fishers, or are traders and processors also part of the community? What is the role of external stakeholders such as government or foreign buyers? And finally, what institutional forms are needed to support a co-management strategy?

This chapter examines the changing institutional framework for managing fisheries. It pays special attention to fisherfolk community participation and its effect on management effectiveness, fish quality, sustainability of the resource and the health and well-being of fishing communities. It draws on two main data sources. The first source is data collected in

Industrial clusters and innovation systems in Africa: Institutions, markets and policy, Oyelaran-Oyeyinka and McCormick (eds), United Nations University Press, 2007, ISBN 978-92-808-1137-7

1998 from anglers, fish traders and small-scale and industrial fish processors (Mitullah, 1999). The fishers, traders and small-scale processors all operated at Uhanya Beach, one of the larger fishing beaches on the Kenyan side of the lake. The industrial fish processors were located in Kisumu and Nairobi. The second source of information for this chapter was additional reading, information gathering and interviews with officials in the Fisheries Department, cooperative society, beach association and two NGOs, one (Osienala) operating locally and the other (ECOVIC) operating regionally. Discussions were also held with a few fisherfolk communities in Uhanya. The chapter also benefited a regional seminar, Sharing Experiences on Poverty Alleviation, organized by Africa Institute for Capacity Development (AICAD) and the Local Agri-Food Systems Conference held in Montpellier, France.

Understanding fisheries management

Earlier research examined fishing in Lake Victoria from the point of view of enterprise clusters and incipient industrialization (McCormick, 1999; Mitullah, 1999). Although the cluster was considered a "complex industrial cluster" because of the interaction of firms of different sizes, it showed little evidence of collective efficiency. The study yielded four major findings: first, that external economies were weak; second, that joint action among the fishermen was ineffective; third, that the joint action of the industrial processors worked for a time, but did not persist; and finally, that there were no common associations.

Although the findings were of interest, they did not easily translate into proposals for remedial action. This may be because the collective efficiency model, which was developed out of the experience of manufacturing industry clusters, is not sufficient to explain the challenges that arise when part of the cluster consists of primary producers depending for their livelihoods on a shared resource. Moreover, although the collective efficiency model recognizes the importance of market access and vertical linkages leading to the market, it is not suited to a full analysis of linkages throughout the production-marketing system.

We, therefore, turn to two additional bodies of literature: works on common-pool resources and the growing literature on value chains.

Common-pool resources

Common-pool resources (CPRs) are resource systems that are both commonly available and subject to depletion or degradation by improper use. More specifically, CPRs include natural and human-constructed re-

Box 10.1 The tragedy of the commons

Hardin (1968) argues that economically rational, individualistic decision-making by users of a common resource will inevitably lead to a tragedy. "Picture a pasture open to all," said Hardin. Each cattle owner will want to maximize gains by keeping as many cattle as possible. But eventually, the carrying capacity of the land will be reached because for each herder, the utility of adding one more animal to his herd is +1. But all of the herders will share the costs of overgrazing, so the herder's loss will be only a fraction of −1. Thus, the herder's rational decision, according to Hardin, "is to add another animal to his herd. And another and another.... But this is the conclusion reached by each and every rational herdsman sharing the commons. Therein is the tragedy."

sources in which exclusion of beneficiaries through physical and institutional means is especially costly, and exploitation by one user reduces resource availability for others (Ostrom and Field, 1999).

Fisheries are a prime example of a common-pool resource. Except for enclosed fish farms, fisheries are open and available to many users. The resource is fugitive: The fish you do not catch today may be caught by someone else tomorrow, encouraging fisherfolk to catch as many as possible rather than try to conserve the resource (Berkes et al. 2002).

Most serious concern about common-pool resources is traceable to Hardin's (1968) seminal article, "The Tragedy of the Commons", in which he asserted that users of the commons are caught in an inevitable process that leads to the destruction of the very resource on which they depend (see box 10.1). Hardin later argued that there were only two solutions to the problem: socialism, in which government imposes good behaviour on those sharing the commons, and a private enterprise system that would replace the common-property system with one of private property rights (Hardin, 1978; Smith, 1981; Welch, 1983).

Critics of Hardin's position have argued that for thousands of years, people have self-organized to manage common-pool resource. Furthermore, users are still devising good long-term, sustainable institutions for governing such resources (see, for example, Ostrom, 1990; Ostrom and Field, 1999; Sekhar 2000).

These critics have pointed to two clear flaws in Hardin's argument. The first is the assumption that all potential users have free and open access to the common resource. In fact, "common property" is not necessarily everyone's property (Berkes et al., 2001; Ciriacy-Wantrup, 1975). Common (or communal) property refers to a specific type of property rights, while open access implies a condition of no property rights at all.

The second flaw in the Hardin argument is that it ignores the social relations that characterize resource users throughout the world (Berkes et al., 2001). As suggested above, resource users over the centuries have developed institutions – rules, norms and customs – governing the use of their common property resources. These are usually deeply rooted in the organization of the community, relying, for example, on clan elders for enforcement and the settlement of disputes. These ensure that individual users do not act as individualistic utility maximizers, but are guided by social values and norms stressing responsibility to the community.

These arguments point to the importance of property rights regimes. To understand the management of common-pool resources, one must know the rules governing their use as well as who makes and who enforces those rules. Four types have been distinguished (see Berkes et al., 2001; Ostrom and Field, 1999):

1. Open access, characterized by the absence of enforced property rights;
2. Group (communal) property, in which resource rights are held by a group of users who can exclude others;
3. Individual (private) property, in which resource rights are held by individuals (or firms) who can exclude others;
4. Government property, in which a government that can regulate or subsidize use holds the resource rights.

Open access regimes are most susceptible to "tragedy". This is because, unless there are very few users, resource depletion by over-use is likely. Other regime types, in contrast, have rules and regulations, which, if properly enforced, can protect the resource from irresponsible use.

Empirical studies show that no single type of property regime works efficiently, fairly and sustainably in relation to all CPRs (Ostrom and Field, 1999). It is therefore crucial to identify the regime that will work best in a given situation. Fisheries management is as much about people as it is about fish and eco-systems. To be effective, therefore, it must take into account the social, economic and political realities of the people using and/or affected by the resource. This realization has led fisheries managers to shift their emphasis away from maximizing the catch to sustaining stocks and eco-systems (Berkes et al., 2001; Jansen et al., 1999).

One strategy that has gained favour is rooted in the vast development literature on participation (see Chambers, 1997; and http://www.ids.ac.uk/particip/). Co-management – as the term suggests – is a partnership in which government, the community of fishers, external agents and other stakeholders share the responsibility and authority for making decisions about the management of a fishery (Berkes et al., 2001). The various forms of co-management combine aspects of communal and government property regimes.

The considerable CPR literature provides considerable insight into the problems and potential solutions of many of the problems arising in the management of such resources. Detailed studies of local institutions designed to manage and preserve common resources highlight the factors that are critical to the organization, sustainability and adaptability of such resources. This literature, however, tends to focus on the users and the immediate social setting within which they work (Ostrom and Field, 1999). Thus, the analysis considers the local community, the local and national governments and other local and national institutions. Yet, in the case of export fisheries, groups that are more distant can exert considerable pressure on the fisherfolk and their resources. To understand this, we turn to the literature on global value chains.

Global value chains

As outlined in chapter 2, a typical value chain consists of four stages: design, supply, production and distribution. Take, for example, the case of frozen fish fillets. The product is "designed" by those who decide which type of fish will be used, whether the fish will be pre-cooked or fresh-frozen, how it will be packaged and so on. The supply stage involves procuring the fish from fisherfolk and acquiring other inputs such as water, salt, preservatives and cooking ingredients. The fillet is then produced by cleaning, washing, cutting, packing and freezing. The final stage – distribution – involves transferring the product through various channels, such as wholesalers and retailers, to the final consumer.

The distinction made in the value chain literature between "buyer-driven" and "producer-driven" chains is useful for this analysis. In buyer-driven chains the buyer of the product rather than its producer exerts the greatest control on the chain's structure and the product's characteristics. Certain food products are increasingly recognized as falling into this category. Recent research on horticulture exports to Europe and the UK, for example, documents the power of the supermarkets in determining product type and quality (see, for example, Dolan, 2002). We will argue that Kenya's Nile perch industry is similarly buyer driven, especially in the chain ending in Europe. In this case, the European Union (EU) is acting as a mediator and standards enforcer between its companies and the Kenyan producers.

Conceptual framework

The concepts and theories found in the common-pool resource literature are central to the following analysis of the changes that are taking place in the Lake Victoria Nile perch industry. Two types of institutions are fundamental to the understanding of the fisheries: the property rights regimes that are or have been in place, and the norms, rules and regulations that are used to manage and preserve them.

In addition, we recognize the fact that most of the perch caught by Kenyan fisherfolk is destined for the European market. This makes the EU a key player who cannot be ignored in the framing of improved management systems. This calls for including in the conceptual framework the notion of a value chain as a set of linked value-adding activities that are influenced or governed by powerful actors within the chain.

Lake Victoria fisheries

As background for the chapter we first examine the trends in fish catch and fish exports from the Lake Victoria fisheries, and then look briefly at how fisheries were managed in the pre-commercial era and how this shifted when government became involved.

Catch and export trends

Lake Victoria is the second-largest freshwater lake in the world, with an area of 68,000 sq km. It is relatively shallow with a maximum depth of 84 metres and a mean depth of 40 metres. The three East African countries share it. The proportion of the Lake for each of the countries is 6, 45 and 49 per cent for Kenya, Uganda and Tanzania, respectively. Nile perch (*Lates niloticus*) is not indigenous to Lake Victoria, but was introduced by the colonial government in 1954 as a means of enhancing the fisheries (Bokea and Ikiara, 2000; Mitullah, 1999).

The introduction and maturation of the Nile perch has contributed to the rapid growth of the Lake Victoria fishing industry. As late as 1981, less than 1,000 metric tons of Nile perch was landed annually; by 1993, total production in the three countries was close to 363,000 tons with 29 per cent landed in Kenya and the rest in Tanzania and Uganda (Goulding, 1997).

Nile perch constitutes over half of the fish landings by weight and nearly three-quarters by value. In 1995, Lake Victoria fisheries yielded 181,888 metric tons of fish, valued at 4.7 million Kenyan shillings. Of this, 102,546 metric tons, valued at KSh3.3 million, was Nile perch (Mitullah, 1999: 5). The balance was mainly tilapia (*Oreochromis niloticus*) and the small, sardine-like omena (*Rastrineobala argentea*). Since much of the latter is retained for domestic consumption, it is estimated that at least 90 per cent of exports of fish and related products are Nile perch (Bokea and Ikiara, 2000).

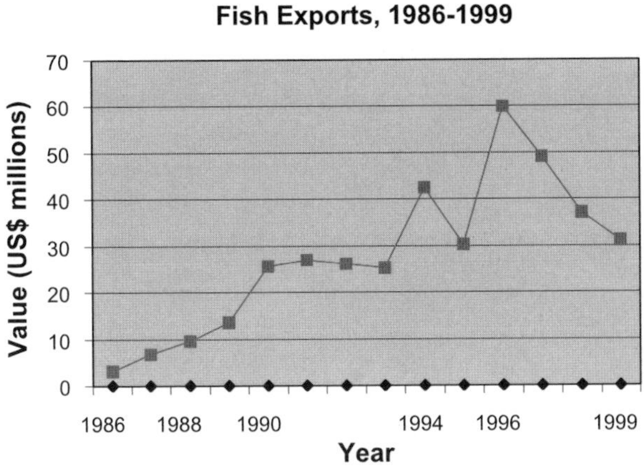

Fish Exports, 1986-1999

Figure 10.1 Fish exports. Source: Statistical abstracts, various years

Fish exports grew rapidly between 1986 and 1996 as markets in the developed countries, especially in the European Union, opened (Spencer et al., 2000). In 1986, the value of Kenya's fish exports was US$3.1 million (see figure 10.1). This grew more than ten-fold to US$42.5 million in 1994, then dipped to US$30.2 million in 1995 before peaking at US$59.9 million in 1996. Between 1996 and 1999, exports dropped by 42 per cent to US$31.1 million, mainly as a result of successive bans on Lake Victoria fish imposed by the European Union (EU).

The EU first banned fish exports from all three East African countries in 1996 following the death of two people in Spain who had eaten salmonella-infected fish exported from Uganda (Mitullah, 1999). The ban was later lifted, but was re-imposed in 1997 after an outbreak of cholera in the Lake region. Again the ban was lifted, only to be renewed in 1999 when pesticide residues were discovered in fish coming from Lake Victoria. Apparently, some anglers, desperate to increase their catch, had begun using pesticides to kill or numb fish.

Exports dropped by 29 per cent in a single year, from US$59.9 million in 1996 to $US49.1 million in 1997. The price of perch also plunged as industrial processors stopped buying fish. Exporters sought other, less fussy markets in the Middle East and elsewhere. Industrial fish processors also began to work individually and together to improve fish handling at all levels to meet the stringent EU standards (Mitullah, 1999).

The ban triggered a critical look at the quality of fish and general management of Lake Victoria fisheries by all stakeholder groups. Fish handling, from point of capture to the market, had to be addressed. The EU inspection missions that followed the bans revealed the unsanitary conditions and poor handling of fish at beaches. The missions also noted the poor disposal methods of fish skeletons and meat trimmings and the substandard factory conditions (Mitullah, 1999a). It is these concerns that have contributed to various institutional responses, which are discussed in this chapter.

The indigenous management system

In order to understand the role fisherfolk communities play, it is worth appreciating the management strategies they applied before external interventions. The fisheries at that time could be categorized as communal property. The clan elders protected that property by establishing and enforcing rules that stated who could fish, when they could fish and what means they could use. The management of fisheries was integrated into the culture and traditions of local communities (Owino, 1999). There was an agreement that fisheries resources had to be managed judiciously and in a sustainable manner. There were rules and regulations safeguarding fishing activities. The clan elder was the custodian of these rules, and any newcomer who wanted to access fisheries had to go through a process of evaluation. Owino observes that "The right to fish was invested in clan elders whose jurisdiction was not only land but also covered the water near the shore. The powers of the elders remain a legacy to date by the very naming of almost all beaches after them." The prefix *ka-* (a Luo word meaning "belonging to") followed by a name of an individual is how most beaches around the shores of Lake Victoria are named.

The communities strictly observed seasonal closures, which occur during the long rains falling between February and May and short rains between September and December. The closed season was known by the clan to be the breeding periods for fish. If any fishing was to be done, it had to occur far offshore because fish came close to the shore to breed. Many of the clans insisted on use of large-meshed equipment (*ohunga*) during the rains, to avoid the capture of fingerlings.

Other restrictions included ownership of canoes and fishing gears. At any one beach, only two fishermen were allowed to own beach seine nets. These individuals had to be of high integrity and had to be willing to give fish to members of the community who were lacking. Fishing was restricted to those who were more than 20 years old and married, as these were considered to be responsible enough to adhere to rules and regulations for conserving the resource.

Fishing was limited to areas near the shore within wetlands and river mouths (Geheb, 1996). The type of fishing gear and equipment available to communities influenced this. Sufficient fish could be found along the shoreline so there was no need to fish beyond the shoreline. Water beyond the shoreline was open to anybody, although available technology was limited, and the waters had strong currents and were infested with crocodiles and hippos (Owino, 1999).

It was common to have immigrant fishermen who stayed for different durations depending on their interest and engagement. The treatment of immigrants was unique. On arrival, such individuals had to report to a clan elder, give details of where they came from, and declare the type and amount of their gear. After the evaluation, they would be required to adhere to the rules and regulations of the local community and stay within the community. This system began collapsing with colonial introduction of formal rules and regulations, which were punitively enforced. The brutal enforcement of regulations relating to fisheries resource shifted responsibility away from the fisherfolk communities into the hands of the state. This changed the property status of the Lake from communal property to state property (Geheb, 1997).

Central government and management of fisheries

One of Hardin's (1978) solutions to the "tragedy" of managing common resources is to bring in an external "Leviathan". This, combined with the general tendency of newly independent African countries to vest central governments with the management of most resources, led to recommendations that government control natural resource systems (see also Ostrom 1990: 9). Kenya is no exception. Until the era of multi-party politics, the government had almost full control of all public institutions and resources. This ostracized most stakeholders from participating in mobilization, planning and management of resources. This section examines policies and institutions of central government management.

The first institutions to manage fisheries were set up during the colonial period. The colonial government established Lake Victoria Fisheries Service (LVFS) in 1947 to manage the fisheries and assist the fishermen. This organization was charged with licensing fishers and ensuring that the right fishing gear was used. It had strict and punitive procedures of enforcement, although it failed to convince the fisherfolk that it was possible to fish all the fish from the lake. The communities failed to understand the reason behind enforcement and continued to use improper gear. This was made worse by a lack of adequate fisheries staff and funding for effective enforcement of regulations. It was the failure to effectively enforce the fishing regulations on fishing gear that brought about the idea of complementing existing stocks with perch to prevent the collapse of the Lake Victoria fishery.

The failure of LVFS to enforce regulations resulted in its disbandment in 1960 and the handing over of fisheries responsibilities to the Lake

Victoria Fisheries Union. The union lasted only until 1964, when the control of fisheries was given to the new Department of Fisheries in independent Kenya. This was the era of populist politics and policies; there were no legally endorsed regulatory measures and the department had limited impact. It aimed at appeasing citizens who had suffered in the hands of colonial masters. The years from 1964 to the early 1970s were characterized by the absence of formal regulations, with informal regulations determining the nature of exploitation of fisheries. The new government did not concentrate on conservation of fisheries as a resource but laid emphasis on marketing and technological improvements. Provisions for management were not clear, thereby creating a lapse in enforcement of regulations. This partly contributed to the corrupt practices experienced in the industry.

As the fisheries became commercialized in the mid-1970s, the relations along the global perch market chain became complex and competitive. Most actors were interested in the gains without being keen on management and sustainability of the resource. In response to the competitive nature of the fisheries, and the dramatic changes brought about by the global perch market boom, the government of Kenya adopted a new Fisheries Act in 1989. The government needed to deal with questions relating to how the new production and processing should be organized and how to strike a balance between fish going for export market and local market.

The Fisheries Act (CAP 378–380) outlines the rules and regulations of the management of Lake Victoria fisheries. It spells out who can fish, where, when and how. The Act gives certain responsibilities to fish scouts: control of illegal fishing gear and methods, dealing with net theft, providing security, collecting fish statistics and checking the licensing of boats and gear (Owino, 1999).

Apart from the Fisheries Act, several other Acts govern the management of fisheries. These include the Cooperative and Land Use Management Acts and provisions of the Department of Social Services of the Ministry of Home Affairs, Heritage and Sports that govern the operations of self-help groups. Cooperatives have been important organizations for agricultural production, primary processing and marketing of agricultural, livestock and fisheries commodities. They serve as vehicles for mobilization of rural and urban savings, which in turn supports productive activities.

Before the new Cooperative Societies Act and Sessional Paper No. 6 of 1996, on Cooperatives in a Liberalised Economy, the government supported the cooperative movement through direct assistance and subsidized services. Under the new Cooperatives Act and the Sessional Paper, the cooperatives are supposed to be free enterprises expected to compete with other private commercial entities in the market (Republic of Kenya, 2002). The impact of this change is still to be assessed, as fishermen continue to opt out of cooperative societies to form groups under the Department of Social Services of the Ministry of Home Affairs, Heritage and Sports. This creates conflict between the two ministries, each struggling to have control over the groups.

Conflict between the two ministries arises because the Fisheries Act provides for the management of beaches by the Fisheries Department, while the Cooperatives Act allows the Cooperative Societies to levy a fee from every quantity of fish sold, but does not obligate the cooperatives to ensure efficient management of the fisheries. The fisheries officers collaborate with the beach associations to undertake this task. The various Acts and provisions are not clear on the responsibilities and relationships among actors. This partly contributes to conflict among the actors, especially between the cooperatives and Department of Social Services officers. These two organizations are key in the management of beaches and marketing of fish. They work closely with the fisheries officials who handle technical aspects of fisheries management.

The new Act and the Sessional Paper are expected to improve the operations of the cooperatives and deal with existing conflicts between the ministry in charge of Cooperatives and the Ministry of Home Affairs, Heritage and Sports. This should enable the government and other stakeholders to deal with the challenges facing the industry, especially those related to the export market and its impact on the livelihoods of fisherfolk.

Current livelihoods and long-term sustainability

Livelihoods are commonly defined as the capabilities, assets (including both material and social resources) and activities required for a means of living (Moser and Norton, 2001). A livelihood is identified as sustainable when it can cope with and recover from stresses and shocks and maintain or enhance capabilities and assets both current and in the future, while not undermining the natural resource base (Carney, 1998; Chambers and Conway, 1992). Principal assets available to the rural poor tend to be land and water (Sobhan, 2001). The fisherfolk communities around the shores of Lake Victoria have relied on the lake resources, especially fishing, for decades. While many of them do have land as an asset, their economic livelihoods are largely based on fishing. It is in this context that this section of the chapter examines the conflict between current livelihoods and long-term sustainability of Lake Victoria fisheries.

Struggle for livelihoods

Rural people typically rely on multiple sources of income to receive their livelihoods. For the fisherfolk households around Lake Victoria, these sources may include cash from sales of fish, farm income, wages from employment, earnings from business and remittances from household members working in urban areas or abroad. Fisherfolk also supplement their cash incomes by drawing directly on the lake for food. Several of these sources have been threatened by changes in Kenya's economic situation and by factors directly related to the commercialization of the fisheries.

The general decline in the Kenyan economy, combined with increases in the cost of basic services such as education and health care, has had an impact on the well being of many households. The Kenyan economy has experienced poor economic performance during the last two decades. The expectations for better economic prospects for the 1990s following the commencement of macroeconomic stabilization measures were not realized. Problems of declining donor funds, poor governance, poor weather and infrastructure, depressed investments, declining tourism activities and poor performance of the manufacturing sector reduced the gross domestic product (GDP) growth to 2.5 per cent between 1990 and 1995 and to 2 per cent between 1995 and 2000 (Kenya, 2002). The downward trend continued until 2000, when the change in GDP growth reached negative 0.3 per cent. Since 2001, there has been improvement, with growth rates of 0.8, 1.2 and 1.8 per cent in 2001, 2002 and 2003, respectively (Republic of Kenya, 2002, 2003, 2004). It is too soon to know whether this represents a real turnaround or simply a slowing of the country's decline. The livelihoods of most households, especially those living in rural areas, have hardly improved. In 1999, incidence of poverty was estimated at 52 per cent with certain regions recording poverty incidence of 60 to 62 per cent (Kenya, 1999). The population living below the poverty line has since increased to 56 per cent, with rural areas having higher figures (Economic Commission for Africa, 2004).

Among other things, this decline means that household income from employment, business and cash crops has stagnated or declined in most parts of Kenya. Changes associated with the Structural Adjustment Programmes of the early 1990s have also had an impact on households' well being. With the introduction of cost-sharing in schools and medical facilities, many people found themselves struggling to find additional cash, simply to maintain their standard of living. Those unable to raise additional funds saw their standards of living fall. The National Coalition Government (NARC) has addressed these two areas by having a policy of free primary education and compulsory health insurance for all Kenyans. The latter is in the process of being made operational.

Nyanza province, the location of Lake Victoria, is one of the worst-hit poverty areas in Kenya. The Kenya Human Development Report notes that the province is poor; its indicators of mortality, health facilities, safe water, sanitation, communication and transportation (UNDP, 2001) are among the worst in the country. Problems in this province are compounded by the high incidence of HIV/AIDS that results in lost incomes and high medical expenses. Growing poverty throughout Kenya has clearly had an impact on the fisherfolk of Nyanza Province. Reduced incomes and increasing expenses give them a strong incentive to maximize their catch. If carried to an extreme, this could result in the sort of tragedy envisioned by Hardin (1968). To understand what needs to be done to arrest such a tragedy, we need to examine factors contributing to the declining fish supply and the management of fisheries.

Declining fish supply

The supply of Nile perch has been declining since about 1991 (Bokea and Ikiara, 2000). The catch, measured in metric tonnage landed, declined by 22 per cent between 1991 and 1996, despite a substantial increase in fishing effort. Furthermore, the size of fish caught has steadily declined. Factors contributing to the reduction of fish supply include over-fishing; illegal fishing gear, including trawlers, which destroy nursery grounds; the perch poaching most smaller fish; and water hyacinth weeds spreading and interfering with the water system. Over-fishing comes because of the failure of fishers to observe regulations, in particular the one relating to "closed season", a period when fishing is forbidden in specified areas. It also occurs when they are too many fishermen fishing in limited waters, as is the case on the shores of Lake Victoria. Kenya has only 6 per cent of the Lake but by 1993 there were about 82,300 fishermen (Kenya, 1994) on the limited water body. By the year 2000, this number had reduced to 30,000 (interview, Fisheries Department). This is partly due to the reduced number of fish in the lake, which is forcing fishers to pursue alternative economic activities.

Second, use of illegal gear by artisan fishermen who do not own motorized boats for deep lake fishing has had a negative impact on the resource. Most of these fishers use small-size fishing net mesh, which results in catching "baby perch". Under-size fish are not returned to the water, but are sold to small-scale processors. While the large-scale industrial processors do not buy "baby perch", they have continuously reduced the sizes of fish they process due to the declining fish sizes. Most processors operate below capacity, with many processing under-size perch. Discussions with the Department of Fisheries quality control manager revealed that about 80 per cent of fish being processed are between 30 and

45 cm, while the regulations require sizes of between 50 and 85 cm. A 50 cm fish weighs about 1.5 kg, but the majority of fish processed are below this size.

Third, the feeding habits of the perch have been blamed for the declining fish supply (Asila and Ogari, 1988; Bwathondi, 1985; Okeyo-Owuor, 1999; Reynolds and Greboval, 1988). Goldschmidt (1992) has observed that the introduction of the perch into Lake Victoria has caused the destruction of about 65 per cent of *Haplochromis* species. Okeyo-Owuor attributes the lack of native fish species to the "shattering" impact of perch predation on native fishes, which have been virtually wiped out, while Ogari indicates that the perch has almost eliminated endemic species and turned cannibalistic, feeding on juvenile perch. The predator nature of the perch can be attributed to the mere fact that all big fish feed on small fish. The only escape for small fish is to avoid areas dominated by big fish. The indigenous *Haplochromis* in Lake Victoria mingled with the perch and eventually disappeared.

Fourthly, the spread of the water hyacinth may have contributed to the declining fish supplies. This view, however, remains controversial. The fisherfolk have argued that since the invasion of the weed, native species that had been depleted have returned. On the other hand, observers have noted that the weed interferes with fishing, especially free movement in the lake and fish landing sites.

Poor management of Lake Victoria fisheries has exacerbated the problem of declining fish supplies. We turn now to an analysis of the institutions and practices of management, noting that these have changed significantly with the transformation of the fisheries from a subsistence to a commercial activity.

Commercialization of the fisheries

The last two decades of the twentieth century witnessed the commercialization of the Lake Victoria fisheries. "Commercialization" as a concept in this study signifies the transformation of a fishery from an activity that is primarily subsistence to one that is primarily commercial. The transformation involves a number of specific changes, as depicted in table 10.1. The poverty of the fisherfolk, the commercialization of the fisheries and the ineffectiveness of the Kenyan government threaten to bring about a second change to a "free for all" or open-access regime.

Commercialization has involved at least six separate transformations. The first is the shift from a multi-species fishery comprising 300 species of fish to a fishery consisting of just 3 species, one of which dominates commercial fishing (Bokea and Ikiara, 2000; Ogutu-Ohwayo, 1990; Witte

Table 10.1 Impact of commercialization on fisheries management

Transformation	Impact on Management
Focus on Nile perch	Loss of bio-diversity
Presence of outsiders	Clan management systems no longer appropriate or effective
	Outsiders need to be incorporated into management system
Urbanization of beaches	Significant non-fishing activities
	Women's involvement, especially in processing and trading
	Pollution
Rise of large-scale processors and traders	New ethnic dimensions
	Change in power balance
	Change in economic balance
	Loss of fish for local consumption
Heightened competition	Over-fishing
	Development of market for "baby" perch
	Cooperative no longer sole buyer
	Lack of joint action
Emergence of EU market	Further change in power balance
	Significant rise in quality standards required for participation in export market
	Need for "Competent Authority" to negotiate with EU and ensure quality of fish

et al., 1992). Geheb (1997) observes that some 80 per cent of the multi-species belonged to the smaller *Haplochromis* (locally referred to as *fulu*) flock. Other species included mainly two larger species of the Nile tilapia (*ngege* and *mbiru*), the lung fish (*kamongo* or *mamba*), the cat fish (*mumi*) and *Labeo victorianus* (*ningu*) and *Rastrineobola argenta* (*omena*).

Since the beginning of the 1970s the commercial value of the perch has overshadowed other species. Hundreds of fish species have disappeared, as both government and fisherfolk communities focused on the perch. At the introduction of the perch in 1954, it was argued on the one hand that *Haplochromis* had little commercial value, and it was deemed a "trash fish". On the other hand, it was observed that where the perch was a native, it co-existed with tilapia species and therefore did not pose a threat to commercially important tilapia stocks in Lake Victoria (Anderson, 1961).

There were also counter-arguments to the introduction of the perch by those who contended that the perch was not efficient. The amount of fish a Nile perch has to eat to produce a single kilogram of flesh is far greater than the amount of vegetative matter a tilapia has to eat to produce an equal amount of flesh (Fryer, 1960). The commercial aspect of the perch seems to have won the day, making it a dominant species in the lake. The tilapia also has commercial value, but it has nevertheless declined in relative importance from 23 per cent of landings in 1990 to only 6.5 per cent in 1996 (Bokea and Ikiara, 2000). The third type of fish, omena, has gained in commercial importance with the introduction of a fish meal-based animal-feeds industry in Kenya in the 1990s.

The second transformation has been the growing presence of outsiders in the fishing communities. Among a sample of 30 fishers covered in a study of Uhanya Beach, only 8 came from the locality. The rest were drawn from several districts of Nyanza province as well as from Uganda and Tanzania (Mitullah, 1999a). Household censuses of the residents of the beach also showed that the majority of residents were outsiders who had come to Uhanya for business. Most of them had maintained their links with their home areas where they belonged to either business-related associations or kinship/local-area associations. Most of those questioned felt that it was not important to come from the local area.

When outsiders were few, they were easily integrated into existing clan authority systems. As they have increased in numbers, clan management systems were no longer appropriate or effective. Local communities believe that many problems facing them, including depletion of fish by use of illegal gear, mismanagement of fishing cooperatives and immoral behaviour prevailing within the beaches, are the result of the collapse of the indigenous management system.

As the clan management system declined, the institutions of government grew in importance. As we will see in the next section, however, these proved to be inadequate to the task of managing the fisheries effectively. Consequently, communities were unclear about whether they should follow the state regulations or the informal clan rules and regulations. This created a regulatory vacuum, thereby establishing a condition of open access that threatens the very existence of the fisheries (Geheb, 1997).

Thirdly, commercialization has changed the nature of the fisheries, especially at landing beaches. Increased population and urban forms of development began to occur as different actors moved into the beaches. These include trading fish, retailing food and household goods, selling prepared food and offering various consumer services. Notably absent, however, are social services such as schools, health care and infrastructure. Housing, which is quite important for outsiders, quickly became a commercial asset within the beaches. Most of the dwelling units, however, are poorly constructed and lack basic facilities such as toilets and bathrooms. They are largely composed of one room constructed of mud (or corrugated iron sheets) floors and walls with different forms of roofing materials. Most of the settlements do not have electricity or an adequate road network. The road network is problematic during rainy season and interferes with both fish marketing and general transport of passengers and commodities.

Women as well as men have taken up business activities at the beaches. At first, women were able to buy good quality perch or tilapia, which they processed at the beaches by frying or sun drying and sold either locally or in nearby towns. The commercialization of the Nile perch and depletion of tilapia supplies has changed this. Many women now have access only to the leftovers from the fish processing plants. In Obunga, Kisumu District, for example, over 800 women make their living by deep-frying fish skeletons (Mitullah, 1999).

A serious consequence of the increased activity is the pollution of the beaches. The lack of sanitary facilities is the main culprit, but also problematic are the lack of garbage collection, the increased vehicle traffic and the introduction into the area of chickens and goats.

Fourthly, commercialization of Lake Victoria fisheries has attracted large-scale industrial fish processors and different types of traders. Others attracted include middle persons, outsider fishermen and hired fishing crews who do not own any gear but work for absentee fisherpersons. The latter are a unique category of actors attracted by commercialization. They purchase fishing gear and equipment and hire fishermen and skilled managers to run their business ventures while they stay away from the investment and only make occasional visits.

The large-scale industrial processors and traders form a dominant class of investors. The large-scale processors in particular are making significant profits from the global perch market. By 1999, there were 22 firms, with 15 located around Lake Victoria, 4 in Nairobi and 3 in Mombasa (Mitullah, 1999b). At the beginning of the perch boom most of these firms were located in Nairobi and Mombasa. However, the increase in fishing requirements and the opening of the foreign market pushed a number of firms to relocate to the shores of Lake Victoria (Abila and Jansen, 1997). Since our study in 1999, new factories have come up while others are dormant.

The introduction of large-scale processors into the fishery has drastically altered the social, economic and political balance. The processors are ethnically different and economically and politically more powerful than the local fisherfolk. In 1998 the factories ranged in size from 35 to over 200 workers. Most were owned by Kenyan Asians. Of three African-owned factories, only one was owned by a person from the Lake region. One large-scale trader was also from the local area, but others were non-locals based in Nairobi and other distant towns. Perhaps more important than the ethnic difference is the shift in the power balance among the various actors. The large-scale processors and traders have the power to determine prices and to give or withhold necessary inputs.

Ogutu has argued that the large-scale industrial processors are virtually becoming the owners of equipment and mortgaging the fishermen. He argues further that the reluctance of commercial banks to extend credit to ordinary fishermen reduces their ability to compete (Ogutu, 1988). Cooperatives, which should provide alternative finance, are generally weak, while the informal credit by traders and intermediaries, which is dominant in Asia, is not well developed within the fishing clusters of Lake Victoria (Mitullah, 1999a). Market dynamics compel the cooperatives to enter into a patron-client relationship with the large-scale processors and traders. These relationships include credit, supply of gear and purchase of fish in the lake. During the pre-perch era, most of the fishing gear was owner-operated, with the owners in charge of the boats and fishing operations. Others who worked with such owners possessed their own gear (Jansen, 1997). Commercialization has almost reversed the pattern with as many as 83 per cent of men participating in fishing activities being merely crew, owning neither the vessel nor the fishing gear (Asowa-Okwe, nd).

Fifthly, commercialization has resulted in heightened competition, which has in turn created new challenges for fisheries management. The first has already been discussed. The competition for fish has encouraged the use of improper gear and methods. In desperation for fish, fishers have used improper sizes of nets and at times chemicals, while the large-scale industrial fish processors have used trawlers, which are prohibited in Lake Victoria Kenya waters. The improper gear and methods have contributed to the depletion of fish quantities because they are not selective. In particular, the use of chemicals for catching fish has been one of the worst experiences of the Lake Victoria fisheries. It not only captures fish, but also makes fish a health hazard. This is an outcome of a thoughtless competition and exploitation of a common pool resource.

As a result of this, a market has developed in "baby perch", i.e., perch that are smaller than the allowed size. Although their processing for local consumption provides a short-term solution to the lack of food security in the region, it undermines the long-term viability of the fishery and thus poses a serious management problem.

Another consequence of heightened competition is the development of new buyers. Private traders have emerged to compete with the cooperative for fish. Some of these operate independently, but many are buying agents for particular industrial fish-processors. Working hand-in-hand with the large-scale processors, they serve to hold down the price of raw fish (Mitullah, 1999).

Heightened competition has also affected the industrial fish processors. These were observed to be secretive and highly suspicious of one another (Mitullah, 1999). As a result, they were very reluctant to work together even on issues of mutual concern. However, as discussed later, the European Union ban on fish from East Africa pushed the processors to start the Association of Fish Processors and Exporters of Kenya (AFIPEK) (Henson and Mitullah, 2004).

The last aspect of the transformation of the Lake Victoria fisheries is the emergence of the EU as the prime export market. This poses at least three challenges to the management of the fisheries. The first is that the power balance discussed above has been further changed with the addition of a powerful external buyer to the value chain. Because of its economic power, the EU can exert pressure on every other actor, from the industrial processors down to the individual fisherfolk. Its ultimate weapon – one that it has used on Kenya three times in the past five years – is to ban imports of fish from particular places.

As a result of this power, the EU has been able to raise the quality standards required for participation in the export market. These standards affect not only the processes at the exporting factories but also the handling of the fish in the boats, on the landing beaches and while in transit. Furthermore, the EU has been able to require the governments of exporting countries to name a single "Competent Authority" to negotiate with the EU and to ensure the quality of any fish coming from that country.

The entry of large-scale industrial fish processors and their agents into the market has meant no fish for households and other traders unless the large-scale processors have enough fish. The level of household consumption of fish has changed during the last ten years. The Food and Agriculture Organisation (FAO) has warned about the detrimental effects a large export of fish may have on people who depend upon fish (Greboval, 1992). Household consumption has not only been complicated by perch exports, but also the fact that the indigenous fishing communities prefer tilapia to the Nile perch, which species' predation has reduced the number of the former. Jansen (1997) observes that many of the consumers living in the fishing communities near the lake dislike the "oily and fat fish". This has been changing as food insecurity becomes intensive, and better forms of local fish processing develop.

Jansen (1997) points out that fishers are no longer able to take fish home for consumption and fish consumption is just a few times a week while before commercialization it was part of the daily diet. Other studies (Bokea and Ikiara, 2000; Owino, 1999) done with the support of ICUN (the World Conservation Union on Lake Victoria fisheries) show the deprivation of the fisherfolk communities of their local resource as the global markets take control. The fisherfolk have had to adopt new strategies, which include a three-pronged approach to livelihoods, concentrating on fishing, farming and informal employment.

The transformation itself is neither good nor bad. The problem is that the institutions necessary to support the transformation failed to develop appropriately. Partly this is related to the general corruption that crept into government and private institutions from the late 1970s, exacerbated in the 1990s by general economic decline that resulted in a drop of real salaries paid to government officials.

Fisheries challenged

Meeting export-market requirements, especially those governing food exports to European countries, is a challenge for any developing country. This section describes in some detail the particular requirements imposed by the EU and then discusses some of the problems faced by the fishery, especially government actors.

Challenges of export-market requirements

The liberalization of trade in agricultural and food products has shifted attention on technical measures such as food safety regulations, labelling requirements and quality and compositional standards (Spencer et al., 2000). While liberalization is expected to open markets, those participating in the chain are recognizing that technical measures can act, either explicitly or implicitly, as a barrier to trade in a similar manner to tariffs and quantitative restrictions (Messerlin and Zarrouk, 1999; Sykes, 1995; Vogel, 1995).

The emergence of the European Union market as a buyer-driven value chain established mandatory standards for those interested in selling to the market. This caused a change in the power balance. The three East African countries did not have a chance to bargain but had to respond to the EU health safety regulations by revising fishing regulations in order to integrate the EU requirements under EU Hygiene Directive 91/493/EEC.

The EU hygiene directive covers the entire supply chain: fish and fishery products, fishing vessels, health checks and certification, quality of water and laboratory and methods of analysis and limits. These regulations are said to be more stringent than those required by other markets such as Israel, Japan, Singapore and the United Arab Emirates. In Kenya, an area of concern has been hygiene standards on boats and landing sites, many of which lack jetties, potable running water, cooling facilities and fencing.

The EU requirements have an effect on the quality of fish, and hence the emphasis by the EU on a Competent Authority (CA) that ensures that fish destined for export complies with EU hygiene requirements. The European Commission undertakes spot checks of the CA to ensure that task is done satisfactorily.

During the year 2000 the Department of Fisheries of the Ministry of Agriculture and Rural Development became the CA responsible for quality assessment under the Fish Quality Assurance Regulations 2000. The responsibilities of a CA include assessment of hygiene levels in the boats, landing sites and processing factories; certifying fish exports; and monitoring lake pollution for heavy metals and pesticides, among others. The CA is also responsible for testing samples of fish and water quality from factories and beaches. This is aimed at ensuring that beaches and processing factories are hygienically managed, water is treated and has no pathogens and fish collection points have sanitation facilities, are fenced, paved and with adequate drainage system.

The EU requires that the CA use an accredited laboratory for analysing water and fish samples. The Kenyan government still does not have a single laboratory for testing microbiological and pesticide residues. The CA, with the support of the Lake Victoria Environmental Programme funded by the World Bank and other donors, has constructed a fish quality-control laboratory in Kisumu. The facility undertakes the quality-control checks and monitoring (Samaki News, 2002). Meanwhile, a number of laboratories have been used for analysing water and fish samples, although it took a while to find an institution with a laboratory capable of analysing pesticide residues in an manner acceptable to the EU. After a number of assessments, the EU accepted Kenya Plant Health Inspection Service laboratory as having the necessary capacity and capability for accurate pesticide residue analysis.

Although the government, in collaboration with other stakeholders, has been developing strategies for responding to the EU requirements and efficient co-management of fisheries, there has been difficulty in addressing all the issues. This is because of poor economic performance, fisherfolk's attitude, conflicts of interest and corruption among others. Upgrading landing sites is costly, but absolutely necessary for continued export to the EU. Reliable estimates put the average cost of meeting basic requirements at a single landing beach at US$100,000. The basic requirements are fencing, banda, a potable water supply, rudimentary fish handling equipment, paving, toilets and cold boxes. Further improvements, including electricity supply, an ice-making plant, access road upgrading and a landing jetty, raise the investment to over US$300,000 per site (Henson and Mitullah, 2004). The government cannot afford to undertake such investments for all beaches, but has committed itself to work closely with the private sector and donors to develop a realistic plan for improvement of fishing infrastructure (Kenya, 2003).

Problems of enforcement

Both the Fisheries and Cooperative departments have failed to efficiently serve the fisherfolk and manage beaches. Owino (1999) observes that the Fisheries Act has not been effectively implemented. This is mainly due to poor remuneration for fisheries staff, especially the scouts, and lack of an enabling environment for performing their duties (Abila, 1998; Geheb, 1997). The fish scouts are few, over-worked and poorly paid. In 1999 the salary of a fish scout was equivalent to US$50–60 per month, while the bribes a fish scout received to allow fishermen to go against the provisions of the Act amounted to US$250 (Owino, 1999).

Corruption has been a major problem in Kenya and has largely contributed to poor governance experienced in most public institutions. The phenomenon permeates the entire socio-economic and political fabric of the nation and poses problems of monumental proportions to its future (Kibwana et al., 1996). Since the shift to multi-party politics, a number of initiatives are in place to address corrupt practices. They include the Kenya Anti-Corruption Authority (KACA) which was disbanded on the grounds that it was unconstitutionally established, and a Parliamentary Select committee on Corruption and other related committees (Kibwana et al., 2001). There has also been a call for the establishment of an ombudsman to deal with mal-administration, especially in public institutions (Mitullah et al., 1998). Since the disbanding of KACA, the government has enacted the Anti Corruption and Economic Crimes Act of 2003. The Act established the Kenya Anti-Corruption Commission (KACC), which has replaced KACA. KACC is a neutral body with powers to investigate and prosecute corruption cases and is answerable to Parliament (CLARION, 2004).

Taking the above into consideration, the fisheries are not an exception in corrupt practices. Mal-administration in public institutions is common in Kenya and includes bias, neglect, inattention, delay, incompetence, ineptitude, perversity, turpitude and arbitrariness, among other problems. In an attempt to bypass some of these malpractices, the public get lured into engaging in corrupt practices, such as bribing the fisheries officials to either facilitate processes they want concluded or to go against rules and regulations.

The gains in the global perch market have exposed the scouts to manipulation as they attempt to implement provisions of the Fisheries Act. Mitullah's study revealed that the fish scouts were themselves going against the provisions of the Act. They not only condoned the use of improper gear and methods, but some of them owned boats and used improper gear and methods themselves. Fish landed by those using improper gear and methods was sold and processed with the full knowledge of the scouts, while others bribe them to go against the closed fishing and spawning period (Mitullah, 1999b).

Trawling, which was banned, was being done with the knowledge of senior fisheries and government provincial administration officers (Mitullah, 1999b). Although Owino (1999) argues that the real wage of fish scouts was higher before the perch boom, it seems the scouts, like many others, have been keen on making gains out of the perch. In any case, before the perch boom, the Lake Victoria fishery was largely a subsistence economy. It could hardly sustain the fishers and their households. This explains why there was no abuse of office by fish scouts before the commercialization of the fisheries.

The other shortcoming of the Fisheries Act is the lack of integration of the fisherfolk in the management of fisheries, a responsibility that was inherent among the fisherfolk communities. During the year 2000, a meeting of stakeholder groups, including the fisherfolk, was convened in order to agree on a co-management approach to the fisheries. The Permanent Secretary, Ministry of Agriculture and Rural Development participated in the meeting. The meeting observed that the absence of stakeholder participation in fishery management had contributed to the poor management, especially of beaches. During the meeting, consultations were made with fisherfolk on how to deal with use of improper gear, poaching and quality control issues. This was a landmark meeting in terms of addressing the issues affecting the industry.

Apart from the shortcoming of the fisheries officials, retrenchment of civil servants has made the situation worse. The fish scouts have been retrenched, leaving a single scout responsible for six beaches. This is an enormous task considering that the beaches are not close to each other and the scouts do not have any means of transport. At the same time, the cooperatives have been very weak, partly due to the tight control by the government in the past, and their inability to efficiently serve the membership. The current development plan has observed that the cooperative sector is faced with weak marketing structures, poor management and leadership capacity and a weak capital base (Kenya Development Plan, 2002).

Changing fisheries management

The ban on fish exports, challenges of export requirements and the desire to access global markets have contributed to changes in the management of fisheries. This sub-section highlights some of the problem areas of management and how stakeholders are addressing the major issues of concern.

The failure of institutions charged with fisheries management has resulted in a search for improved management approaches that integrate all stakeholder groups, including the fisherfolk. The government, through the Fisheries Department, is addressing the issue through co-management. This includes training fisheries officers, a pilot project covering 16 beaches, establishment of a Beach Management Committee and Beach Improvement Units. These processes are largely driven by the Department of Fisheries. A number of non-governmental organizations (NGOs) and community-based organizations (CBOs) are also working with the fisherfolk and the government in addressing the issues.

In total, 20 beach inspectors have been trained to manage the handling of fish and ensure proper sanitation at the 10 beaches where fish for exports is expected to be sourced. The 10 beaches fall among the 16 pilot beaches. At the same time, the Common Market for Eastern and Southern Africa and FAO have been offering training to senior fisheries inspectors on quality management systems. So far, there is no specific training institution for fisheries, as the one institute established for these purposes in Naivasha has been converted into a wildlife-protection training institute.

The government has designated 16 beaches for improvement, of which 10 are set aside as landing sites for fish destined for exports. The beaches will be paved; have soak pits, septic tanks and drainage systems to accommodate sipping trucks. Unpaved compounds attract flies and can possibly pollute water and fish, while sand is a physical hazard to food.

Ten million Kenyan shillings have been allocated for building the capacity of the fisherfolk within the 16 pilot beaches. So far, training of fisherfolk and other stakeholders on management and appraisal of activities has been done. The trainings have exposed the fisherfolk to the requirements for good fisheries management. This includes awareness of fish quality and appropriate gear and methods, as well as training on how to change leadership within existing local governance structures. Overall, the trainings emphasize the need for fisherfolk to take full management of the fisheries. They should not wait for government or other external actors but should ensure that the bad fishing practices stop, sanitation on the beaches is satisfactory and sustainable management systems are in place.

Through training, the fisherfolk communities are expected to come up with action plans on how they want to manage the fisheries. This approach to management and the on-going training are the first stakeholder approach to co-management of fisheries. Similar approaches are being encouraged in other beaches, but without any direct funding. If these pilot sites prove successful, the Fisheries Department expects to extend the programme to some of the other 298 listed landing beaches on Lake Victoria. However, the fisheries officials conducting the trainings have lamented that it takes a long time to change the community's way of thinking and undertaking their activities. While this may be valid, indigenous approaches of managing fisheries have to be recognized and integrated in the new forms of managing fisheries.

Lake Victoria Management Programme (LVMP) has been assisting the fisheries department in managing fisheries. Since its establishment, the organization has been providing support to fisherfolk communities. The support has included fencing of beaches, improving road networks, sanitation and construction of toilets and dispensaries. Some of the facilities developed, such as dispensaries, are still to be equipped and put in full use. During our follow-up survey, LVMP was providing patrol boats, to be used for ensuring security and conservation of Lake resources. This is expected to also reduce the use of improper gear and methods.

The fisheries officers in charge of Beach Management Units have been worried about how to ensure sustainable management of fisheries. It has been observed that at a practical level the fisheries department has to deal with two conflicting forces – ensuring livelihoods of fishing communities who rely on fish caught using improper gear and methods, and enforcing the regulations in order to sustain the resource. This point was elaborated by noting that it is difficult to sustain fisheries and maintain a human face. The latter implies flexibility in enforcing regulations by allowing survivalist fisherfolk to keep on using improper gear and methods. This is a conflict that can be solved only by closely working with the fisherfolk and coming up with a compromise situation that is respected by all parties.

Another step has been the establishment of a Beach Improvement Committee (BIC). The committee is expected to look into the issues related to the ten fish landing beaches designated for sourcing fish for exports and is charged with identifying what needs to be improved per the EU requirements for fish exports. Some of the thoughts and options being examined include levying the processors a fee for beach improvement. However, the primary concern of the department is the limited fish supply. The committee is composed only of the officials of the Fisheries Department and the large-scale industrial processors. Having a BIC limited to fisheries officials and fish processors is not sustainable. All actors involved in fisheries, especially the key primary stakeholder group (fisherfolk), have to be part of the improvement team.

Toward co-management

Policies and management of the fisheries in Kenya are changing. The current Development Plan indicates that one of the sector policy priorities will be co-management for cost-effective utilization and management of fishery resources (Kenya Development Plan, 2002). The plan further observes that there will be devolution of planning and decision-making in the fisheries management to the fisheries stakeholders through co-management. Other planned strategies include improvement of basic infrastructure for fishing, fish landing, fish processing, transportation, storage and capacity building through provision of extension services and training of stakeholders, among others. This section discusses some of the local emerging institutions in fisheries management and reflects on the issue of co-management. In particular, it examines how the fisherfolk are involved in the management of fisheries using different forms of institutions.

Emerging institutions

Apart from the planned policy interventions, some public and civil institutions are emerging. The government and related arms, bilateral donors, international agencies, cooperative societies and civil society organizations, including community-based organizations, are all engaging in management of fisheries. Even the industrial processors have joined to deal with the critical issues facing them. Most of these institutions recognize the fisherfolk as the centrepiece of strategies aimed at improving the management of Lake Victoria fisheries.

While there are many spontaneous strategies being put in place for managing fisheries, the landmark was the meeting between the government fisheries officials and fisherfolk communities in 2001. During the meeting, which was graced by the Permanent Secretary, Ministry of Agriculture and Rural Development, the fisherfolk came up with proposals for managing Lake resources. They identified breeding grounds and poor fishing methods. They further requested the government restrict fishing of some fish species, which was immediately done. However, discussions with the fisherfolk at the beaches noted that although the ban had minimized illegal fishing, in some areas poaching continued. At Uhanya beach, the beach association argued that the ban was problematic since it covered only Kenya and not the other two East African countries. In their analysis, outsiders (Ugandans and Tanzanians) were making gains on the Kenya ban.

Management of the Lake Victoria fisheries needs combined and coordinated effort of the three countries. This is what the Lake Victoria Fisheries Organisation (LVFO), LVMP and East Africa for Management of Lake Victoria Resources (ECOVIC) are attempting to do. The East African Communities adopted the convention for establishing LVFO in 1994. The convention came to force on 30 November 1999 with the main objective of fostering cooperation among the three East African countries. The organization's key objective is to harmonize national measures for the sustainable utilization of living resources of the lake and to develop and adopt conservation and management measures. The organization is charged with a number of responsibilities, including the proper management and optimum utilization of the fisheries and other resources of the lake (LVFO, 2003).

ECOVIC is a membership-based organization with members drawn from the fisherfolk-registered CBOs and NGOs. It has headquarters in Arusha, Tanzania, and representatives in each district bordering the lake. The establishment of the organization was influenced by Osienala (Friends of the Lake), a Kenyan NGO that has been working with fisherfolk communities for the last decade. ECOVIC was conceptualized in a meeting for East Africa held in 1998 and formally registered in 2000. Currently the organization is in the process of establishing its various organs. The organization has a goal of addressing socio-economic and political issues of the fisherfolk, with a major focus on advocacy and lobbying.

Apart from the joint efforts of CBOs and NGOs, individual fisherfolk communities are making deliberate efforts to address issues relating to Lake resources, including the management of beaches. Under co-management strategy, the fisherfolk communities are to actively participate in the management of the Lake Victoria resources. A number of examples of such initiatives exist. In Takawiri Island the fisherfolk initiative has realized employment of 40 people to manage the beach, built eight classrooms and hired three teachers. The community is also educating 30 orphans and has opened a special account for future orphans. They are also building a dispensary and are planning to construct a water system for the island. Another fisherfolk initiative is illustrated by the Kanam Fisherfolk Community Development Network. The network is composed of communities drawn from a number of beaches who owe their origin to one forefather, Anam. The network aims at developing Kanam areas and is supported by Homa Hills Centre and a group of consultants.

The EU threat to large-scale industrial processors resulted in the formation of an association, the Kenya Association of Fish Processors and Exporters (AFIPEK), registered in May 2000. The association works closely with the government in ensuring that the quality standards are achieved and respected. The association has participated in a number of interventions aimed at sustainable management and quality control. Some of these include the drafting and launch of the Kenyan fish industry code of practice; the testing, compliance and verification of the quality control conditions which led to the lifting of the ban on fish from Lake Victoria; and the rehabilitation of the fish landing beaches along the shores of Lake Victoria (Samaki News, 2002).

These initial management efforts, combined with the various government-facilitated actions, have potential to improve management of Lake Victoria fisheries, as reflected in the conclusions below.

Conclusions

In approximately three decades, the Lake Victoria fisheries have been transformed from a predominantly subsistence resource to one that is integrated into a global value chain. In this process, the combination of poverty in the fishing community, heightened competition and an ineffective regulatory regime threatened to turn the resource into an open access regime and, ultimately, into a tragedy. There are signs, however, that tragedy can be averted.

The evidence discussed in this chapter indicates that the institutions necessary for co-management of Lake Victoria Fisheries are emerging. The government has recognized the need to involve all stakeholders in management of the fisheries resource. This is being done through a combined effort of the government, international organizations and the civil society organizations. In particular, steps are being taken to involve the fisherfolk once again in management of the resource. Through these joint efforts, the fisherfolk are being sensitized, trained and involved in the planning and management of fisheries. So far, response from the fisherfolk is positive. This is expected to increase their access to Lake Victoria fisheries and to assist in resolving the conflicting forces of sustainable fishery management of fisheries and the livelihoods of fisherfolk communities who rely on fish caught using improper gear and methods.

External buyers are also exerting considerable influence as discussed in the section dealing with challenges of export requirements. At the same time, the industrial fish processors, who are key to the chain and have a bigger stake, have begun working with each other through their association. They are also working with the government through the Beach Improvement Committees and with other stakeholders to ensure that the global market requirements are met. These are signs that most of those participating in the global export chain are making attempts to respond to global market requirements or risk falling out of the chain.

In spite of the concerted efforts, many problems remain. The unequal power of the different stakeholders and corruption that pervades Kenyan society could result in a perverse outcome. Of particular concern is the unregulated growth at the beaches and the inability to provide relevant services and infrastructure, maintain law and order and ensure moral behaviour. Urban populations within the beaches do not have recreational options and often turn to alcohol and casual social relations, which are problematic in this era of HIV/AIDS. At the same time, urban life within the beaches has further marginalized the fisherfolk who are not performing well in the global export perch chain. They view the outsiders residing within the beaches as the cause of their marginalization and no longer take steps to integrate them into their communities.

Among the fisherfolk communities and in the global market perch chain, women are quite disadvantaged. As observed in the section dealing with commercialization of the fisheries, they have been reduced to processing skeletons and other fish waste, selling perch rejected by industrial fish processors or "baby perch" poached by equally marginalized fishermen. Co-management strategies have to ensure equity of access to the fisheries resource and protect the interests of all stakeholders but with a keen interest on the fisherfolk.

These conclusions reveal the need for further research in three particular areas. First, there is need for continued tracking of the effectiveness of the management of the fisheries at different levels. This will include obtaining data from all stakeholders, but especially the fisherfolk, about their level of satisfaction with changes made. Secondly, there is need to know more about fisherfolk's livelihood strategies and level of household income and well-being, and last the need to trace the fish value chains from their origins in Lake Victoria to the destinations in various countries in order to identify the value addition at each stage. Such an analysis might assist the fisherfolk to understand the dynamics of the chain, obtain a larger share of the chain profits, and change their attitude on the management of the fisheries as a common pool resource.

REFERENCES

Abila, R. O. (1998) "Four Decades of the Nile Perch Fishery in Lake Victoria: Technological Development, Impacts and Policy Options for Sustainable Utilisation", in G. H. Howard and S. Mutindi, eds, *Water Hyacinth, Nile Perch and Pollution: Issues for Ecosystem Management in Lake Victoria*, Nairobi: IUCN EARO, 26–48.

Abila, R. O. and Eirik G. Jansen (1997) "From Local to Global Markets: The Fish Exporting and Fishmeal Industries of Lake Victoria – Structure, Strategies and Socio-economic Impacts in Kenya", IUCN Report No. 2, Nairobi.

Anderson, A. M. (1961) "Further Observations Concerning the Proposed Introduction of Nile Perch into Lake Victoria", *East African Agricultural and Forestry Journal* 26(4): 195–201.

Asila, A. A. and J. Ogari (1988) "Growth Parameters and Mortality Rates of Nile Perch (*Lates niloticus*) Estimated from Length-Frequency Data in Nyanza Gulf (Lake Victoria)", Fish. Rep. 389, Nairobi: FAO, 272–87.

Asowa-Okwe (nd) "Capital Conditions of Fish Labourers in Lake Kyoga and Lake Victoria Canoe Fisheries in Uganda", in Mahmood Mamdani and Joe

Oloka-Onyango, eds, *Studies in Living Conditions, Popular Movements and Constitutionalism*, Jep Book 2.

Berkes, F., R. Mahon, P. McConney, R. Pollnac and R. Pomeroy (2001) *Managing Small-scale Fisheries*, Ottawa: International Development Research Centre.

Bokea, C. and M. Ikiara (2000) "The Macroeconomy of the Export Fishing Industry in Lake Victoria (Kenya)", IUCN Report No. 7, Nairobi.

Bwathondi, P. O. J. (1985) "The Future of Floating Cage Culture in Tanzania", paper presented at IFS aquaculture meeting in Africa, Kisumu, Kenya, 7–11 October.

Carney, D. (1998) "Implementing the Sustainable Rural Livelihood Approach", in D. Carney, ed., *Sustainable Rural Livelihoods: What Contributions Can We Make?* London: Department for International Development, 3–23.

Centre for Law and Research International (CLARION) (2004) *Kenya State of Corruption Report*, Issue No. 10, Nairobi: CLARIPRESS.

Chambers, R. (1997) *Whose Reality Counts? Putting the Last First*, London: Intermediate Technology Publications.

Chambers, R. and G. Conway (1992) "Sustainable Rural Livelihoods: Practical Concepts for the 21st Century", Discussion Paper 296, Sussex: Institute of Development Studies.

Ciriacy-Wantrup, S. V. and R. C. Bishop (1975) "'Common Property' as a Concept in Natural Resources Policy", *Natural Resources Journal* 15: 713–27.

Dolan, C. and J. Humphrey (2002) "Changing Governance Patterns in the Trade in Fresh Vegetables between Africa and the United Kingdom", paper presented at a workshop on Export Horticulture and Livelihood Strategies, Nairobi, Kenya, 30 April.

Economic Commission for Africa (2004) "Economic Report on Africa", ERA.

Fryer, G. (1960) "Concerning Proposed Introduction of Nile Perch in Lake Victoria", *East African Agricultural and Forestry Journal*, April.

Geheb, K. (1997) "Regulators and Regulated: Fisheries Management Options and Dynamics in Kenya's Lake Victoria Fishery", Ph.D. thesis, University of Sussex, School of African and Asian Studies.

Goldschmidt, T. (1992) "Reproductive Strategies, Subtrophic Niche Differentiation and the Role of Competition for Food in *Haplochromide cichlids (Pisces)* from Lake Victoria, Tanzania", *Annales-Musee Royal de l'Afrique Centrale Sciences Zoologiques (Belgium)* 257: 119–131.

Goulding, I. (1997) "Perch on a Precepice", *Sea Food International*, April.

Greboval, D. and P. Mannini (1992) "The Fisheries of Lake Victoria: Review of Basic Data", UNDP/FAO Regional Project, Inland Fisheries Planning RAF/87/099/WP/16/92, Rome: Food and Agriculture Organisation (FAO).

Hardin, G. (1968) "The Tragedy of the Commons", *Science*, 162: 1243.

Hardin, G. (1978) "Political Requirements for Preserving Our Common Heritage", in H. P. Brokaw, ed., *Wildlife and America*, Washington, D.C.: Council on Environmental Quality, 310–17.

Henson, Spencer, Ann-Marie Brouder and Winnie Mitullah (2000) "Food Safety Requirements and Exports of Perishable Products from Developing Countries: Fish Exports From Kenya to the European Union", *American Journal of Agricultural Economics* 82(5): 1159–69.

Henson, S. and W. V. Mitullah (2004) "Kenyan Exports of Nile Perch: The Impact of Food Safety Standards on an Export-Oriented Supply Chain", Policy Research Working Paper 3349, Washington, D.C.: World Bank, June.

Jansen, E. G. (1997) "Rich Fisheries – Poor Fisherfolk: Some Preliminary Observations about the Effects of Trade and Aid in the Lake Victoria Fisheries", Socio-economics of the Nile Perch Fishery of Lake Victoria Project Report No. 1, Nairobi: IUCN-EARO.

Jansen, E. G., R. O. Alila and J. Owino (1999) "Constraints and Opportunities for 'Community Participation' in the Management of the Lake Victoria Fisheries", Report No. 6, Nairobi: IUCN Eastern Africa Programme.

Kenya, Republic of (1994) "Welfare Monitoring Survey II, Basic Report", Nairobi: Central Bureau of Statistics.

Kenya, Republic of (1994) "Siaya District Development Plan 1994/96", Nairobi: Government Printer.

Kenya, Republic of (1999) "Welfare Monitoring Survey of 1997", Nairobi: Government Printer.

Kenya, Republic of (1999) "National Poverty Eradication Plan, 1999–2015", Nairobi: Government Printer.

Kenya, Republic of (2002a) "Development Plan 2002–2008", Nairobi: Government Printer.

Kenya, Republic of (2002b) "Economic Survey 2002", Nairobi: Government Printer.

Kenya, Republic of (2003a) "Economic Survey 2003", Nairobi: Government Printer.

Kenya, Republic of (2003b) "Economic Recovery Strategy for Wealth and Employment Creation, 2003–2007", Nairobi: Government Printer.

Kibwana, Kivutha, Wanjala Smokin and Okech-Owiti (1996) *The Anatomy of Corruption in Kenya: Legal, Political and Socio-economic Perspective*, Nairobi: Claripress.

Kibwana, Kivutha, S. Kichamu Akivaga, Lawrence Murugu Mute and Morris Odhiambo (2001) *Initiatives against Corruption in Kenya: Legal and Policy Interventions 1995–2001*, Nairobi: Claripress.

Lake Victoria Fisheries Organisation (LVFO) (2003) "The Role of Regional Cooperation with Reference to Lake Victoria", paper presented at a workshop on a Comprehensive Fisheries Policy and Fisheries Strategic Plan, 2–5 June, Commercial Bank Management Centre, Nairobi.

McCormick, Dorothy (1999) "African Enterprise Clusters and Industrialization: Theory and Reality", *World Development*, 27(9): 1531–52.

Messerlin, P. A. and J. Zarrouk (1999) "Trade Facilitation: Technical Regulations and Customs Procedures", paper presented at the Conference on Developing Countries in a Millennium Round, Geneva, September.

Mitullah, Winnie (1999a) "Lake Victoria's Nile Perch Fish Cluster: Institutions, Politics And Joint Action", IDS Working Paper 87, Brighton: Institute of Development Studies, University Of Sussex.

Mitullah, Winnie (1999b) "Fishing and Fish Processing Cluster at Lake Victoria, Kenya", Nairobi: University of Nairobi, Institute for Development Studies.

Mitullah, Winnie, L. M. Mute, Kivutha Kibwana and Wanjala Smokin (1998) *The Case of Ombudsman in Kenya*, Nairobi: Claripress.

Moser, Caroline and Andy Norton (2001) "To Claim Our Rights: Livelihood Security, Human Rights and Sustainable Development", concept paper prepared for the Workshop on Human Rights, Assets and Livelihood Security, and Sustainable Development.

Ogutu-Ohwayo, R. (1990) "The Reduction of Fish Species Diversity in Lakes Victoria and Kyoga (East Africa) following Human Exploitation and Introduction of Non-Native Species", *Journal of Fish Biology* 37, Supplement A, 207–208.

Okeyo-Owuor, J. B. (1999) "A Review of Biodiversity and Socio-economic Research in Relation to Fisheries in Lake Victoria", Report No. 5, Nairobi: IUCN Eastern Africa Programme.

Ostrom, E. (1990) *Governing the Commons: The Evolution of Institutions for Collective Action*, Cambridge: Cambridge University Press.

Ostrom, E. and C. B. Field (1999) "Revisiting the Commons: Local Lessons, Global Challenges", *Science*, 284: 5412.

Owino, John P. (1999) "Traditional and Central Management Systems of Lake Victoria Fisheries in Kenya", Socio-Economics of Lake Victoria Fisheries, Report No. 4, Nairobi: IUCN.

Reynolds, J. E. and D. F. Greboval (1988) "Socio-economic Effects of the Evolution of Nile Perch Fisheries in Lake Victoria: A Review", CIFA Tech. Paper 17.

Samaki News (2002) Newsletter of the Department of Fisheries, Draft Copy, 1(1).

Sekhar, N. U. (2000) "Decentralised Natural Resource Management: From State to Co-Management in India", *Journal of Environmental Planning & Management* 43(1): 124–40.

Smith, R. T. (1981) "Resolving the Tragedy of the Commons by Creating Private Property Rights in Wildlife", *Cato Journal* 1: 439–468.

Sobhan, Rehman (2001) "Correcting Structural Injustices: Refocusing the Agenda for Poverty Eradication", Dhaka: Centre for Policy Dialogue.

Sykes, A. O. (1995) *Product Standards for Internationally Integrated Goods Markets*, Washington, D.C.: Brookings Institution.

UNDP (2001) "Human Development Report 2001", New York: United Nations Development Programme.

Vogel, D. (1995) *Trading Up: Consumer and Environmental Regulations in Global Economy*, Cambridge, Mass.: Harvard University Press.

Welch, W. P. (1983) "The Political Feasibility of Full Ownership Property Rights: The Case of Pollution and Fisheries", *Policy Sciences* 16: 165–80.

Witte, F., A. Goldschmidt, P. C. Goudswaard, W. Ligtvoet, M. J. P. Van Oijen and J. H. Wanink (1992) "Species Extinction and Concomitant Ecological Changes in Lake Victoria", *Netherlands Journal of Zoology* 42(2–3): 214–32.

11

Government support and enabling environment for inter-firm cluster cooperation: Policy lessons from South Africa

Mike Morris and Glen Robbins

The last decade of the twentieth century witnessed the emergence of a considerable body of research and academic writing making the case for theorists, government policymakers and implementers, organized business formations and firms to pay more attention to matters of inter-firm cooperation, networks, regional collaboration and clusters.[1] From renewed interest in the innovative regions of northern Italy to industrial districts in Brazil and California's Silicon Valley, studies suggested that the character of inter-firm relationships within regions and between regions would reveal new insights into firm competitiveness and thereby offer fertile ground for new types of industrial development policies as well as new types of policy-related interventions. This work had its roots in examinations such as those of new economic geography by Krugman (1991, 1995), Piore and Sabel's New Industrial Districts (1984), incisive critiques of the decline of Fordist mass-production systems (Best, 1990) and the consequent attention given to alternative models of production in regions that had never adopted Fordist modes of organizing production or were exhibiting post-Fordist behavioural characteristics (Kaplinsky, 1994). Terms such as "collective efficiency" (Schmitz, 1999a) and "industrial clusters" (Porter, 1990) have contributed to legitimizing the attention given to regions and their characteristics in an increasingly globalized environment. In the past few years this work has evolved with studies into inter-firm learning and innovation (Bell and Albu, 1999; Maskell et al., 1998) as well as having been influential in value-chain analysis of the prospects of regional and sub-regional clusters of

Industrial clusters and innovation systems in Africa: Institutions, markets and policy, Oyelaran-Oyeyinka and McCormick (eds), United Nations University Press, 2007, ISBN 978-92-808-1137-7

economic activity (Humphrey, 1995; Kaplinsky et al., 2001; Morris and Barnes, 2004; Nadvi and Schmitz, 1999).

What is under-emphasized in the literature on clusters, networking, learning and inter-firm cooperation is proper consideration of the specific role of government (through its different levels of national, state/provincial and local) in creating what Helmsing (2001) has called the "enabling environment" to foster dynamic firm clustering. Not only in terms of providing a framework of policy and strategy but also, perhaps especially so, in creating the institutional mechanisms to either make networking, learning and cooperation happen or simply supporting and reinforcing such processes when they have already occurred. This issue of how government can create a cluster-enabling environment is particularly important in developing countries, where globalization creates huge demands and pressures to become internationally competitive rapidly, but conditions are characterized by poor resources, low technology levels, skills gaps, human resource scarcities and serious lack of institutional capacity.

Although not its main focus, this chapter also pays some attention to processes of regionalization, localization and decentralization within nation states. This approach is informed by the core case study, examined in this chapter, which highlights the importance of the local state as opposed to a more traditional focus on roles played by other levels of government. A considerable literature has emerged which examines how processes of global political and economic alignment, combined with demands for more meaningful democracy at a local level, have resulted in limitations being placed on traditional national state economic policy instruments combined with systems of devolving political power to regional and sub-regional entities (Scott, 1998; Storper, 1997; Sugden et al., 2003). These processes clearly have implications for policy frameworks, such as industrial policy, which have traditionally been conceived in terms of national imperatives. They are likely to impact not only the content of policy in an effort to give more regional specificity, but also the manner in which government acts out its policy intentions, the tools it uses and how it engages with actors other than those dominating the national discourse.

This chapter addresses the role of government (at various levels) in fostering dynamic forms of clustering amongst enterprises in developing countries through a case study on South African clusters. It does so by examining, in some detail, the role that government played in the development of two clusters in the automotive industry. Clearly the geographical focus (a middle-income developing country) and sector choice (a relatively high technology- and knowledge-intensive industry) of the case study limits the generalizability of the analysis, especially to other poorer and less state-capacitated African countries. However, we hope that the detailed nature of the discussion offers some important potential lessons for other developing countries.[2]

The structure of the chapter is as follows. In the opening sections we discuss some of the key issues regarding the importance of clustering, and then outline the public policy literature on the role of government in fostering clustering in developing countries, including the few African examples we have managed to unearth. Having drawn out some of the public policy proposals for how government has or should be operating in fostering clustering issues we turn to the concrete case of South Africa, the most developed and capacitated state on the continent, to see how things have operated there. The following sections first outline the rhetoric of government policy to assess how appropriate and effective it has been in its own terms. We then move into a detailed discussion of implementation of this policy agenda using the only two successful cases of clustering in South Africa we have found. In doing so, the chapter uses the evolution of South Africa's post-apartheid industrial policy and the positive and negative experiences of two well-functioning automotive clusters to throw some light on this central question: What is the role of government in fostering clustering in developing countries? Particular attention is paid to assessing the degree to which both the discourse and more importantly the practice of government policy – through the Department of Trade and Industry (DTI) – has come to recognize the importance of fostering inter-firm cooperation and encouraging social capital formation amongst key actors in specific regions. This examination is conducted using the tools outlined in the literature of inter-firm learning and networking approaches to fostering effective competitive responses by firms. It then goes on to draw from the experience of two South African case studies of such networks operating – the automotive benchmarking clubs and the Durban Automotive Cluster.[3] It argues that despite some attempts to reposition the DTI and its activities in the terrain documented in the literature, such processes to foster firm-based processes remain marginalized and generally under-appreciated in its policies and, using the case study material, in the institutional manner in which it is structured. The chapter concludes with some general public policy recommendations, which are, we hope, applicable to other developing countries, especially in Africa.

The evolution of post-apartheid industrial policy in South Africa

South Africa's post-apartheid government inherited an industry-policy framework founded on the protectionism of import substitution industrialization and heavily biased toward a minerals-energy complex. Supported by demand-side policies, the apartheid government had succeeded in embedding a series of distortions that, at great cost to the South African taxpayer, had been maintained in the face of increasing global policy shifts toward liberalization and the consequent opening up of economies. In a context where the new (post-apartheid) government needed to move rapidly to secure the confidence of major trading partners and to confront structural economic weaknesses, it immediately introduced a raft of reform measures focused on monetarist austerity and liberalization of trade regimes. In this regard, the first few years of the new Department of Trade and Industry was thus marked by the attention given to the dismantling of protectionist support systems (through aligning South Africa with the imperatives of the Uruguay Round) and rolling back of distorting and costly schemes such as GEIS (the General Export Incentive Scheme). As a result, despite a considerable body of industrial policy work recommending a range of discrete and innovative interventions, such as that represented by the Industrial Strategy Project (Joffe et al., 1995), trade reform matters tended to pre-occupy the DTI.

The publication of the Growth, Employment and Redistribution (GEAR) document, in 1996, reinforced the critical focus of opening up the economy to further competition in order to enable South African manufacturers to access global markets. It also proposed a scheme of export-orientation that would be supported by the DTI though a set of supply-side measures. Significant institutional attention has been expended by the DTI in rolling out various incarnations of these supply-side measures. These were matched with a series of sectoral initiatives in support of sectors undergoing major structural change, the most prominent being autos and clothing/textiles (Barnes et al., 2004; DTI, 2002).

Furthermore, the DTI placed considerable emphasis on supporting an environment conducive to the growth of micro, small and medium-sized enterprises. Schemes were also developed to create a variety of measures where firms would have access to credit, facilities, training and other forms of support. Such reforms were reinforced by a series of adjustments of the labour-relations framework that moved to substantially improve basic conditions of employment and institutionalize key elements of the industrial relations process.

Hirsch and Hanival (1998) outline five key pillars of the DTI's industrial policies and programmes in the late 1990s. The first of these was investment support to ensure investment processes coordination with a particular emphasis on foreign direct investment. The second pillar outlined was trade policy (major trade liberalization and reform processes through the Uruguay Round of the General Agreement on Tariffs and

Trade, GATT) to force manufacturers to become internationally competitive and improve the economy's export orientation. Thirdly, government highlighted the importance of technology policy to foster improved technology dissemination and acquisition in order to improve competitiveness. A series of funds were set up that encouraged firms to provide matching investment to secure improved technological outcomes. The programmes also offered incentives for improved cooperation between higher educational institutions and firms. Fourthly, the DTI also placed considerable emphasis on working with partner government departments (Labour and Education) to facilitate a more innovative and comprehensive system to upgrade human resources and foster manufacturing firms' competitiveness.

Finally, and most importantly for our purposes, was the DTI perspective on strategic and informational leadership. This was founded on a view that "competitive advantage must also be derived from intra and inter firm cooperation" (Hirsch and Hanival, 1998: 7). The DTI saw a role for itself in facilitating intra- and inter-firm processes to ensure strategic information exchange between the stakeholders as well as to enable greater plant-level collaboration within supply chains and amongst firms in similar sectors. The case for this, as suggested by Hirsch and Hanival (1998) was based on work by leading firm-change theorists such as Michael Porter (1990) and Michael Best (1990).[4] In line with some of this thinking, the DTI began to highlight the importance of exogenous factors as essential to firms' ability to compete, the importance of collaborative inter-firm processes in their ability to succeed on matters such as training, supply chain cooperation and a variety of other aspects. Hence, informed by similar initiatives in other countries, the DTI embarked on a process to encourage the formation of nationally driven "cluster" processes and aimed to boost intra- and inter-firm cooperation lacking in many South African firms through matching grant schemes, such as the Sectoral Partnership Fund and the Workplace Challenge.

Together, these points of focus presented major delivery challenges. Not only was the structure of the DTI outdated, it was also short of the requisite skills. Nevertheless, substantial progress was made on key elements of the programme. Much attention was placed on investment-support initiatives and the DTI's trade work peaked with the conclusion of the SA-EU Free Trade Agreement. Specific sector focuses were dominated by the automotive sector's Motor Industry Development Programme (MIDP) initiative. This initiative was seen as a successful integration of trade, investment and strategic approaches whereby South Africa witnessed unprecedented investment by global original equipment manufacturers (OEMs) and exports increased substantially. For many, the competitiveness of the global automotive sector and its advanced technological and skills requirements reflected a significant maturing of both South African industrial policy and manufacturing capacity.

The publication of the Micro-economic Reform Strategy (MRS) and the Integrated Manufacturing Strategy (IMS) by the South African Department of Trade and Industry, during the course of 2002, heralded an important milestone in the State's approach to industrial policy matters. These documents provided, for the first time since the 1994 elections, a comprehensive record of DTI industrial policy-related perspectives and intentions that would guide the DTI in the first decade of the new millennium. To quote from the document,

> It is the view of the dti (sic) that the way to achieve this (high growth, employment and equity) is through a strategy that takes a systematic approach to eliminating constraints in our economy and improving its efficiency. Co-ordinated and concerted actions have to be taken to maximise the potential within our domestic economy, integrate beneficially into the global economy and build competitiveness based on an increased knowledge intensity, value addition, wider and more equitable participation in the economy and regional production systems. At the core of the accelerated trajectory is knowledge intensity, which means utilising and developing the knowledge and skills of our people in order to integrate ICTs, technology, innovation and knowledge-intensive services into the functioning of the economy as a whole. (DTI, 2002: 3)

The Micro-economic Reform Strategy identified a role for the DTI in supporting firms' endogenous transformation. The imperative behind this shift was an analysis that suggested that macro-economic stability and trade policy alignment with major trading partners was necessary but insufficient on its own to enable South African firms to assert themselves in competitive global markets. The MRS highlighted the requirement that firms engage in continuous competitiveness review and adjustment in order to engage effectively with global economic processes. In a context where state machinery, in the form of the DTI, had been aligned with macro objectives, the MRS proposed a new alignment with micro tools and processes.

In identifying its role, the DTI once again drew on Porter-type conceptions of moving from comparative advantage to competitive advantage, with the policy specifying a requirement for "new sources of competition" to be secured (DTI, 2002b; Kaplan, 2003). These "new sources" are identified as, firstly, marshalling and capturing advantages enabled by information and communication technologies (from both a process and product perspective); secondly, embracing new approaches to responsiveness to secure time and efficiency advantages; and thirdly, integrating domestic processes in global production value chains to the advantage of "national socio-economic objectives".

In enabling the advance of these focus areas, the IMS proposes six sets of integrated interventions:

- Improving market access to developed countries and building trading opportunities in the South;
- Enhancing the integration, relative cost-effectiveness and policy alignment in Southern Africa Development Community production processes;
- Taking maximum advantage of beneficiation (adding value through downstream processing) opportunities;
- Stressing equity and economic participation;
- Developing knowledge-intensity and services integration in the economy; and
- Focusing on global value chains and local horizontal interconnections between enterprises and facilitating value-adding networking to increase competitive capabilities – what it obscurely calls "facilitating integrated value matrices" (DTI, 2002b: 22–26).

The strategy then explains how this approach will impact the DTI's operation and its intended role, as its core business is framed so as "to provide strategic leadership to the economy and to provide value-added products and services" (DTI, 2002b: 28). The DTI will focus on improving government performance in relation to economic processes in the country, the promotion of competitiveness in particular sectors and the delivery of broad-based support measures (such as schemes to help companies register trademarks). With regard to proposed sector activities, the DTI indicates an eagerness to form partnerships and advises that sectors without cohesive organizational processes will not meet the support criteria. The DTI also emphasizes partnerships with other government institutions and spheres of government. However, there is no explicit indication of plans to decentralize activities and to facilitate the building of discrete local knowledge and cluster networks.

The South African DTI's policy approach to clusters and networking in a context of decentralization pressures

As the DTI has done little in terms of documenting its policy intent and activities, it is difficult to measure how it matches conceptually and in implementation to the clustering and networking requirements outlined in the literature. To examine this issue it is necessary to draw on available DTI documentation as well as documentation produced by those who have worked for and with the DTI in the past decade or so (Hirsch and Hanival, 1998; Kaplan, 2003; Kaplinsky and Morris, 1997).

In its early post-democratization phase (1994–1999), the DTI developed a considerable level of interest in the facilitation of national level clusters to improve the competitiveness of key sectors aligned with its export-oriented goals. In practice, the DTI began to roll out a series of supply-side support programmes that were seen as less distorting than demand-side interventions that had prevailed prior to the onset of democracy. Through sponsoring detailed sectoral analyses, the DTI shared research with industry leaders and brought together select representatives of suppliers, buyers, related and supporting industries, government and at times competitors – referred to by Michael Porter's Monitor Company as a cluster.[5] This entailed aligning "kick-start" funding with active support and involvement of DTI staff in cluster processes that commonly closely aligned themselves with national industry associations of the relevant sectors and involved high-level participation of dominant companies. The DTI worked to popularize the concept of clusters through hosting a series of workshops with key sector groups in the main manufacturing regions. These were, in some instances, further supported by funds and facilitation from the DTI's Spatial Development Initiatives (SDI) projects that could allow nascent cluster processes to take on more of a regional character. However, whilst the studies and their related dissemination processes contributed to the development of a shared strategic perspective of various country industries, they did not, in most instances, translate into any sustained collective action by the stakeholders concerned.[6]

Despite considerable state funding, high-level involvement of dominant industry players and considerable direct attention of policymakers, the successes of the DTI's direct association with cluster processes were muted. Despite the failure of many of the national processes to sustain themselves beyond initial research phases and of regional processes to become more self-sufficient, the exercise by the DTI is seen to have had some benefits. It resulted in a substantial escalation of working relationships between firms involved and DTI officials that benefited both parties. The DTI officials had an opportunity to be exposed to industry knowledge and insights to inform their policy choices and industry players gained an improved understanding of the DTI and its programmes and policies. However, these impacts were undermined by the inability of the DTI to retain its sector-specific staff and the constant process of departmental reorganization, which resulted in remaining personnel being shifted to other positions or departments.

The launching of the DTI's Sectoral Partnership Fund in the second half of the 1990s created an opportunity for sector stakeholders at a more discreet sectoral and regional level to work to build a collective agenda around matters of competitiveness. However, the bulk of applications through the scheme resulted in one-off projects rather than sustained networking (e.g., stainless steel and jewellery clusters) or, where networking was sustained, it did not extend beyond single-issue processes (e.g., PE Auto Cluster with its focus on logistics). The DTI's creation of a dedicated team to promote cluster initiatives yielded little more than further analytical studies and workshops. Industry participants in these processes often complained of a DTI obsession with setting cluster agendas and of failing to recognize the importance of shared governance of processes and building trust. An example of this can be seen in processes that sought to establish a cluster-type partnership between key industrial chemical stakeholders in the Durban region. The overriding government interest was for collective action to boost investment and exports, whilst industry participants called for the process to prioritize resolving environmental management issues.

Participants in these cluster processes originating in national processes identified the following as core weaknesses:[7]

- DTI's attempts to impose an agenda on firms;
- The lack of a relationship (trust)-building process;
- Lack of evidence of "quick wins";
- A cluster model founded on national priorities as opposed to localized common concerns between firms, leaving firms disconnected from the agenda;
- A government-driven governance model without the creation of real partnerships; and
- Lack of credibility/knowledge of DTI facilitators.

The result of this less-than-spectacular engagement with cluster processes was that the DTI took less of an interest in what were conventionally framed as cluster processes or inter-firm networks. The loss of skilled staff who had acquired detailed sector knowledge and built relationships with some industry role players may have contributed to this decision. However, this loss of interest in such processes by the DTI did not prevent other role players continuing to seek opportunities in inter-firm cooperation.

At the turn of the millennium the DTI underwent a sustained period of restructuring to finally shed the institutional baggage of apartheid-era industrial policies. It also shifted away from cluster processes which were viewed as excessively resource-intensive and seen to yield less tangible results than more direct interventions on an individual basis with leading sector players. Whilst the latest policy offerings re-emphasize the thrust toward clusters, it remains a concept founded on strategic national processes with key role-players in day-to-day implementation terms (DTI, 2002b).

A further complication, and one that likely hindered significant advances on industrial policy content and innovation in South Africa from its early post-apartheid formulations, has been the highly centralized

approach of the DTI, which has resulted in very little meaningful interaction with other spheres of government and even less "grassroots" interaction with firms in their specific locations. The result has been little
inter-governmental co-ordination and a policy orientation with a strong
top-down delivery bias.

Within this context it is noteworthy that the DTI has shown very little
direct interest in processes relating to decentralization, both for its own
benefit (in terms of improving its intelligence base) and for its customers'
benefit. It has also not truly realized how important localized processes
and various networks can be to local, regional and even national economic development, as illustrated in studies referred to in this chapter.
In this regard its programmes and activities can still be characterized as
highly centralized, macro-level, generally not informed by the dynamics
of space and place and offering little in terms of support to networking
and clustering activities on a discrete regional basis.

The very limited provincial and local government service offerings to
firms in specific locations is even more of a concern in light of the highly
centralized DTI delivery systems. A pilot programme by the DTI to roll
out the delivery of its Export Marketing and Investment Assistance
(EMIA) scheme to 24 service centres around the country (in the form of
export councils, chambers of commerce and provincial government trade
and investment bodies) is a marked departure from the bulk of DTI programmes which remain administered at a national level (Business Day,
2003). But it appears that this EMIA roll-out is driven more by an
attempt to increase successful take-up of the scheme, rather than to improve service delivery alignment with regional and local players and deliver enhanced continuous learning opportunities for these role-players,
including the DTI and the applicant firms.

In other circumstances, where effective regional and local-level
economic development processes exist, this might not be a problem.
However, outside of the large metropolitan local authority structures,
South Africa is characterized by relatively weak provincial and local
government administrations and hence these entities struggle to make
themselves consistently relevant to businesses in their regions.[8] A more
comprehensive regional focus by the DTI could contribute to resolving
this gap. The recent interest the DTI is showing in local economic-
development policy processes and regular contact between provincial
and national trade and industry structures may herald such a shift, but
to date these have received very little meaningful institutional attention.

The problem is that DTI discourse is long on complex policy issues and
short on the institutional processes required for successful implementation. This is a serious problem in developing countries like South Africa,
which lack institutional capacity and sufficiently skilled personnel in gov-

ernment to ensure the implementation of strategies. Without detailed thought on the necessary institutional arrangements required for implementing policy there is little guarantee that the fine policy words will ever translate into effective results. It is therefore not surprising that firms and consultants consistently complain about the difficulties in accessing the supply-side measures found in government's industrial policy.

A final problem that has arisen with respect to these policy initiatives is clearly understanding and specifying who is to do what. The DTI was charged with providing "strategic leadership ... and ... value-added products and services" (DTI, 2002b: 28). But is it realistic to expect the DTI and its civil servants to provide the services required to facilitate inter-firm cooperation or raise competitiveness levels? Is this not the domain of the "business services" sector? Should it not be the task of those private consultancy firms that help firms restructure and achieve world-class manufacturing in their operational performance, providing training for manufacturing excellence, facilitating learning and networking?

Industrial policy has been designed for a new competitive and cooperative manufacturing economy, but has it been designed to create a holistically enabling environment? Certainly on the financial side funds have been earmarked to support and assist firms on various matching grant schemes with the buzzwords "public-private sector partnerships". But are the only parties that need to be brought to the table government and manufacturing enterprises? Is this a partnership based on two or three parties? What about the consulting firms, the business services enterprises, the industry facilitators, all of whom are supposed to provide the actual support for industrial restructuring, cluster facilitation and network learning to ensure firms either individually or collectively make the transition toward international competitiveness. The real problem is that the DTI has not tried to close the magic triangle and build a relationship between itself providing a framework and financial assistance; the enterprises receiving financial support and requiring practical value-added services and knowledge assistance; and the business-services sector providing the range of facilitating and practical value-added restructuring services. By suggesting that somehow government will provide the necessary "value-added services", the new DTI policy has allowed a central question concerning the enabling environment to slip away: How does industrial policy build an effective business-services sector to assist enterprises in building this new manufacturing economy?

The DTI itself makes the case that,

It is clear that a wide range of policies have been developed and new approaches initiated since 1994. It is difficult to judge the exact impact of these initiatives, given the time lags in their effects being felt, and the absence or inadequacy of monitoring and evaluation systems. Despite this, it is clear that through a combination of policy interventions and an array of external and internal forces, there have been significant structural changes in our economy, demonstrated in our industrial performance. (DTI, 2002b: 14)

The operative and salient part of the quotation lies in the revealing statement that "it is difficult to judge the exact impact ... given ... the absence or inadequacy of monitoring and evaluation systems". Without adequate monitoring it is impossible to assess the impact of such policy initiatives and difficult to evaluate whether any general improvements in industrial performance stem from any of the government's strategic interventions.

Finally what is missing in the state's policy discourse is an analysis of the institutional arrangements required to implement policy frameworks. In fact, a case could be made that whilst it is often clear when the state is obstructing network formation and clustering, it is less clear what the state should be doing to create a flourishing environment for such processes. Hence the more cynical are often heard to argue that the less a government does to intervene and participate in such processes, the more they are likely to thrive. This is ironic, given that many of those shying away from a more active role for government started off as passionate protagonists of centralized industrial intervention and have been driven by bitter experiences of bureaucratic bungling into a decidedly reluctant embrace of a more central and direct role for government. However, the issue may be more of disaggregating the different levels of possible government intervention and the difference between direct and indirect roles than a blanket embracement or rejection of a role for government. It may well be more a matter of finding new ways of working with firms and other public and private partners, at appropriately different levels of government, to enable it to be relevant in a positive manner to such processes. It may also be that involvement in such processes is less about state-led policies being jammed down the throats of facilitators and manufacturing enterprises and more about government engaging in its own learning and response cycles in such processes. And finally, it may be that that a core element of becoming relevant in this framework of operation requires the state to embrace the decentralization of its industrial-policy activities where appropriate, as it is often at the local level that the state needs to find a place for itself in cluster and networking processes.

However, understanding such issues, especially of the necessary institutional arrangements required of government, requires a concrete analysis of real situations, of the actual setting up and functioning of real clusters and learning networks. It is to this end that we turn to a concrete analysis of the two case studies to see what lessons can be distilled about the government's role in fostering clusters and learning networks.

The case of the auto sector cluster activities

The auto benchmarking clubs

During the mid-1990s the South African automotive sector was in the midst of a substantial crisis. The Uruguay Round-related reduction of tariff protection, behind whose protection a domestic industry had prospered, contributed significantly to this crisis in which the volume of imported vehicles and components increased whilst performance and productivity gaps in OEMs and component producers made successful entry into global markets as exporters a difficult, if not impossible, exercise. However, the DTI's development of a sector-specific restructuring support programme, the Motor Industry Development Programme (MIDP), soon began to encourage significant OEM production-for-export commitments in some of the country's major firms (initially Volkswagen and BMW). Whilst the structuring of the MIDP favoured the OEMs, the programme contributed significantly to an output turnaround and hence created a window of opportunity for the OEMs' suppliers to realign themselves with new opportunities.

Research conducted by academics from the former University of Natal, in the form of comprehensive performance benchmarks of local Durban-based suppliers' performance, spurred the formation of a nascent partnership between the researchers and a handful of firms. The researchers, acting as external intermediaries, formed a separate business services company (Benchmarking and Manufacturing Analysts, see http://www. bmanalysts.com) and became cluster facilitators. The Sector Partnership Fund leveraged matching finance from government (65 per cent) and auto firms (35 per cent) to create the KZN Auto Benchmarking Club, which became operational in January 1998 after a successful seven-month struggle to break through government red tape and access financial support. This regionally based continuous-improvement cluster was designed to help firms learn how to upgrade their operational performance in order to approach the international competitiveness frontier. In a few years, based on its operational success, two other sister clusters were formed in the Eastern Cape and Gauteng (Barnes and Morris, 1999; Morris and Barnes, 2004).

These clubs have proved to be highly successful continuous-improvement clusters. This is determined by a number of criteria, including increased knowledge sharing as firms shared their experiences through workshops and firm visits; learning as the newsletters diffused to other layers of management within firms; significant improvement in operational performance; increasing membership growth; and financial self sufficiency as government withdrew its financial support.

The clubs are primarily based on firms' desire for ensured continuous improvement and operational performance enhancement in order to become more internationally competitive through their membership. Therefore the best quantitative indicator is the impact they have had on the competitiveness of the cluster members as measured by improvements in club member firms' operational performance. Although a wealth of information is available and is shared with firms on a regular basis, only the overall summary (table 11.1) of progress in Club member firms' process upgrading, both in relation to their own improvements and relative to an international sample of benchmarked firms, is presented.

It is clear that the impact of these clubs on operational performance has been significant even if the South African components sector has also some way to go to reach the global frontier. With the exception of delivery reliability to customers, progress for all of the measures in South Africa has been significant. Generally speaking, the South African component firm performance increase is better where internal factors (work-in-progress control, training, absenteeism) are involved than where they are dependent on external factors (raw material inventories, supplier performance). From a value chain perspective this suggests that the growth of learning is still predominantly in the first-tier components suppliers and has not yet diffused up the value chain. Some of inventory control weakness is due to logistic problems along the value chain, especially with regard to incoming materials (minimum-sized import quantities, problems at the ports) and distance to the export market (for stocks of finished goods). In general there are clear indications that significant process upgrading has occurred and the firms are becoming more internationally competitive. Clearly external factors have also contributed, but the members argue that the cooperation, knowledge sharing and learning embedded in the operations of the clubs have played a major and critical role in the process.

However, from the key question is how we assess the new government's institutional levers in assisting the process. On the positive side it is clear that without the existence of a sympathetic industrial policy incorporating the ability of the service providers to access financial support for clustering – i.e., the Sector Partnership Fund – this network would never have seen the light of day. However, the inability of government to come to grips with implementing the appropriate institutional arrangements to create a truly enabling institutional environment also nearly killed the cluster.

Table 11.1 Learning and operational-performance change of firms in clusters

Critical success factors	Key performance indicators	South African firms			Comparator firms	
		1998/99	2001	Improvement 1998/99–2001	Western Europe	Emerging economies
Cost control	Total inventory (days)	62.6	42.0	32.8%	31.2	38.6
	Raw material (days)	32.3	21.8	32.7%	17.2	19.2
	Work in progress (days)	12.4	8.2	34.3%	5.3	8.6
	Finished goods (days)	17.8	12.1	32.0%	8.6	9.5
Quality	Customer return rate (ppm)	3270	1240	62.0%	549	624
	Internal reject rate (%)	4.9	3.9	20.7%	1.9	3.5
	Supplier return rate (ppm)	2198	18518	16.0%	8319	13213
Flexibility	Lead time (days)	19.9	17.9	9.9%	16.8	12.0
	Supplier on time (%)	78.7	82.2	4.5%	92.2	92.3
	On time delivery to customers (%)	92.2	92.7	0.6%	96.1	93.5
Capacity to change	Training spent as % total remuneration	1.3	2.0	56.2%	1.3	3.1
	Absenteeism (%)	4.4	4.0	9.4%	4.2	5.7

Source: Benchmarking and Manufacturing Analysts (http://www.bmanalysts.com)

One of the most striking difficulties experienced in the establishment and initial functioning of the Club was the institutional difficulties associated with the government's supply-side support. The DTI may have radically broken with import-substituting industrialization, but the bureaucratic structure of the government's Department of Trade and Industry remained intact. Whilst new policies were put in place there was insufficient re-conceptualization of the new policies' deployment implications and hence reconfiguring of its institutional arrangements to ensure that implementation followed the policy shift. As such, the supply-side support measures that replaced the previous protective regime were so immersed in bureaucratic red tape that it was extremely difficult for firms to access them. The international competitive demands placed on firms that relied on some level of government support rendered the long lead times associated with its previous operations inadequate. The knowledge implications of its shift in policy also required retraining government staff from "paper pushers" to agents-of-change fully attuned to the competitive demands facing South African firms.

Whilst it was therefore very easy obtaining formal government support for the Club, given its new policy reorientation and industrial-development agenda, it was extremely difficult obtaining the practical supply-side support required for the establishment of the Club. This is borne out by the fact that the Club was launched seven months later than originally envisaged and that it took nearly five months from the Club's launch to receive the first disbursement of government money. Moreover, as time progressed, the clubs discovered that providing a 65 per cent subsidy proved a double-edged sword. The DTI invariably took between three and six months to reimburse incurred expenditures. Consequently, service providers who facilitated Club activities constantly experienced cash flow crises. In 2003, when the DTI finally reneged on promises to provide more secure long-term funding, these clubs were faced with collapse. In 2004 they abandoned seeking any national DTI support and became completely self-financing from member firm payments. This was not without its problems but it did finally seem to solve the continuously recurring cash flow crises engendered by government.

However, as if in order to drive the point of bureaucratic bungling home, the DTI's cumbersome rules and procedures have made it as difficult to end state support as it was to maintain it. The rules required an audit as the final step and, although funds were not allocated in the initial budgets for this process, the DTI informed the clubs in writing that they would fully cover the sector performance fund (SPF) closure-auditing costs. Despite this assurance, when the invoices were sent to the DTI they claimed that their rules only allowed them to pay 65 per cent of costs. Notwithstanding the four months taken to decide this and the additional 20 per cent interest charges incurred by clubs and service providers for late payment, the DTI induced a further cash flow crisis by reneging on a further 35 per cent of the auditing costs to wind down their own SPF mechanism.

The Durban Auto Cluster

In 2001 a significant development occurred when the Durban Metropolitan Council's Economic Development Department took high-level interest in the potential of widening the scope of KZN's Benchmarking Club into a broader cluster speaking to a wide variety of automotive problems in the region. Municipal seed funding was provided, resulting in the launch of the Durban Auto Cluster in January 2002 based on four foci – supplier development, logistics, human resources development and operational performance.[9]

Early collective gains, such as more favourable freight rates and shared training infrastructure and programmes, soon encouraged firms to extend the DAC's scope by contributing increasing levels of funding. Since its formal establishment the cluster has grown to incorporate in excess of 35 firms and sources the bulk of its funding from firm contributions. It has developed an array of programmes ranging from highly technical specialized training interventions that might benefit a handful of firms to more generic initiatives such as programmes to support new entrants into the sector – especially for emerging black-owned firms. It is widely viewed as an example of a highly effective cluster (Bessant et al., 2003).

The governance structure of the cluster involves the firms electing an executive supplemented by local, provincial and (nominally) national government representatives. This executive guides the facilitators' work and allocates resources according to the needs of the firm-driven working groups associated with each programme area of the cluster. Although the cluster in its present form is reliant on some public-sector support, it has had an alternative plan for some time that would enable it to continue operating the bulk of its activities without any direct government support.

The Department of Trade and Industry has offered inconsistent support and shown erratic interest in the workings of the DAC. This has translated into DTI representatives rarely participating in the cluster's Durban-based activities and DTI contributing the smallest portion of public-sector contributions to the DAC since its establishment. This "distance" between DTI staff responsible for sector activities and the DAC, aggravated by substantial staff turnover and associated loss of experience, has been felt in a number of ways by the DAC participants and facilitators. Responses to applications for funds are not dealt with in a timely manner and, as those dealing with the applications have little direct experience of the cluster or its participants, have often been misunderstood. Requests for more direct involvement in cluster processes have often been met with the response that the DTI has a responsibility to maintain some distance from regional processes and to direct its attention to strategic national activities. These perspectives remain common today despite the fact that the cluster is arguably the most successful in terms of the number of firms involved and the level of partnership funding committed from firms, and in terms of the diversity of active programmes.

In similar fashion to the experience of the auto clubs, and stemming from the same base problem, this "distance" is further complicated by the DTI's internal procedures relating to funding of such initiatives. Applicants must meet criteria that are too precise to allow the necessary flexibility for facilitating such firm-based processes. Lengthy application procedures create considerable periods of uncertainty and payment delays can easily derail activities and result in loss of confidence by participants. Furthermore, the fact that facilitating firms such as Benchmarking and Manufacturing Analysts have to pay VAT on invoice (not in and of itself a problem created by the DTI) and not on receipt of government funds can place further pressures on the viability of start-up processes in clusters. This causes participants to invest excessive amounts of time seeking resource certainty where such conditions are made worse by delays.

Irregular participants from the DTI's automotive sector division or from the Durban office of the DTI expressed considerable surprise at the scale and scope of the DAC activities and repeatedly made the point that the experience could offer valuable pointers to evolving national government perspectives on policy and associated implementation. However, this enthusiasm was not converted into more formal and tangible endorsement. Informal recognition of the DAC took place in the form of requests that DAC facilitators participate in various DTI processes aimed at defining national policy agendas. The existence of the DAC reinforced the credibility and authority of the DAC facilitators in their engagement with national policy processes, but once again this did not yield any more substantial direct DTI engagement with the local processes.

The DAC was fortunate to be able to source considerable support through the erstwhile Durban Metropolitan Council's Economic Development Department (now the eThekwini Municipality) and, for a time but with similar inflexibility, the KZN Department for Economic Development and Tourism. This was beset by delays and uncertainty, as well as by policy directives that required the DAC to focus attention on matters it did not initially see as its core businesses, issues of emerging policy framework as opposed to immediate needs of firms. For instance, the KZN Department for Economic Development and Tourism expressed the desire to support a process that featured more active involvement of black economic empowerment concerns and black-owned businesses. They struggled with the timeframes the DAC suggested would be in order for the support of enterprises marginal to the rapidly globalizing auto sector. The continuous struggle to get various government players to agree to provide some sort of subsidy to the cluster's running costs and to its core businesses of competitiveness support programmes remains today – despite very obvious signs of early gains and signs of willingness by the DAC participants to engage with new policy directions.

It is also important to note that the DAC processes were not undertaken under any industry association banner. Earlier Benchmarking Club processes had revealed that industry associations were caught up in lobbying exercises and issues relating to national collective bargaining processes. They had traditionally kept their noses out of firms' internal operations – with the exception of industrial relations matters. By and large, the industry associations, in their regional form, supported the cluster activities and it was also made clear that their role was in no way being directly threatened. No direct association endorsement was sought as the cluster focused on inclusiveness as a key principle and avoided being directly associated with any one industry body.

This sensitivity about the nature and form of associations also extended to the involvement of OEMs, and in particular Toyota South Africa, in the processes. Compared to other cluster initiatives in the auto sector in the country, the emphasis in the DAC was on the interests of the layers of suppliers to the OEMs. Whilst Toyota's express support for the efforts of the DAC were sought from its start, it was agreed by all that Toyota would be an active participant, but not exercise any dominant responsibilities in the process. This enabled suppliers to feel comfortable working together on strategies to ensure they could improve their negotiating position in relation to the automotive value chain dominated by the OEMs. It also enabled Toyota to continue to pursue its own corporate strategies without any sense of threat to its commercial imperatives.

The DAC continues to move from strength to strength as it develops more complex programmes and these have become more closely integrated with the firms' day-to-day operations. It has also begun work to build some networks of cooperation with auto firms in other regions through the benchmarking club activities. Whilst it has developed in a unique context, it remains an example of activities that remain marginal to the DTI's agenda and yet offer the potential for the DTI to reposition itself in future policy and implementation activities.

Conclusion: Lessons based on the South African case

What then can we learn from this experience of two somewhat specific South African automotive case studies that can be generalized to government's role in fostering clusters in Africa? Clearly there are huge differences between the clusters discussed here and those in the other chapters. There are obvious and important differences that make South Africa stand apart from many other African countries. Firstly, the South African economy is much more developed than that of most other African economies. Furthermore, the characteristics of the automotive sector and its dominant global value chain means that many issues and problems are of a different order. Moreover, the case studies discussed here are, in many respects, of a different nature compared to other clusters discussed in most of the African cluster literature. The nature, dynamics and structure of the these two automotive clusters – scale, level of capital and technology intensity, export orientation and knowledge intensity – seem more similar to those in industrialized countries than most clusters in much poorer and underdeveloped parts of Africa. Yet there is value in trying to learn from activities that are closer to the international frontier, for if these seemingly more advanced examples exhibit problems, then it is surely relevant to clusters in the rest of Africa that are striving to adopt strategies and follow paths to make them more internationally competitive.

The South African government's industrial policy on clusters recognizes the value of encouraging firm-level cooperative interactions. However, the content and tone of the bulk of the DTI's policy frameworks remain somewhat immune from the influences of insights gained from both international (including other developing countries) and domestic experiences that suggest the value of reorientation of industrial policy interventions toward the facilitation of networking and clustering activities. The case studies illustrate how such processes can improve the learning capabilities of the role-players (including government) and critically offer the potential of measurable performance impacts where firms can utilize the platforms created by networks and clusters to upgrade their performance.

How government undertakes policy implementation processes is often as relevant (if not more so) than the policy itself. In South Africa we have witnessed central government, through the DTI, managing processes of trade reform, sector-specific industrial programmes and macro-policy adjustment with considerable skill and insight. However, whilst a sector-industry programme such as the MIDP has been much lauded as turning around the fortunes of the South African automotive industry, it has not expressly incorporated programmes to facilitate networking and clustering activities that have a reach beyond OEMs and major first-tier suppliers. International experience suggests that networking and clustering have much to offer in terms of improving the reach and depth of benefits of nationally driven resource-sustainability programmes and attention-intensive industrial policy interventions such as the MIDP. Furthermore, sectors without the focus that DTI lavished on the MIDP have struggled to obtain the attention of central government around networking and clustering. Unfortunately, these have too often been associated with the need for large-scale and short-term leverage impacts as opposed to continuous platform assessment and renewal cycles that predominate in case studies on networks and clusters. It is clear that the development of regionally rooted cluster processes can have a meaningful impact on significant numbers of firms' ability to upgrade their performance in the face of pressures of global competition. This is borne out by extensive international experience, as well as by the case studies of the auto benchmarking clubs and the Durban Auto Cluster. This raises the issue that perhaps the problem lies in where, in the various levels of government, the responsibility for such regionally based clustering and networking initiatives is located.

At a more general level, and of pertinence to other developing countries, a number of lessons for the role of government – in relation to industrial policy and practice – emerge from the preceding sections. These are documented here as contributions to an ongoing debate on the nature of industrial policy and the institutional framework to ensure implementation, as well as how to relate these to its processes of localization and decentralization and the increasing recognition of forms of firm-based networking.

In formulating national policy and implementation frameworks, governments need to recognice a number of major issues in responding to this:

- The initiative for these processes is often one that emerges from local processes and is rarely a successful product of national cluster interventions. The reason for this revolves around the need for interventionist bodies to be institutionally embedded and intimate with local firms, facilitators and supporting organizations.
- Participation by dominant players in the national market does not guarantee cluster sustainability; in fact, it can often have the opposite result as such interests seek to exercise narrow corporate interests rather than the more broad sector or economic interests.
- Enabling business participants to define an agenda for a cluster process, based on comprehensive research and informed facilitation, is essential. This requires government support programmes, such as they might exist, to be tailored to generic cluster risk-reduction activities as opposed to rigid state policy requirements.

- Supporting the private sector and creating public-private partnerships require government to recognize, support and reward the important role of the business services sector in delivering direct interventions that raise industry competitiveness levels, which government requires but is incapable of doing so itself.
- A lack of consistent participation by government officials in such processes creates confidence and communication gaps which undermine the potential for mutual learning between firms and different spheres of government.

A lack of coordination and interaction between government spheres weakens both the policy content and the implementation effectiveness of government interventions. This is particularly important in light of the critical nature of local insights in making cluster processes work. Key issues in this regard include:

- From a national perspective, policy development should ideally be informed by varying conditions in the different regions and by regular direct interactions with the supposed beneficiaries of such interventions – namely, the firms themselves. Failure to participate in regional grassroots processes undermines the potential government benefit of learning from firm networks by reducing the exposure of responsible officials to firms and their issues.
- The corollary of this need for institutional embeddedness and intimacy with local stakeholders, facilitators and firms is that it is usually better to have government institutions involved in creating or maintaining clusters that operate at a lower level than the national structures. Whether this should be provincial or local government depends on the resource capabilities of the various institutional levels. In large urban areas it is usually the metropolitan government that has existing capacity, is more attuned with the local sector situation and has the greatest incentive to ensure that local economic development initiatives get off the ground. In rural areas and country towns, local municipalities are nothing more than services collection agencies and the provincial government has a major role to play in assisting firms to join up into learning networks.
- Lack of a policy delivery presence at a local level results in a substantial disconnection between national policy and the effectiveness of its implementation. Distant and unresponsive bureaucratic structures do little to enhance the essential relationship-building in the uptake of national-level priority programmes. Barriers of space and consequent reductions in levels of contact between firms and government officials do little to enhance the trust and mutual learning that has been seen as an essential ingredient in successful networking and clustering processes.

- Poor interaction between national, provincial and local government spheres reduces the potential for the sharing of insights and strategies that can improve allocations of state resources and contribute to more informed interventions. The tendency for national government to concentrate competitiveness resources in its own hands and then set up bureaucratically obstructive accessing mechanisms has a debilitating impact on firms' and cluster facilitators' ability to gain from networking arrangements. Likewise, this hierarchical relationship between provincial and local government can have the same effect. This is especially true where metropolitan or city governments are better placed, i.e., institutionally embedded and able to express the necessary institutional intimacy, to make appropriate decisions regarding firms and the capabilities of local service providers or facilitators.
- Government has to understand the difference between policy formulation, policy design, policy promotion and policy implementation. Policy formulation is usually undertaken by externally based researchers or consultants and involves drawing on research and formulating a set of policy principles and guidelines, which are adopted with suitable modification by government. Policy design requires translating this into a legal framework, which then becomes the codified policy of the government – a process which is undertaken by bureaucrats and legislative experts. Policy promotion is the dissemination of the policy to all interested stakeholders inviting them to participate. Policy implementation is ensuring that the bureaucratic processes are in place to easily deliver on the various policy promises and ensure that the policy objectives are met. This requires the government department(s) to reorganize internal institutional arrangements, train staff, change civil servant mindsets, speed up processes and so on in order to ensure that the policies can be easily accessed, the various activities (whether they be funding or reporting or concrete interventions) delivered to the relevant parties in the correct time frames and the results monitored and evaluated. Unfortunately, most policy processes stop at policy promotion as government bureaucrats assume dissemination equals implementation and the crucial issue of ensuring that the placement of necessary institutional arrangements to implement the objectives is ignored.

Enhanced inter-firm and firm-institution networking processes reduce the pressure on government officials to have the capacity and knowledge to provide leadership in the development of industrial policy points of focus and interventions. In a context where government capacity is often given as a reason for policy failure, the following points are relevant:

- Whilst there are certain benefits to having a competent and informed government bureaucracy, both international and South African experience has illustrated how fairly minor and uncomplicated government interventions can create conducive networking conditions where the actions of the government participants rapidly become marginal to the long-term effectiveness of the networking processes. In such a context government can focus on improving its accessibility and extracting knowledge insights from such processes to inform future policy and thereby become more demand- than supply-oriented.

- Other institutions relevant to such networks, be they parastatals, tertiary institutions, business organizations or private service providers, also need to align themselves to support and contribute to networks in which partnerships become essential. Such partnerships contribute to better market or policy alignment and have the potential to make optimum use of available resources.

Finally, the maturing of an industrial policy and delivery framework needs to be accompanied by considerable rethinking of the role of different government spheres and other institutions in the effective development of future policy and the nature of its delivery. "Flexibility", "rapid-change", "service excellence", "knowledge-intensity" and "demand-driven" are terms not often associated with government bureaucracies, but can and do make their presence felt in discrete networking and clustering activities. Government actions can contribute to the creation of obstacles or to improving its capability as an informed enabler. This should not be confused with a case to withdraw the state from the industrial policy arena. Rather it should be seen in the light of improving the allocation of existing and future resources to enable the state to improve its own knowledge resources (essential for sound policy) through improved learning and partnerships. In turn, it can convert this insight into more effective interventions through engagement with groups of firms operating in a supportive framework rather than individual firms disconnected from sector and value-chain processes. The South African experience points to the potential should the state at all levels seek ways to engage in networking processes with firms, not as a director of activities but as a stakeholder with an interest in learning and seeking collective responses to challenges.

Notes

1. We are indebted to incisive and helpful comments from Justin Barnes, Jo Lorentzen and Jorg Meyer-Stamer and for research support provided by Leanne Sedowski.
2. In addition to limitations that might arise from the case study it is also important that this chapter be considered in light of critical issues raised by Humphrey and Schmitz (2002) on matters of inter-firm relations and the governance of value chains. The nature of the interaction between firms is a fundamental thread running through the literature on firm

clusters and networks, but limitations of space prevent a more thorough treatment of the subject matter in this chapter with its focus on government policy.

3. Both authors have been participants in processes to develop post-apartheid industry policy in different spheres of government activity and have been active participants in the case studies analysed in the article. The chapter is therefore informed not only by analysis of secondary material but also through knowledge gained through participant observation.

4. The Monitor Company, Michael Porter's consultancy company, was a provider of strategic research to the DTI during this phase (see http://www.monitor.com).

5. For further information on the approach of the Monitor Company see Michael Fairbanks and Stace Lindsay (1997) *Ploughing the Sea*, Harvard Business School Press, Boston.

6. Processes were initiated in sectors such as jewellery, aluminium, stainless steel, heavy mining equipment, automotive components, tourism and minerals processesing.

7. Personal interviews and feedback to Glen Robbins who was at the time working in the Durban Metro responsible for initiating these processes.

8. The exceptions are the Western Cape provincial authority and Gauteng, but the latter is peculiar in that the province consists essentially of three large metropolitan areas.

9. For more information on the Durban Auto Cluster, see http://www.bmanalysts.com/dac_home.htm.

REFERENCES

Barnes, Justin and Mike Morris (1999) "Improving Operational Competitiveness through Firm Level Clustering: A Case Study of the KwaZulu-Natal Benchmarking Club", Working Paper 24, Durban: University of Natal, School of Development Studies.

Barnes, Justin and Julia Johnson (2004) "Sectoral Overview of the Automotive Industry in the eThekwini Municipality and Broader KZN province," unpublished research note produced for eThekwini Municipality by B&M Analysts (www.bmanalysts.com).

Bell, M. and A. Albu (1999) "Knowledge Systems and Technological Dynamism in Industrial Clusters in Developing Countries", *World Development* 27(9): 1715–34.

Bessant, John, Raphie Kaplinsky and Mike Morris (2004) "Industrial Policy in Developing Economies: Developing Dynamic Comparative Advantage in the South African Automobile Sector", *Competition and Change* 8(2): 153–172.

Best, M. H. (1990) *The New Competition: Institutions of Industrial Restructuring*, Cambridge, Mass.: Harvard University Press.

Business Day Magazine (2003) July.

Department of Trade and Industry (2002) Annual Report, South Africa.

Helmsing, Albert H. J. (2001) "Externalities, Learning and Governance: New Perpectives on Local Economic Development", *Development and Change*, 32(2).

Hirsch, Alan and Stephen Hanival (1998) "South African Industrial Policy", TIPS annual conference paper, available through http://www.tips.org.za/.

Humprey, John (1995a) "Trust and the Transformation of Supplier Relations in Indian Industry", in C. Lane and R. Bachman, eds, *Trust Within and Between Organizations*, London: Oxford University Press.

Humphrey, John (1995b) "Industrial Reorganization in Developing Countries: From Models to Trajectories", *World Development*, 23(1).

Humphrey, John and Hubert Schmitz (2000) "Governance and Upgrading: Linking Industrial Cluster and Global Value Chain Research", IDS Working Paper 120, Brighton: University of Sussex, Institute of Development Studies.

Joffe, Avril, David Kaplan, Raphie Kaplinsky and David Lewis (1995) *Improving Manufacturing Performance in South Africa: Report of the Industrial Strategy Project*, Cape Town: UCT Press.

Kaplan, David (2003) "Manufacturing Performance and Policy in South Africa – A Review", TIPS/DPRU Annual Conference paper, available through http://www.tips.org.za/.

Kaplinsky, Raphie (1994) *Easternisation: The Spread of Japanese Management Techniques in Developing Countries*, London: UNU/Frank Cass.

Kaplinsky, Raphie, G. Gereffi, J. Humphrey and T. Sturgeon (2001) "The Value of Value Chains: Spreading the Gains from Globalisation", Sussex: IDS.

Kaplinsky, Raphie and Mike Morris (1997) "The Formulation of Industrial Policy in South Africa: A View from the Edge", Working Paper 15, Durban: University of Natal, School of Development Studies.

Krugman, Paul (1991) *Geography and Trade*, Cambridge, Mass.: MIT Press.

Krugman, Paul (1995) *Development, Geography and Economic Theory*, Cambridge, Mass.: MIT Press.

Maskell, Peter, Heikki Eskelinen, Ingjaldur Hannibaldson, Anders Malmberg and Eirik Vatne (1998) *Competitiveness, Localized Learning and Regional Development: Specialization and Prosperity in Small Open Economies*, London: Routledge.

Morris, Mike and Justin Barnes (2004) "Policy Lessons In Organising Cooperation and Facilitating Networked Learning in Value Chains and Industrial Clusters", available at http://www.Ukzn.Ac.Za/Csdsv.

Nadvi, Khalid and Hubert Schmitz (1999) "Clustering and Industrialisation", *World Development* 27(9).

Piore, Michael and Charles Sabel (1984) *The Second Industrial Divide: Possibilities for Prosperity*, New York: Basic Books Publishers.

Porter, M. E. (1990) *The Competitive Advantage of Nations*, New York: Macmillan.

Schmitz, Hubert (1999a) "Global Competition and Local Co-operation: Success and Failure in the Sinos Valley, Brazil", *World Development* 27(9): 465–83.

Scott, Alan (1998) *Regions and the World Economy*, London: Oxford University Press.

Storper, Michael (1997) *The Regional World*, London: Guildford.

Sugden, Roger, Rita Hartung Cheng and G. Richard Meadows (2003) *Urban and Regional Prosperity in a Globalised New Economy*, Cheltenham: Edward Elgar.

12

Institutional support for collective ICT learning: Cluster development in Kenya and Ghana

Banji Oyelaran-Oyeyinka, Kaushalesh Lal and Catherine Nyaki Adeya

The traditional technology policy framework advances two broad reasons for supporting small firm activities.[1] The first is the perceived market failure in the labour and technology markets and the second is the high incidence of weakness in or absence of markets and institutions in developing countries (Lall, 2001; Metcalfe, 1994). As most analysts agree, there is pervasive market failure in developing countries, while widespread institutional[2] disarticulation exerts far greater impact on small rather than large producers. Institutional weaknesses raise transaction costs that thereby constrain firms from taking advantage of market opportunities, while market failures[3] limit access to markets and innovation possibilities.[4] From a policy perspective, small and medium-sized enterprise (SME) expansion generates employment in ways that create positive externalities due to their wider geographic spread and quantitatively larger numbers. Support to SMEs is therefore seen as a way of attenuating the negative effects of unemployment and to generate economic growth.

While the development of small and medium-sized firms[5] remains central to the economic development of African countries, they have not fulfilled their expected mandate due to a number of well-known structural constraints (Pyke and Sengenberger, 1992). Small firms lack the managerial and technological capabilities that are routinely internalized by large firms. In the 1980s, the exposure of African industry to international competition further laid bare the structural fragility of the region's industrial system. The policy response to the internal resource scarcity of SMEs and recent competitive pressures were attempts by state and private agencies to develop institutions and services to promote

Industrial clusters and innovation systems in Africa: Institutions, markets and policy, Oyelaran-Oyeyinka and McCormick (eds), United Nations University Press, 2007, ISBN 978-92-808-1137-7

competitiveness within small firms. Central to this approach is the effort to upgrade product quality, improve design and packaging, and raise the overall human skills of firms through real service provision (Pyke, 1994; Schmitz, 1992). Service delivery is hamstrung by an array of agencies that are themselves technically weak, poorly funded and largely ineffectual. The shortcomings in the types of public intervention lead analysts to private options to eliminate policy biases (Hallberg, 2000). However, most alternative prescriptions still require considerable state action. These alternatives include eliminating market failures that led to cost disadvantages, restricting access to markets, facilitating access to information, removing discriminatory practices against small producers and improving public goods.

In the recent past, there has also been a move toward greater systemic support, in contrast to the previous traditional technology policy dealing with the conception of firms operating in isolation. This view suggests that small and medium-sized enterprises and clusters in developing areas will need sustained systemic support to cope with the new competitive domestic and global market (King, 1999; Levy, Berry and Nugent, 1999; Pietrobelli and Rabellotti, 2004; Pyke and Sengenberger, 1992). Greater systemic coordination in the provision of infrastructure and information would lead to gains in collective efficiency. The aim of the study reported in this chapter is to examine the role of institutional support and the ways clusters in two African countries learn through collective support. In doing this we attempt to answer the question of whether clustering as an industrial-organization strategy fosters collective learning and promotes enterprise performance.

The chapter is organized as follows: In the following section we describe the objectives and present the characteristics of the clusters in the two countries and the analytical framework. The next section reports the statistical findings and the final section provides a summary and conclusion.

Objectives of the chapter

Micro and small enterprises (MSEs) dominate clusters in Africa. They have increasingly gained prominence as a channel and potential means for employment generation, poverty reduction and industrial regeneration in Kenya and Ghana. In Kenya, MSEs employed about 3.7 million people in 1999, which grew to 4.2 million people in 2000, representing an 11.9 per cent annual growth rate (GoK, 2001). In aggregate terms, the urban areas absorb the greatest number of MSE workers, representing nearly two-thirds (64.4 per cent) of total MSE-sector employment (GoK, 2002). From the available statistics, MSEs' contribution to GDP was estimated at 18.4 per cent (CBS et al., 1999). During the same period that the MSEs realized this growth, it was noted that a number of them suffered from "low productivity leading to low incomes and hence low potential to provide a viable vehicle for poverty reduction" (GoK, 2002). Consequently, a number of interventions such as credit services, training, technology upgrading and marketing were attempted, though with little success.

An important debate that currently preoccupies policymakers and scholars alike is the role of information and communication technologies (ICTs) in promoting the growth and competitiveness of MSEs. There has been little systematic study on the role ICTs play in enhancing the productivity and market reach of MSEs. In sub-Saharan Africa (SSA), there is hardly any evidence of whether and/or how ICTs are being used in MSEs. Many governments have developed and are still developing policies to enhance the productivity of enterprises in clusters. However, in the case of Africa there is a curious gap in these policy developments, especially with the clear omission of ICTs. The chapter derives from a study conducted of Kamukunji and Kariobangi clusters in Kenya and Suame Cluster in Ghana and was designed to assess MSEs'[6] potential to absorb information and communication technologies and to explore the effect of clustering on MSEs' ability to utilize ICTs effectively. The main objectives of the study are:

- To examine cluster characteristics as well as the formal and informal institutions that provide technological support in the adoption of ICTs;
- To investigate the contributions of human development institutions in producing a workforce of desired skills for the cluster;
- To assess the degree of ICT adoption due to the clustering effect;[7] and
- To identify impediments to ICT diffusion in clusters.

Cluster characteristics in Ghana and Kenya

Suame Cluster (also known as "Suame Magazine") is located in the heart of Kumasi (northern Ghana). Kamukunji cluster lies within Nairobi, 3 kilometres from the Central Business District (CBD). Comparatively poor people live here and most work within the informal sector. Kariobangi is a rapidly expanding cluster about 15 kilometres to the east of Nairobi. Unlike in Kamukunji and Suame, no scholarly research has been done in Kariobangi cluster. Even though the two enterprise clusters in Kenya are geographically separated, they are comparable in enterprise size and contextual factors such as infrastructure, historical development and extent of government and non-governmental support activities.

We know of no specific policies to introduce ICTs in clusters; collective learning seems to have arisen as a response to collective needs. Entrepreneurs have been known to find substitutes in the absence of state policy and inadequate public goods (Brautigam, 1997). Our aim is to analyse the role of formal and informal institutions for learning in these clusters. These include the commonly named Business and Communication Centres in Suame operated by private-sector enterprises. Generally, these centres offer the following services at a fee: telephone calls, facsimile and word- and data-processing services. Ghana Telecom has installed a number of public telephone booths within and outside the cluster, although they are insufficient in comparison to the cluster's population. The Business and Communication Centres in Ghana are similar in structure and nature of business to the Telephone Bureaus in Kenya. Access to a variety of ICT services within the Kamukunji and Kariobangi clusters is limited, except telephone services, which are widely available from telephone bureaus. In addition to telephone booths, there are a few communal ICT centres providing computer services, although service can sometimes be erratic.

Analytical framework

The literature on cluster performance and innovation suggests that development of an enterprise knowledge base in clusters results from the flow of knowledge from external and internal sources (Beaudry et al., 2000; Kline and Rosenberg, 1986; McCormick, 1998; Oyelaran-Oyeyinka, 2003). The creation and use of knowledge depends on the type of clusters. Dynamic clusters use external and internal knowledge sources for innovation and skill upgrading while less dynamic clusters rely heavily on external sources. Expectedly, non-innovative or static clusters may not be equipped with sufficient knowledge infrastructure to enable firms to carry out innovations. However, the innovative capability of firms and clusters cannot be attributed to inter- and intra-firm flows of knowledge alone; it is equally influenced by internal firm factors such as the attitude of owners or managing directors (MDs) of firms. The characteristics of MDs, including entrepreneurship, education and knowledge base, are critical variables. Collective learning and skill upgrading facilities are more relevant for clusters of SMEs. For instance, the idea of Collective Service Centres was adopted as a means to provide small and medium-sized firms with economies of scale in the municipality of Modena in Italy. The centres were primarily responsible for providing information, a key requirement of the New Competition (Best, 1990).[8] A theoretical framework encompassing these characteristics and other factors that determine cluster performance is depicted in figure 12.1. It is a model of how support systems contribute to the technological capability building efforts of firms.

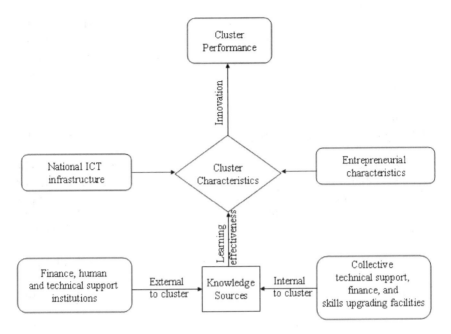

Figure 12.1 Theoretical framework

The framework shows that external and internal knowledge derive from several institutions such as technical, financial and skill-upgrading institutions, although we were not able to capture finance in our analysis due to lack of data. The greater the sources of knowledge, the more effective the learning processes and the higher the propensity for better cluster performance. Since the study focuses on the adoption of ICTs and cluster performance, we included the role of national ICT infrastructure. The adoption of ICTs is significantly influenced by local and national ICT infrastructure (Lal, 2001).

Bivariate and multivariate techniques are used to examine the effects of collective learning opportunities on cluster performance. Bivariate analysis relates firms' characteristics to the degree of ICT adoption while firm performance is analyzed in multivariate framework using ordinary least square models.

Methodology and data

Research methods
The research design focuses upon three sets of explanatory factors for the extent to which MSEs may absorb and utilize ICTs effectively: those related to the technology, to labour supply and learning and to clustering.

Clustering provides opportunities for positive demonstration effects that enable entrepreneurs to master new technology and facilitates interactions that promote joint problem solving, troubleshooting and innovation in adapting the technology to their own needs. These hypotheses were tested in Ghana and Kenya.

Sampling

The target population was MSEs in a specific cluster: Kamukunji and Kariobangi in Kenya and Suame in Kumasi, Ghana. The technique employed was a stratified sampling method. The justification for this technique was that the stratum of interest, which is enterprises in the cluster utilizing ICTs, was perceived to be a small percentage of the total population. General random sampling would not be appropriate. In order to capture as much of the user population as possible, the researchers proceeded to:

1. Conduct a survey of which enterprises in the clusters actually have ICTs in-house and identify the type of ICTs in question;
2. Conduct a survey of the enterprises that do not have ICTs in-house but utilize external facilities of other enterprises in the cluster and/ or use other centralized facilities, such as cybercafés and telecentres. How far do they travel to use these resources? Does the resources meet their needs? Do they plan to have their own in-house? And, if so, why?
3. Find out which enterprises in the clusters do not use or are unaware of these new technologies.

Sampling for this study was carried out at three levels: geographic (cluster), sector and enterprise. Geographically the study covered two clusters, purposively sampled due to their dominance in size, number of diverse MSE activities and presence of local-level associations that support MSEs.

After purposive sampling of the two Kenyan clusters, the variety of enterprises represented within each of the clusters was examined. It was noted during this exercise that enterprises engaging in similar activities tend to group together within the clusters. As such, cluster sampling was adopted to select the study sample from the study sites. The samples were equally stratified on the basis of the three sectors of business activity: manufacture, trade and services, with the enterprise as the unit of analysis. Additionally, thirteen commercial ICT providers within the clusters were sampled for the study, eight in Kariobangi and five in Kamukunji. Given the study's focus on the impact and potential of ICT at the enterprise level, interviews were conducted with the owners, managers or owner-managers of the MSEs as well as the commercial ICT service providers within the clusters.

In Suame a base map, obtained from the Town and Country Planning

Department, was used to carry out a participatory mapping exercise within the cluster, using a transect walk. This was necessary to help the research team identify where the various activities occurred and to note the peculiar differences within the zones. The transect walk helped the research team re-group the existing zones within the Suame Magazine cluster and to facilitate the administration of the questionnaires. Consequently, the research team came up with six research zones within the general cluster using the road networks in the cluster.

The research process

This study used both secondary and primary sources of information. Secondary data was gathered by reviewing relevant published academic works as well as documentation by various development institutions. In particular, reports by international agencies including local NGOs were reviewed. Primary data were collected at two levels.

The first level involved a scoping exercise of two clusters located in Nairobi, which the project intended to use as case studies. The scoping exercise was conducted to record basic facts about the two clusters relevant for developing research instruments, to know the types of activities going on within the clusters, to develop a sampling frame for enterprises as a unit of analysis and to map the study area.

The second level of primary information gathering included liaison and sharing information from the scoping exercise with the Ghana team participating in the comparative study. The Kenya team travelled to Ghana for a planning meeting in May 2001, which enabled the team to visit the Suame cluster used as a case study by the Ghana team. The meeting in Ghana shared the outputs of the scoping exercises in Kenya and Ghana and discussed issues of methodology, including tentative research questions, instruments and research timetable. It was agreed that both teams should use similar research questions and instruments to facilitate cross-cluster comparability.

The third step involved developing country-specific research instruments through a consultative process involving both teams and based on the discussions held in Ghana. The information sharing process included a member of the Ghana team travelling to Kenya in December 2001 to work with the Kenyan team. The final step in the process involved two members of each of the two teams travelling to UNU/INTECH in Holland in March 2002 to work with the Research Coordinator to finalize country reports.

Data collection

Quantitative data were collected using semi-structured questionnaires from September to October 2001. These were complemented by key informant discussions/interviews and observation. Four research assistants were engaged for information gathering.

A pre-testing of the instrument was completed and appropriate adjustments made. The outcomes of the Kenyan and Ghanaian pre-tests were incorporated into the final instrument. The principal investigators reviewed the filled-in instruments daily after fieldwork. The teams also conducted focus group discussions to follow up on some of the issues that came up during the interviews, which also served as a learning process for the owners of the enterprises and for the researchers. After the field data collection, a codebook was developed for the responses to the instrument's open-ended questions. These were discussed and harmonized between the Kenyan and Ghanaian teams. A common database using similar coding was developed for data entry.

Firm-specific variables included history of firms, product profile, type of ICTs used, ownership of ICTs, potential benefits of ICTs, size of firms and financial data. The cluster-specific data was related to presence of technological support and skill upgrading in- and outside clusters, training institutions owned by associations and individuals and the type, frequency and duration of training provided by the existence of institutions. Although available electricity is a crucial part of ICT infrastructure, no information on this aspect was collected because this is part of national information infrastructure, which is beyond the scope of this study. Although firms shared a lot of information with the researchers, firm-specific financial data and information about financial institutions in clusters was difficult to come by. The main ICT tools used by firms were: fixed and mobile telephone, facsimile, computers, computer-aided design/computer-aided manufacture (CAD/CAM) technology, e-mail and the Internet. These technologies were measured on a binary scale, i.e., 1 for users of these technologies and 0 for non-users. Subsequently, a composite ICT index was computed for each firm by taking the average of all the technologies used by firm. We have used this ICT index as a measure of the intensity of ICT adoption by firms in the analysis. The average number of ICT tools used by firms can approximate user intensity because the ICT tools covered in the study are ordinal in nature. For instance, an Internet-using firm requires a computer, a telephone and e-mail as part of its internal infrastructure. On the other hand, firms that do not use e-mail and the Internet could do with a stand-alone computer facility. For this reason, the ICT index of an Internet-using firm should be higher than that of telephone– or stand-alone-computer–using firms, though they are using only one tool. Similar argument can be extended for CAD/CAM-using firms because by extension, all the CAD/CAM-using firms were users of all other ICT tools covered in this study. Hence CAD/CAM-using firms have the highest ICT index values, being the most advanced users of ICT tools.

Hypotheses

H₁: The provision of collective technical, information and skills upgrading facilities leads to higher performance in clusters

For small producers in relatively poor African countries, the cost of staying competitive in skill-based and technology-driven markets is enormous. For this reason, small enterprises require support for skill upgrading. There are two main implications. First, it means that support for autonomous firm-level technical change should be sought from a much wider variety of sources. Within firms, the sources include production lines and machine shops among others, rather than focusing exclusively on research and development (R&D). Second, external support services crucial to the growth of firms come from public and private sources including private associations. The knowledge acquired contributes to improving old vintage plants that promise as much economic return as investment in new vintage plants. Innovation is expected to lead to higher enterprise performance.

Collective skills- and information-upgrading support to industry vary in the depth of service. In developing countries, research and development institutions (RDIs), universities and technical institutes, local engineering consultants and foreign partners provide support to domestic industry. In addition, there are institutions providing information and metrological services (standards, testing and quality control). Three forms of institutional support, namely, public and private services and network associations are possible. Government support is delivered through technology centres or public RDIs with broad mandates to assist SME innovation. Private associations are voluntary trade and manufacturing organizations supported through membership dues. Service providers from the private sector operate as consulting organizations and deliver services at a cost.

H₂: Qualification of owners is related to the types of technologies adopted, with consequences for innovation and cluster performance

In SMEs, owners or MDs take almost all the decisions rendering the decision-making processes very different in SMEs compared to large firms with an established hierarchy. For this reason, decision-making processes in small firms are highly influenced by the knowledge and academic qualification of enterprise owners, while in large firms no single individual is responsible for decisions taken due to the hierarchical nature of firms. Therefore, the skill acquisition process[9] in small firms follows a different trajectory. Small enterprises tend to employ less-qualified persons and subsequently seek to upgrade skills by on-the-job training. However, the crucial question is the type and the adequacy of training provided. A relatively more qualified manager is in a better position to decide on the suitability of a particular training for workers. We hypothesize that MDs with engineering degrees would choose ICT-based learning processes and would favour training workers in advanced ICTs.

H₃: Cluster performance is correlated with higher levels of new-technology usage

Cluster performance is proxied by the performance of individual firms, which are dependent on the availability of ICT infrastructure and skill-upgrading facilities in a cluster. The emergence of new technologies has led to significant shifts in the skill composition of industrial labour and heightened the debate on technology-skill and capital-skill complementarity (Bound and Johnson, 1993; Goldin and Katz, 1998). Skill-bias technical change means that "skilled or more-educated labor is more complementary with new technology or physical capital than is unskilled or less educated labor" (Goldin and Katz, 1998: 694n). Given the technology-skill complementarities, the introduction of ICTs has significant skill implications for developing countries' firms learning to produce for domestic and external markets. The successful adoption of e-business tools is likely to enhance individual worker productivity in the so-called modern sectors such as electronics and general machinery sector. In the more traditional sectors such as textiles, clothing and foods, there is a propensity for significant rise in product quality and more precise processing. To achieve the goal of better quality products, firms are obliged to undertake greater training and investment in skills and knowledge upgrading. The implications for long-term industrial competitiveness in developing countries are thus evident regardless of the sectors where countries have comparative advantage.

The reason for the labour force's rising skill content is the accelerating rate of technological change, which induces the demand for a better-educated and skilled workforce (Arrow, 1962; Nelson and Phelps, 1966).[10] Sectors that experience rapid technological progress are inclined to hire better-educated workers because this group have far less need for training in basic skills and as such constitute a ready innovation asset within firms. The corollary is that technological change will in turn stimulate the demand for more knowledge-intensive and skilled labour. The adoption of new technologies employing high-speed computers coupled with advanced telecommunications technologies has not only resulted in relatively lower transaction costs but also increased intra- and inter-firm integration functions. Firms earn high profit margins through low-wage and low-skills production as well as through fast delivery of customized products and services to customers. The scope advantage of small firms, be they manufacturers of batch orders or subcontractors to larger firms, has been significantly enhanced by new technologies. We therefore hypothesize that the adoption of higher level of ICTs will result in better cluster performance.

Statistical results

It was necessary to analyse the data in bivariate and in multivariate frameworks because greater degrees of freedom were available in bivariate tests but did not capture the interaction of other variables on ICT adoption. On the other hand, multivariate testing permits an examination of the composite role of several indicators at the cost of degrees of freedom. The results are presented in the sections that follow.

Bivariate analysis

Table 12.1 presents the ownership and use of ICT tools by sample firms in Kenya and Uganda. The table shows that use of ICT tools by sample firms is higher than ownership in both the countries. For instance, fixed telephone is used by 79 per cent in Ghana and 92.2 per cent in Kenya, whereas the ownership is 22 per cent and 24.4 per cent, respectively, in the countries. As expected, the use of mobile telephones is much less compared to fixed lines in both the countries. However, whereas the ownership pattern is the same in Kenya, it is much higher (40 per cent) in Ghana.[11]

The use of facsimile varies substantially in two countries. Only 5 per cent of the sample firms used facsimile in Kenya compared to 15 per cent in Ghana, where there is also greater ownership of facsimile. It is clear from table 12.1 that ownership rate of ICTs tools other than fixed telephones in Ghana was much higher than in Kenya while the use of ICTs other than facsimile is similar in both countries. The relatively

Table 12.1 Ownership and use of ICTs

Country →	Kenya		Ghana	
Technology	Ownership	Usage	Ownership	Usage
Fixed telephone	24.4%	92.2%	22%	79%
Mobile telephone	24.4%	41.1%	40%	44%
Facsimile	1.7%	5.0%	15%	15%
Stand-alone computer	2.2%	10.6%	8%	9%
E-mail	1.1%	4.4%	3%	4%
Internet	0.6%	2.8%	1%	1%
CAD/CAM	0%	0%	0%	1%

Table 12.2 Skill intensity and the use of ICTs

Country	ICT index			Total firms
	<0.25	0.26–0.50	>0.51	
Ghana				
Yes	31 (57.4)	26 (83.9)	5 (100.0)	59
No	4 (7.4)	–	–	3
No employees	14 (25.9)	5 (16.1)	–	17
Total firms	54	31	5	90
Kenya				
Yes	60 (53.6)	39 (69.6)	8 (66.7)	107
No	41 (36.6)	16 (28.6)	4 (33.3)	61
No employees	9 (8.0)	1 (1.8)	–	10
Total firms	112	56	12	190

Note: Figures in parentheses are column percentages.

widespread use of ICT tools reveals there is evidently demand, but resource-poor small firms are unable to own the facilities themselves. In table 12.2 we present the distribution of firms according to the intensity of ICT use and the availability of a skilled workforce. MDs of sample firms were asked whether they have workers with sufficient and desired skills for effective use of new technologies. The response was recorded on a binary scale. Table 12.2 shows a positive association between the degree of ICT adoption and the opinion of MDs regarding the availability of a skilled workforce. For instance, in Ghana, 57.4 per cent of MDs' relatively well-trained workforce used less advanced[12] ICTs (ICT index < 0.25) whereas all the MDs of advanced ICT-using firms confirmed they have workers with the desired skills.

Similarly, owners in Kenya whose skilled workers had demonstrable ability to use ICT tools were more inclined to have adopted more advanced ICTs, but 33.3 per cent of MDs who did not have workers with the desired skill level still adopted advanced ICT tools.

The results presented in table 12.3 show the nature and availability of internal and external skill-upgrading facilities. The table is based on the actual practices adopted by all sample firms and shows that apprenticeship[13] training within clusters is the most common source of skill upgrading in both countries. That MDs of 71.1 per cent of firms in Ghana and 96.1 per cent of firms in Kenya found internal apprenticeship the most accessible mode of skill upgrading illustrates this fact. However, the data also suggest that Suame cluster in Ghana has more internal formal training institutions than clusters in Kenya. This is reflected by 6.7 per cent of MDs in Ghanaian firms reporting the existence of formal training institu-

Table 12.3 Availability of skill-upgrading facilities

Sources	Type	Country →	Ghana	Kenya
Internal	Formal training institutions		6 (6.7)	1 (0.6)
	Apprenticeship		64 (71.1)	173 (96.1)
	NGO		1 (1.1)	–
External	Formal training institutions		3 (3.3)	76 (42.2)
	Apprenticeship		1 (1.1)	41 (22.8)
	NGO		4 (4.4)	1 (0.6)
	Formal organizations		–	12 (6.7)

Note: Figures in parentheses are column percentages.

tions in Suame while merely 0.6 per cent of MDs of Kenyan firms acknowledged the presence of internal training institutions.

The two prominent training centres in the Suame cluster that provide institutional training are the Suame Intermediate Technology Transfer Unit (ITTU) and the National Vocational and Technical Institute. Apart from these two formal training institutes are private collective service centres. Enterprise owners, especially those in vehicle servicing and trading, are trained through apprenticeship and on-the-job training. Ninety per cent of the respondents have acquired necessary skills through this mechanism. Three forms of training providers were identified. These are formal learning institutions, the master craftsman and non-governmental organizations (NGOs). The master craftsmen provide training to 90 per cent of the workers and the majority of employees and entrepreneurs receive training on-the-job as apprentices. Only 8 per cent of the 71 respondents received training from formal training institutions and just 2 per cent from NGOs. These training providers are responsible for both internal and external training. Other formal training institutions located outside the cluster provide for only a small proportion of the skills acquired.

The situation is exactly the opposite with regard to availability of external training institutions. A fairly large number of firms (42.2 per cent) reported that outside institutions are the main sources of skill upgrading in Kenya while the percentage of firms that share this view in Ghana is merely 3.3 per cent. This is because Suame has a fairly good share of internal cluster facilities compared with the two clusters in Kenya. Another distinguishing aspect is that apprenticeship is regarded as a relatively more important source of skill upgrading in Kenya compared to Ghana.

Table 12.4 presents the association between the intensity of ICT adoption and the participation of workers in ICT training programmes.

Table 12.4 Participation in ICT training programmes

| Country | ICT index | | | Total firms |
	<0.25	0.26–0.50	>0.51	
Ghana				
Yes	3 (5.6)	3 (9.7)	5 (100.0)	11
No	50 (92.6)	28 (90.3)	–	78
Total firms	54	31	5	90
Kenya				
Yes	5 (4.5)	3 (5.4)	3 (25.0)	11
No	106 (94.6)	53 (94.6)	9 (75.0)	168
Total firms	112	56	12	190

Note: Figures in parentheses are column percentages.

Participation in training programs is determined largely by the attitude and vision of the MD. If MDs appreciate the utility of training programs in relation to the type of ICTs adopted by firms, it is very likely that the owner will send their workers for training. The availability of training programs within the cluster is another factor that can influence the decision to provide worker training. The table shows that MDs of advanced ICT users among Ghanaian firms are inclined to provide training while MDs of low-intensity ICT-using firms have fewer propensities to do so. This is reflected in the responses: MDs of all the advanced ICT-using firms encouraged their workers to participate in ICT training programs whereas a mere 5.6 per cent of MDs of low-intensity ICT-using firms sent their workers for training. The skill-bias of educated owners thus plays an important part in the skill acquisition efforts of the enterprise.

The relation between worker participation in training and the intensity of ICT adoption in Kenya is noticeably different from that of Ghana. A large number of Ghanaian firms (75 per cent) that did not send their workers for training adopted very advanced ICT tools. Four to five per cent of MDs of low-intensity ICT-using firms sent their workers for training. Apart from these factors, there could be other country-level reasons related to the mode and utility of specific training programs that could explain the low level of participation by Kenyan firms.

Table 12.5 presents the distribution of firms according to the intensity of ICT adoption and the perception of various benefits of their use. Although ICT adoption literature suggests numerous benefits, such as augmented competitiveness, flexibility in product designs and just-in-time (JIT) delivery systems, we have considered the benefits indicated by the sample firms. The results presented in table 12.5 suggest that there is positive association between the benefits and the intensity of ICT use that is

Table 12.5 Benefits of using ICTs

Country	ICT index			Response rate
	<0.25	0.26–0.50	>0.51	
Ghana				
Time management	36 (66.7)	27 (87.1)	3 (60.0)	66 (73.3)
Cost effectiveness	24 (44.4)	18 (58.1)	3 (60.0)	45 (50.0)
Enhanced profits	19 (35.2)	13 (41.9)	4 (80.0)	36 (40.0)
Increased sales	11 (20.4)	11 (35.5)	4 (80.0)	26 (28.9)
Exposure to wider markets	14 (25.9)	12 (38.7)	5 (100.0)	31 (34.4)
Total firms	54	31	5	90
Kenya				
Time management	79 (70.5)	53 (94.6)	10 (88.3)	142 (74.7)
Cost effectiveness	43 (38.4)	35 (62.5)	7 (58.3)	85 (44.7)
Enhanced profits	22 (19.6)	16 (28.6)	9 (75.0)	47 (24.7)
Increased sales	34 (30.4)	27 (48.2)	8 (66.7)	69 (36.3)
Exposure to wider markets	34 (30.4)	23 (41.1)	7 (58.3)	64 (33.7)
Total firms	112	56	12	190

Note: Figures in parentheses are column percentages.

uniform across both countries. For instance, better time-management is considered one of the benefits of ICT use. It was expected that MDs of advanced ICT-using firms could manage their time more productively than others. However, the results presented in table 12.5 do not support this argument. In Ghana, only 60 per cent of MDs among various levels of ICT-using firms reported that ICT adoption contributed to better management of time. In Kenya, 88.3 per cent of advanced ICT-using firms attributed better time-management as a benefit of ICT adoption, while 94.6 per cent of mid-level ICT-using firms credited ICT adoption contributing to better time-management. The results suggest that adoption of more advanced ICT tools does not proportionately contribute to better time-management.

Other benefits, such as cost-effectiveness, enhanced profits, increased sales and access to a wider market, are positively related to the degree of ICT adoption in Ghanaian sample firms. For instance, 80 per cent of advanced ICT-using firms reported increased sales due to ICT adoption while only 20.4 per cent of low-intensity ICT-using firms shared the same views. Except for the benefit-to-cost effectiveness, the result is similar in Kenyan firms. Nearly 63 per cent of mid-level ICT-using firms found the adoption of ICTs cost-effective while a lower proportion (58.3 per cent) of advanced ICT-using firms expressed this perspective.

The knowledge and disposition of the owner decisively influences technological change in small producers. Enterprise owners tend to finance

Table 12.6 Education level of MDs and the adoption of ICTs

Country Level of education	ICT index			
	<0.25	0.26–0.50	>0.51	Total firms
Ghana				
None but literate	4 (7.4)	1 (3.2)	–	5 (5.6)
4–8 years	39 (72.2)	22 (71.0)	1 (20.0)	62 (68.9)
9–12 years	11 (20.4)	6 (19.4)	4 (80.0)	21 (23.3)
13+ years	–	2 (6.5)	–	2 (2.2)
Total firms	54	31	5	90
Kenya				
None but literate	1 (0.9)	–	–	1 (0.5)
1–3 years	2 (1.8)	–	–	2 (1.1)
4–8 years	35 (31.3)	11 (19.6)	–	46 (24.2)
9–12 years	69 (61.6)	30 (53.6)	4 (33.3)	103 (54.2)
13+ years	5 (4.5)	15 (26.8)	8 (66.7)	28 (14.7)
Total firms	112	56	12	190

Note: Figures in parentheses are column percentages.

investment largely by their own savings and may also be resource-constrained. Small firms would therefore not invest without clearly perceived benefits. In turn, the perception of MDs of technology adoption is significantly affected by their academic qualifications and experiences. Given the nature of the study's sample firms, we examined the relationship between MDs' qualifications and the degree of ICT adoption with the number of years schooled used as a proxy of education. The results are presented in table 12.6.

As expected, the MDs' education level is positively associated with the degree of ICT adoption in Ghana and Kenya. From table 12.6, MDs of low-level ICT-using firms who studied up to 8 years represent 72.2 per cent where only 20 per cent of MDs with similar qualification adopted advanced ICTs in Ghana. The situation is reversed where MDs are more qualified (9+ years). Only 20.4 per cent of MDs with 9 or more years of schooling adopted a low level of ICTs while 80 per cent of MDs with similar qualifications adopted the most advanced ICTs. The association between ICT-adoption and the qualification of MDs in Kenya is similar to that of Ghana. However, table 12.6 shows that, in general, Kenyan firms were being managed by more qualified MDs.

Multivariate analysis

After the bivariate analysis the data was analysed in separate multivariate frameworks for Kenya and Ghana. Ordinary least square (OLS) tech-

INSTITUTIONAL SUPPORT FOR ICT LEARNING 285

Table 12.7 Determinants of the adoption of ICTs in Kenyan SME clusters

Models →	I	II	III	Remarks
	Dependent variable: ICT index			
Independents				
Constant	0.218	0.233	−0.153	
Time management	0.014 (0.394)	0.011 (0.308)		Does your enterprise derive quality time management?
Cost-effective	0.010 (0.376)	0.011 (0.402)		Does your enterprise derive cost effectiveness?
Profit margins	0.095*** (3.564)			Does your enterprise derive enhanced profits?
Cost-benefit	−0.012 (−1.207)	−0.014 (−1.439)		How is the balance between the cost and benefits of ICTs?
STO		0.049* (1.882)		Does your enterprise derive increased sales due to ICTs?
MD education			0.079*** (5.345)	Managing Director's education
Use your ICTs in clusters			−0.021* (−1.725)	Do enterprises around you use your ICTs?
Use of within clusters (neighbour)			0.029 (1.453)	Do you use the ICT facilities of neighbouring enterprises?
R-square	0.131	0.075	0.202	
Degrees of freedom	151	152	177	

Note: *** → 1%; ** → 5%; * → 10% level of significance

nique is used in identifying firm- and cluster-specific factors that influenced adoption of ICTs. We analyzed Kenya and Ghana data separately because clusters in both countries differ substantially in terms of collective skill-upgrading facilities, provision of ICT training institutions and the availability of technological support within clusters. Parameter estimates of OLS models for Kenyan and Ghanaian data are presented in tables 12.7 and 12.8, respectively. The explanatory power of the equations is not very high because the list of explanatory variables is insufficient to explain the adoption of ICTs. Other possibilities are not available on the dataset and hence cannot be included in the analysis.

Table 12.8 Determinants of adoption of ICTs in Ghanaian SME cluster

	Dependent variable: ICT index		
Models →	I	II	Remarks
Independents			
Constant	0.613	0.147	
Time management			Does your enterprise derive quality time management?
Cost-effective			Does your enterprise derive cost effectiveness?
Profit margins	−0.817** (−2.270)		Does your enterprise derive enhanced profits?
Cost-benefit	0.058 (0.642)		How is the balance between the cost and benefits of ICTs?
STO	0.430** (2.169)		Does your enterprise derive increased sales due to ICTs?
MD education		−0.012 (−0.531)	Managing Director's education
Cluster effect		0.154*** (2.881)	Do you have physical access to ICTs owned by the agencies within the cluster?
Use your ICTs		−0.053** (−2.406)	Do enterprises around you use your ICTs?
Use neighbour's		0.020 (0.500)	Do you use the ICT facilities of neighbouring enterprises?
R-square	0.291	0.286	
Degrees of freedom	22	56	

Note: *** → 1%; ** → 5%; * → 10% level of significance

We carried out three estimations of the ordinary least square model in order to overcome multi-collinearity problems. From table 12.7, profit margins, sales turnover and MDs' qualification emerge as significant in influencing the degree of adoption of ICTs. The cluster-specific variable that played a decisive though negative role in the adoption of ICTs is inter-firm cooperation. Cooperation is represented by a firm's use of neighbouring firms' ICTs. This is an important validation of the assumption of benefits accruing to co-locating firms. The drawback to collaboration is that advanced users of ICTs tend not to share their facilities with neighbouring firms. The most widely expressed view is that firms are reluctant to share facilities with competitors and want to retain corporate confidentiality. Table 12.7 also shows that perceived benefits such as improved time management and cost effectiveness were not significant in influencing the decision to adopt advanced ICT tools. The results are similar to the bivariate results where only a few advanced ICT-using firms reported benefits due to ICT adoption.

Regression analysis results for Suame cluster data are presented in table 12.8. It is seen from the table that two variables, sales turnover and cooperation with firms, play similar roles in influencing the adoption of ICTs in the Kenyan cluster. The surprising result is that, unlike Kenya, profit margins emerged negatively significant in Ghana. This is contrary to what we found in the bivariate analysis (table 12.5). The plausible explanation for this result lies in the degree of freedom of estimates. Results in table 12.5 are based on 36 firms while 22 firms are included in the regression analysis. Other firms were dropped as data for regression analysis when one or more other independent variables were missing.

Another surprising result is that MDs' education was not significant in influencing the degree of ICT adoption. This might be because highly qualified owners that adopted mid-level ICT tools managed only a few firms. Table 12.8 also shows that one of the cluster-specific variables, "use of ICT infrastructure owned by agencies within cluster", has played a crucial role in ICT adoption. This finding supports our hypothesis that the existence of technological support institutions within the cluster encourages adoption of new technologies, which in turn contributes to cluster dynamism. This point again supports the hypothesis that collective service provision in the proximity of firms fosters use of new technologies. From appendix 12.1, Suame cluster has better equipped ICT service-providing organizations within it than the clusters in Kenya.

Discussion of results

Statistical and econometric results presented in this study suggest that cluster performance, brought about by the adoption of new technologies by firms within it, depends on two sets of factors. One set are the firm-specific characteristics: academic qualification and knowledge of MDs, skill intensity of the workforce, motivation of MDs to provide workers with regular training for effective use of new technologies, sales turnover and profit margins. The second set of factors consists of cluster-specific variables: the presence of training and collective internal technological support institutions and the benefits of inter-firm sharing of facilities. The adoption of ICTs depends indirectly on the local and national ICT infrastructure since these provide the backbone for firm and individual ICT use. However, systematic investigation of the impact of ICT infrastructure on firm-level ICT adoption within MSE clusters in Kenya and Ghana was not possible because the relevant data was not available.

The study found a considerable gap in ownership and use of ICTs in Kenyan and Ghanaian sample firms. We propose two main reasons for this. One, firms do not own ICT tools due to the complexity of technologies relative to their level of operation. And second, ICT tools are very costly. Low capacity utilization is also regarded as hindering the decision to purchase new technologies. Keeping in mind the type of technologies in question in this study, low capacity utilization may well be irrelevant. Such a wide gap in ownership and usage of new technologies provides justification for collective service initiatives in industrial clusters. One of the prime reasons behind the cluster-oriented approach to industrial development is to share resources that are economically unviable for individual firms to own. Clusters in both countries have sought to attenuate the problem of small-producer isolation by collective services such as provision of training and technological support institutions.

The study also finds evidence that MDs are more inclined to train workers if facilities are readily available within the cluster. Skill-upgrading activities relate positively to MDs' education level; higher-qualified MDs are more inclined to train their workers. This may be attributed to their understanding of technologies and perceived benefits as higher-qualified MDs are in a better position to understand the potential benefits of new technologies. Taking collective actions and organizing orientation programs to MDs can expose owners to new technologies. This should widen the understanding of less-qualified MDs so they might appreciate the use of new technologies in their core business activities. It is expected to encourage new technology adoption and consequently collective actions can lead to better cluster performance.

Firm-specific factors that emerged significant in determining the degree of adoption of ICTs are in line with the existing literature (Drew, 2003; Lal, 2002). The relationship with size of operation and intensity of new technologies used is bidirectional. Firms with larger size of operation are better-equipped to adopt new technologies, as they have sufficient financial resources. The adoption of more advanced technologies contributes to higher sales turnover as is evident from this study. MDs' knowledge and educational background is important in the adoption of new technologies by SMEs because the decision to adopt lies with the owner, unlike in large firms where decision-making is group-based. More informed and knowledgeable MDs are in a better position to do the cost-benefit analysis of new technologies. Consequently, firms managed by professionals are expected to be early adopters of new technologies. Although it may not be possible to send less-qualified personnel for formal training, orientation programs can augment their understanding. Cluster initiatives in this regard can boost the adoption of new technologies. The emergence of MDs' education as a significant determinant of the adoption of ICTs supports our hypothesis.

The emergence of cluster-specific variables as determinants to new-technologies adoption is an important contribution to the existing literature. The findings validate our hypotheses and suggest that cluster performance can be improved by joint actions in the form of technological and human resource development support. In addition to the presence of specific organizations providing training is the incidence of inter-firm knowledge-flows through the provision of training and exchange of information. The survey found that 60 per cent of the enterprises provide training for other enterprises within the cluster. Of this, 80 per cent provide technical training while 18 per cent provide marketing training. This is an important finding since most apprentices are unable to afford the fees charged for basic training. Some enterprise owners admitted that the trainees find it difficult to pay training fees and those trainees are obliged to pay in-kind through services to the master craftsman. This practice of providing financial support to the apprentices conforms to other clusters in Kumasi and the country in general.

Collective actions are also needed to make new technology economically viable. This was achieved in Suame cluster in Ghana by establishing ICT service providers. Corresponding efforts have not been made in Kenyan clusters. On the other hand, the Suame cluster has more internal formal training institutions compared to Kenya, where firms resort to high-cost external service providers. Consequently, a large number of MDs of advanced ICT users adopted new technologies despite lacking workers with desired skills. In this sense, they took a risk in adopting new technologies. Establishing more skill-upgrading institutions within clusters where entrepreneurs could receive advice and services can reduce this risk factor in adoption of new technologies.

Summary and conclusions

The study analyses data collected from the Suame cluster in Ghana and the Kamukunji and Kariobangi clusters in Kenya, which are predominately MSEs. Firm- and cluster-specific data was collected though a semi-structured questionnaire, which was then analysed in bivariate and multivariate frameworks. Firm- and cluster-specific factors emerged as significant determinants of ICT adoption, while ICTs drive cluster performance in increasingly competitive domestic and global markets. The firm-specific factors are: MDs' knowledge and educational background, increased sales turnover, higher profit margins and inclinations of MDs in upgrading workers' skill. The cluster-specific factors are represented by the availability of internal skill-upgrading facilities, existence of technological supporting institutions within the cluster and provision of formal training institutions.

The findings of the study suggest that a number of policy measures need to be taken by governments in developing countries to improve the competitiveness of micro and SMEs. We suggest that state policy encourage greater private-sector participation in setting up training and information service centres within clusters. These institutions could provide need-based skills for better use of new technologies. It is also recommended that MDs of micro and SMEs be encouraged in the process of workforce skill upgrading by organizing orientation programs to raise MDs' awareness of new technologies. Additionally, there is need to subsidize the cost of new technology equipment so that new technologies become economically viable for small firms. This could be achieved through technology-service organizations with simple services such as e-mail and general Internet access. These institutions could be useful in searching function- and job-specific ICT tools that are not only expected to be efficient but also cost effective. Such collective cluster initiatives are expected to result in better cluster performance.

Appendix 12.1 Nature and composition of clusters

Country	Cluster	Average firm size	Major activities	ICT infrastructure
Ghana	Suame	5 workers	Manufacturing; vehicle repair; metalworking; sale of engineering materials; sale of automobile spare parts; sale of foodstuffs	Telephone calls; facsimile; word- and data-processing service
Kenya	Kamukunji	2 workers	Artisans; vehicle repair; sale of new and second-hand clothes; foodstuffs	Telephone and computers (limited access)
	Kariobangi	4 workers	Tailoring; panel beating; woodwork; shoe-making; food processing; building construction; motor wiring; motor vehicle repair, welding and painting	Telephone and computers (limited access)

Notes

1. We wish to acknowledge the contribution of Winnie Mitullah, who coordinated the study in Kenya with Rudith King and George Obeng, both of whom coordinated country-level studies in Ghana. UNU-INTECH and the International Institute for Communication and Development (IICD) funded the country studies.

2. We follow the definition of institution provided by North (1996): "Institutions are the rules of the game of a society or more formally the humanly devised constraints that structure human interaction. They are composed of formal rules (statute law, common law, and regulations), informal constraints ... and the enforcement characteristics of both." However, as Nelson (2002) correctly observes, to see physical and social technology as "constraints" is problematic. He illustrates: "A productive social technology is like a paved road across a swamp. To say that the location of the prevailing road is a constraint on getting across is basically to miss the point. Without a road, getting across would be impossible, or at least much harder."

3. Markets fail due to the problems of "asymmetric information" and the so-called "appropriability" factor. On the former, the difficulties in obtaining information on borrowers lead to the rationing out of such agents, notably small producers, by lenders in the financial markets. Concerning the latter, the inability of firms to capture the full benefits, for instance, of research and development investment and worker training, often leads to under-investment in these activities relative to what is socially optimal. See Biggs (2001) for empirical evidence from developing countries.

4. Markets fail due, in large measure, to problems related to "asymmetric information" as well as appropriability of inventive gains.

5. Small firms play an important role in the economy of both developing and advanced countries. Countries have formulated various policies to support SMEs.

6. The abbreviation "MSEs" is used comprehensively to include the micro and small enterprises as well as the entrepreneurs. Sometimes the word "MSEs" is used interchangeably with the word "cluster".

7. Clustering effect manifest in the benefits of both co-location and purposive inter-firm collaboration. Clustering policy initiatives are specific meso- and micro-level actions deriving from policy to foster the production and innovation activities of the cluster. Such policies target the group rather than individual small enterprise.

8. As Best explains it "By cooperating in the provision of services with substantial economies of scale, small firms can maintain their independence in production without being reduced to subcontractors for products designed in the central office of a giant firm" (Best, 1990: 225).

9. Siegel et al. (1997) suggest that three types of skill empowerment may result when a firm adopts advanced manufacturing technologies: training, changing employees' job responsibilities and creating new jobs and career opportunities for employees.

10. According to these authors, experience gained in the process of operating a given technology or new technology results in increased efficiencies and as such an educated workforce will be more amenable to learning complex technologies.

11. Mobile telephony was only being introduced in Africa at the time we carried out the survey.

12. As can be seen from the definition of the ICT index presented earlier, the lower index value means the firm is using low-end ICT tools such as telephone (fixed and mobile). Larger index values suggest that the firm is using more complex ICT tools such as computers equipped with office-management and CAD/CAM systems. Firms with highest ICT index values are the users of the latest ICTs such as e-mail and the Internet.

13. Apprenticeship is premised on a system of learning-by-watching and learning-by-doing on the job. This system involves the master-apprentice relationship and is traditionally a very important mode of skill acquisition among small producers.

REFERENCES

Arrow, Kenneth J. (1962) "The Economic Implications of Learning by Doing", *Review of Economic Studies* 29(3).
Beaudry, C., S. Breshi and G. M. P. Swann (2000) "Clusters, Innovation and Growth: A Comparative Study of European Countries", in C. Beaudry, S. Breshi and G. M. P. Swann, eds, *Clusters, Innovation and Growth: A Comparative Study of European Countries*, Harwood Academic Publishers.
Best, M. H. (1990) *The New Competition: Institutions of Industrial Restructuring*, Cambridge, Mass.: Harvard University Press.
Biggs, T. (2001) "Is Small Beautiful and Worthy of Subsidy?" *Literature Review*, Washington, D.C.: World Bank.
Bound, J. and G. Johnson (1992) "Change in the Structure of Wages in the 1980s: An Evaluation of Alternative Explanations", *American Economic Review* 82: 371–92.
Brautigam, D. (1997) "Substituting for the State: Institutions and Industrial Development in Eastern Nigeria", *World Development* 25(7): 1063–80.
Central Bureau of Statistics (CBS), International Center for Economic Growth (ICEG) and K-Rep Holdings, Ltd. (1999) *National Micro and Small Enterprise Baseline Survey 1999: Survey Results*, Nairobi, Kenya: Central Bureau of Statistics (CBS), International Center for Economic Growth (ICEG) and K-Rep Holdings Ltd.
Drew, S. (2003) "Stategic Uses of E-commerce by SMEs in the East of England", *European Management Journal*, 21(1).
Government of Kenya (GoK) (2001) "Poverty Reduction Strategy Paper for the Period 2001–2004", Nairobi, Kenya: Government Printers.
Government of Kenya (GoK) (2002) "National Development Plan", Nairobi, Kenya: Government Printers.
Goldin, C. and L. Katz (1998) "The Origins of Technology-Skill Complementarity", *Quarterly Journal of Economics* 113.
Hallberg, Kristin (2000) "A Market-Oriented Strategy for Small and Medium-Scale Enterprises", Discussion Paper No. 40, Washington, D.C.: World Bank.
King, K. and S. McGrath (1999) *Enterprise in Africa: Between Poverty and Growth*, London: Intermediate Technology Publications.
Kline, S. J. and Nathan Rosenberg (1986) "An Overview of Innovation", in R. Landau and N. Rosenberg, *The Positive Sum Strategy*, New York: National Academy Press, 275–305.
Lal, K. (2001) "Institutional Environment and the Growth of Indian IT Industry", *Information Society*, 17.
Lal, K. (2002) "E-Business and Manufacturing Sector: A Study of Small and Medium-Sized Enterprises in India", *Research Policy*, 31(7).

Lall, S. (2001) *Competitiveness, Technology and Skills*, Cheltenham, UK and Northampton, Mass.: Edward Elgar.

Levy, B., A. Berry and J. B. Nugent (1999) *Fulfilling the Export Potential of Small and Medium Firms*, Boston: Kluwer Academic.

McCormick, Dorothy (1998) "Enterprise Clusters in Africa: On the Way to Industrialization", IDS Discussion Paper 366, Nairobi: University of Nairobi.

Metcalfe, J. S. (1994) "Evolutionary Economics and Technology Policy", *Economic Journal*, 104(425).

Nelson, Richard R. (2001) "On the Uneven Evolution of Human Know-How", ISERP Working Paper 01–05, New York: Columbia University, Institute for Social and Economic Research Policy.

Nelson, R. R. and E. Phelps (1966) "Investments in Humans, Technological Diffusion and Economic Growth", *American Economic Review* 56.

North, D. C. (1996) "Economic Performance through Time", in Lee J. Alston, T. Eggertsson and D. C. North, eds, *Empirical Studies in Institutional Change*, Cambridge: Cambridge University Press.

Oyelaran-Oyeyinka, B. (2003) "Knowledge Networks and Technological Capabilities in the African Manufacturing Cluster", *Science, Technology and Development*, 8(1).

Pietrobelli, Carlo and Roberta Rabelotti (2004) "Competitiveness and Upgrading in Clusters and Value Chains: The Case of Latin America", paper presented at DTI/UNIDO Competitiveness Conference, Pretoria, South Africa, 7–11 June.

Pyke, F. (1994) "Small Firms, Technical Services and Inter-Firm Cooperation", Research Series No. 99, Geneva: International Institute for Labour Studies.

Pyke, F. and W. Sengenberger, eds (1992) *Industrial Districts and Local Economic Regeneration*, Geneva: International Institute for Labour Studies.

Schmitz, Hubert (1992) "On the Clustering of Small Firms", *IDS Bulletin* 23(3): 64–69.

Siegel, D. S., D. Waldman and D. W. Youngdahl (1997) "The Adoption of Advanced Manufacturing Technologies: Human Resource Management Implications", *IEEE Transactions on Engineering Management* 44.

13

Conclusion and policy implications

Banji Oyelaran-Oyeyinka and Dorothy McCormick

This book examines the incidence and role of clusters in Africa as a viable and increasingly important form of industrial organization. The previous chapters have presented a set of case studies that analyse clusters in different sectors and at different levels of economic development. We brought these cases together in an attempt to improve our understanding of how local clusters can be transformed into local systems of innovation (LSI) and, furthermore, how local clusters can be better connected to global actors.

We believe that an improved understanding of clusters and innovation is important for at least three reasons. First, the economies of African countries consist largely of small and medium-sized enterprises, many of them specializing in traditional sectors such as furniture, clothing, fabricated metal products and food processing. Second, as a result of liberalization that opened up the economies of most African countries, small firms must now compete in both domestic and regional markets with a wide variety of cheaper and, in many cases, higher-quality alternatives. These are imported, not only from the traditional European and North American suppliers, but also from Asian mass-producing suppliers of intermediate and finished goods. The third reason for the study of clusters and innovation relates to the second. If African-based companies are to access demanding customers in an unpredictable global environment, firms and clusters have to introduce new products, raise quality, lower costs and improve delivery speeds. In short, they must learn both to innovate and to be efficient in all aspects of their businesses.

Industrial clusters and innovation systems in Africa: Institutions, markets and policy, Oyelaran-Oyeyinka and McCormick (eds), United Nations University Press, 2007, ISBN 978-92-808-1137-7

The case studies have presented us with detailed information about how some clusters have fared in this effort. This chapter does not attempt to summarize all of these findings, but rather to examine what appears to be the common ground for clusters and innovation systems. We first highlight the findings that seem to be most relevant.

Empirical findings: Some highlights

Clusters are geographically and sectorally bounded groups of producers. One clear lesson from the case studies is that, despite this common definition, not all clusters are equal. In some clusters many firms are continuously learning, changing and innovating, while other clusters seem to be stuck in traps of poor markets, low-quality products and a lack of imagination. The authors of the case studies used one or more of the three theoretical frameworks presented in chapters 2 and 3 in their search for explanations for these differences. Although the frameworks were applied differently in the nine case-study chapters, certain of their elements have emerged repeatedly as critical for the establishment, operation and – most importantly – the growth, upgrading and innovation potential of the clusters studied. We discuss the elements under four broad headings: origins, location and agglomeration economies; market access and market relations; joint action, supporting institutions and power; and information, knowledge and learning.

Origins, location and agglomeration economies

Many examples in this volume and elsewhere support North's (1990) simple contention that "history matters". This led us to expect that the origins of a cluster would condition its future direction including its innovation potential. Many of the case studies trace the history of the clusters under study, showing how they began, how they grew, whether they moved (or were moved) from one place to another, and what type of support and/or challenges they had along the way. Broadly speaking, it is possible to distinguish between "constructed" and "spontaneous" clusters. Spontaneous clusters just happen, usually when one or two businesses of a particular type are joined by others, until over a long or short time, a cluster is formed. The Otigba computer cluster (Oyelaran-Oyeyinka, chapter 6) is an excellent example of a fast-growing spontaneous cluster that seems to have thrived with little government support. The emergence of an information-technology hardware cluster in a very late-industrializing environment in such a self-organizing fashion merits a close examination. Conventional wisdom suggests that poor countries are unlikely to be host to high technology, let alone doing so within the organization of small and medium-sized enterprises. But not only has the evolution of the Otigba cluster proceeded largely without direct support from the state, it has grown in a decidedly hostile institutional and arid infrastructural environment. From Oyelaran-Oyeyinka's account, the strength of the cluster was the very early emergence of a private association of highly educated entrepreneurs of component suppliers, buyers, clone builders and parts and components traders. The cluster has quickly transformed into an intensely competitive environment and a local milieu that provides a significant knowledge base for building a future computer-hardware cluster.

Domiatt (El-Shahat, chapter 7) and the Lake Victoria fish clusters (Kiggundu, chapter 8, and McCormick and Mitullah, chapter 10) took longer to develop, but also began spontaneously. Like Otigba, Domiatt consists of self-organizing micro, small and medium-sized enterprises that grew from entrepreneurial cultures combined with a specific skill base, in this case artisanal rather than high technology. The fish clusters, on the other hand, have evolved as new markets for the resources found in Lake Victoria. Although government was not directly involved in their origins, government action was important in their ability to respond to changing market conditions.

Constructed clusters are those that have been "built", usually by government authorities, to house businesses. These range from fully serviced industrial parks to micro and small enterprise (MSE) sites, such as the Mwenge and Gerezani clusters in Tanzania described by Musonda (chapter 5). Some of these are the product of government efforts to remove spontaneous clusters to less congested parts of cities and towns, while a few, like Gerezani, trace their origins to government initiatives to expand industrial manufacturing after independence.

Although typologies such as spontaneous and constructed clusters are fraught with difficulties, they can be helpful in understanding the dynamics of cluster building and the path affecting their present development. Our cases do not offer the last word on whether constructed or spontaneous clusters are more likely to turn into innovation systems, but the fact that the most dynamic clusters grew up spontaneously is an important finding. The finding must, however, be treated with caution as it clearly does not hold in all cases. The Uhuru Market textile cluster (McCormick and Kinyanjui, chapter 4) had fairly spontaneous origins, but is much less dynamic than the computer, shoe or auto clusters. The fact that its transformation process was gradual and many of the original entrepreneurs have left the market may account for this cluster's present lack of dynamic networking.

That clusters are geographically bounded by definition implies that their location may be important. This is an aspect of clustering that usually receives little attention. Clusters exist in a multi-dimensional space. They are located in particular places, but may be linked both globally and locally to firms and clusters elsewhere. In some cases, the global linkages may actually be stronger than those within the cluster or between the cluster and other local actors. Tracing such linkages can be very important for understanding knowledge flows into and out of the cluster.

Equally important is the actual physical location of the cluster. Most of our cases are located in cities or large towns. Only in the Kenyan case of Shinyalu (McCormick and Kinyanjui, chapter 4) do we find a truly rural cluster, though many others exist in Kenya and elsewhere. One of the main results of a rural location in the African context is poor or non-existent infrastructure, which severely limits the scope for innovation in production, services and marketing. Lack of electricity, for example, means that certain types of production machinery cannot be used. Without electricity, clusters are likely to lack services such as telephones, photocopying machines and computers. Poor rural roads make obtaining supplies and getting products to market costly and difficult.

The current case studies reveal that co-location does not always result in the expected external economies and, furthermore, that even when present, these may not contribute significantly to cluster upgrading. The Uganda fish clusters, for example, show that although labour effects were initially positive, skills were insufficient for further upgrading (Kiggundu, chapter 8). These same clusters benefited from the emergence of specialized suppliers, but could not resolve the problems of diminishing quantities of their most important supply: fish. Technology spillovers, which are potentially the most important externality for fostering innovation, were predictably strong in places like Otigba, where the core technology driving activity was a computer assembling process with technology acquired through apprenticeship and tacit knowledge.

Finance is an intermediate input that has received little attention in the case studies, perhaps because most MSEs are self-financing by necessity, even if not by choice. Nevertheless, in two instances finance was explicitly mentioned. The Otigba cluster established inter-firm credit facilities (Oyelaran-Oyeyinka, chapter 6). Cluster interviewees claimed faster production and delivery service as a result of this arrangement. Kiggundu (chapter 8) points to the availability of pre-shipment finance as a driver for learning. Firms that might otherwise be excluded from the demanding export markets are able to participate because some buyers are willing to finance their exports.

Market access and market relations

Product markets are crucial to the understanding of cluster operations and innovation. The cases point to three important aspects of markets: market access, demanding customers and standards.

Although earlier work on African clusters identified market access as an almost universal benefit of clustering on the continent, the case studies in this book have provided more nuanced information. Market access appears to be an important benefit in clusters such as the Otigba IT cluster, which is rapidly developing a regional reputation as a place for IT solutions, and the well-established Domiatt furniture cluster (Oyelaran-Oyeyinka, chapter 6, and El-Shahat, chapter 7). However, market access was not seen as a major benefit for the Ugandan fish exporting clusters (Kiggundu, chapter 8), and the rural textile cluster actually suffered by being tied to poor local markets (McCormick and Kinyanjui, chapter 4).

These findings suggest that for clusters the issue is more than simple access. They raise questions about the nature of buyers, the capabilities of producers, and the institutions governing exchange. The value-chain literature suggests that firms and entire value chains will upgrade in response to demanding customers (Gereffi, 2001; Kaplinsky and Morris, 2001). Most of the examples given in this literature point to export markets, but the case studies in this book demonstrate that clusters do not need to be directly involved in exporting to benefit from demanding customers. The Durban Automotive Cluster (DAC) produces mainly for the South African market, which, like many in Africa, has been liberalized to the extent that anything sold there must compete with products from all over the world. This means that the South African consumer is increasingly demanding, and the cluster has had to improve quality and productive efficiency simply to keep its customers (Lorentzen et al., chapter 9). Similarly, McCormick and Kinyanjui (chapter 4) point out that while it can be difficult for very small producers to reach export markets, high-volume local buyers, such as hospitals, schools, supermarkets and the government, may be demanding enough to encourage their upgrading.

The notion of demanding customers is closely linked to that of standards. The standards imposed by the European Union on fish from Lake Victoria constitute one example of how a buyer can bring about change in a cluster (Kiggundu, chapter 8, and McCormick and Mitullah, chapter 10). The changes ranged from the improvement of beach landing facilities to new rules on the disposal of waste products by the processing factories, but were all designed to regain the chain's access to the EU market.

Joint action, supporting institutions and power

A key theme in this book as well as in earlier cluster studies is that clusters succeed best when actors work together to achieve common aims. Joint action involving firms, government and public- or private-support institutions appears to be a critical ingredient for the development of innovative clusters. Several different forms of joint action were mentioned in the cases. The most basic were subcontracting, collaboration and the sharing of information (Musonda, chapter 5). Joint action in Otigba (Oyelaran-Oyeyinka, chapter 6) took the form of inter-firm credit facilities, technical support, knowledge sharing and joint warehousing of goods. The cluster clearly benefited from the early emergence of a private association of highly educated computer entrepreneurs. In several clusters, a sectoral or cluster-level business association provided an effective platform for addressing issues affecting the cluster. The relative success of the Uganda fish cluster was attributed to joint efforts for process upgrading, in particular the speed and decisiveness with which business operators and policymakers coordinated their efforts to learn and acquire new knowledge crucial to the upgrading process (Kiggundu, chapter 8). ICT adoption in Ghana and Kenya (Oyelaran-Oyeyinka et al., chapter 12) was related to the availability within the cluster of skill-upgrading facilities, technology-support institutions and public or private ICT-training institutions.

The case of the KwaZulu-Natal Benchmarking Club is unique among the cases reported in both its structure and its activities (Lorentzen et al., chapter 9). Made up of auto component firms, their main buyer and academic researchers, the Club studied members' performance, set benchmarks, tackled problems and encouraged each other to upgrade. This required considerable time and commitment on the part of each member. Firms had to disclose sensitive production and financial information. Researchers had to turn the data into usable benchmarks and feed it back at regular intervals to the firms. Trust in the process and in one another grew slowly. Throughout its existence the Benchmarking Club focused on the performance of individual members. It eventually evolved into the larger Durban Automotive Cluster (DAC), which had the broader objective of developing collective responses to the competitive challenges facing the industry in the area. The case highlights the importance of two ingredients to joint upgrading efforts: trust and external knowledge inputs.

Efforts at joint action may benefit some individuals or groups more than others. The case study of Domiatt shows how certain institutions – chambers of trade and commerce, institutions in the banking sector –

have been opportunistically used to advance and buttress the showroom owners and wood sellers' power nexus (El-Shahat, chapter 7). This increased their power at the expense of the artisanal workshops. The showroom owner appropriates the profits associated with the artisans' new designs, but does not invest any of it into the artisanal workshops or into development of his own new designs. McCormick and Mitullah (chapter 10) point out how the rise of large-scale processors and traders during the commercialization of the Lake Victoria fisheries changed the power balance at the lake and how later the emergence of the EU as the most powerful external buyer changed it further. They also note power imbalances – in this case gender-based – even within relatively disadvantaged groups such as the fisherfolk. These imbalances have clear implications for learning. When the more powerful actors choose not to share knowledge or invest in productive resources, innovation in the cluster may be stifled. The reverse seems also to be true. When more powerful actors are interested in upgrading and supportive of training and knowledge sharing, positive benefits are likely to accrue. For example, one of the key variables in ICT adoption was the managing director's interest in upgrading workers' skills (Oyelaran-Oyeyinka et al., chapter 12).

Information, knowledge and learning

Much of our discussion thus far has attempted to understand how innovation is facilitated, shaped or constrained by a range of variables connected with general cluster operation and success. We now look more specifically at variables usually associated with innovative behaviour – information, knowledge and learning – to see how they have affected innovation in the cases. The three tend to be intertwined and to be made visible through formal and informal institutions.

The cases reinforce a finding from the study of individual enterprises, namely that what an entrepreneur already knows is important. The knowledge may be academic or practical; it may have been acquired in school, through formal training or on the job. The case of academic knowledge – specifically the level of education an entrepreneur brings to the business – has been well documented. It is related both to the nature of the business and to its size and complexity (Kinyanjui, 1992; Mead, 1999). In our cases, we see that result replicated at the cluster level. The Otigba computer cluster is in a high technology sector and the cluster itself shows great diversity in the availability of production and related services. Both of these are highly unusual occurrences in a low-income African country. Not surprisingly, this cluster was formed by university graduates and, as Oyelaran-Oyeyinka points out, one of its great strengths was the early emergence of a private sector association of highly educated entrepreneurs from firms of various specializations. Education of the entrepreneurs is also a key factor in the adoption of ICT (Oyelaran-Oyeyinka et al., chapter 12).

On the other hand, clusters formed by skilled, but less-educated, entrepreneurs tend to operate within their craft specialization. This seems to be equally true of shoe, handicraft, furniture and woodworking, metal fabrication and textile clusters in all of the countries (chapters 4, 5 and 7). The Tanzanian government's establishment of a college for handicrafts in recognition of their commercial and cultural value is one example of a new initiative attempting to strengthen craft production (Musonda, chapter 5).

At least as important as the knowledge base that entrepreneurs bring into the cluster is the learning that happens within the cluster. The existence of internal or nearby technical training institutions that are willing to work with cluster entrepreneurs is a benefit that should help clusters upgrade. The fact that our findings do not highlight any such institution, however, suggests that entrepreneurs may not perceive them as useful or that the training institutions do not make much effort to offer programmes relevant to the businesses in nearby MSE clusters.

The positive examples of ongoing learning in clusters differ from the traditional training models. The learning of the Durban Auto Cluster (Lorentzen et al., chapter 9) was clearly different from the usual cluster-learning models on several scores. First it was aimed at decisionmakers, firm owners and government officials, rather than operatives or technicians. Second, it had a clear focus on performance benchmarking and was therefore tailored to the participants' needs. Third, the process was interactive, with researchers, business people and government officials all involved as teachers, resource people and learners. The involvement of resource people external to the Durban Auto Cluster should also be noted. External input is most positive when those receiving it recognize its relevance. This was documented, not only in Durban, but also in the Ugandan fish clusters, where Kiggundu claims that learning from foreign specialists was important for both product and process upgrading, and in Otigba, where at least one entrepreneur has gone out of the country to acquire specialized training.

These positive learning experiences contrast sharply with those of other clusters in which technology seems stuck. The market and available infrastructure are often rightly blamed for low technology and poor product quality in African clusters (McCormick and Kinyanjui, chapter 4). The market argument is that, as consumers are poor and unable to pay for better-quality items, producers continue to make what they are certain to sell. The infrastructure argument, on the other hand, is simply that in many lines of production it is difficult or even impossible to achieve high quality without benefit of electricity to operate specialized machinery. These arguments, though valid in many instances, tell only part of the story. Our cases reveal that technological learning may also fail to happen because it has been thwarted by the opportunistic behaviour of some cluster actors (El-Shahat, chapter 7). By taking artisan designs without paying for them or providing constructive feedback to the artisan, Domiatt's showroom owner breaks a learning loop and contributes to learning stagnation.

Summary

The origins and locations of clusters are important. They establish certain directions and place a cluster within a particular geographical space and institutional framework, but a cluster's origins should not be viewed as determining its fate. The cases reveal, for example, that although spontaneity and flexibility are key to innovative behaviour, so-called spontaneous clusters can get stuck in low technology and spontaneity can exist in a variety of settings. There is no clear evidence that constructed clusters cannot attract innovative firms if appropriate policies are in place and those organizing the clusters make an effort to do so. Location of a cluster in a developing country is significant for well-known reasons. The usual pattern of low wages and abundant labour combined with poor infrastructure and a weak institutional framework offers both locational advantages and disadvantages. Clusters can use their cost advantage to compete in external markets, but they need to be wary of being caught in a race to the bottom that jeopardizes their own profits and their workers' well-being. This danger is all the more real given that one of the disadvantages of location in many competing developing countries is an almost inevitable power imbalance between external buyers and the cluster's producers.

The cases confirm the theoretical insight that the most important agglomeration economy for innovation is technological spillovers. They also point to another agglomeration benefit that is rarely discussed in the literature, namely that it is easier for the authorities to provide basic infrastructure to clustered than to dispersed firms, thus making it possible for them to use higher level technologies. The cases also suggest, though with too little evidence, that agglomeration might help in the attraction or creation of better financial infrastructure.

The cases confirm that demanding markets are important for innovation and cluster upgrading. They also suggest that "demanding markets" admit of different degrees. The local supermarkets that are demanding markets for a *jua kali* cluster in Kenya may demand less in terms of product quality, delivery times or labour standards than export markets, but they can serve as an essential first step in the cluster's upgrading process. To promote innovation, markets need to be demanding enough to challenge old thinking and old ways of doing things.

Analysis of efforts such as the Durban Auto Cluster suggests that clusters can reap particular benefits from joint activities focused on upgrading. Lobbying for infrastructure or tax incentives can be done by local business associations and may have a significant impact, especially on clusters that lack basic necessities. More ambitious efforts can be difficult to undertake given firms' understandable fears and reservations about sharing sensitive information. These must be approached slowly and with great patience to gauge whether sufficient trust can be built among participants to make the action possible.

Examination of levels of education and training in the various clusters suggests that prior learning provides a base for innovation and may limit its possibilities. Clusters consisting of entrepreneurs with only primary school education are more likely to innovate in traditional than in high technology fields, for example. Nevertheless, innovation appears to be much more related to a process of ongoing learning than to the levels of previous education and training of cluster entrepreneurs. The major challenge for building innovative clusters is to establish positive incentives that encourage new learning and its practical application to products and processes in the cluster. A second challenge is to remove or re-shape institutions that thwart learning or allow its benefits to go to those who will not keep it alive.

Implications for theory

The case studies point to three factors as most important in bringing about this continuous learning: demanding markets, positive joint action and institutions capable of moderating and focusing power imbalances. It is clearly not enough for enterprises to exist side by side within some defined geographical space. Markets that demand new or higher quality products create the most basic innovative pull for the formation or transformation of enterprise clusters. In some cases, such as Otigba, this is complemented by the push factors of education and prior technological knowledge. Market opportunities alone, however, are unlikely to create an innovative cluster. For innovation to take place at the level of the cluster, firms must learn from each other, pressure the authorities for the infrastructure, tax benefits and other things needed to support innovation and work together in ways appropriate to the sector and general level of cluster development. Finally, clusters need good institutions both internally and externally, which can be counted on to promote innovative behaviour and protect the interests of those with less power.

At one level, one can say that these theoretical implications hardly break new ground. What is new is the weight that the analysis of the case studies has allowed us to place on these particular three variables. This weight enables us to identify with greater certainty policy directions that should foster innovative clusters. It is to these policies that we now turn.

Implications for policy and practice

Our aim in drawing out implications for policy and practice is to provide guidance to government, private sector associations and non-governmental organizations (NGOs) offering services to MSE clusters for policies, approaches and, to a lesser extent, specific interventions that may help clusters to innovate. Even in this era of liberalization and government downsizing, government has a critical role to play in industrial development generally and cluster development in particular. The issue is not *whether* government should be involved in cluster development, but *when* and *how* it should act. We therefore first recall some of the general lessons that the cases offer for government policy and practice. We then turn to more specific recommendations, organizing this discussion around the three main variables identified in the previous section. Our suggestions are not exhaustive, but are instead meant to give ideas that can be developed further.

Lessons for government

The first lesson for government is that collaborative policy development is likely to result in better policies and more useful interventions than policy development "from on high". This is most clearly demonstrated in the Durban Auto Cluster (Lorentzen et al., chapter 9, and Morris and Robbins, chapter 11) and the Lake Victoria Fish Cluster (McCormick and Mitullah, chapter 10), but can also be seen in several other cases. A competent and informed government bureaucracy is important, but government needs to interact on an equal footing with business people, association officials and other stakeholders. Such interactions should not be limited to once-a-year budget inputs, but should include mechanisms for ongoing communication about a variety of issues relevant to cluster development.

The second lesson is that effective policy implementation usually requires changes in government institutions. Some of these may be fairly straightforward, such as the establishment of a "cluster desk" in the Ministry of Industry. Others, however, are more substantial and range from reorganizing key government departments to enable them to work more effectively with clusters, to seeking a fundamental reorientation in the attitudes and mindsets of civil servants toward private-sector development (Morris and Robbins, chapter 11).

The third lesson is that most clusters are embedded in a local as well as a national economy. Morris and Robbins (chapter 11) argue that the need for institutional embeddedness and closeness to local stakeholders, facilitators and firms implies that it is usually better to involve local rather than national government in creating and maintaining clusters. Sometimes, however, an export cluster needs a national profile or is evolving in response to national initiatives, making it necessary to involve the national authorities or structures. This points to the need for coordination between national and local levels. Without such coordination, policy and related interventions are weakened if not rendered totally ineffective.

Finally, even in the cases of clusters that appear totally spontaneous, government usually plays some role. The Otigba computer cluster, for example, emerged spontaneously through the efforts of entrepreneurs, acting individually and together in the association. Nevertheless, certain nearly invisible forms of government support were present. These include the existence of basic electricity service in the cluster, the encouragement of students in public universities and other tertiary institutions to take up placements in cluster firms, and the participation of Nigeria in ECOWAS, which has made it easier for businesses to engage in cross-border trade and training activities. Identifying such hidden forms of support can be an important first step toward working more closely with clusters and facilitating their development.

In sum, government is one of several players. It cannot – and should not – act alone and it may not even take the lead. At the same time, these four lessons can also serve as principles for the involvement of other actors with clusters. Donors, NGOs and researchers, among others, would do well to act collaboratively, be ready to change their own attitudes and mindsets, coordinate their actions with other players, and recognize and build on existing forms of support.

Essentials of an innovative cluster

We now turn to more specific issues surrounding the development of innovation in clusters and address the three essential variables identified in our model.

Markets are essentially private-sector institutions and current wisdom suggests that they should not be subject to undue interference. Nevertheless, export and other demanding markets are often difficult to access and potential new entrants may need support in order to obtain necessary information, make contacts, meet relevant standards, secure financing and deal with the paperwork required to conclude transactions. The Ugandan and Kenyan fish clusters (Kiggundu, chapter 8, and McCormick and Mitullah, chapter 10) offer good examples of what government can do. In an interactive process, local and national government, support organizations and the private sector learned how to meet the new sanitary and phytosanitary standards required by the European Union. Every key actor has had to change the way it did things in order to reach this goal. In Uganda, the effort was spearheaded by government using resources from UNIDO and the World Bank and drawing on local training and standards institutions. In Kenya, the government is also taking the lead, but it is trying to facilitate a process that will lead to stakeholder co-management. Much of the strategy rests on training key actors, including fisheries officers, inspectors and fisherfolk, in improved methods of fishing and preservation.

The fish cluster cases have important lessons for other clusters attempting to access demanding markets. The first is that securing accurate market information concerning both its location and requirements is an essential first step toward market access. Firms seeking access may need help not only in getting the information itself but, more importantly, in tapping into regular sources of information such as Web sites, electronic mailing lists and conventional printed material. Associations, and in some cases NGOs, can help by gathering this information and making it available either freely or for a fee. Alternatively, they can set up training programmes to teach firms to find it themselves. For the building of a truly innovative cluster, this latter approach is better as it gives firms the tools they need to find creative solutions to their market problems. The second lesson is that different actors can ease market access by bringing their own particular expertise to bear on specific problems and bottlenecks. Direct action by the national government may be necessary when the problem involves other governments. NGOs are often good at providing training but for the long term it can be better to involve national or local training institutions. Business associations, local government, universities and others may be called on to address other aspects of the problem. The third lesson is that similar problems may exist in neighbouring countries. These countries may have taken action that can be imitated or that may have an impact on the problem at home. The fourth lesson is that clusters' market issues vary greatly from one sector to another and may require specialized knowledge. The final lesson about markets and market access is that working together can enable actors to do things they could probably not do alone. This takes us to the next crucial variable: joint action.

An innovative cluster will be characterized by high levels of collaboration and interaction between and among producers, suppliers, service providers and others within and outside the cluster. In some cases, such as Otigba, this collaboration appears to arise spontaneously. In others it is missing and may need to be facilitated. The cases point to two main types of facilitation: direct facilitation and the provision of incentives. The Durban Auto Cluster is a good example of direct facilitation by a group of academics-turned-consultants (Lorentzen et al., chapter 9). Once formed, the DAC itself became a facilitator of horizontal and vertical information sharing by both firms and government. It also worked toward establishing a functioning and growing local supplier infrastructure involving firms of varying sizes, experience, international exposure and strategic orientation from different tiers of the supply chain.

The other way to promote joint action is to offer incentives. These might include tax breaks, such as deductions for association membership dues, or access to infrastructure or other resources for firms agreeing to work together. Our cases show little evidence of the successful use of such incentive programmes, but they remain theoretically appealing because they allow firms to choose to collaborate depending on their own priorities.

We also note that there are some disincentives to collaboration and some instances in which joint action has perverse outcomes. The DAC members were initially wary of sharing their financial information for fear that it would be used against them by competitors. They were also sceptical about the value of interacting with government officials. Some of Kenya's potential jua kali association members are prevented from joining by lack of information (McCormick and Kinyanjui, chapter 4). Others are deterred by stories of financial mismanagement by officials. The Domiatt case demonstrates that in conditions of unequal power, firms can be forced into exploitative relationships (El-Shahat, chapter 7). Innovative behaviour in such cases is thwarted for lack of an appropriate institutional framework. This brings us to the third requirement for an innovative cluster: the existence of institutions that promote and reward innovative behaviour.

Clusters need strong institutions, both within and outside the cluster, that promote and reward innovative behaviour. They also need ways of dealing creatively with institutional change. The cases provide some examples at international, national and local levels. We saw, for example, the way in which changes in the European Union's rules triggered responses by fish clusters in both Kenya and Uganda. The clusters and the national governments, with more or less success, created new processes, upgraded their physical infrastructure, and changed their own institutions in order to regain access to the lucrative EU markets. The story of the

DAC is set against a backdrop of profound institutional change in South Africa. Politically, the change was from apartheid to the New South Africa; economically, it was from import substitution to market liberalization. Other countries and clusters experienced the shock of structural adjustment policies, which liberalized their main markets and forced them to look elsewhere. Clusters also operate in the context of local formal and informal institutions that promote or discourage innovation.

Conclusions

This volume has explored a wide range of theoretical, empirical and policy issues. In the end we conclude that the three frameworks presented in chapters 2 and 3 remain useful for analysing clusters. Not all of the variables contained in them are, however, equally relevant for the understanding of how clusters learn and innovate. The analysis of the cases points to three – demanding markets, joint action and the institutional framework – as critical for the development of innovative clusters. Based on this, we made some suggestions for policies and approaches that we believe will foster the development of innovative MSE clusters.

Our conclusions underscore two other important points. First, from a theoretical perspective they show that any framework used for analysing innovation in clusters needs to pay serious attention to the role of the state and the nature and distribution of power. Second, from a policy perspective, the findings show the limitations of trying to graft best practices from one context onto programmes for another. Policies can certainly draw on others' experience, but they must be specifically designed for the local reality.

Do we now know all there is to know about clusters and innovation? Far from it. Although the cases have been instructive, there remains much more to learn. Despite the remaining knowledge gaps, we can say with some certainty that a profile of the innovative cluster in Africa is emerging. It is our hope that this profile will be a useful tool for entrepreneurs and those who support them with research, policy and specific interventions.

REFERENCES

Gereffi, Gary (2001) "Beyond the Producer-driven/Buyer-driven Dichotomy: The Evolution of Global Value Chains in the Internet Era", *IDS Bulletin* 32(3): 30–40.

Kaplinsky, Raphael and Mike Morris (2002) "A Handbook for Value Chain Research", report prepared for the International Development Research Centre, available at http://www.ids.ac.uk/Ids/Global/.

Kinyanjui, Mary Njeri (1992) "Small and Medium Sized Manufacturing Enterprises in Central Kenya: Structure, Role and Location", Ph.D. thesis, Cambridge University.

Mead, Donald C. (1999) "MSEs Tackle Both Poverty and Growth (But in Differing Proportions)", in Kenneth King and Simon McGrath, eds, *Enterprise in Africa: Between Poverty and Growth*, London: Intermediate Technology Publications.

North, Douglass (1990) *Institutions, Institutional Change and Economic Performance*, Cambridge: Cambridge University Press.

Index

Africa
  cluster failure, reasons for, 63
  collective efficiency, weak, 158
  infrastructure fragility, 269, 297
  institutional environment, fragmented,
    66
  market failure, 269
  SME clusters, 270, 294
Africa Institute for Capacity Development
  (AICAD), 212
African Growth Opportunity Act (AGOA),
  50
agglomeration
  cluster, 5–6, 83, 302
  self-organizing, secondary, 11
  Uganda fish processing, 160, 163, 164, 166
  urban MSEs, 82
Anti Corruption and Economic Crimes Act
  of 2003, 232
apartheid era, 57, 190, 251
Association of Telecommunications
  Companies of Nigeria, 121

Beach Improvement Committee (BIC), 235
Beach Improvement Units, 234, 238
Beach Management Committee, 234, 238
Beach Management Units, 235
Beta Computers (Nigeria), 109, 116
Brazil, 51

Business and Communication Centres
  (Ghana), 272
business associations, 23, 299

Capetown wine cluster
  apartheid period, 57
  appellation system, location-based, 56
  innovative cluster, 55–56, 56f3.3
  South Africa, 1t3.2, 50, 51t3.2
CDI (Centre for the Development of
  Industry), 168, 181
CFC (Common Fund for Commodities), 174
CFC/FAO/COMESA/LVFO project, 174
chain governance, 26–28
chain upgrading, 30-31
Changamwe cluster (Mombasa), 70
cluster
  agglomeration, 5–6, 83, 302
  analysis, levels of, 9t1.1
  analysis, weakness in, 6–7
  business associations, 23, 168, 299
  business system, 21–22
  co-location, 6, 297
  constructed, 47f3.1, 48, 295, 296, 302
  customers, demanding, 298
  defined, 4box1.1, 5, 20
  desk, 304–305
  education and training, 303
  electricity, role of, 67, 75, 302

310

An innovative cluster will be characterized by high levels of collaboration and interaction between and among producers, suppliers, service providers and others within and outside the cluster. In some cases, such as Otigba, this collaboration appears to arise spontaneously. In others it is missing and may need to be facilitated. The cases point to two main types of facilitation: direct facilitation and the provision of incentives. The Durban Auto Cluster is a good example of direct facilitation by a group of academics-turned-consultants (Lorentzen et al., chapter 9). Once formed, the DAC itself became a facilitator of horizontal and vertical information sharing by both firms and government. It also worked toward establishing a functioning and growing local supplier infrastructure involving firms of varying sizes, experience, international exposure and strategic orientation from different tiers of the supply chain.

The other way to promote joint action is to offer incentives. These might include tax breaks, such as deductions for association membership dues, or access to infrastructure or other resources for firms agreeing to work together. Our cases show little evidence of the successful use of such incentive programmes, but they remain theoretically appealing because they allow firms to choose to collaborate depending on their own priorities.

We also note that there are some disincentives to collaboration and some instances in which joint action has perverse outcomes. The DAC members were initially wary of sharing their financial information for fear that it would be used against them by competitors. They were also sceptical about the value of interacting with government officials. Some of Kenya's potential jua kali association members are prevented from joining by lack of information (McCormick and Kinyanjui, chapter 4). Others are deterred by stories of financial mismanagement by officials. The Domiatt case demonstrates that in conditions of unequal power, firms can be forced into exploitative relationships (El-Shahat, chapter 7). Innovative behaviour in such cases is thwarted for lack of an appropriate institutional framework. This brings us to the third requirement for an innovative cluster: the existence of institutions that promote and reward innovative behaviour.

Clusters need strong institutions, both within and outside the cluster, that promote and reward innovative behaviour. They also need ways of dealing creatively with institutional change. The cases provide some examples at international, national and local levels. We saw, for example, the way in which changes in the European Union's rules triggered responses by fish clusters in both Kenya and Uganda. The clusters and the national governments, with more or less success, created new processes, upgraded their physical infrastructure, and changed their own institutions in order to regain access to the lucrative EU markets. The story of the

DAC is set against a backdrop of profound institutional change in South Africa. Politically, the change was from apartheid to the New South Africa; economically, it was from import substitution to market liberalization. Other countries and clusters experienced the shock of structural adjustment policies, which liberalized their main markets and forced them to look elsewhere. Clusters also operate in the context of local formal and informal institutions that promote or discourage innovation.

Conclusions

This volume has explored a wide range of theoretical, empirical and policy issues. In the end we conclude that the three frameworks presented in chapters 2 and 3 remain useful for analysing clusters. Not all of the variables contained in them are, however, equally relevant for the understanding of how clusters learn and innovate. The analysis of the cases points to three – demanding markets, joint action and the institutional framework – as critical for the development of innovative clusters. Based on this, we made some suggestions for policies and approaches that we believe will foster the development of innovative MSE clusters.

Our conclusions underscore two other important points. First, from a theoretical perspective they show that any framework used for analysing innovation in clusters needs to pay serious attention to the role of the state and the nature and distribution of power. Second, from a policy perspective, the findings show the limitations of trying to graft best practices from one context onto programmes for another. Policies can certainly draw on others' experience, but they must be specifically designed for the local reality.

Do we now know all there is to know about clusters and innovation? Far from it. Although the cases have been instructive, there remains much more to learn. Despite the remaining knowledge gaps, we can say with some certainty that a profile of the innovative cluster in Africa is emerging. It is our hope that this profile will be a useful tool for entrepreneurs and those who support them with research, policy and specific interventions.

REFERENCES

Gereffi, Gary (2001) "Beyond the Producer-driven/Buyer-driven Dichotomy: The Evolution of Global Value Chains in the Internet Era", *IDS Bulletin* 32(3): 30–40.

Kaplinsky, Raphael and Mike Morris (2002) "A Handbook for Value Chain Research", report prepared for the International Development Research Centre, available at http://www.ids.ac.uk/Ids/Global/.

Kinyanjui, Mary Njeri (1992) "Small and Medium Sized Manufacturing Enterprises in Central Kenya: Structure, Role and Location", Ph.D. thesis, Cambridge University.

Mead, Donald C. (1999) "MSEs Tackle Both Poverty and Growth (But in Differing Proportions)", in Kenneth King and Simon McGrath, eds, *Enterprise in Africa: Between Poverty and Growth*, London: Intermediate Technology Publications.

North, Douglass (1990) *Institutions, Institutional Change and Economic Performance*, Cambridge: Cambridge University Press.

Index

.